The Cowboy in Country Music

ALSO BY DON CUSIC

Gene Autry: His Life and Career
(McFarland, 2010)

*The Trials of Henry Flipper,
First Black Graduate of West Point*
(McFarland, 2009)

The Cowboy in Country Music

An Historical Survey with Artist Profiles

DON CUSIC

McFarland & Company, Inc., Publishers
Jefferson, North Carolina, and London

LIBRARY OF CONGRESS CATALOGUING-IN-PUBLICATION DATA

Cusic, Don.
The cowboy in country music :
an historical survey with artist profiles / Don Cusic.
p.   cm.
Includes bibliographical references and index.

ISBN 978-0-7864-6314-5
softcover : 50# alkaline paper ∞

1. Country music—History and criticism.
2. Country musicians—United States—Biography.
3. Cowboys—Songs and music—History and criticism.
I. Title.
ML3524.C86   2011   781.64209—dc23   2011021772

British Library cataloguing data are available

©2011 Don Cusic. All rights reserved

*No part of this book may be reproduced or transmitted in any form
or by any means, electronic or mechanical, including photocopying
or recording, or by any information storage and retrieval system,
without permission in writing from the publisher.*

Cover image and design by David Landis (Shake It Loose Graphics)

Manufactured in the United States of America

*McFarland & Company, Inc., Publishers
Box 611, Jefferson, North Carolina 28640
www.mcfarlandpub.com*

Acknowledgments

In writing this book, I am grateful to all those I interviewed who are subjects of chapters: Wes Tuttle, Marilyn Tuttle, Monte Hale, Riders in the Sky, Michael Martin Murphey, Ray Price, Johnny Cash, Johnny Western, Red Steagall, Don Edwards, Rex Allen, Jr., Lynn Anderson, Ian Tyson, Sons of the San Joaquin, Ray Benson, Wylie Gustafson, R.W. Hampton, Waddie Mitchell and Chris LeDoux. I must also thank those who possess a great knowledge of western music and have shared it with me. These include O.J. Sikes, Ranger Doug Green, Packy Smith, Hal Spencer, Jon Guyot Smith and numerous others whom I may be forgetting, I met and talked with at Western Music Association and Western Writers of America meetings. John Rumble at the Country Music Foundation, Don Reeves at the National Cowboy and Western Heriage Museum in Oklahoma City, Scott O'Malley with the Scott O'Malley Agency, Paul Lohr with Frontier Management and free lance writer Vernell Hackett were always helpful when I needed help.

I must thank my assistant, Molly Shehan, for her constant help in my working life. To the folks who work on *The Western Way*—Jim Sharp, Wendy Mazur, Lindalee Green, Marsha Short, Rick Huff, Marvin O'Dell and O.J. Sikes—I owe a great deal of thanks. Mickey Dawes got me involved in editing *The Western Way* and Sherry Bond was an integral part of getting the magazine up and running. The folks at the Western Music Association, especially Jon Messenger, Curly Musgrave, and Bob Fee have been supportive.

Table of Contents

Acknowledgments v
Preface 1
Introduction: Cowboys and Country Music 5

1. Roundin' Up Radio	11
2. Gene Autry and The Phantom Empire	18
3. The Big Three: Gene, Roy and the Sons of the Pioneers	25
4. Dale Evans, Queen of the West	33
5. Girls of the Golden West	39
6. Louise Massey and the Westerners	41
7. Patsy Montana	44
8. Ray Whitley	47
9. Guitars, Cowboys and Country Music	50
10. Andy Parker and the Plainsmen	54
11. Foy Willing and Riders of the Purple Sage	56
12. Jimmy Wakely	60
13. Johnny Bond	65
14. Rosalie Allen	72
15. Cindy Walker	73
16. Marilyn Tuttle	75
17. Smiley Burnette	79
18. Stuart Hamblen	82
19. Tex Ritter	86
20. Wesley Tuttle	89
21. Monte Hale	94
22. Rex Allen	97
23. John Wayne	100
24. Bob Wills, King of Western Swing	108

Table of Contents

25. Bing Crosby and Country Music	112
26. Riders In The Sky	114
27. Flying W Wranglers	119
28. Michael Martin Murphey	121
29. Ray Price	129
30. Marty Robbins	142
31. Johnny Cash	146
32. Johnny Western	154
33. Red Steagall	160
34. Don Edwards	164
35. Rex Allen Jr.	170
36. Lynn Anderson	176
37. Ian Tyson	181
38. Sons of the San Joaquin	187
39. Asleep at the Wheel	193
40. Wylie and the Wild West	197
41. R.W. Hampton, Riding for His Own Brand	202
42. Waddie Mitchell, Cowboy Poet	209
43. Chris LeDoux	216
44. George Strait	218
45. Country Music, Cowboys and the West	224
46. The West on the Music Charts	232

Bibliography 251

Index 257

Preface

You don't hear much about western music these days if you live on the east side of the "Big River." But on the other side of the Mississippi there are around 200 Western Festivals annually where singers sing western songs, cowboy poets recite poetry, and people dress in western garb, giving visitors a taste of the Legendary West. That "taste" involves everything from authentic meals cooked by chuck wagons to horseback rides to western clothing and jewelry.

Since 2001 I have been editor of *The Western Way*, the quarterly magazine of the Western Music Association. During that time I have interviewed and written about the leading performers in western music as well as the major historical figures in western music. Many of the chapters in this book were originally published in *The Western Way*.

The first "western" songs were folk songs, sung by cowboys. During the 1930s, the "singing cowboy" emerged in the movies, led by Gene Autry, Roy Rogers, the Sons of the Pioneers and Tex Ritter. These movie cowboys sang songs written for the movies, often by professional songwriters, as well as folk songs.

The singing cowboy gave country music its first positive image; prior to the singing cowboy, the image of the country music performer was that of a "mountaineer" or "hillbilly." The movie cowboy was a romantic hero, taken away from the real cowboy's job of looking after cattle and dressed up in fancy clothes and given a guitar and a song, which he often sang to a pretty girl. The working cowboy was a laborer doing difficult work for wages; the movie cowboy was a "star" who captured the imagination of youngsters all over the nation.

The cowboy became an important part of country music because of his clothes; country singers found that cowboy hats, boots and jeans had an appeal to country audiences. Through the years, country music split into different directions; there was Western Swing, which was Big Band country, honky-tonk music, bluegrass and the smooth, pop oriented sound that became mainstream country music. Still, many country singers persisted in dressing western even if they'd never ridden a horse or seen a cow.

Country music has gone through various stages where the male performers have dressed in sports coats, tuxedoes, rhinestones, torn jeans and T-shirts and business suits—but it always comes back to the look of the cowboy. That is why I state in this book that the cowboy is the most enduring symbol of country music. Put a cowboy hat on a guitar and you think "country music."

In this book I begin with the historical cowboy and how he became a romantic hero. There is a chapter on early western songs, some of folk origin and others written for the stage. It is essential to cover the pioneers in this genre: Gene Autry, Roy Rogers, the Sons of the Pioneers, and Tex Ritter. I cover some lesser known cowboy singers as well, from the "last" singing cowboy, Rex Allen, to more marginal figures like Wesley Tuttle, Monte Hale and Foy Willing and Riders of the Purple Sage. I profile the women singers, from Dale Evans to Louise Massey, Patsy Montana and the Girls of the Golden West.

The singing cowboys played a major role in popularizing the guitar, so there's a chapter in this book on the history of the guitar and how it relates to singing cowboys.

There are chapters on the major artists in contemporary western music, such as Riders in the Sky, Michael Martin Murphey, Don Edwards, Red Steagall and Rex Allen Jr. These artists often have roots in—or at least a connection to—country music but have chosen to sing about the West and live a western "lifestyle," which involves singing about the West, dressing "western" and sometimes living and working on a ranch.

Finally, I have a chapter on George Strait, the most "western" of contemporary, mainstream country singers. There are also chapters on the country and pop charts that trace the evolution of western songs from the early 20th century through the singing cowboys, the television westerns and on into modern country music.

Some of the individuals have died since I interviewed them and wrote these articles; in many cases, I did the last interview with them. Many of those in this book are nearly forgotten today, but they were each a major figure in their day and leave a legacy in western music. Each one is an important part of the history of western music and deserves to be remembered. Western music itself, which nearly died out until a revival began in the late 1970s, also deserves to be remembered for its contributions to the great body of American music. That's why this book was written.

The theme of this book is the importance of the image of the cowboy in country music. There are 47 chapters, each about a different artist or some aspect of western music, so there is some overlap. And some readers will surely point out things I missed. This book is not written as a straight narrative but rather consists of a collection of pieces that tell about western music from slightly different angles.

Within the western music community there is an insistence that there is a huge difference between "country" music and "western" music and those in "western" music are continually frustrated that fans don't see the difference. Personally, I view western music as a branch or offshoot of country music, just as bluegrass is. Others see a total separation between "country" and "western," with the primary difference being that "western" music is the more positive and more "pure" of the two.

Back in the 1960s there was an ongoing dialogue about the difference between "folk" and "country" music. Those outside these fields tended to lump them together; those within the walls of these communities saw a huge difference. The same situation confronts the family of western music. Part of the difficulty is a resistance to change; country music is loyal to the market, while western music is loyal to a sound and image. Country music changes with each generation and incorporates the sounds of pop music as it grows and attracts new, young adherents. Western music sees itself as timeless, embracing the sounds of country music of the 1940s and 1950s but rejecting both the sound and topics of contemporary country, which deals with a contemporary world. In the western music community, there is a resistance to the contemporary world, although the Internet has made it possible for those who love western music to find this music, and other fans, even though they live miles apart.

In western music, many performers still live in a past that embraces the singing cowboy movies and television filled with the western shows of the late 1950s. In many ways, western music is the country music they used to love. But western music does have a distinctive character, embracing the morals and values during the "family era" of the 1950s and a music whose lyrics celebrate the beauty of the West and the distinctiveness of the American cowboy.

In the twenty-first century, western music is alive and well but it has grown old. In order for the music to last, it must attract young people and that's a difficult chore when over 80 percent of Americans live in the suburbs and the cowboy on television and in the movies is, mostly, a thing of the past. Still, if the cowboy is the enduring symbol of country music, he is also the enduring symbol of America. The cowboy is one of only two unique American characters developed in entertainment (the other is the minstrel show performer). One can't help but believe that a character this unique will live on through the years and that music by, about and for cowboys will continue to be written and performed, even though real life working cowboys are few and far between.

Introduction: Cowboys and Country Music

The cowboy is the most enduring symbol of country music. The image of the cowboy permeates country music; country artists often wear cowboy hats and boots and sing about being a cowboy. Although contemporary cowboys tend to ride in pickup trucks instead of on horses and live in the suburbs rather than on ranches, the idea that a freedom loving, independent, going-his-own-way type of individual who doesn't care what society allows or others think is a "true cowboy" is embraced by many people in the country music community.

Those outside of country music also link cowboys with the music, often referring to "country-western" music—an outdated term—to describe contemporary country music. Advertisers and marketers take advantage of the fact that cowboys and country music are linked; look at a picture of a cowboy hat on a guitar, or cowboy boots beside a guitar, or a band dressed in cowboy hats and western garb and anyone looking at the photo is bound to think "country music."

By the beginning of the twentieth century, the image of the cowboy as a romantic hero was part of American culture. But the cowboy as a hero wasn't exactly the same cowboy who drove cattle up the trails in the nineteenth century; that cowboy was a low-paid hired worker who had a mostly boring though sometimes dangerous job. For the cowboy to become a romantic hero, the cattle had to be taken out of the picture, and this was done by show business.

The first step towards turning cowboys into heroic figures came with the dime novels, so named because they were short novels—about 30,000 words or about 100 pages if they were printed as a paperback today—that sold for a dime. In the era before electronic media, when print media was the mass media, those ten-cent novels served almost the same purpose then as movies do today. In addition to dime novels, there were "pulp magazines" that printed western stories; those served the same basic function as weekly TV series do today.

Buffalo Bill was a hero in early dime novels, as were other real life figures such as Calamity Jane, Wild Bill Hickok and others, but the dime novel stories rarely had anything to do with most real life exploits. Many of their stories were written by easterners who simply made up stories about the Wild West.

Buffalo Bill Cody took advantage of his depiction in the dime novels; he was attracted to show business and went East to appear and tour in a play, *Scouts of the Plains*. However, Cody always returned to the West, where he worked as an Indian scout or guide. In 1882 the town of North Platte, Nebraska, where Cody lived, asked him to organize a celebration for July 4. Cody organized the "Old Glory Blowout," which was part rodeo and part Wild West show. Actually, it was the forerunner to both the rodeo and his Wild West Show. Cody offered cash prizes for cowboys to compete in various events, expecting to attract about a hundred cowboys. He was surprised that over a thousand competed. There was also a buffalo hunt and some staged spectacles, which led to Cody's organizing a Wild West Show in 1883 which toured the United States and Europe for the next twenty-five years.

At first the Wild West played one-night stands but began playing long engagements on permanent grounds in 1886 with their summer-long engagement on Staten Island in New York. In 1887 Cody toured Europe and received international acclaim when he made a royal command performance before Queen Victoria in London on May 11, 1887. Cody reached the height of his fame in 1893 at the Chicago World's Fair when he set up the Wild West Show in a lot across from the fair's entrance and enjoyed huge crowds. At this point there were about 300 people and 500 horses in the show.

Cody hired Buck Taylor and made him the "King of the Cowboys," who rode to the rescue of those in distress during dramatic attacks on the stagecoach during the show. And, of course, Buffalo Bill Cody, dressed in his western garb, was an authentic cowboy hero himself for all the world to see.

During the first few years of the twentieth century there were two people who made a major contribution to the popularity of cowboys. The first was Theodore Roosevelt, who became president in September 1901 after President William McKinley had been assassinated. Roosevelt had lived in the West during the 1880s and wrote about it; he was widely known as "the cowboy President" and his connection with the West (and the Rough Riders) brought a lot of attention to cowboys and the West and gave them both a degree of respectability in eastern circles. The second person was Owen Wister, a Harvard classmate of Roosevelt's, who wrote a novel, *The Virginian*, which became one of the most popular novels of all time. This novel was not only a best-seller, but was also influential, as the character "The Virginian" established the prototype of a western hero.

By the end of the nineteenth century, Thomas Edison had invented the movie camera and early, crude movies were made and shown in vaudeville houses. Edison made short films of Buffalo Bill Cody and Annie Oakley shooting guns and in 1898 there was a movie about three minutes long entitled *Cripple Creek Bar-Room* that consisted of some actors dressed as cowboys standing around a saloon, re-creating a western scene.

The first "feature" movie was only ten minutes long and was done in 1903 by Edwin S. Porter, who worked for Edison. This movie was a western, *The Great Train Robbery*, and was filmed in the wilds of New Jersey. This movie is considered the first to have a plot, and the plot became fairly standard: bad guys rob a train and tie up a girl on a railroad track, good guy saves the girl from an oncoming train and goes to a saloon where he confronts the bad guys, who are shooting at some tenderfoot's feet making him dance, but the good guy saves everything and brings justice to the outlaws.

Broncho Billy Anderson was the first actor to create a western hero/character with his films, which began around 1908 and were finished by 1920; he was also the first to film in California, settling near San Francisco. The movie which established Hollywood, California, as a major location for movies was a western, *The Squaw Man*, directed by Cecil B. DeMille and released in 1913. With the establishment of the movie industry in California, and the production of westerns there, the creation of the "image" of the modern cowboy was linked to California.

During the silent movie era several cowboy stars emerged. The first major cowboy movie star was William S. Hart, who starred in western movies he wrote and directed from 1915 to 1925. Hart's silent movies were sentimental and romantic but also authentic; he dressed in rough garb and the sets were dusty. Hart was extremely popular with audiences during the silent era, which saw major western movies like *The Covered Wagon* (1923), *The Iron Horse* (1924), *Three Badmen* (1926), and *North of '36* (1926). Clearly, there was an appeal for westerns as the movie industry developed. After William S. Hart, Tom Mix dominated. Mix differed from Hart because, while Hart insisted on realism with his clothing and sets, Mix moved towards escapism; this meant that Mix dressed in fancy clothes no cowboy ever wore riding the dusty range. There was an element of "glamour" and "show biz" in movie cowboys after Tom Mix. In many ways, it was Tom Mix who showed movie cowboys how to dress for the screen and changed the image of the American cowboy, at least for the movies.

Tom Mix (photograph courtesy of Packy Smith).

When the "talkies" came in, heralded by *The Jazz Singer* in 1927, many producers and directors of westerns believed it was impossible to have westerns with sound because of the problems with filming outdoors; however those problems were overcome and in 1929 the first major "talkie" western, *In Old Arizona*, appeared. The story featured the Cisco Kid, played by Warner Baxter, who earned an Academy Award for his role. Other early important sound westerns were *The Virginian* (1929) starring Gary Cooper and *Cimarron* (1931), which won the Academy Award for best picture.

Sound westerns weren't regularly made until after 1932 because of technical problems that had to be solved by sound engineers and because most movie houses were not fully converted to sound until that time. By this point there had emerged in Hollywood two types of movies produced by studios: the "A" movies were big budget films, while the "B" movies and serials were made more cheaply. There were several reasons for this. First, the major studios owned the "first run" theaters in American cities; smaller towns and "second run" theaters were owned and run by independent operators. This meant that "A" films had a built-in audience for their release, but a lot of small towns and smaller theaters would not get the films. Second, movies were the major entertainment outlet after they replaced vaudeville, and people who went to the movies on a Saturday wanted to see several movies, perhaps a serial (which usually ended in a "cliff-hanger" to be continued the next week), a newsreel, a short full-length movie and then an "A" movie. Thus there was a demand for the "B" movie ("B" can stand for either "budget" or a notch below "A"). This is important because most westerns were "B" movies, so the impact of westerns on American culture was mostly through this genre.

There was much debate when sound was introduced about whether it would actually work or not. Many people believed silents were just fine; besides, there were a lot of immigrants in major cities who couldn't understand English but could appreciate a silent movie. But singing was different; in fact, in *The Jazz Singer*, the dialogue is shown like that of a silent movie and only the singing is heard.

It is natural that people wanted singing incorporated into cowboy movies because they were being incorporated in other movies; the advent of sound breathed new life into this old format. The first to incorporate singing in a cowboy movie was Ken Maynard, one of the most popular cowboy stars in the late 1920s and early 1930s. He first sang in *Wagon Master* (1929); then in a short Tiffany film, *Voice of Hollywood* (1930), he played his fiddle and sang a song. In *The Fighting Legion* (1930) a trio sang a saloon song and in two other movies from 1930, *Song of the Caballero* and *Sons of the Saddle,* Maynard sang and accompanied himself on fiddle and banjo. He sang in several other movies before he left Universal Studios and signed with Mascot, a small company known for its serials. Maynard wanted to continue featuring singing in his cowboy pictures but wasn't a particularly strong singer; also, he had problems with alcohol and was often belligerent and difficult to work with. So when *In Old Santa Fe* (1935) was cast, another singer was hired.

Ken Maynard (photograph courtesy of Packy Smith).

Gene Autry was a successful singer on *National Barn Dance* on WLS in Chicago and recorded for the American Record Company, which was owned by Herbert J. Yates. Yates also owned Republic Pictures, which merged with Mascot, so Yates owned the movie company as well. *In Old Santa Fe* marked the movie debut of Gene Autry.

On Maynard's next film, *Mystery Mountain,* the actor proved to be too difficult and the decision was made to fire him; however, the producers waited until the film was completed before they gave Maynard the news. This meant that a serial, *Phantom Empire,* was set for production but there was no "star." The movie company decided to let Autry star in the series although they did not expect any great things from him. Autry did not look like the usual movie cowboy star, most of whom came from Wild West shows and rodeos. But the serial was already written so they decided to go ahead. Further, they decided to cast him as his real name, "Gene Autry," to capitalize on his success as a recording and radio artist rather than give him a character's name; it was hoped this would sell tickets in the South and Midwest where these "B" westerns had their prime market. Autry's debut proved a huge success and launched him as a star, beginning with his first feature film, *Tumbling Tumbleweeds,* in 1935.

This coincided with a trend in songwriting that began when songs were first heard in movies. At the end of the 1920s, movie studios began purchasing publishing companies and "Tin Pan Alley" shifted to Los Angeles, where songwriters wrote for Hollywood movies instead of Broadway musicals. For the singing cowboy movies this meant that professional songwriters now wrote cowboy songs, using the popular song format with western themes and lyrics.

New York songwriters had written "cowboy" songs before the movies to capitalize on the popularity of the West, but it was not until the singing cowboys of the 1930s and 1940s that the songwriting machine really cranked up. This made a huge difference for the music industry. First, it took cowboy songs away from the folk tradition and put them into the popular song tradition; second, it took country music out of the South, where it was considered a regional music, and spread it nationally; third, it showed songwriters and publishers there was money to be made in country music with the right outlet; fourth, it changed the image of country music, which used to be that of "hillbilly" and "hayseeds" performers to a singer wearing cowboy attire; and fifth it gave cowboy music a huge body of songs created for popular culture. More than any other source, the singing cowboys from the Hollywood movies of 1935–1950 were responsible for the sound, image and number of cowboy songs. Without the singing cowboys, country music would have remained a small folk genre and never merged with popular songwriting and mainstream popular music.

SOURCES:

Cusic, Don. *Cowboys and the Wild West: An A to Z Guide from the Chisholm Trail to the Silver Screen*. New York: Facts on File, 1994.
Dary, David. *Cowboy Culture: A Saga of Five Centuries*. Lawrence: University Press of Kansas, 1981, 1989.
Everson, William K. *History of the Western Film*. Secaucus, NJ: Citadel Press, 1969.
Green, Douglas B. *Singing in the Saddle: The History of the Singing Cowboy*. Nashville: Country Music Foundation Press and Vanderbilt University Press, 2002.
Loy, R. Philip. *Westerns and American Culture, 1930–1955*. Jefferson, NC: McFarland, 2001.
Malone, Bill. *Country Music U.S.A.* Austin: University of Texas Press, 1968.
Malone, Bill C. *Singing Cowboys and Musical Mountaineers: Southern Culture and the Roots of Country Music*. Athens: University of Georgia Press, 1993.
Slatta, Richard. *Cowboys of the Americas*. New Haven, CT: Yale University Press, 1990.
Tuska, Jon. *The Vanishing Legion: A History of Mascot Pictures, 1927–1935*. Jefferson, NC: McFarland, 1982.

1
Roundin' Up Radio

There is no such thing as "western music," although there are western songs. Western songs are defined by their lyrics, and a prevailing definition would state that they deal with the West and western culture, particularly cowboys. There are several types of western songs: (1) songs of the working cowboy; (2) songs of the beauty and grandeur of the West; (3) songs from the Tin Pan Alley songwriters who wrote for the singing cowboy movies; and (4) contemporary songs that picture the cowboy as a freedom loving cuss who is independent, strong, and manly, and who adheres to a basic code of the West loosely defined as self-centered individualism with a conscience. These are important distinctions when discussing what is referred to as "western music" on the radio airwaves during the 1922–1953 period. Briefly, the earliest "western" on radio was western songs, sometimes performed by authentic cowboys. This evolved to performers who dressed in western clothing—and presented a western image but did not necessarily embrace the western lifestyle—and sang a wide variety of music and songs on the radio. To put it in cowboy terms, we're looking at a long line of cowboy boots that begins with a dirty, mud-caked boot with cow manure on the bottom and goes through a series of boots that become cleaner and neater until we end with a custom made boot with colorful insignia and polished to a high shine.

The earliest western songs from the nineteenth century, corresponding to the era 1865–1890 when cowboys drove cattle to the railheads, were primarily songs by and about working cowboys. Prior to the development and popularity of radio and recordings, these songs were collected in print form. The two most important collections of western songs published in the late 19th and early 20th centuries are Jack Thorp's *Songs of the Cowboys* and John Lomax's *Cowboy Songs and Other Frontier Ballads*.

During the 1920s, with the advent of the radio and recording industries, western songs began to be heard by large audiences. Early radio programming was a smorgasbord of talks, lectures, music and drama; its major concern was filling up air time while trying to figure out how to make money with the new medium. Taking its cues from vaudeville, which consisted of a variety of acts, radio developed programming that consisted of a wide variety of shows—drama, comedy, musical—to fill up the air time.

Since about half the nation was rural, and most of the rest lived in towns—there were very few big cities—radio stations considered the rural audience an important market. Songs known as "old familiar" or "folk" tunes—which later came under the umbrella of what became known as "country music" and which encompass folk songs, string bands, bluegrass, gospel and western—were part of this programming. In general, the performers, audience, and music were all considered "rural" and western songs fit here.

Saturday night had once been radio's "dead" night, but rural music found a home, playing to listeners after they'd finished their week's work. These shows were called "barn dances," which were actually variety shows aimed at a rural audience. They offered a smattering of entertainment and included old folk songs, barbershop quartet numbers, songs from the minstrel and vaudeville stages, novelty numbers, Gay nineties sentimental songs, cowboy songs and newer songs written by performers. There were harmony groups, comedians, instrumentalists, novelty acts and square dancers. These shows embraced western singers.

The term "barn dance" was first used with a rural music show in January 1923 when a square dance show began at WBAP in Fort Worth, Texas, led by fiddler M.J. Bonner. Sometime around 1925 WBAP carried a regular Friday night barn dance.

By 1922 WSB out of Atlanta had rural performers on the air; the most famous was Fiddlin' John Carson, whose 1923 recording of "Little Ole Log Cabin Down the Lane," b/w "The Old Hen Cackl'd and the Rooster's Gonna Crow," essentially began the commercial country music recording industry.

In Chicago at WLS, a station owned by Sears, Roebuck and Co., a barn dance began on April 19, 1924, held at the Sherman Hotel. The show was created by WLS executive Edgar L. Bill and one of its first announcers was George D. Hay, who later began the Grand Ole Opry. At this first *National Barn Dance* old time fiddler Tommy Dandurand, with square dance caller Tom Owen, re-created the old fashioned country barn dance.

On October, 1, 1928, Prairie Farmer Publications purchased WLS from Sears and the station increased its wattage from 500 to 5,000. By this time the Barn Dance ran five and a half hours (7:35 P.M. to 1 A.M.) on Saturday nights. Burridge D. Butler, publisher of *The Prairie Farmer*, managed in a paternalistic style and the show became highly moralistic and family-oriented during his years at the helm.

The most popular performer on WLS during the 1920s was Bradley Kincaid, known for singing old folk standards such as "Barbara Allen"; he also sang some old western songs. Kincaid stayed at WLS from 1926 to 1929, during which time he became the first country radio artist to publish a songbook, *Favorite Mountain Ballads and Old Time Songs* (1928). Kincaid left WLS in 1929 and moved to WLW in Cincinnati, then on to Pittsburgh, Schenectady, New York, New York City and Boston during the 1930s. Arkie, the Arkansas Woodchopper, whose real name was Luther W. Ossenbrink, cultivated the image of an outdoorsman but recorded about a dozen cowboy songs and, according to Douglas B. Green in his book, *Singing in the Saddle*, may have paved the way for Gene Autry as a singing cowboy at WLS.

The "official" beginning of the *WSM Barn Dance* in Nashville was November 28, 1925, when George D. Hay, who headed the original *National Barn Dance*, hosted fiddler Uncle Jimmy Thompson. *WSM Barn Dance* changed its name to the *Grand Ole Opry* in 1927.

There were few western singers on the radio in this first era of rural programming. Perhaps the most famous during the 1920s was Otto Gray & His Oklahoma Cowboys on KFRU in Bristow, Oklahoma, which became KVOO in Tulsa. The group later moved to KFJF in Kansas City. Otto Gray was neither a singer nor a musician, but he financed, fronted and managed the top western group of the 1920s. Gray, who performed as a trick roper during their live shows, began his performing career in 1918 as Otto & His Rodeo Rubes. In 1924 he took over management of the Billy McGinty Cowboy Band and changed their name to Otto Gray and his Oklahoma Cowboys. During the 1928–1932 period, Gray's group toured extensively in addition to their work on radio, but did not record much, so their legacy has not been well preserved. Gray was so successful in his day that he became the first cowboy entertainer to appear on the cover of *Billboard* magazine. Although their image was western, their musical performances reflected the pop music of the 1920s, including a healthy dose of novelty numbers. Two of Grey's members, Zeke Clements and Whitey Ford ("the Duke of Paducah") became well known performers after Grey's group disbanded.

There were some radio performers doing western songs during the 1920s. Jules Verne Allen, who had been a working cowboy, performed on WFAA in Dallas, KFI and KNX in Los Angles and WOAI and KTSA in San Antonio during the 1920s, calling himself "the Original Singing Cowboy," "Longhorn Luke" and "Shiftless." Verne also published a songbook in the 1920s, *Cowboy Songs Sung by Longhorn Luke and His Cowboys*; later, in 1933, his *Cowboy Lore*, consisting of 36 cowboy songs, was published. In 1926, John Crockett, "the Cowboy Singer" had a local program over KMJ in Fresno, California.

In terms of western songs, the 1920s are known for the earliest recordings of numerous cowboy classics. One of the biggest sellers during this era was "When the Work's All Done This Fall," recorded by Carl Sprague for Victor in 1925. But western "stars" during the 1920s were on the movie screen, not on the radio or recordings. That, however, changed during the next decade.

During the 1930s, radio became the major way that rural music was heard by listeners, replacing the phonograph of the 1920s. For performers, radio had a profound impact; no longer were amateurs who played music on the side part of the game. Professional entertainers emerged and, as rural music became more commercial, rural performers had careers instead of an avocation. Also, because radio demanded a huge repertoire, no longer could a musician or group get by with just a few tunes. Audiences no longer accepted the tunes they had been hearing for years; performers either had to compose new songs or find songs from professional songwriters. This affected western performers because audiences soon grew tired of hearing the same old cowboy songs over and over.

The new carbon microphones demanded a new type of singing; gone was the belt-'em-out style and in was the crooning sound where singers sang softly with emotion. The most popular singers, like Bing Crosby, Jimmie Rodgers and, later, Gene Autry, developed an easy-going, conversational vocal style that appealed to listeners, who felt it was accessible and sincere.

The first national exposure for western songs came with *Death Valley Days*, an NBC show sponsored by Borax. John I. White, who billed himself "The Lonesome Cowboy," sang old cowboy songs on the show from 1930 until 1936.

Any discussion of western singers on the radio must center on Gene Autry, especially after his popularity in the singing cowboy movies from 1935 on. Autry was not the first western singer, nor was he the last; he was not an "authentic" cowboy and some didn't even like his singing (he was criticized for being "too slick"). But Gene Autry was the biggest and most influential western singer in the history of this music and, because of his popularity and success, he inspired a number of others to become western singers, or singers who dressed in western clothing.

By 1931, Autry was performing over KVOO in Tulsa, Oklahoma, and had been recording since October 1929. He performed a wide variety of music; his recordings ranged from Jimmie Rodgers songs (or songs that sounded like Jimmie Rodgers songs) to mountain ballads and hillbilly tunes. His biggest hit, recorded about two months before he joined WLS, was "That Silver Haired Daddy of Mine." Known as "Oklahoma's Singing Cowboy," Autry appeared on shows on WLS in addition to *National Barn Dance*. Since WLS reached into the Midwest, or the "prairie" country, the addition of a western singer—or a singer dressed in western clothing—made sense.

By the end of 1933, performers at WLS, in addition to Gene Autry, included Lily May Ledford, "the fiddlinest girl to ever come out of the mountains," Georgie Gobel, "the littlest cowboy," who played the ukulele dressed in a cowboy costume, Patsy Montana and the Prairie

Ramblers (who changed their name from the Kentucky Ramblers), Denver Darling in a trio with George "Shug" Fisher and Hugh Cross, Joe Maphis, the DeZurik Sisters with their Swiss-style yodeling, Red Foley, the Girls of the Golden West, and Lulu Belle and Skyland Scotty, who did songs like "Chewing Chawing Gum," "How Many Biscuits Can You Eat?" and two songs Scotty wrote, "Have I Told You Lately That I Love You?" and "Remember Me."

WLS in Chicago became known for their "western" performers, led by Gene Autry, who left the station in 1934 to go to Hollywood. A number of other acts who played important roles in the singing cowboy movement began at WLS. These include Autry's sidekick, Smiley Burnette, Rex Allen, Eddie Dean, Bob Baker, the Willis Brothers, Patsy Montana, Bob Atcher, the Girls of the Golden West, Louise Massey and the Westerners, and the Prairie Ramblers. Other acts soon began wearing western clothing and singing western songs.

There was a lot of what later became known as "country" music—which included western singers and western songs—on radio in the 1930s; in 1932 there was the *Iowa Barn Dance Frolic* on WHO in Des Moines, and the Kentucky Ramblers were on WOC in Davenport, Iowa, where a young announcer named Ronald Reagan was working. Tex Owens had his own show as "The Texas Ranger" and was also a member of the *Brush Creek Follies* on KMBC in Kansas City, Missouri. In 1933 Texas Jim Lewis was on WJR in Detroit. Lewis formed a band called the Lone Star Rangers, later renamed the Lone Star Cowboys, and in Halifax, Nova Scotia, Hank Snow sang on CHNS. In 1934 the Swift Jewel Cowboys were on WMC in Memphis.

In 1932 in New York City, *Bobby Benson's Adventures* began on CBS. This show, which ran into the 1950s, featured a 12-year-old boy's adventures on the B-Bar-B Ranch, where the foreman was Tex Mason, sometimes played by Tex Ritter. Ritter (and others) sang western songs on this program.

Ritter also appeared with the Lone Star Rangers on WOR and later on *Cowboy Tom's Roundup*, a daily children's show, and hosted *Tex Ritter's Campfire* on WHN in 1932 in New York. Beginning in 1933, Ethel Park Richardson hosted a weekly program from New York on NBC, *Hillbilly Heart-Throbs*, that featured guests such as Tex Ritter, Frank Luther, Zora Layman, Carson Robison, Texas Jim Robertson and the Vass Family. In 1933 Foy Willing did a radio show sponsored by Crazy Water Crystals in New York, and in 1934 Patsy Montana and the Prairie Ramblers moved to WOR, New York, from WLS for a year before returning to Chicago. Also in 1934, Tex Ritter was the featured performer on the *WHN Barn Dance* in New York and hosted the show with Ray Whitley. The next year Texas Jim Lewis and his Lone Star Cowboys were at the Village Barn.

The Beverly Hill Billies were the first rural music stars in Los Angeles. They first appeared on KMPC on April 6, 1930, created by KMPC announcers Glen "Mr. Tallfeller" Rice and John McIntire. The group was a huge success on radio and began recording for Brunswick in April 1930. In September 1932 the group joined KTM.

Providing competition for the Beverly Hill Billies was the *Hollywood Barn Dance* and Stuart Hamblen's *Lucky Stars* program on KFWB, both established in 1932. In 1934 the Sons of the Pioneers were on KFWB. Along with Gene Autry, the Sons of the Pioneers were the most successful and influential western singers. Their trio harmony sound was adopted by a number of groups who performed rural music. The Sons of the Pioneer wrote classic western songs, especially Bob Nolan, who penned "Tumbling Tumbleweeds" and "Cool Water." Founding member Len Slye later changed his name to Roy Rogers and became a singing cowboy star in the movies. Although they appeared in a number of singing cowboy movies, the Sons of the Pioneers kept a steady presence on radio through their own shows, recordings, and transcriptions.

The Sons of the Pioneers made early use of a kind of syndication for performers when they recorded transcriptions. These 12 to 16 inch discs held 15 minutes, or "a show's worth," and the Sons recorded a number of these and sent them out to radio stations via a transcription service. These transcription services provided a programming service to radio stations, an alternative to the barn dances that popularized western songs and performers in the 1930s.

Just across the Texas border in Mexico rural music was getting a boost from Border Stations, established there beginning in 1930 when XED began broadcasting from Renosa, Tamaulipas. The station was originally owned by Will Horwitz, a Houston theater owner and philanthropist. Jimmy Rodgers played there. Then Dr. John R. Brinkley moved in.

Dr. John Romulus Brinkley grew rich and famous in Milford, Kansas, by pioneering the implementation of slivers of billy goat sex glands into humans to "rejuvenate" their sex drive. In 1930 he ran for governor of Kansas and almost won, but soon after the election he was run out of the state by medical authorities. In 1931 he established XER (later XERA) just across the border from Del Rio, Texas, in Villa Acuna, Mexico, a 100,000 watt station. Then he purchased XED and changed its call letters to XEAW.

In 1933 Brinkley gave up the goat gland business and began a controversial prostate treatment. His radio stations, and others on the Mexican border such as XEPN in Piedras Negras and XENT in Nuevo Laredo, came about because Mexico had been denied United States broadcasting licenses; Canada and the United States divided these up among themselves, leaving Mexico out. These outlaw stations, which broadcast from 50,000 to 500,000 watts, blanketed the United States.

During the 1930s there were about a dozen "border blaster" stations playing records and transcriptions as well as hosting live shows. Singers going by the names Utah Cowboy, the Lonesome Cowhand, Cowboy Max, the Rio Grande Cowboys, Cowboy Slim Nichols, Cowboy Jack, Tex Ivey and His Original Ranch Boys, and Doc Schneider and His Yodeling Texas Cowboys were an important source of western songs for the airwaves. Listeners also heard the Carter Family, Patsy Montana, the Pickard Family, Pappy O'Daniel's Hillbilly Boys, Roy "Lonesome Cowboy" Faulkner, Buck Nation, Red River Dave, Jesse Rodgers (a distant cousin of Jimmie) and others. Perhaps the most popular singing cowboy was Nolan "Cowboy Slim" Rinehart, whose theme song was "Roaming Cowboy."

In 1934 WSM was awarded "clear channel" status, which meant that no other AM station in the country could operate on the 650 slot on the radio dial. That same year Zeke Clements, an alumnus of Otto Gray and His Oklahoma Cowboys, became the first Opry act to wear cowboy clothing.

In 1932 there were five radio stations in Kentucky: the largest was WHAS in Louisville, an NBC affiliate with 25,000 watts. In 1934 J.L. Frank moved from Chicago to Louisville, and the following year at WHAS were Cousin Emmy, the Callahan Brothers, and Clayton McMichen. J.L. Frank was the driving force at WHAS in Louisville and a great concert promoter. In early 1935, before he moved to Hollywood, Gene Autry performed regularly on WHAS. In 1936 J.L. Frank formed the group the Golden West Cowboys, led by Pee Wee King, and moved to Knoxville and then, in 1937, to Nashville to join the Grand Ole Opry.

The turning point for western singers on the radio occurred when Gene Autry went West to Hollywood in 1935 and starred in his first singing cowboy movie, *Tumbling Tumbleweeds*. Autry's success during the 1935–1940 period inspired countless other singers to wear western clothing and sing western songs. Because of Autry's success, what later became known as "country music" moved from the image of the musical mountaineer to the singing cowboy.

By the 1930s, Atlanta was the second largest city in the South (behind New Orleans) with a population over 350,000. The powerhouse station in Atlanta was WSB, which increased its power to 5,000 watts in 1930, then to 50,000 watts in 1933. On Monday, January 3, 1936, they began the *Cross Roads Follies*, the first program that featured a cast of rural performers. Acts on WSB included the Texas Wranglers (with fiddle player Boudleaux Bryant) and Santa Fe Trailers as well as Curly Fox and the Tennessee Firecrackers, and Ernest Rogers.

On June 1, 1937, Pee Wee King and the Golden West Cowboys, managed by J.L. Frank, joined the Grand Ole Opry and introduced the trumpet, drums and electric guitar to the show. Also, their spiffy western outfits and well organized touring were reminiscent of the Big Band organizations.

In 1936 Louise Massey & the Westerners were on NBC's *Log Cabin Dude Ranch* in New York and were a headline act at the Waldorf-Astoria, the Rainbow Room and others venues. In September 1937 Denver Darling moved to New York and performed on WOR and at the Village Barn in Greenwich Village.

In 1936 the Sons of the Pioneers had shows on KFOX and KRKD in Los Angeles before settling in at KHJ on Peter Potter's *Hollywood Barn Dance*. In Texas the *Crazy Water Crystals Show* began from Mineral Wells' Crazy Hotel; the show was broadcast on NBC and featured the Light Crust Doughboys. The Crazy Water Crystals company was owned by Carr P. Collins and named for an alleged cure of two insane ladies in the 1880s. In 1936 the company sponsored *Saturday Night Stampede* on Fort Worth's WBAP and a live show from Ranger Junior College that featured Jules Verne Allen singing songs such as "Cowboy's Lament" and "Santa Fe Trail." In 1937, Doc Williams and Big Slim and the Lone Star Cowboy (Harry McAuliffe) joined the *WWVA Jamboree* in Wheeling, West Virginia.

After Gene Autry's success in the movies, more and more country singers began wearing western clothing and adopting western names for radio programs. Still, a western singer remained only part of these "barn dances," which continued to seek a wide variety of entertainment for rural audiences. Historian Bill C. Malone noted the following:

> By the end of the 1930s the cowboy or western impulse had become a refuge for country entertainers, or their managers, who sought a respectable or more up-to-date alternative to the hillbilly image. Cowboy costuming was decidedly more romantic than any kind of clothing associated with rural plain folk life, and western-cut suits could in fact suggest the more dignified and hence more prosperous milieu of the rancher. Many of the cowboy songs, especially those from Tin Pan Alley, tended to be more sophisticated in style and structure than the typical hillbilly offerings.
>
> [Malone continues] Individual cowboy singers bearing names such as Red River Dave, Powder River Jack, the Yodeling Ranger, Cowboy Slim, the Lonesome Cowboy, Montana Slim, Patsy Montana and the Texas Drifter vied with cowboy bands and singing groups who called themselves Radio Rangers, Radio Cowboys, Cowboy Ramblers, Westerners, Mountain Rangers, Driving Pioneers, Trail Blazers, Range Riders, Riders of the Purple Sage, Sons of the Pioneers, Oklahoma Cowboys, Bar-X Cowboys, 101 Ranch Boys, Golden West Cowboys, Girls of the Golden West, Prairie Ramblers and on and on.

Malone succinctly notes that, by World War II, "the cowboy had won the day in country music."

The "western" shows on radio after 1940 were dominated by Gene Autry and his *Melody Ranch* program, sponsored by Doublemint Chewing Gum on the CBS network. On this show, as well as on Roy Rogers' radio shows, a wide variety of music was sung—everything from western classics to the pop hits of the day.

The barn dances in radio were still going strong in the post–World War II era and there were certainly a healthy number of western songs performed by western performers during this period. In 1944 *Billboard* magazine estimated there were 600 regular rural-oriented radio shows in the United States and they reached an estimated 40 million people. That same year, a movie, *National Barn Dance*, was produced by Paramount that featured Jean Heather,

Charles Quigley, Robert Benchley and Mabel Paige, with performances by Pat Buttram, Joe Kelly, Lulu Belle & Scotty, the Dinning Sisters, the Hoosier Hot Shots and Arkie, the Arkansas Woodchopper.

A survey at the end of World War II indicated that WLS was the most important and most influential rural radio show. However, in 1946, Alka-Seltzer dropped its sponsorship of *National Barn Dance* and the show did not have network exposure again until 1949, when the Phillips Petroleum Company sponsored the show on ABC. However, *National Barn Dance* continued to broadcast on the airwaves.

After World War II, what evolved as "western" music was primarily defined by the performers. If western music is defined by the performers rather than by the songs—in other words, if someone dresses western (cowboy hat, boots, western themed outfits), projects the "image" of a cowboy, and accepts the "cowboy attitude"—then the field of "western" can be much broader and all kinds of music may be considered "western."

In 1955, barn dances were still on radio, primarily because the rural areas in the United States received television later than the urban areas. In 1955 rock and roll emerged with Bill Haley and the Comets' hit recording of "Rock Around the Clock." In 1956, Elvis sold ten million records, and radio increasingly looked to rock and roll for programming. WLS lasted until 1960, when it was sold to American Broadcasting-Paramount Theaters, which changed the station's musical format to rock'n'roll. The *WGN Barn Dance* emerged a few months later, using a number of WLS performers, and this show lasted until 1971.

In the early 1950s, radio barn dances began to make the transition to television; some of the earliest were the *Midwestern Hayride* from Cincinnati; *The Ozark Jubilee* from Springfield, Missouri; Connie B. Gay's *Town and Country Time* from Washington, D.C; and Al Gannaway's *Stars of the Grand Ole Opry* from Nashville. Soon, however, the barn dance format gave way to pop-type variety shows hosted by "stars" such as Eddy Arnold, Red Foley and, later, Johnny Cash and Glen Campbell.

By 1955, the singing cowboy movies were finished and no more were made. Although Gene Autry and Roy Rogers made the transition to television during the 1950s, these shows did not have the impact on music that movies did, with the exception of the song "Happy Trails," the theme song for Roy Rogers and Dale Evans. (Autry's theme song, "Back in the Saddle Again," became a hit from his radio shows, which started before World War II.)

The next group of well-known western songs came primarily from television shows such as *Maverick, Bonanza, Cheyenne, Ballad of Davey Crockett, Legend of Wyatt Earp, The Ballad of Paladin* and *The Rebel Johnny Yuma* or from movie soundtracks, such as "Theme from *High Noon* (Do Not Forsake Me, Oh My Darlin')," "The Magnificent Seven," and "The Good, the Bad and the Ugly." Most of these songs received no radio airplay or were hits on pop radio.

After 1960, the appearance of cowboys on TV and in the movies was curtailed. The pioneers of western music ended their entertainment careers, or at least did not appear as "mainstream" entertainers, although some could still be found in Las Vegas or working the state and county fair circuits. The major way that western songs, or songs with a western theme, have gotten on the radio since the 1960s has been when country artists recorded them.

SOURCES:

Malone, Bill. *Country Music U.S.A.* Austin: University of Texas Press, 1968.
Malone, Bill C. *Singing Cowboys and Musical Mountaineers: Southern Culture and the Roots of Country Music.* Athens: University of Georgia Press, 1993.
Morris, Edward. "New, Improved, Homogenized: Country Radio Since 1950." In *Country: The Music and the Musicians.* New York: Abbeville Press, 1988.
Wolfe, Charles K. "The Triumph of the Hills: Country Radio, 1920–1950." In *Country: The Music and the Musicians.* New York: Abbeville Press, 1988.

2

Gene Autry and *The Phantom Empire*

There's no argument that Gene Autry was the first singing cowboy star; however, his first feature, *Tumbling Tumbleweeds*, released in 1935, is credited with being the vehicle that launched the singing cowboy into movie theaters and Autry into movie stardom. Actually, it was a serial that Gene Autry did earlier, *The Phantom Empire*, which both launched the singing cowboy as a movie hero as well as Autry into movie stardom.

When film critics speak of *The Phantom Empire*, they generally focus on its mixture of science fiction and westerns. In fact, in terms of science fiction, it was a pioneer serial, arriving at theaters a year ahead of Buck Rogers and other sci-fi serials. Obviously, the success of *The Phantom Empire* inspired Mascot and other film companies to pursue these futuristic serials for Saturday morning fare.

What has been overlooked is the importance of this serial to the singing cowboy genre. This serial was the introduction of the singing cowboys to movie audiences.

The idea for singing cowboy movies came from Nat Levine, founder and owner of Mascot Pictures, after he saw the Ken Maynard film, *Strawberry Roan*, based on the cowboy song by Curley Fletcher. In that film, Maynard sang twice and played the fiddle.

Ken Maynard was a major western star and had sung in several of his previous movies. Levine contacted Maynard and offered him $10,000 a week to join Mascot; however, Maynard elected to remain with Universal, which had signed him in March 1933 to replace Tom Mix as their western star.

Levine had ambitious plans for 1933. Mack Sennett's lot on Ventura Boulevard in the San Fernando Valley had gone into receivership and Levine negotiated a lease with an option to purchase. There were plans for Mascot to produce 12 features and four serials during that year, beginning with *Burn 'em Up Barnes*, a 12 episode serial on auto racing.

Because it was difficult for independent filmmakers to obtain credit—banks were loathe to lend to them—Levine met regularly with Herbert Yates, owner of Consolidated Films, a film processing company. Levine and other independents depended heavily on credit for the film processing from Yates in order to make their pictures. Levine and Yates met at Yates' office in New York to discuss the upcoming Mascot Productions. During this meeting, Levine may have discussed the idea of having Ken Maynard star in singing cowboy movies, although Maynard was still with Universal. At this point, it is possible that Yates brought up Gene Autry's name as a suggestion for Levine's consideration when casting a movie. Yates owned the American Record Corporation, which Autry recorded for. Autry appeared regularly on

WLS in Chicago and *National Barn Dance*, giving him much exposure to radio audiences in the Midwest, and he also sold a lot of records through the Sears, Roebuck catalogue.

Gene Autry and Nat Levine probably met for the first time in September 1933 in Chicago when Levine was either on his way to New York or returning to Los Angeles. Levine was not impressed with Autry as a western film star because the movie producer did not feel Autry was masculine enough. Western film stars had generally come from rodeos or Wild West shows and their "image" was one of being a rough-hewn individualist. Gene Autry, anxious to break into the movies, apparently wrote Nat Levine a number of letters after their Chicago meeting, asking for a chance to appear in films.

Nat Levine still had the idea of creating singing cowboy pictures but was occupied with his other productions. Levine did not feel Gene Autry was the right person for that role, but apparently he did not find anyone else he felt was right for it either. That all changed after a confrontation between Ken Maynard and Carl Laemmle, head of Universal Studios. Maynard had gone over budget on seven movies and Laemmle was not impressed with *Smoking Guns*, the film Maynard had just finished. That confrontation resulted in Maynard walking off the Universal lot and accepting Levine's offer to join Mascot.

This caused a sudden change of plans for Nat Levine, who now had a major cowboy star for Mascot features. Levine probably went to New York to discuss this new development with Herbert Yates and obtain film processing credit. Gene Autry's name again came up during the conversation and Levine decided to have a sequence in the movie where Autry would sing a song and call a square dance. Since Gene Autry was known throughout the Midwest because of his appearances on WLS and *National Barn Dance*, it stood to reason that having Autry in a film was a good investment. On the flip side, if Autry didn't work out, there wasn't much lost.

Levine apparently met with Autry again in Chicago—probably in late spring 1934—and informed the singer that a scene in the Ken Maynard movie would be written for him. The only catch was that Maynard would have to meet Autry first and approve of the singer.

In the summer of 1934, Gene Autry, his wife, Ina Mae, and Smiley Burnette drove to California in Autry's Buick, probably arriving in early to mid–August. On the way out, Smiley Burnette wrote several songs while sitting in the back seat of Autry's car, including "Ridin' Down the Canyon." Autry gave Smiley $5 for the copyright so they are listed as cowriters.

In Hollywood, Autry's meeting with Ken Maynard to get the star's approval went well and filming was set to start in September. On September 4 Mascot signed Autry to a "term" contract, giving him $100 a week for his debut appearance in a movie. The movie was *In Old Santa Fe* and Autry's part was to perform, accompanied by Smiley Burnette, a square dance and sing "Someday in Wyoming." Smiley Burnette did "Mama Don't 'Low No Music in Here," playing all the instruments in the band. Autry then sang "Down In Old Santa Fe."

In Old Santa Fe had contemporary elements in an old West setting. During the film, the leading actress, Evalyn Knapp, drove a sports car and some characters wore clothing that was a mixture of East and West as Maynard battled big city gangsters. This mixture of the Old West infused with modern devices—cars, airplanes, radios, etc.—probably originated with Nat Levine, who needed fresh ideas for the western and wanted a more contemporary setting.

After *In Old Santa Fe* finished filming in late September, Autry and Burnette had small roles in Maynard's next project, a serial *Mystery Mountain*. There were no songs in this serial; Autry and Burnette drove a wagon and benefited from being in the right place at the right time. After the filming of *Mystery Mountain*, Autry and Burnette returned to Chicago for personal appearances and radio shows.

In Old Santa Fe was released on November 15, 1934, and the first chapter in *Mystery Mountain* was released on December 1. But before *Mystery Mountain* finished filming, Levine and Maynard clashed and Levine fired Maynard. That solved one problem for Nat Levine but created another because Maynard was scheduled to star in another serial, *The Phantom Empire*.

Fortunately, Nat Levine had worked with Gene Autry on *In Old Santa Fe* and knew he was a talented singer, so Levine told his scriptwriters to alter the plot of *The Phantom Empire* and tailor it to allow Gene Autry to sing in most chapters. He called Autry back from Chicago. Autry and Burnette returned to Hollywood in early December to film *The Phantom Empire* and completed the filming late that month and returned to Chicago.

On Saturday, February 23, 1935, the first chapter of *The Phantom Empire* was released. On that same day, Gene Autry was in Chicago on *Sears Junior Roundup*, broadcast at 10:00 A.M. on WLS. A month later Autry was in Louisville, where he rejoined J.L. Frank, his booking agent while in Chicago. In Louisville Autry appeared twice daily on WHAS and toured in the area. Meanwhile, a new chapter of *The Phantom Empire* appeared each week.

Gene Autry (photograph courtesy of Packy Smith).

The Phantom Empire took advantage of Autry's success on radio, and his dude ranch in the film is known as "Radio Ranch." There are two basic settings: the Radio Ranch of Autry and the underground city of Murania, ruled by Queen Tika. In the first chapter, titled "The Singing Cowboy," which runs about 30 minutes, the opening scene consists of a group of cowboys chasing a stagecoach. It looks like a hold up and indeed it is, as the "outlaws" turn out to be musicians who demand their musical instruments from the stopped stagecoach. After they receive their instruments, the musicians back Autry singing "Uncle Noah's Ark," which features the backing musicians making animal noises as Autry sings about the animals.

After the song, there is a radio drama, acted out on-screen, and then the basic plot for the serial unfolds: an airplane lands containing some devious people, led by Professor Beetson, looking for radium. They quickly surmise that the only reason people are in the area is to listen to the popular Gene Autry sing on his *Radio Ranch* program; therefore, they must get rid of Autry.

As this plot unfolds, Autry relaxes on the porch and sings his hit song, "Silver Haired Daddy of Mine." There is a "Junior Thunder Riders Club" comprised of youngsters who pick up radio signals from Murania, a civilization located beneath the earth. Autry is enticed to lead the group of conniving visitors to Thunder Valley, where he is ambushed and left unconscious on the ground.

Meanwhile, some of the devious visitors run across a Muranian and shoot him; however, when they return to recover the body, the Muranian has disappeared because other Muranians carried him to their underground city. The Muranians look amazingly like humans but must wear a helmet/mask when on the surface of the earth because they cannot breathe the air.

Queen Tika rules Murania, and her kingdom has a device like a television whereby she can dial up a picture and see what is happening on Earth. She concludes these visitors are up to no good, in danger of discovering her kingdom; therefore the Muranians must get rid of Gene Autry, because he is the reason people are in Thunder Valley. So that's two groups wanting to get rid of Gene Autry.

Autry, meanwhile, recovers from his ambush and is discovered by Frankie and Betsy Baxter, the two leading kids with the Junior Thunder Riders. They all mount horses and take off, pursued by Muranians, until they get to the top of a hill, where they tie a rope to a tree and then lower themselves below the rim where the Muranians won't see them. The Muranians' horses run across the rope, breaking it, and the chapter ends with Autry and the two Baxters falling into what looks like a bottomless area to sure death. Oh no! how will Gene Autry survive this?

The second chapter begins with a review of the first episode; however, in the replay, Autry and the kids tumble down the side of a mountain but grasp a small tree, allowing them to stay on a ledge and avoid the bottomless fall. The other members of the club find them, toss a rope across a chasm and Gene and the two kids manage to get out of their tight situation by going hand over hand on the rope.

Gene Autry must broadcast his Radio Ranch show each day at two o'clock or else "we'll lose our contract." Nobody ever explains exactly what this contract is, but it gives Autry a strong incentive to get back to Radio Ranch each day to sing his song on a broadcast.

In the second chapter, Autry sings "Oscar and Pete," with Smiley Burnette playing the part of Oscar. It is a humorous song and is done while Queen Tiki watches on her TV-like apparatus. A radio drama follows, with a shoot-out where the stagecoach driver falls to the ground. The actors are supposed to be shooting blanks, but the stagecoach driver—father of Frankie and Betsy—is dead. The question of who shot him seems to be answered when a real bullet is discovered in Gene Autry's rifle. On-screen, the viewer sees a hand slip a bullet in the rifle. Autry is thus falsely accused of a crime—a device that will be used over and over in his later movies.

The sheriff arrives from town to arrest Autry, who escapes in order to find "the real killer." Autry is chased by the sheriff and his posse, the Muranians (who of course want to eliminate him) and an airplane piloted by a devious person with Frankie and Betsy hidden in the back. The sheriff shoots Autry, who falls off his horse, while the Muranians launch a rocket at the plane, which hits the plane and explodes as Frankie and Betsy look on in horror. Thus ends the second chapter: HORRORS? ALORS! ARE ALL THE GOOD GUYS GONE?

The Phantom Empire is now available on video and DVD, so one can watch each chapter right after another. If watched this way, the viewer will notice that the beginning of the following chapter recaps the ending of the last chapter but is slightly different, explaining how the hero has survived what looked like an impossible situation. The third chapter of *The Phantom Empire* begins with the radium bomb launched by the Muranians coming towards the airplane, but the two kids—Frankie and Betsy—have enough time to put on parachutes and jump from the plane.

In many of Autry's features, there is a scene where he changes clothes with another character to protect his identity and mislead others. In this serial Autry changes clothes with the plane's pilot (who is unconscious). In Murania, Queen Tika is concerned the "surface people" will discover her kingdom and destroy their perfect civilization. However, there is a subplot in Murania: Argo, the chief executioner, is plotting to overthrow the queen by saving those condemned to death by the queen. These victims were to be killed by 200,000 volts of electricity directed at them; however, Argo had devised a trap door, which dumps the victims to a room below as the electricity is turned on.

There are a lot of "just in time" events in this serial (and in Autry's movies) where Autry escapes or crooks are discovered or the plot hinges on someone arriving or something being discovered at the very last minute.

In chapter three there is no music—except for Smiley Burnette playing the harmonica—and this chapter ends with Autry driving a car with no brakes, pursued by the bad guys, and plunging off a cliff.

In chapter four it is discovered that the "Junior Thunder Riders" saved Autry just before the car went off the cliff. These Junior Thunder Riders are all youngsters, dressed in capes and wearing small buckets on their head with a horn-like device attached on top. Obviously, there was not a large budget for wardrobe.

In the midst of everyone chasing him, Gene Autry manages to get back to Radio Ranch for his broadcast in chapter four, hiding in a wagon of straw. He broadcasts from a barn—a secret hideaway of the youngsters' club—after a cowboy quartet performs "Ain't No Need to Worry." Then Autry sings "Uncle Henry," finishing his song just as the bad guys bust down the barn door. This chapter ends with an explosion in a secret cave which should lead to Autry's escape—except the door has been locked, trapping Autry.

Well, as it turns out at the beginning of chapter five, the Junior Thunder Riders arrived just in time to unlock the door and let Autry and the two kids escape. Smiley Burnette shows his comic genius in this episode, dressed as a woman while he and "Pete" transport the radio equipment to another hideout so Autry can broadcast again. Autry gets entangled in a fight with a Muranian, knocks him out, then changes clothes with the Muranian and joins the real Thunder Riders from Murania, so called because every time this group of underworld horsemen appear, their hoofbeats sound like Thunder. Hence the name of Thunder Valley, where the entrance to the cave is located that leads to Murania.

In Murania, Gene Autry is hauled before Queen Tika and informs her that her kingdom is damp and musty, "better suited for rats," and that his "business is singing—it makes you feel good to sing." Interestingly, the Muranians need special masks in order to breathe on the surface of Earth but Autry does not need a special mask to breathe in Murania. Neither do other "surface humans" who enter.

Autry is sentenced to the death chamber by Queen Tika and this chapter ends with Autry facing bolts of electricity. In chapter six, it turns out that Argo allowed the cowboy to slip through the trap door, thereby joining the revolution against Queen Tika. But Autry escapes from this room, fights more Muranians, and communicates from a control room in Murania via a television screen with the kids at Radio Ranch. Although there are no TV cameras anywhere, the Muranians can dial into different places throughout their own kingdom as well as on Earth's surface.

A radium bomb, sent from Murania towards the kids on Radio Ranch, turns and crashes into the control room, where Autry has been knocked unconscious after fighting a Muranian as this chapter ends. OH NO! THIS IS SURELY THE END OF GENE AUTRY! BUT WAIT

In chapter seven, Autry is sent to the "Reviving Chamber" so he can be brought back to life and tell the queen, who has found out about the rebellion, who the "traitor" is. Autry stirs, speaking a strange language. Just before a scalpel enters his skull for brain surgery he awakens, then all the lights go out, plunging everyone and everything into total darkness. ARGO DOES NOT WANT THE QUEEN TO LEARN IT IS HIM BEHIND THE REBELLION! Meanwhile, during the confusion Autry escapes—after fighting more Muranians—but ends up trapped on a ledge in Murania, surrounded by Muranians! There were no songs in chapter seven.

Chapter eight begins with Autry fighting the Muranians in hand-to-hand (or sword-to-sword) combat before he arrives back on the earth's surface, where he is chased by Muranian Thunder Riders. Autry and the two kids then discover where the mad scientist and his cohorts are plotting, but they have to get back to Radio Ranch for the broadcast. They're NOT GOING TO MAKE IT BACK ON TIME so they hijack the scientist's airplane and Autry sings "I'm Getting a Moon's Eye View of the World" over the radio from the cockpit.

After the song ends, the engine sputters, the pilot grabs the gun from young Frankie—who is both working the electronic gear for Autry to broadcast and holding a gun on the pilot—grabs a parachute and bails out. Gene Autry then jumps into the cockpit and starts piloting the plane, but the plane crashes into a canyon. ALAS! ALORS! IS THIS THE END OF GENE AUTRY?!!?

Chapter nine begins with that final descent of the plane; however, young Frankie and Betsy manage to jump out just before the plane crashes, while Gene rides it down. The bad guys discover Autry unconscious and would kill him. But he is wearing a Muranian outfit, so they save him so he can show them the entrance to Murania. The kids also end up in Murania standing before the queen, who sentences them to a lifetime of confinement in the Lower Dungeon. But, of course, the kids escape and are roaming around Murania while Autry is at the special entrance to Murania, unable to get the door open to save the kids. And the kids are in terrible shape; they have found the Master Control Room where RADIUM BEAMS ARE BEAMING THEM TO DEATH!!

Chapter ten opens and it is revealed that Gene Autry has managed to get back to Murania with Oscar (Smiley Burnette) and Pete—two comic sidekicks. The Muranians shut off the radium beams before Autry and his two sidekicks—who dress as robots—arrive in Murania where Autry again appears before the queen in his cowboy outfit (all black with white piping, no hat, but a single holster gun and fancy boots). Autry refuses to tell the queen who saved him from certain death unless she releases Frankie and Betsy. The queen tunes in her TV set and hears Argo plotting against her; Autry then tells the queen about the rebellion and the queen offers a deal: she'll release Autry and the youngsters if the rebellion is quashed and her kingdom is returned to her.

There are more fist fights, with Gene winning against insurmountable odds, then losing now and then as Argo captures the queen while Autry lands unconscious on a conveyer belt where robots are applying a blowtorch to machinery that passes. It looks like the end of Gene Autry as chapter ten concludes!

Chapter eleven begins with the kids and Oscar and Pete (dressed as robots) arriving to pull Gene off the conveyor belt JUST IN TIME. A radium gun that can melt mountains is roped by Gene, who heads off to rescue the queen. The forces of the rebellion execute the royal consort and are ready to execute the queen. Oscar and Pete, in a comedy of errors, manage to enter the Master Control Room and turn on every switch except the right one (to allow Autry to open the secret trap door in the Death Chamber) until Oscar falls onto the right switch, opening the door JUST IN TIME. But Autry is in the beams of a deathly ray gun as this chapter ends, once again facing certain death. THERE IS NO WAY TO ESCAPE THIS TIME!

In the last chapter of *The Phantom Empire*, Oscar and Pete pull Autry out of the ray gun's deathly ray JUST IN TIME. The Queen allows Gene and his cohorts to escape, but turns down his offer to escape with him, preferring to die with her people. The rebellion destroys Murania, which melts amid huge explosions as the good guys escape. On the surface, Autry tracks down Professor Beetson, the mastermind behind all of the evil doings, and the professor confesses all to Gene, assured no one will believe Autry's tale. BUT WAIT! Frankie has gotten a special gizmo from Murania which allows him to pull up the professor's confession on a

TV screen while the sheriff watches! OH WOWIE ZOWIE! This allows Gene to no longer be falsely accused of Frankie and Betsy's father's murder!

Meanwhile, back at Radio Ranch, Gene sings "Uncle Noah's Ark" again, while the band members provide animal noises. Gene then signs off, says goodnight and yodels a melodic phrase as the serial ends.

WHEW! Talk about cliff-hangers! A young person in the 21st century would no doubt find the whole serial way too hokey with all the gizmos and gadgets on the obvious stage set of Murania. But for a ten-year-old rural fan in 1935, this was exciting stuff. There was lots of action, a suspension of disbelief, and the constant wondering of HOW IN THE WORLD IS GENE AUTRY GOING TO GET OUT OF THIS MESS?

Contemporary film critics tend to dismiss serials; those cliff-hangers—and solutions—are much too implausible. But this serial opened the door for two genres that developed during the 1930s: science fiction stories and singing cowboys.

The success of *The Phantom Empire* (it became the third highest grossing serial in the history of Mascot) and the positive reaction Autry received from fans—who wrote to Mascot about him—both pleased and surprised Nat Levine. This led Levine to conclude that the idea of a singing cowboy feature was viable and that Gene Autry had the potential to be a movie star. Levine called Autry back to Hollywood and arranged for the scriptwriters to meet Autry and develop a script for a full-length feature film.

Gene Autry signed a contract with Mascot on May 17, 1935. He moved to Los Angeles and began filming his first feature, *Tumbling Tumbleweeds*, that summer. Just before the filming began, Herbert Yates arranged a business deal whereby Mascot and some other independent film companies combined their resources to create Republic Productions, with Levine as head of production.

The first movie released under the new Republic arrangement was a singing western, *Westward Ho!*, starring John Wayne. The Singing Rangers, who sang "Covered Wagons Rolling West," were comprised of singing actors, not a "name" singing group. In the movie, John Wayne sang "The Girl That I Love in My Dreams" to a young lady—but the voice was dubbed in (probably sung by Jack Kirk) because, in real life, Wayne could not sing.

This proves, once again, how influential *The Phantom Empire* serial—and Gene Autry—was to moviemaking even before his first starring feature was released. John Wayne filmed *Westward Ho!* at the same time Gene Autry was filming *Tumbling Tumbleweeds*, while Warner Brothers was filming a singing western starring Dick Foran, scheduled for release around the same time Autry's first feature was released in September 1935.

Gene Autry went on to star in 91 singing cowboy movies, then starred on a radio program, Melody Ranch, and a television program, *The Gene Autry Show*, in addition to having a string of hit recordings. But his career as a singing cowboy star in films really began with the science fiction-western serial *The Phantom Empire*.

SOURCES:

Cusic, Don. *Gene Autry: His Life and Career*. Jefferson, NC: McFarland, 2007.
George-Warren, Holly. *Public Cowboy No. 1: The Life and Times of Gene Autry*. New York: Oxford University Press, 2007.
Green, Douglas B. *Singing in the Saddle: The History of the Singing Cowboy*. Nashville: Country Music Foundation Press and Vanderbilt University Press, 2002.

3

The Big Three: Gene, Roy and the Sons of the Pioneers

It has been many many years since Gene Autry made his first appearance in a movie and the Sons of the Pioneers (with Roy Rogers as a member) made their first recordings. And yet, they still remain "The Big Three" in western music; indeed, contemporary western music remains defined by these three artists, whose paths first intersected during The Great Depression.

On August 8, 1934, the Sons of the Pioneers recorded four songs for Decca Records: "Way Out There," "Tumbling Tumbleweeds," "Moonlight on the Prairie" and "Ridin' Home." The following month, Gene Autry filmed a scene in a Ken Maynard movie, *In Old Santa Fe*. Autry and Smiley Burnette performed for about ten minutes in the movie and then appeared briefly in a Maynard serial for Mascot Pictures. In December, Autry starred in a Mascot serial, *Phantom Empire*, that pioneered the singing cowboy genre. By December 1934, "Tumbling Tumbleweeds" by the Sons of the Pioneers had been released and was considered a hit.

Gene Autry was already a star when he got to Hollywood; he had been in Chicago since late 1932, appearing on WLS, the 50,000 watt powerhouse. Autry's records and the "Gene Autry Round-Up Guitar" were sold in the Sears catalog and his appearances on *National Barn Dance*, broadcast over WLS every Saturday night, gave him a huge following in the Midwest. Autry's success came quickly, but it was certainly not "overnight."

Gene Autry was born in Tioga, Texas, and grew up there and in southwest Okalahoma (his family moved back and forth across the Texas-Oklahoma border). Autry obtained a job as a relief telegrapher with the Frisco Railroad and was stationed in Tulsa, Oklahoma, where he appeared on KVOO. He began his recording career in 1929 in New York with old "folk" and Jimmie Rodgers songs; in the earliest part of his career, Autry was a Jimmie Rodgers imitator. Autry recorded for both Victor and the American Record Company. The latter had an agreement with Sears to license recordings to the mail order firm to be sold under the Sears' label, "Conqueror," in their catalog. Autry's records sold well through Sears and led to his moving to Chicago in December 1932.

In Chicago, Autry's biggest hit was "Silver Haired Daddy of Mine," a country song about mountain shack where his dear old dad lived. But Autry began to dress like a cowboy in Chicago and cultivated a western image. In 1934 he had the opportunity, negotiated by Nat Levine, owner of Mascot Pictures, and Herbert Yates, owner of the American Record label, to go to Hollywood and appear in the Ken Maynard film, *In Old Santa Fe*.

Maynard was fired by the studio after starring in a serial (where Autry and Burnette appeared briefly), which led to the opportunity for Autry to become a movie star. *Phantom Empire* had originally been written for Maynard, but after the actor was fired, the studio was stranded with a script and a production schedule but no star. Enter Gene Autry.

Phantom Empire was released in February 1935 and the 12-week serial brought Autry a lot of attention. The studio quickly realized that Autry could carry a movie and plans were made to bring him back to Hollywood (he had gone to Chicago, then Louisville after filming to continue with radio shows and personal appearances). The first feature film starring Gene Autry was *Tumbling Tumbleweeds*.

The Sons of the Pioneers appeared in that movie with Autry, titled after their hit song, but by this time the group had already appeared in several other movies. Leonard Slye—later known as Roy Rogers—was in the group, along with Tim Spencer and the song's writer, Bob Nolan. The driving force behind the early Sons of the Pioneers was Leonard Franklin Slye, who was born in Cincinnati, Ohio; after living in Portsmouth, then Duck Run, Ohio, his family moved back to Cincinnati, where Leonard and his father worked in a shoe factory. In the summer of 1930, the Slye family visited their daughter, Mary, who had moved to California; they returned to Cincinnati but the following year Leonard Slye moved to Southern California to stay.

This was 1931, the depths of the Great Depression, and Slye took any odd job he could find in California; he worked at a golf course, drove dump trucks and worked road construction. Meanwhile, his family back in Ohio sold their property and moved west to join their son. After a short while, Len (as he was known) and his father found themselves out of work. Len wanted to make a living playing music, so he and his cousin Stanley billed themselves as "The Slye Brothers" and played wherever and whenever they could—everything from dances to house parties. Stanley soon gave up—it was a frustrating way to make a living—but Len joined a band, Uncle Tom Murray's Hollywood Hillbillies. In Inglewood there was an amateur radio show, *Midnight Frolic*, on Saturday nights and Len auditioned for the show but did not do well during the broadcast. However, after the show the manager of the Rocky Mountaineers called and offered him a job with that group, singing and playing guitar. The group had a weekly radio show on KGER in Long Beach.

Len Slye wanted to form a singing group because he loved harmony, so he ran an ad for a singer in the *Los Angeles Examiner*; Bob Nolan answered the ad. Robert Clarence Nobles was born in New Brunswick, Canada, but moved to Boston to attend school. His father, Harry Nobles, had joined the United States Army during World War I and then, after the war, retired to Tucson, Arizona, where, at the age of 14, Bob joined him.

The southwestern landscape, with its deserts, had an immediate and profound impact on Nolan. He began to seriously compose poems and wrote the poem that eventually became the song "Cool Water." In 1929, Nolan moved to California, joining his father.

Nolan was working as a lifeguard when he answered the newspaper advertisement placed by Len Slye for a singer who could yodel. The two sang duets with the Rocky Mountaineers; deciding they needed a third voice they added Bill "Slumber" Nichols, a friend of Nolan's. Frustrated with their lack of progress, Nolan quit the group in mid-1932 and worked as a golf caddy at the Bel Air Country Club; during this period, while at his apartment, he wrote "Tumbling Tumbleweeds."

After Nolan quit the group, Slye ran another ad, which was answered by Tim Spencer. Vernon "Tim" Spencer was born in Webb City, Missouri, but moved with his family to New Mexico when he was a child, then to Oklahoma where he became involved in school musicals and purchased a banjo ukulele. He began entertaining in and around Tulsa; then, after finishing school, he moved to Los Angeles to try to break into the movies.

In August 1932 the trio of Tim Spencer, Len Slye and Bill Nichols performed with the Rocky Mountaineers and Benny Nawai and the International Cowboys on KFAC and KGER. Under the name "O-Bar-O Cowboys" they went on a tour of the Southwest from June to September 1933. After the tour the group disbanded, but Slye and Spencer agreed to try again and persuaded Bob Nolan to join them as "The Pioneer Trio," which evolved into "Sons of the Pioneers."

At the end of 1933 this trio was performing under two names, the Pioneer Trio and the Gold Star Rangers. In early 1934 they added fiddler Hugh Farr. Around this same time they were introduced on radio by announcer Harry Hall as the Sons of the Pioneers because Hall felt the young group looked more like "sons" than "pioneers."

Sons of the Pioneers (photograph courtesy of Packy Smith).

By the time the Sons of the Pioneers had their first recording session, they were performing as the staff band on KFWB and appeared in local clubs nearly every night. Late in 1934 the Sons of the Pioneers began recording a number of transcriptions for Standard Radio, which were sent to radio stations. In mid-1935 they added Hugh's brother, guitarist Karl Farr, and continued recording transcriptions for Standard Radio. This group—Slye, Nolan, Spencer and the Farr Brothers—are known as the "original" Sons of the Pioneers.

The group appeared in their first movie, *Radio Scout*, in May 1935, then appeared in *Slightly Static*, *Bronco Buster* (an Oswald the Rabbit cartoon) and *The Old Homestead*, released in August 1935. They appeared in *Way Up Thar* with Joan Davis, released in November 1935. Leonard Slye had a small role in *Tumbling Tumbleweeds*, Gene Autry's first feature film and the group was in two pictures for Columbia with cowboy star Charles Starrett, *Gallant Defender* and *The Mysterious Avenger*.

In February 1936 they were in *Song of the Saddle*, a singing cowboy movie starring Dick Foran; in July they appeared in *Rhythm on the Range*, starring Bing Crosby, and in November they were in another Dick Foran movie, *The California Mail*, followed by *The Big Show*, which starred Gene Autry.

By this time, Gene Autry had established himself as the top singing cowboy star in Hollywood. About two weeks after the release of *Tumbling Tumbleweeds*, the movie *Melody Trail* was released, then two more movies quickly went into production. *The Sagebrush Troubadour* was released in November and *Singing Vagabond* was released in December. In 1936, eight Gene Autry movies were released; the year concluded with *The Big Show*, filmed at the Texas Centennial in Dallas and released in November, and *The Old Corral*, which was released in December. The Sons of the Pioneers had a prominent role in *The Big Show* and in *The Old Corral*. A young actor going under the name Dick Weston appeared in that movie. Dick Weston was Len Slye.

Len Slye was ambitious. He saw the success Gene Autry, Tex Ritter, Dick Foran and others achieved as "singing cowboys" in the movies, and he decided to try his luck. In 1936 he auditioned for the role of a singing cowboy at Universal but lost out to Bob Baker. Slye continued working with the Sons of the Pioneers and that group signed with Columbia Pictures and appeared in a Charles Starrett film, *The Old Wyoming Trail*, released in November 1937.

In the fall of 1937 there were rumbles from Republic Pictures that Gene Autry was unhappy; in fact, there were stories that Autry planned to leave Republic and sign with another studio. This prompted studio owner Herbert Yates to look for someone to replace Gene Autry as a singing cowboy star. Republic apparently considered Tex Ritter, Stuart Hamblen and Red Foley, but none of these singers were signed. Republic also conducted some auditions, hoping to find an "unknown" and make him a singing cowboy star.

Len Slye certainly wasn't an unknown at Republic, but he had, for some reason, been overlooked. Slye was in a store in Glendale having his cowboy hat cleaned when he heard about the auditions; apparently someone who planned to audition had come into the store. Slye headed to the Republic lot but could not get in; he hung around until groups returning from lunch began filtering through the gate. Slye joined them but was stopped by the security officer; however, just as he was stopped, Sol Siegel, a producer for Republic, happened to walk by. Siegel knew Slye as a member of the Sons of the Pioneers and also as Dick Weston, but for some reason he had not thought of Slye when they were casting about for a new singing cowboy.

Slye auditioned by singing "Hadie Brown," which showed off his yodeling prowess, and the Sons of the Pioneers hit, "Tumbling Tumbleweeds." On October 13, 1937, Len Slye signed with Republic for $75 a week. He approached Columbia about getting released from his contract from them—as a member of the Sons of the Pioneers—and they agreed.

The Republic executives knew they had landed someone who was not just a promising movie star but was also an established recording star with his group, so they signed the Sons of the Pioneers to the American Record Company (which Yates also owned) and eight days after Rogers signed as an actor the group—comprised of Rogers, Bob Nolan, Lloyd Perryman, the Farr Brothers and Sam Koki on steel guitar—went into a Los Angeles studio and recorded seven songs. On October 26 they recorded 11 songs; two days later they recorded four more songs. The Sons of the Pioneers finished this set of recordings in mid-December when they recorded 14 songs over two days—mostly gospel material.

The 36 songs the group recorded included "Love Song of the Waterfall," "Song of the Bandit," "Cajon Stomp," "Cowboy's Night Herd Song," "That Pioneer Mother of Mine," "Hadie Brown," "Hold That Critter Down" and "The Touch of God's Hand." In the latter part of 1937 Slye, as Dick Weston, was cast in a Three Mesquiteers movie, *Wild Horse Rodeo*, and was then cast in an Autry picture, *The Old Barn Dance*.

After completing *The Old Barn Dance* at the end of 1937, Autry vowed not to make anymore movies for the studio until they increased his pay; at this time he had interest and offers from two other studios—Twentieth Century-Fox and Paramount. *The Old Barn Dance* was released in January 1938 while Autry was on the road doing personal appearances. Autry remained out of Hollywood while legal wrangling between Republic and Autry's attorneys took place. A script had been written for Autry, *Washington Cowboy*, and production was set to start—but there was no Autry. Republic decided to cast their new singing cowboy in the starring role. First, they changed his name to Roy Rogers; the memory of Will Rogers was still strong and "Roy" seemed to go well with "Rogers."

The film was rewritten for Rogers and retitled *Under Western Stars*; it starred Rogers along with Gene Autry's regular sidekick, Smiley Burnette, as Frog Millhouse. The movie was released on April 15. In the film Roy Rogers sang "Dust," a song credited to Johnny Marvin and Gene Autry, which had been intended for *Washington Cowboy*.

Gene Autry returned to Republic in mid–May and resumed his position as the top star at Republic. In 1939 five Autry pictures were released during the first half of the year. In July, Autry left for an overseas tour that included London, Liverpool, Dublin, Glasgow, and Danzig. During these appearances, Autry was mobbed like later rock stars would be.

Backstage in Dublin, Autry first heard the song "South of the Border," which became a major hit for him and also the title of a movie. The crowds in Dublin caught the attention of P.K. Wrigley, owner of the Wrigley Chewing Gum Company, who wanted to sponsor a radio program to advertise Doublemint gum. When he returned to Chicago, Wrigley set in motion a series of events that culminated in Autry's radio show, *Melody Ranch*, that began in January 1940 and ran for 16 years on CBS.

During the time Autry was in Britain, *Colorado Sunset*, and *In Old Monterey* were released. *Rovin' Tumbleweeds* was released in mid–November and *South of the Border* was released on December 15. The song and the movie were so successful with audiences that Republic made plans for a second movie, *Down Mexico Way*, the title coming from the second line in the song.

Roy Rogers also starred in a series of movies for Republic: in 1939 there were nine films and in 1940 he starred in seven films—but not always as "Roy Rogers." He was in nine films in 1941—again, usually playing a character. He was still under the shadow of Gene Autry, but at the end of 1941, the United States declared war on Japan and Germany. Gene Autry enlisted in the Army Air Corps in 1942 after completing several films, but Rogers remained out of the service during World War II with deferments engineered by Republic and because he had two children.

During the War Herbert Yates decided to put a major promotion behind Roy Rogers and commissioned his writers to write a movie titled *King of the Cowboys*. Rogers starred in this film, released in April 1943, and from that point forward was billed as "King of the Cowboys." In 1942 the musical *Oklahoma* premiered on Broadway and Republic head Herbert Yates saw it; when he walked out of the theatre he was determined that the Roy Rogers movies would contain elaborate musical production numbers like *Oklahoma* did.

The Sons of the Pioneers continued to maintain their popularity through recordings, radio appearances, radio transcriptions and appearances in movies; by late 1936 they had joined *Peter Potter's Hollywood Barn Dance* and had a regular spot on KFOX in Long Beach, on KRLD in Los Angles and, as the Gold Star Rangers, on KMTR before they settled on KHJ in Los Angeles.

In 1936 Tim Spencer left the group and was replaced briefly by Charlie Quirk, then by Lloyd Perryman; in 1937 Pat Brady replaced Rogers and remained with the group as bass player and comedian. In 1938 the Sons of the Pioneers began a syndicated radio show, *Sunshine Ranch*, over KNX and the Mutual Broadcasting System. At this point the group consisted of Nolan, Spencer (who had rejoined the group), Perryman, Brady, and the Farr Brothers. They also continued appearing in Starrett movies through early 1941 and wrote a number of songs for western films.

In 1940 the Sons of the Pioneers moved to Chicago, where they stayed for a year as members of the NBC network show, *Uncle Ezra's Radio Station*, a 30-minute show on Saturdays that was an offshoot of *National Barn Dance*. The show ran from July 13, 1940, until June 28, 1941. During their time in Chicago, the Sons of the Pioneers recorded about 200 songs on transcriptions for NBC's Orthacoustic Recording Division.

In September 1941 the group returned to Los Angeles and joined the Camel Caravan for a tour of military bases on the West Coast. Also in 1941 the group signed to do a series of transcriptions for Dr. Pepper with singers Dick Foran and Martha Mears. This was broadcast over the Mutual System and lasted until the end of World War II.

During World War II, Pioneers Lloyd Perryman and Pat Brady joined the service. Perryman was replaced by Ken Carson and Shug Fisher replaced Pat Brady, after Deuce Spriggins had filled in briefly. During World War II, the Sons of the Pioneers, consisting of the trio of Spencer, Nolan and Carson, with Shug Fisher and the Farr Brothers, worked extensively with Roy Rogers, appearing in over 40 westerns with him.

Lloyd Perryman and Pat Brady rejoined the group in 1945; they signed a recording contract with RCA and became "Bob Nolan and the Sons of the Pioneers." In early 1949, Tim Spencer retired from the Pioneers; a few months later Nolan also retired. Ken Curtis replaced Spencer, and while Tommy "Spike" Doss replaced Nolan. Lloyd Perryman assumed leadership of the group, which had a further change when Pat Brady left to join Roy Rogers as his sidekick in movies and on television.

Roy Rogers became the top singing cowboy star during World War II and never relinquished that title. In 1944 he starred in *The Cowboy and the Senorita*; his costar was a pretty big band singer named Dale Evans. Roy Rogers and Dale Evans also starred in four other movies in 1944; in 1945 they starred together in five films. In 1946 they starred together in seven films and in 1947 they appeared together in two movies released that year. However, those two films had been completed in 1946, and Dale's contract with Republic ended at the end of that year.

Dale decided she didn't want to continue starring in cowboy pictures; she had ambitions to be a major actress in musicals and those Roy Rogers movies kept her typecast as a western heroine. So she left Republic but then re-signed when they agreed to cast her in nonwestern films. She did two for Republic: *The Trespasser* and *Slippy McGee*. Fans wrote to Roy, to Dale and to Republic, requesting Roy and Dale be paired again but Roy's costar in four movies was Jane Frazee. There were big changes in the personal life of Roy Rogers; his wife, Arline died after giving birth to their son, Roy Rogers Jr. ("Dusty") in November 1946. After Arline's death, Roy and Dale began spending time together. Dale's marriage to musician R. Dale Butts was ending and Roy and Dale's friendship blossomed into a romance. On December 31, 1947, they were married in Oklahoma at the Flying L Ranch.

In early 1948, Dale Evans made a commitment to the Christian faith; later that year, Roy Rogers did the same. The couple starred together in movies again, beginning with *Susanna Pass*, *Down Dakota Way*, and *The Golden Stallion*, all in 1949, then three more in 1950. Roy then had other costars in his movies until *South of Caliente* at the end of 1951.

Roy Rogers and Dale Evans were billed as "King of the Cowboys" and "Queen of the West" as they toured together, costarred in their television and radio shows and recorded together. Roy Rogers was never as successful as a solo recording artist as he was with his group, the Sons of the Pioneers, and he was never as successful as Gene Autry, who had Christmas hits—"Here Comes Santa Claus" and "Rudolph the Red Nosed Reindeer"—at the end of the 1940s and beginning of the 1950s. Roy did have an impressive string of hits on country jukeboxes but his real success came through his television show and personal appearances in the 1950s.

After World War II, Gene Autry starred in several pictures at Republic before he formed his own production company at Columbia, where he finished his movie career. Autry's radio show, *Melody Ranch*, was on CBS radio on Sunday evenings and he developed *The Gene Autry Show* for television.

In 1950 the Sons of the Pioneers began a radio program, *The Lucky U Ranch*; both Nolan and Spencer made appearances on the show. The group sang in the movie classic *Wagons West*, which later became the basis for the popular TV show *Wagon Train*.

In February 1953 Shug Fisher and Ken Curtis left the group and began the *Lucky U* radio and TV program. Dale Warren then joined the group and Deuce Spriggens replaced Fisher. Also in 1953, the Pioneers left RCA after eight years, but the label signed Bob Nolan. The group signed with Decca in 1954 before returning to Victor in February 1955 with the old trio of Spencer, Nolan and Perryman. Doss and Warren were left out, although Ken Curtis was brought back to sing for Spencer while Spencer ran the day-to-day activities of the group. Pat Brady was also brought back to replace Deuce Spriggens; this is the group that recorded for Victor from 1955 to 57.

In 1954, twenty years after the genre was established, the singing cowboy movies ended with *Phantom Stallion* starring Rex Allen. By that point, Gene Autry and Roy Rogers were both on television with shows that ran into the 1960s. Along the way, other singing cowboy stars emerged: Tex Ritter, Jimmy Wakely, Rex Allen and Monte Hale. But when fans of singing cowboys look back on the golden age of that genre, they always see The Big Three.

Roy Rogers (photograph from the author's collection).

Gene Autry's TV program and radio show ended in 1956 but he continued to tour until 1960, then became owner of the Los Angeles Angels and spent the rest of his life as a baseball team owner and a businessman. Roy Rogers and the Sons of the Pioneers continued to perform and record; Rogers starred in a movie, *MacKintosh and T.J.*, in 1975 but, for the most part, the era of the singing cowboy was gone.

Those who grew up watching Gene Autry and Roy Rogers in the movies and on TV or hearing the Sons of the Pioneers on radio have plenty of opportunities to relive that past through their old movies or recordings, which are plentiful. The Autry office in Los Angeles has done an excellent job of restoring Gene's movies and overseeing the re-release of his recordings. There are plenty of Roy Rogers movies and CDs available as well, although the restoration process and marketing haven't been on the same level as the efforts for Autry.

Technology has provided a wonderful way of capturing the music and movies of the past and saving them for today, so it is not hard to surmise that many years from now the music of Gene Autry, Roy Rogers and the Sons of the Pioneers will still be the defining sound of western music.

SOURCES:

Autry, Gene. *Back in the Saddle Again.* With Mickey Herskowitz. Garden City, NY: Doubleday, 1976.
Cusic, Don. *Gene Autry: His Life and Career.* Jefferson, NC: McFarland, 2007.
George-Warren, Holly. *Public Cowboy No. 1: The Life and Times of Gene Autry.* New York: Oxford University Press, 2007.

Green, Douglas B. *Singing in the Saddle: The History of the Singing Cowboy*. Nashville: Country Music Foundation Press and Vanderbilt University Press, 2002.

O'Neal, Bill, and Fred Goodwin. *The Sons of the Pioneers*. Austin: Eakin Press,

Rogers, Dale Evans. *Rainbow on a Hard Trail: Her Story of Life and Love*. With Norman B. Rohrer. Grand Rapids, MI: Fleming H. Revell, 1999.

Rogers, Roy, and Dale Evans. *Happy Trails: Our Life Story*. With Jane Stern and Michael Stern. New York: Simon & Schuster, 1994.

____ and ____. *Happy Trails: The Story of Roy Rogers and Dale Evans*. With Carlton Stowers. Waco, Texas: Word Books, 1979.

Warren, Dale. Phone interview with author on September 17, 2002.

White, Raymond E. *King of the Cowboys, Queen of the West: Roy Rogers and Dale Evans*. Madison: University of Wisconsin Press/Popular Press, 2005.

4

Dale Evans, Queen of the West

There have been a lot of singing cowboys but there's only been one "Queen of the West."
Dale Evans is the only female to emerge as a star in the "singing cowboy" genre of westerns. Since her debut in a singing western in 1944, there have been a number of ladies who sang—and still sting—songs of the west, and some of them are mighty good. But Dale Evans remains "The Queen of the West."

Ironically, Dale Evans was a very reluctant western star. In fact, if she had her way back in the 1940s when she began starring in western movies, she would have been a big band singer starring in Broadway musicals. But it didn't turn out that way.

Frances Octavia Smith was born October 31, 1912, in Uvalde, Texas, to Walter and Betty Sue Smith. In nearby Italy, Texas, her father farmed and ran a hardware store. During her growing up years Frances had piano lessons and did well at school, skipping several grades. Around 1920 Walter and Betty Sue, with their two children, Frances and Hillman, moved to Osceola, Arkansas, located on the Mississippi River about 40 miles north of Memphis.

In 1927, Frances was madly in love with Thomas Frederick Fox and the two high school sweethearts ran off and got married; she was 14 and he was 18. The young couple moved in with his parents in Blytheville, Arkansas, but the marriage did not work out; however, they had a son, Thomas Fox Jr., born November 28. Meanwhile, Walter and Betty Sue Smith had moved to Memphis and they invited their daughter and young grandson to join them. On Easter 1928, Frances and Tom did so. The Smiths offered to adopt Tom, but Frances would not hear of it. He was her son, she loved him and she was committed to raising him.

At 17, Frances Fox was a divorced single mom who needed to find a way to support herself and her child. She longed to sing and write songs but the practical side of her realized she needed a steady job. She enrolled in a business school and obtained a job with an insurance company.

Her big break came one day as she sat at her desk "staring vaguely at an accident claim form in my typewriter. I was trying to think up words to fit a tune I had just composed, when the boss walked in. He stood there looking at me for a moment, and then he exploded. 'Young lady, I think you are in the wrong business!'"

As the young mom began to type quickly, her boss walked away, then came back and asked, "How would you like to sing on a radio program?" The insurance company was a sponsor for a program and the boss arranged for her to make a guest appearance; she sang "Mighty Lak a Rose" on that Friday night debut on WREC.

After that performance, Frances Fox had a regular job singing for "experience, no pay."

She also performed at various functions around Memphis where she "learned to meet and face the public." She also moved up to WMC, one of the top stations in Memphis.

The divorce of Thomas and Frances Fox was granted in September 1929. In November 1930, eighteen-year-old Frances married August Wayne Johns, 22, and the couple moved to Chicago. Frances wanted to break into show business in a city that was second only to New York as a center for entertainment. Again, Frances obtained a position with an insurance company, but things did not work out on this first trip to Chicago. In 1932 she moved back to Texas where her parents now lived. Suffering from malnutrition and anemia, she spent two weeks in the hospital. She also had an abusive husband, adding to her woes.

Frances landed a job at WHAS in Louisville in the fall of either 1933 or 1934; there she performed as "Marion Lee." Joe Eaton, the program director for the station, decided to change her name. "He informed me that my name would thereafter be Dale Evans," she remembered. "'That's a boy's name!' I indignantly informed him but Joe wouldn't budge. He told me of a beautiful actress in the era of silent films whose name was Dale Winter. He wanted me to be Dale in honor of her. The surname Evans was added simply because Joe decided it was euphonious. It could roll easily off the lips of radio announcers."

In May 1936, Dale divorced August Johns. Still working for WHAS for $30 a week (where she had apparently met Gene Autry during the time he appeared there in spring 1935), Dale landed a spot on the *Early Bird* program on WFAA in Dallas. Her son, Tommy, lived in Texas with his grandparents; Dale visited on the weekends. Meanwhile, Robert Dale Butts, whom Dale had met in Louisville, moved to Dallas and also went to work at WFAA as a pianist and arranger. On September 20, 1937, Butts and Dale, whose legal name was now Frances Octavia Johns, were married in Dallas, Texas.

In 1936, Dale Evans saw Roy Rogers for the first time. Rogers was with his group, the Sons of the Pioneers, appearing at the Texas Centennial where Gene Autry was filming his movie, *The Big Show*, which featured the Sons of the Pioneers as guests. Tom Fox remembers he was at the centennial, with his mother and had "just thrown up in her hat." The two walked past where the Sons of the Pioneers were and when Dale saw Roy she remarked, "What a pleasant looking young man."

In 1939 Robert Dale Butts (always referred to as "R. Dale" by his wife) and Dale Evans moved to Chicago. Butts went to work as an arranger for NBC while Dale sang with the Jay Mills Orchestra at the Edgewater Beach Hotel. She then obtained a job with the Anson Weeks Orchestra and toured throughout the Midwest and West Coast with this group.

In 1940 Dale was back in Chicago, living with her son, her husband and his parents while performing in the supper clubs at the Blackstone, Sherman and Drake hotels. She sang on WWBM radio and on network shows for NBC and CBS. She also had her own show, *That Gal from Texas*, broadcast over CBS.

In 1940, "out of the blue one afternoon ... I received a telegram from an agent in Hollywood," remembered Dale. "He asked for photographs. If he liked them, he would arrange a screen test." Dale remembers she "laughed as I read the telegram. I had no desire whatever to go to Hollywood. I was aiming at stardom in Broadway musical comedies." The telegram was sent by Hollywood agent Joe Rivkin, who sent several more before Dale answered. She then "had the assigned glamour photos taken and sent the best of the batch" to Rivkin.

The agent wired back: "Take a plane immediately for a screen test at Paramount Studios." So Dale caught a plane from Chicago to Hollywood. Travel by plane was not as common—or as comfortable—in 1940 as it was at the end of the 20th century, and "ten feet off the ground, on our way to cruising altitude, I developed a severe earache and suffered with it all night long," said Dale. "In those days airplanes had no pressurized cabins to compensate for high altitudes," she remembered. "A flight attendant dropped warm oil into my ears. Nothing helped. I slept not a wink and could eat no breakfast because of nausea."

After landing, she saw "a thin man pacing up and down on the tarmac.... I'd read in a book that all agents are nervous and high-strung." After introducing herself she noticed "an incredulous look on his face. 'Oh, no!' he exclaimed. Are you 'Dale Evans?'" After replying that she was, he ordered her to take off her sunglasses then mumbled, "Well, you certainly don't look like your pictures."

After putting her luggage in his car he was driving down the road when he noticed Dale's wedding ring. "You didn't tell me you were married!" he said. "You didn't ask," she replied. He asked her how old she was and the twenty-eight-year-old singer replied "twenty-two." He insisted she say "twenty one.... And you are single. Understand?"

The two drove up to the Hollywood Plaza Hotel where Rivkin took her to the beauty salon and ordered an operator to "see what you can do with her." As Dale recalled it, "The beautician gave me a stinging facial massage ... [and] tinted my light brown hair with an auburn rinse and sent me off to dress for a luncheon with Mr. Meiklejohn, a casting director for Paramount."

She put on a black dress and was curtly informed by Rivkin that "in Hollywood you wear bright colors, with flowers" before she was ushered into Meiklejohn's office. Looking her over with a critical eye, the casting director noted, "I'm a little worried about the nose. A trifle too long for the chin" and then asked if she danced. Rivkin quickly replied, "Dance? She makes Eleanor Powell look like a bum" before Dale corrected him, saying, "No, Mr. Meiklejohn, I can't dance. I can't even do a time step."

"Bill Meiklejohn almost blew his top when he heard that," said Dale. "He gave Joe Rivkin the kind of icy stare that would have frozen a polar bear into silence." The casting director then told her that he was looking for someone to play opposite Bing Crosby and Fred Astair in the movie *Holiday Inn*, but "since I could not dance, I couldn't fit the part."

From the lunch, Dale went to the wardrobe department, then to a drama coach who "picked a scene from Marlene Dietrich's picture *Blue Angel* and told me that MacDonald Carey was to play opposite me," said Dale. For two weeks, she worked hard, rehearsing the part, and tried to lose some weight.

She had to lie about being married and having a son until, she said, "I could stand it no longer. I walked up to Joe Rivkin and told him that I had to talk to him right now before things went any further." She then informed him she was twenty-eight and had a twelve-year-old son who lived with her. Rivkin said immediately, "You will have to send him away to school." Dale refused, so Rivkin then said, "Tom is your brother. Do you understand?"

Dale remembers that she "didn't like it but at least this ruse gave me a chance to have Tom with me in Hollywood ... so I said, 'It's all right with me if it's all right with Tom.'" Tom agreed but told her "you can do anything you want, Mother, as long as I myself don't have to lie."

Back in Chicago, Dale received a call from Rivkin that Paramount had turned her down but Twentieth Century-Fox wanted to sign her for $400 a week. R. Dale, Dale, Tom and R. Dale's parents then moved to Los Angeles where they rented a house in 1940. Dale landed small parts in two movies, *Orchestra Wives* and *Girl Trouble*. She then became a featured singer on the *Chase and Sanborn Show* on network radio, which featured Edgar Bergen and Charlie McCarthy with Don Ameche and Jimmy Durante.

Dale Evans had a 43-week run on the *Chase and Sanborn Show* but during that period Joe Rivkin entered the military, so Art Rush took over as her agent. Rush was the personal manager of Roy Rogers, having signed on with the cowboy star in March 1940. Dale had an active singing career, entertaining troops on USO shows at military camps in the United

States; her husband, R. Dale, usually went along and accompanied her on piano. Dale soon had a conflict with Art Rush because he spent so much time with his top client, Roy Rogers, so she left him and signed with Daniel M. Winkler.

Because of Art Rush and Daniel Winkler, Dale Evans was brought to the attention of Herbert Yates, head of Republic Pictures, home of the singing cowboys. In 1943 Dale Evans signed with Republic. Her first film was *Swing Your Partner* with Lulu Belle and Scotty, two stars of the *National Barn Dance* in Chicago. She then appeared in *Hoosier Holiday*, *West Side Kid*, *Here Comes Elmer* and her first western, *War of the Wildcats* (also known as *In Old Oklahoma*), starring John Wayne. She appeared in the 1944 release *Casanova in Burlesque* with Joe E. Brown and *Hitchhike to Happiness*. Her husband was busy arranging songs and scoring films for Republic, while her son graduated from high school and entered the University of Southern California. Both she and R. Dale were busy with their careers, often working together, and the strain began to show on their marriage.

Oklahoma debuted on Broadway in 1942 and was the most successful musical during World War II, with songs like "Surrey with the Fringe on Top," "Oh, What a Beautiful Morning" and "People Will Say We're in Love." Herbert Yates had seen *Oklahoma* in New York and, according to Dale, "decided to expand the female lead in westerns and adopt this format for one of his biggest stars, Roy Rogers." And so Dale Evans was cast in her first film with Roy Rogers, whom she had met briefly while performing at Edwards Air Force Base where he was performing with the Sons of the Pioneers. The film was *The Cowboy and the Senorita*.

Dale Evans (photograph courtesy of Packy Smith).

After their first movie together, the duo starred in three more movies: *Yellow Rose of Texas*, *Lights of Old Santa Fe*, and *San Fernando Valley*. Dale Evans eventually starred in twenty-eight films with Roy Rogers; but she was a reluctant star at first, disliking westerns and wanting to be cast in musicals or at least more "glamorous" films. Before *Song of Arizona* was released, Dale threatened to leave Republic, stating, "A heroine in a Western is always second string. The cowboy and his horse always come first." This was proven in the billing of the Roy Rogers films, where Roy was listed first, his horse Trigger second, his sidekick (usually Gabby Hayes) third and then his leading lady.

In 1945 Dale was named "Queen of the West" as the top ranking western movie heroine. But things were not going well at home. In September 1945, she and R. Dale separated; in October she filed for divorce, which was granted in November 1946.

Meanwhile, she was spending a good deal of time with Roy Rogers and his wife, Arline, and daughters Linda Lou and Cheryl. Roy and Dale filmed *Home in Oklahoma* at the Flying

L Ranch in Dougherty, Oklahoma, then appeared at the Heldorado Rodeo in Nevada while filming *Heldorado* in Las Vegas.

On Monday, October 28, 1946, Roy's wife, Arline, gave birth to Roy Rogers Jr., nicknamed "Dusty." Six days later, on November 3, Arline died of an embolism. Although he was distraught, Roy continued his professional career, performing on the *National Barn Dance* in Chicago and at the Illinois State Fair.

After Roy and Dale starred in *Bells of San Angelo*, she let her contract lapse and went back to radio, appearing on the *Jimmy Durante Show* and the *Garry Moore Show*. Her next movie role was in *The Trespasser* with Bill Bakewell.

Gossip columnists speculated about the relationship of Roy Rogers and Dale Evans, although Roy issued a statement that he "was not getting married anytime soon to anyone."

Roy Rogers was the top western star at this time. Gene Autry had returned from the armed services, appeared in some Republic pictures, then left for Columbia. Republic then upped the budgets for Rogers' pictures and had him appear in elaborate costumes. But at home, Rogers had three children that had to be taken care of so he hired a nanny. He had been married twice (his first had ended in divorce) and Dale had been married three times.

During this period Dale wrote a song, "Don't Fall in Love With a Cowboy," with the line "no matter how much you love a cowboy he will love his horse the best." But it seemed like Dale was ignoring her own advice.

Roy and Dale spent a lot of personal time together although their film careers separated them; Dale was in the movie *Slippy McGee* with Don Barry while Roy continued his personal appearances. In Atlantic City, New Jersey, Dale appeared with the Sons of the Pioneers and Roy drove down from New York, where he debuted his "Roy Rogers Thrill Circus." Roy and Dale had dinner and he asked about her returning to his films but she declined. Meanwhile, fans kept writing to Republic Studios, wanting to see Dale in Roy's films.

Roy Rogers proposed to Dale Evans while they were making a joint appearance at a rodeo in Chicago; both were sitting on horses when Roy took out a ring and asked for her hand. She accepted and they were married on New Year's Eve 1947 in Oklahoma at the Flying L Ranch. Because of a blizzard the two spent the first two weeks of their honeymoon on the ranch.

After their marriage, Dale agreed to join Roy in his pictures, so the two went to see Herbert Yates to inform him of this decision. Yates and Republic resisted having a married couple starring in films together, and Jane Frazee replaced Dale in Roy's films. However, pressure from fans caused the studio to relent, and in 1949 Dale returned to star with Rogers in eight movies. In all, Dale Evans appeared in a total of 38 movies.

From this point forward Roy and Dale starred together in films, on television and on radio. Dale's last movie with Roy was *South of Caliente*, released in 1951. *The Roy Rogers Show* on television followed almost immediately. That show lasted from 1952 to 1957, then the couple hosted *The Roy Rogers and Dale Evans Show*, a musical variety show.

From their marriage forward it was "Roy Rogers and Dale Evans." Their life was filled with career success in movies, TV shows and radio. Ironically, after her marriage she turned down an opportunity to appear in the Broadway musical *Annie Get Your Gun* during its run in London.

Although their professional lives were doing well, the personal lives of Roy Rogers and Dale Evans saw a number of tragedies. In August 1950 they saw the birth of their only child together, Robin, who had Down syndrome. Robin lived only two years. Evans' book, *Angel Unaware*, was a best-selling account of her life. Their adopted daughter, Debbie, died in a bus crash during a church trip when she was 12 and their adopted son, Sandy, died while serving in the army in Germany after a night of heavy drinking. They were sustained during these tragedies by their strong religious faith. Dale had made her Christian commitment in January 1948, just after their marriage, while Roy made his commitment shortly afterward.

During the time Dale was taking care of Robin, she wrote one of the best-known western songs. "Happy Trails" was a phrase Roy Rogers often used when signing autographs. Dale wrote the lyrics one afternoon; "for the melody, I recalled a phenomenon at the Grand Canyon, on the donkey trail from the rim to the river below," said Dale. "As the guide started down the steep path with his donkey and a group of hikers, he would yodel a deep note followed by a high one. Far below at the camp a guide would answer back with the opposite call, starting with the high note and ending with the low one. At the top came 'Da Da De-e-e-e-e.' And at the bottom came the answer with the opposite intonation: 'De-e-e-e Da.'"

Dale Evans wrote 25 songs. In addition to "Happy Trails," she also wrote "Aha, San Antone" and "The Bible Tells Me So," which was a top seller in 1955.

In 1965 Roy Rogers and Dale Evans moved to Apple Valley, north of San Bernardino, where they opened the Roy Rogers and Dale Evans Museum.

During her last years Dale continued to write books on her Christian faith (she wrote a total of 17) and had a religious television program, *A Date With Dale*, on the Trinity Broadcasting Network. The last performance of Roy Rogers and Dale Evans came in 1997, just before their 50th wedding anniversary, at a charity benefit where they sang "Happy Trails."

Both Roy Rogers and Dale Evans both lived long and active lives. When Roy died on July 6, 1998, he and Dale had been married for over 50 years. Dale lived another two and a half years, dying on February 7, 2001, at the age of eighty-eight.

SOURCES:

Green, Douglas B. *Singing in the Saddle: The History of the Singing Cowboy.* Nashville: Country Music Foundation Press and Vanderbilt University Press, 2002.

Rogers, Dale Evans. *Rainbow on a Hard Trail: Her Story of Life and Love.* With Norman B. Rohrer. Grand Rapids, MI: Fleming H. Revell, 1999.

Rogers, Roy, and Dale Evans. *Happy Trails: Our Life Story.* With Jane Stern and Michael Stern. New York: Simon & Schuster, 1994.

_____ and _____. *Happy Trails: The Story of Roy Rogers and Dale Evans.* With Carlton Stowers. Waco, Texas: Word Books, 1979.

White, Raymond E. *King of the Cowboys, Queen of the West: Roy Rogers and Dale Evans.* Madison: University of Wisconsin Press/Popular Press, 2005.

5

Girls of the Golden West

Despite an early bio that claimed the "Girls of the Golden West" hailed from Muleshoe, Texas, the fact is that the two young ladies—Dollie and Millie Good—were born in Mt. Carmel, Illinois, and grew up in East St. Louis. Furthermore, the "girls" had never even been to Texas when that bio was written in 1935.

Before their name was "Good" it was "Goad." They grew up with a mother who loved old songs and sang them around their home. Mildred Fern Goad was born April 11, 1913, and Dorothy Laven Goad was born on December 11, 1915. At an early age, Millie discovered she had an ear for harmony; whatever song her sister sang, Millie could just naturally "hear" the harmony part and sing along.

The name "Girls of the Golden West" was suggested by a family friend; it came originally from an opera by Puccini in 1910 as well as a short story by Bret Harte. The two young ladies adapted that name for their act and changed their own names from "Goad" to "Good" because it sounded better. They first appeared on St. Louis radio stations KIL and KMOX, then moved to the border station XER briefly before going to KFPI in Milford, Kansas, and then WLS, the powerhouse in Chicago that was home to *National Barn Dance*.

When the Girls of the Golden West joined WLS in 1933, they joined an impressive cast that became a "who's who" in western and country music during the ensuing years. During the period 1933–1938, when the Girls were on WLS, other performers on that station included Gene Autry, the Prairie Ramblers, Smiley Burnette, Bradley Kincaid, Lulu Belle and Scotty, Patsy Montana, Lily May Ledford, the Three Little Maids, Linda Parker, Grace Moore, Red Foley and others. Mother Goad sewed the costumes for her daughters and made them ornate, western-styled outfits with fringe and yokes. (In 1934 Millie Good married William "Bill" Joseph McCluskey, an announcer and promoter for WLS. Dolly married Tex Atchison, the fiddle player for the Prairie Ramblers.)

Their first recording session was on July 28, 1933, when they recorded "Colorado Blues" and "Started Out from Texas" for Bluebird. Soon, they did more old cowboy songs: "Old Chisholm Trail," "My Love Is a Rider" and "Cowboy Jack." Then they began writing songs like "Lonesome Cowgirl," "Home Sweet Home in Texas" and their most famous number, "There's a Silver Moon on the Golden Gate." The recording career for the Girls of the Golden West ended in 1938; by this time they had recorded 64 sides, about two-thirds of them western material for Bluebird, the budget label for Victor.

From 1936 to 1938 the Girls of the Golden West were on a program sponsored by Pinex Cough Syrup with Red Foley and Lily May Ledford. In 1937 they left Chicago and WLS and moved to Cincinnati, where they appeared on the *Renfro Valley Barn Dance* show with

John Lair. When Lair's group left for the Renfro Valley in Kentucky, the Good sisters remained in Cincinnati.

The *Boone County Jamboree* was started by WLW in Cincinnati in 1938 and headed by George Biggar, a former executive with WLS in Chicago. Biggar, with booker agent manager Bill McClusky, the husband of Millie Good, built the *Jamboree* into a top barn dance with acts such as Hank Penny, Curly Fox and Texas Ruby, Homer and Jethro, Bradley Kincaid and Hugh Cross in addition to the Girls of the Golden West. They even attracted Lulu Belle and Scotty from Chicago for a brief period. The *Boone County Jamboree* evolved into the *Midwestern Hayride* in 1945. That year, the Girls of the Golden West were voted the most popular act on WLW.

The Girls of the Golden West were a premier harmony duo, in the same league as the Blue Sky Boys and forerunners for other duet acts such as the Delmore Brothers and Everly Brothers. In addition to their western material, the Girls sang a number of sentimental parlor songs and were known for their yodeling and falsetto in harmony. They continued performing until 1949, when they retired, although they reunited for a series of albums for Texas-based Bluebonnet Records in 1963.

Millie Good died on November 12, 1967; Dolly Good died on August 4, 1982.

SOURCES:

Cusic, Don. *Cowboys and the Wild West: An A to Z Guide from the Chisholm Trail to the Silver Screen*. New York: Facts on File, 1994.

Girls of the Golden West. File at First Library and Archive, Country Music Foundation, Nashville, Tennessee.

Green, Douglas B. *Singing in the Saddle: The History of the Singing Cowboy*. Nashville: Country Music Foundation Press and Vanderbilt University Press, 2002.

McCusker, Kristine M. *Lonesome Cowgirls and Honky-Tonk Angels: The Women of Barn Dance Radio*. Urbana: University of Illinois Press, 2008.

6

Louise Massey and the Westerners

In September 1933, *National Barn Dance* on WLS in Chicago went full time on the NBC network on Saturday nights; that same month, Louise Massey and the Westerners joined station WLS. The station knew the appeal of folk and western music. Bradley Kincaid and Arkie the Arkansas Woodchopper had been with the station since the 1920s and Gene Autry had joined at the end of 1931; during 1932 and 1933 Autry became one of the most popular entertainers on WLS.

Gene Autry was never a "member" of WLS or *National Barn Dance*; he was aligned with Sears, which sponsored his programs on WLS. Although Autry appeared on *National Barn Dance* on WLS often and was one of the most popular performers on that show, the station wanted a western act to call their own.

Henry Austin "Dad" Massey was a cattleman and old time fiddler in Hart County, Texas. Dad moved his family to the Hondo Valley in Lincoln County, New Mexico, where he ran the K Bar Ranch near Roswell. "Dad" Massey raised eight children and taught all his children to play music, but only three made it a profession: Louise was born on August 10, 1902; Curt was born May 3, 1910; and Allen was born December 3, 1908.

Milt Mabie's family moved from Iowa to the Roswell area of New Mexico and he and Louise began courting; in 1919 Louise Massey and Milt Mabie married. Since Milt played stand up bass, he was a welcome addition to the family band, which performed locally in the Hondo Valley at schools, parties and civic events as "The Massey Family." Louise Massey also played piano for silent movies at a theatre in Roswell.

In 1928 an agent with the Redpath Lyceum Bureau, a booking agency for the Chautauqua circuit, discovered the Masseys and convinced them to become professional entertainers. At this point the group consisted of Louise as the main vocalist and occasionally piano (although she rarely played on stage), her husband, Milt, on upright bass; brother Curt on fiddle (although he also played trumpet and piano) and brother Allen on guitar and tenor banjo; "Dad" played fiddle. Curt had a great voice and was also a featured singer.

During the next two seasons, the group was booked all over the United States and Canada. "Dad" Massey grew tired of the traveling and quit the group. He advised the group to get with a radio station and settle there. They first joined WIBW in Topeka, Kansas, where they were known as the Musical Masseys, then they moved to KMBC in Kansas City where they hired Larry Wellington (born February 15, 1902), an accordion player who became the only nonfamily member of the group. At this point they changed their name to "The Westerners."

A WLS talent scout in the Midwest heard them on KMBC and hired them for WLS, where they were given a two-year contract. They began broadcasting in September 1933 and the following month began recording for the American Recording Corporation, owned by Herbert Yates. In 1935 the group, who became known as "Louise Massey and the Westerners" because of Louise's popularity as featured vocalist, became regulars on the NBC program *Show Boat*. The group stayed with WLS for over two years, then moved to New York City in 1936 for two years where they appeared on the NBC program *Log Cabin Dude Ranch*, sponsored by Log Cabin Syrup. This show featured music from the Westerners as well as dramatizations of stories of the Old West.

In 1938 the group went to Hollywood where they appeared in the Monogram feature *Where the Buffalo Roam* starring Tex Ritter; they also starred in several movie shorts for Paramount. In 1939 the group moved back to Chicago and WLS where they appeared on the daytime *Plantation Party* show, broadcast on NBC. This show also featured Red Foley and Whitey Ford ("The Duke of Paducah"). From 1941 to 1945 they were stars on the *Reveille Roundup Program* on NBC.

Dressed in full western attire, the group was the real deal; they had grown up on a ranch and knew the western lifestyle first hand. They quickly became one of the most popular acts on WLS and during one month drew over 200,000 letters—a record for WLS acts.

They recorded for the ARC labels, including Conqueror (sold by Sears), Columbia, Melotone, Okeh and Vocalion, for ten years and continued on the CBS owned record company after the network purchased ARC from Yates. During their career they had about 150 songs released, but only about a fourth were western. The talented group recorded polkas, old time fiddle tunes, sacred songs, pop ballads and old folk tunes in addition to their western numbers.

The Masseys were fluent in Spanish and many of their songs have a Spanish tinge. Their most famous song was "My Adobe Hacienda," written by Louise Massey Mabie and Lee Penny. This was recorded a number of times and became an award winning song for BMI, indicating extensive radio and TV airplay. Louise also wrote or cowrote "Rancho Padre," "All Alone Each Night," "Bunkhouse Jamboree," "I'm a Barefooted Mama" and "Old Pinto." "Dude Cowboy" was written by group members Allen, Curt and Larry; "The Honey Song" was written by Curt and Arbie Gibson; "Waltz Time Melody," "Rock and Rye Polka" and "Beer and Skittles" were all written by Larry Wellington; "Song of the Lariat" was written by Milt; "Ridin' Down That Old Texas Trail" was written by Milt and Curt; and "Draggin' the Bow" was written by Curt.

The group disbanded in 1947 when Louise and Milt decided to retire and move back to New Mexico. Larry Wellington stayed in Chicago, where he remained active in music; Allen moved to California where he worked in radio and toured with the Hoosier Hot Shots. Curt, the most successful solo member of the group, worked in radio, TV and recorded as a solo act or with duet partner Martha Tilton. Curt, with a voice reminiscent of Bing Crosby's, wrote the theme song to the popular CBS TV show *Petticoat Junction* in the 1960s; the show starred Smiley Burnette.

Larry Wellington died on May 5, 1973; Allen Massey died on March 3, 1983; Curt Massey died on October 20, 1991; Milt Mabie died on September 29, 1973; and Louise Massey Mabie, who was inducted into the Cowgirl Hall of Fame in Fort Worth in 1982, died in San Angelo, Texas, on June 22, 1983.

SOURCES:

Cusic, Don. *Cowboys and the Wild West: An A to Z Guide from the Chisholm Trail to the Silver Screen*. New York: Facts on File, 1994.
Green, Douglas B. *Singing in the Saddle: The History of the Singing Cowboy*. Nashville: Country Music Foundation Press and Vanderbilt University Press, 2002.

Louise Massey and the Westerners. File at Frist Library and Archive, Country Music Foundation, Nashville, Tennessee.

McCusker, Kristine M. *Lonesome Cowgirls and Honky-Tonk Angels: The Women of Barn Dance Radio*. Urbana: University of Illinois Press, 2008.

7

Patsy Montana

"I Want to Be a Couboy's Sweetheart"—the first country or western record by a woman to sell a million copies—was originally recorded in a New York studio on August 16, 1935, by Patsy Montana for the American Recording Company. The producer on the session was the legendary Uncle Art Satherley, who was also guiding the sessions of Gene Autry, who starred in his first feature film that year.

The song was an immediate hit and established Patsy Montana in a career during which she that saw her become a member of the Western Music Hall of Fame as well as the Country Music Hall of Fame. In the years since that song was first heard, it has become a standard in western music and an inspiration for countless women who have sung western music and set out to follow in the bootsteps of Patsy Montana.

The bundle of energy who became Patsy Montana was born Ruby Rebecca Blevins on October 30, 1908, in Beaudry, Arkansas. In 1910 the family moved to Jesseville, a few miles from Hot Springs, then Hope, Arkansas, where Patsy grew up the seventh child out of a family of ten—and the only girl. When she was in high school she added an "e" to the end of Ruby because she "thought Rubye looked more sophisticated."

In the late 1920s she discovered the records of Jimmie Rodgers and sang his songs. "His music was so different from anything else I had ever heard," she said. "He yodeled and I guess that was a big draw for me. He sang about hard times, railroads and so many things with which I could identify. The sound was rather bluesy, stuff I had heard the black folks singing. At the same time it often sounded all jazzed up," said Patsy in her autobiography. "I loved my Jimmie Rodgers records, and I memorized every one of them."

She graduated from high school in 1928 and the following year moved to California where her brother lived. Wanting to go to college, she entered the University of the West, which later became UCLA, and studied violin and piano. She was also taught to play the guitar by her brother.

In Los Angeles Rubye entered a talent contest where the winner would appear on *Breakfast Club* on KMTR. She performed two Jimmie Rodgers songs and won the contest. That same year she became a member of the Montana Cowgirls trio, earning $7.50 per show.

Stuart Hamblen, who was on a competing station, offered her a job on his show—the top western radio show in L.A.—playing violin and singing with a girl trio. Since one of the other girl's names was Ruthie, Hamblen encouraged Rubye to change her name; so she became Patsy Montana. In 1930 the Montana Girls became regulars with Hoot Gibson's Rodeo and the following year were in the movie *Lightnin' Express*. The other two girls got married and quit performing, so Patsy went on alone.

She made her first recordings on November 4, 1932, with Jimmie Davis in New York.

On those sessions with Davis, who later became governor of Louisiana and also penned classics such as "You Are My Sunshine" and "It Makes No Difference Now," she played the violin, sang harmony and yodeled under the name Rubye Blevins. She recorded four songs with Davis and four songs on her own for Victor. The four songs she recorded on her own were "Montana Plains," "Sailor's Sweetheart," "I Love My Daddy, Too" and "When the Flowers of Montana Were Blooming." "Jimmie Davis flat out told me I needed to ditch the violin and pick up the guitar," she said. "If I intended to sing western music I had to play western music. It had to be the guitar because ... I could not accompany myself on the violin."

Patsy Montana (photograph from the author's collection).

In the summer of 1933 she went to visit the World's Fair in Chicago and met the Girls of the Golden West—Millie and Dolly Good—because her mother had corresponded with them. They informed her that a group on the *National Barn Dance*, the Prairie Ramblers, were looking for a girl singer and were holding auditions that afternoon. For her audition she sang a Stuart Hamblen song, "Texas Plains," and got the job, joining a group that had Tex Atchison on fiddle, Floyd "Salty" Holmes on harmonica, guitar and jug, Chick Hurt on mandolin and Jack Taylor on guitar and bass. The group played the *Wake Up and Smile* show in WLS each morning at 6:30.

In a hotel room alone during a road trip in 1934 she decided to clean out her purse and came across a scrap of paper with "cowboy's sweetheart" on it. That phrase had been jotted down by J.L. Frank, who was booking and managing several acts at WLS, including Fibber McGee and Molly and Gene Autry. Frank thought it would be a good idea for a song and as she sat there, the words came quickly; she used the tune of Stuart Hamblen's "Texas Plains."

The "sweetheart" she was thinking of as she wrote the song was Paul Rose, whom she married on July 3, 1934. Soon after the song was written Patsy and Paul left Chicago and moved to New York where she had her own radio show, *Smile a While*, sponsored by Kolor Bak. In September 1935, she moved back to Chicago and WLS. "I Want to Be a Cowboy's Sweetheart" was an instant hit and she recorded it again for Decca in Chicago on January 26, 1937. This led to her appearance in the Gene Autry movie *Colorado Sunset*, released in 1939.

Radio performers moved from station to station during the 1930s and 1940s, often at the behest of their sponsor. In 1940 Patsy Montana moved to St. Louis, then, in February 1941, to San Antonio. At the end of 1941 she moved to Hollywood, where she sang on KNX. Then in October 1942 she moved back to Chicago to sing on WJJD before rejoining WLS in January 1943.

She purchased her family's old home place, the Box R Ranch, near Hot Springs,

Arkansas, and moved there in 1948 and appeared on a daily radio program on KTHS. She also began performing on *Louisiana Hayride*, driving there for each Saturday night performance where the Patsy Montana Trio followed Hank Williams.

In August 1952 she moved to California, where she remained, although she went back to Chicago briefly in the mid–1950s. For the rest of her life Patsy lived in Rosemead, California, although she continued to travel throughout the United States, performing western music, with "I Want to Be a Cowboy's Sweetheart" her calling card. However, that wasn't her only hit. She also recorded "Montana Plains," "Rodeo Sweetheart," Shy Anne from Old Cheyenne," "I Wanna Be a Western Cowgirl," "The She Buckaroo" and "I Want to Be a Cowboy's Dream Girl."

In 1987 Patsy Montana was inducted into the National Cowgirl Hall of Fame and in November 1989, when the Western Music Association was formed, she was on the first board of advisors, along with such notables as Rex Allen Sr. (chairman), Gene Autry, Roy Rogers, Dale Evans, Chris LeDoux, Ken Griffis, Michael Martin Murphey, Riders in the Sky, Sons of the Pioneers and Bill Wiley.

Patsy Montana was a great yodeler who helped created the image of the yodeling cowgirl and elevated women to a prominent position in country and western music.

Patsy Montana passed away on May 3, 1996, about six months short of her 88th birthday.

SOURCES:

Green, Douglas B. *Singing in the Saddle: The History of the Singing Cowboy.* Nashville: Country Music Foundation Press and Vanderbilt University Press, 2002.

McCusker, Kristine M. *Lonesome Cowgirls and Honky-Tonk Angels: The Women of Barn Dance Radio.* Urbana: University of Illinois Press, 2008.

Montana, Patsy. *Patsy Montana: The Cowboy's Sweetheart.* With Jane Frost. Jefferson, NC: McFarland, 2002.

8

Ray Whitley

Ray Whitley is probably best known as composer of Gene Autry's theme, "Back in the Saddle Again," but this is only a small part of his legacy. He composed numerous other songs, including "Lonely River," "I Hang My Head and Cry" and "Ages and Ages Ago," all popularized by Autry. But his contributions to western music go far beyond his compositions; he was featured in a number of musical shorts and became musical companion to George O'Brien, William Boyd and Tim Holt in numerous B Western films in the 1930s and 40s.

Ray Otis Whitley was born December 5, 1901, in Atlanta, Georgia. In 1906, Whitley's mother died, his father remarried and the family moved to Clay County, Alabama, where Whitley spend his formative years. Right after the end of World War I, he joined the U.S. Navy, where he served as an electrician for three years. He met his future wife in Philadelphia, where he settled after his discharge in 1923. From Philadelphia, he moved to Nitro, West Virginia. He began to play and sing, influenced by the music of Jimmie Rodgers, and moved to New York City in 1929 where he was on the construction crew that built the Empire State Building, the New York subway system and the George Washington Bridge.

During the Great Depression, Whitley decided to try show business after construction jobs dried up. He played the ukulele but, encouraged by his wife, he learned the guitar. He then auditioned for WMCA, where he was accepted and placed with a group, the Range Ramblers, that included Dwight Butcher, Buck and Tex Ann Nation, and Otis Elder. Their radio show was sponsored by the popular laxative, Crazy Water Crystals.

The group moved to WHN in New York where Whitley cohosted the *WHN Barn Dance* with another aspiring singer, Tex Ritter. In addition to the radio show, Whitley performed in and around New York City (including at the prestigious Stork Club) as well as up and down the East Coast. He recorded a number of sides for the American Record Company before moving to Decca in 1936, where he recorded two cowboy tunes, "Saddle Your Blues to a Wild Mustang" and "Wah-Hoo."

Whitley was hired in 1932 to provide entertainment for the World Championship Rodeo. He changed his band's name to the Six Bar Cowboys because that was the name of the ranch owned by Colonel W.T. Johnson, who had hired him for the rodeo. In the band were the Phelps brothers—Earl, Willie and Norman—as well as banjoist Ken Card.

In 1936 Whitley decided to head west to Hollywood because of the success of Gene Autry and the singing cowboys. On his way out, he spent some time on Colonel Johnson's Six-Bar Ranch in West Texas to acquire some cowboy skills; he also performed in Dallas at the state centennial. When Whitley left for the remainder of the trip, his band included Spade Cooley on fiddle and Ken Carson on guitar.

In Hollywood, Whitley's first speaking role was in *Hopalong Cassidy Returns* for Paramount in 1936; then he performed in a series of musical shorts for RKO in 1937. RKO was interested in making singing cowboy movies. Inspired by the success of Republic Pictures, RKO had a good prospect in Ray Whitley for the starring role. However, RKO never developed a singing cowboy series and never cast Whitley in a starring role, although he made 18 shorts for them between 1937 and 1942. He did star as a singing sidekick to George O'Brien in six films and with Tim Holt in twelve others. In 1942 Whitley moved to Universal, where he was cast as a singing sidekick to Rod Cameron.

It continues to amaze and perplex film historians and singing cowboy aficionados that Ray Whitley never had a starring role in a singing cowboy movie. In Douglas B. Green's book, *Singing in the Saddle: The History of the Singing Cowboy*, Green quotes a film historian who states the following: "The general consensus among film historians is that Whitley had far more looks, talent, and charisma than many of the actors who were promoted by studios and starred in Western epics, yet Whitley never made it above the co-starring rung on the Western success ladder."

Between film appearances, Whitley toured as a performer and wrote songs with Fred Rose, who lived with the Whitleys while trying to get his foot in the door as a Hollywood songwriter. Among the songs they wrote were "Lonely River," "Ages and Ages Ago," and "I Hang My Head and Cry." Whitley's most famous song, "Back in the Saddle Again," was first heard in the film *Border G-Men* starring George O'Brien in 1938; in October 1938 Whitley recorded it for Decca. According to Whitley, he got the idea for the title of the song when he received an early morning phone call telling him that a song was needed quickly for a film. Whitley told his wife, "Well, I'm back in the saddle again," and his wife encouraged him to use that phrase as a title.

Ray Whitley (photograph courtesy of Packy Smith).

Later, Autry heard the song, reworked it and used it as his theme song for his *Melody Ranch* radio series. In Whitley's original version, Whitley begins with an instrumental lead-in, then sings the chorus ("whoopee ti yi yo"), while Autry begins with the verse. Autry also altered the melody slightly in the first line of the verse and changed the lyrics in the second verse (from "I sleep out every night" to "you sleep out every night"). Autry reportedly paid Whitley a sum of money (the amount varies between $500 and $750, depending on the source of the story) for the copyright.

Whitley appeared in a total of 54 films, then turned his attention to his musical career. He toured extensively with Tim Holt, then with Monte Hale, and fronted a western swing band. He managed the Sons of the Pioneers and Jimmy Wakely—both briefly—and during the 1950s and 1960s opened a series of businesses. He is known for helping develop the Gibson J-200, which became the guitar of the singing cowboys. He served as an executive for Gene Autry's music publishing and record companies and during the 1970s was popular at western film festivals.

Whitley appeared as a character actor on some of Roy Rogers' TV shows and his last film role was as James Dean's manager in *Giant*, which was released by Warner Brothers in 1956.

Ray Whitely died of diabetic shock on February 21, 1979, while on a fishing trip in Mexico. He was elected to the Western Music Hall of Fame in 1996.

SOURCES:

Green, Douglas B. *Singing in the Saddle: The History of the Singing Cowboy*. Nashville: Country Music Foundation Press and Vanderbilt University Press, 2002.

Vaughn, Gerald F. *Ray Whitley: Country-Western Music Master and Film Star*. Newark, DE: Privately published by the author, 1973.

Whitley, Ray. Country Music Foundation Oral History Project. Interviewer: Murray Nash, June 8, 1978.

_____. _____. Interviewer: Douglas B. Green, March 30, 1975.

_____. _____. Interviewer: Douglas B. Green, July 1, 1974.

9

Guitars, Cowboys and Country Music

The cowboy is the most enduring symbol of country music, and the guitar is the most enduring sound of country music. The guitar—particularly the acoustic guitar strummed to accompany a singer—provides the essential, bare-bones sound of a country or western song.

Radio and recordings played a major role in making the guitar a popular instrument during the 1920s. The first commercially successful recording of what became known as country music was by Fiddlin' John Carson in 1923. Recordings of early string bands, led by the fiddle but often accompanied by a guitar, followed, and in 1924 Vernon Dalhart recorded "The Prisoner's Song," b/w "Wreck of the Old '97," accompanied by a guitar. That record sold over a million copies.

In 1927 in Bristol, Tennessee, the Carter Family—with Maybelle on guitar, Sarah on autoharp and Sarah's husband, A.P., as principal songwriter—recorded several songs for the Victor Company. Jimmie Rodgers, who accompanied himself on guitar, also recorded during those sessions. These acts became two of the most influential acts in early country music. Their recordings were helped by the invention of the microphone, which allowed the guitar to be heard as it accompanied a singer. Without the microphone, the sound of the guitar was often buried underneath other instruments.

WLS went on the air in Chicago in 1924 and *National Barn Dance*, a show aimed at the rural audience, featured string bands. In 1926 Bradley Kincaid joined WLS and sang on daily programs as well as *National Barn Dance* each Saturday night. Kincaid was born in Berea, Kentucky, and received a guitar when his father traded a dog for one. Kincaid sang old folk songs such as "Barbara Allen" accompanied by his guitar and became the first star of WLS. He was incredibly popular with listeners and became the first country radio star to publish a songbook, *Favorite Mountain Ballads and Old Time Songs*, in 1928.

Sears owned the largest mail order business in the country; it was the nation's major retailer and sold radios, phonographs, phonographs, records, instruments, clothes and a host of other objects. Since Bradley Kincaid played a guitar, it seemed logical for Sears to market a guitar endorsed by Kincaid. In 1929 the "Bradley Kincaid Houn' Dog Guitar" was featured in the Sears catalog. The guitar was a standard-sized instrument with a solid spruce top and mahogany body and mahogany neck. The body featured a large mountain hunting scene decal (called "decalomania") on the belly. The fingerboard was ebonized hardwood with pearl dot inlays. The pin bridge was rosewood, and the ladder braced guitar was intended for steel strings. It was manufactured by Harmony, a company owned by Sears. If a customer ordered this guitar they also received a copy of Kincaid's songbook and a pick. Kincaid left WLS in 1929 and moved to WLW in Cincinnati and then to a series of stations, including WSM and the *Grand Ole Opry* in the 1940s.

In 1931 Gene Autry lived in Sapulpa, Oklahoma, and worked as a telegrapher for the railroad. He had made his first recordings in 1929 and continued to record through the years for the American Record Company, which leased its masters to budget outlets. One of those outlets was Sears, Roebuck and Company, which released the records on its label, Conqueror. Autry had started his career as a Jimmie Rodgers imitator; he recorded a number of Rodgers' songs as well as original songs that sounded like they could have come from Jimmie Rodgers. Autry's records sold well, which led Sears to invite him to move to Chicago where they sponsored a number of radio shows on WLS, the station they used to own.

Autry joined WLS at the end of 1932. During that year, Sears introduced the Gene Autry Roundup Guitar, which was, essentially, the Bradley Kincaid Houn' Dog Guitar with a picture of a cowboy rounding up cattle and Autry's signature on the bottom of the guitar's body. The guitar was a standard-sized guitar, manufactured by Harmony, and in 1935 Sears offered an "Old Santa Fe Arch-top" guitar after Autry appeared in Ken Maynard's picture *In Old Santa Fe*. There were some developments in the Gene Autry Roundup guitar, primarily increasing the size of the body. The 1935 model had a spruce top and birch body with a reddish mahogany finish. There were pearl dots on the inlays on the neck. The model lasted until 1930, when it was replaced by a larger guitar.

Guitars were popularized by the singing cowboys of the 1930s and 1940s who generally played a guitar on screen as they sang. Pictures of the singing cowboys, especially Gene Autry, Roy Rogers and Tex Ritter, often showed them holding a guitar; in their movies they are often shown playing the guitar as they sang. Young boys and girls watching these movies— or seeing these pictures—were often inspired to pick up a guitar and learn to play.

There has been no guitar more identified with the singing cowboys than the Gibson SJ-200. The roots of that relationship go back to the late 1930s and Ray Whitley. It has long been acknowledged that Ray Whitley was the major figure in the development of the Super Jumbo 200 (SJ-200) guitar by Gibson. Eldon Whitford, a guitar historian as well as a builder of guitars, said that circumstance evolved from "a relationship Ray Whitley had with Gibson through mail order catalog guitars." Those guitars were the "Ray Whitley Recording King" guitars sold in the Montgomery Ward catalogue.

Whitford also believed "Whitley was the best musician of the singing cowboys" and "put more miles on the road than any of the others." In an article in *Vintage Guitar* magazine, Whitford and David Vinopal point out that "every fall for over 20 years, Whitley was the star of Colonel W.T. Johnson's Rodeo in New York City and Boston, a role he sometimes shared with Autry and Roy Rogers." During one of his appearances at Madison Square Gardens in 1937, Whitley met Guy Hart, who worked for Gibson, and the two became friends.

Whitley had played Gibson guitars for a long time and told Hart the company should build a flat-top guitar that was "fancy" with a bigger body to produce a louder sound with a deeper tone. Whitley also suggested a shorter neck—12 frets to the body—because country singers did not usually play up on the neck. According to Whitfield and Vinopal, Hart told Whitley that Gibson "would build him his dream guitar if he would be willing to help them promote it" and invited Whitley to come to Gibson's plant in Kalamazoo for a week to help with the development of this guitar.

Prior to Whitley's visit, the Gibson luthiers experimented with a bigger bodied guitar and had built several guitars as part of their ongoing experimentation to improve and enhance their models. There was also the matter of the competition. Martin had introduced the D-18 and D-28 guitars in 1934 and they had a wide waist, a 14-fret-to-the-body neck, and a louder, deeper sound. Whitley spent a week in Kalamazoo and Gibson made him a blonde, 12-fret-to-the-body neck and inlaid Whitley's name in pearl on the headstock. This was the first SJ-200 from Gibson for Whitley and he received it in December 1937. Later, he received a 14-fret version and another short neck, this one with a sunburst finish. Gibson also sought to make them "fancier."

Ray Whitley was friends with the other singing cowboys. He spoke with Gene Autry and Tex Ritter and apparently convinced them to order Gibsons, because in the 1938 catalogue there is a picture of those three singing cowboys with Gibson SJ-200s. Autry ordered several, and the "fanciest" Gibson, outlined by a "rope" binding with his name in inlaid pearl on the neck, belonged to him. Gibson also created a smaller version of the SJ-200 for Autry to hold while he was on Champion, his horse. This miniature version of the SJ-200 is seen in a number of Autry photos.

The Gibson SJ-200 was soon seen in the singing cowboy movies, which created sales for Gibson. Singing cowboys (and cowgirls) who owned SJ-200s included Ray "Crash" Corrigan, Bob Baker, Jimmy Wakely, the Girls of the Golden West, and Rex Allen. Red Foley, who appeared in only one singing cowboy movie, owned a Jumbo 400 as well as a J-200. Others connected to singing cowboys who owned an SJ-200 were Merle Travis and Johnny Bond as well as country stars Eddy Arnold, Hank Thompson, Johnny Cash, Emmylou Harris and numerous others.

Whitley's first SJ-200 Gibson met a terrible fate when movie cowboy Tim Holt borrowed Whitley's Cadillac and guitar for a singing gig. Driving down the road, Hart flicked a cigarette outside. However, the cigarette blew into the backseat and before Holt realized it the car and the guitar were on fire. Whitley, a nonsmoker, was not thrilled at the fate of his car and guitar.

Gene Autry, Tex Ritter and Roy Rogers all played Martin guitars when they began and, after Whitley showed his SJ-200, Autry and Ritter switched. Roy Rogers also switched to a Gibson guitar during his 1940s movies, but it was a Super 400, an arch-top guitar.

"Roy Rogers was a pretty good swing guitar player," noted Whitford. "And that Super 400 was the guitar those jazz players loved." The Super 400 was introduced by Gibson in 1934; it cost almost $100 more than their popular L-5 guitar and came during the Great Depression when the Gibson factory had begun making wooden toys in order to stay in business. (The first Super 400 cost $400 with a case; the L-5 cost $305.)

George Gruhn and Walter Carter, in an article in *Vintage Guitar* magazine, state that Gibson developed the Super 400 as a response to a competitor, Epiphone, which began marketing an arch-top 3/8 inches wider than the L-5 in 1931. Martin had also presented its large bodied flat-tops in 1931. According to Gruhn and Carter, the Super 400 "became not only the standard arch-top for players, but the industry leader for a new era of supersized 'jazz' or 'orchestral' guitars" because "musicians ... found the Super 400 to have the power and tone to cut through the sound of the big bands of the 1930s."

Roy Rogers played a Super 400 acoustic arch-top. Perhaps the most famous electric Super 400 was the one played by Scotty Moore, Elvis' guitar player in his early days. Elvis himself played Scotty's Super 400 during his performance of "One Night" on his 1968 "comeback special" on NBC.

Gibson became "the guitar that won the west" by winning over western film stars. Those Gibson SJ-200s that audiences saw on the silver screen and in the live appearances by western and country stars cemented the relationship between Gibson, western and country singers and fans. Those Gibson SJ-200s became as essential to the cowboy "look" as cowboy hats, boots, and fancy outfits.

SOURCES:

Bacon, Tony. *The History of the American Guitar: From 1833 to the Present Day*. New York: Outline Press, 2001.
Chapman, Richard. *Guitar: Music, History, Players*. New York: Dorling Kindersley, 2000.
Evans, Steve, and Ron Middlebrook. *Cowboy Guitars*. Jacksonville, AK: Centerstream, 2009.
Gruhn, George. "Stromberg Master 400." *Vintage Guitar*, December 1, 2005.
_____, and Walter Carter. "Gibson Super 400." *Vintage Guitar*, September 16, 2009.
Johnston, Richard, and Dick Boak. *Martin Guitars: A History*. New York: Hal Leonard, 1988, 1994, 2008.
Whitford, Eldon. Personal interview, October 15, 2009, on phone and via e-mail.
_____, and David Vinopal. "Gibson SJ-200: On the Trail to the Original." *Vintage Guitar*, August 10, 2004.
Wright, Michael. "Bradley Kincaid Houn' Dog Guitar," *Vintage Guitar*, July 7, 2006.
_____. "Harmony: The Parlor Years (1892–1914)." *Vintage Guitar*, January 7, 2002.
_____. "Supertone Gene Autry Roundup 1938." *Vintage Guitar*, January 27, 2005.
_____. "1,000 Years of the Guitar: A Contextual Reflection." *Vintage Guitar*, July 5, 2001.

10

Andy Parker and the Plainsmen

The Western groups that emerged during the 1940s in the shadow of the Sons of the Pioneers were heavily influenced by the pop music of the day. The big band sound of Glenn Miller, Artie Shaw, Benny Goodman, Tommy Dorsey, Jimmy Dorsey, Harry James and others was the sound that dominated that era. The music of singing cowboys Gene Autry, Tex Ritter and Roy Rogers added another important element to the sound; so did western swing music coming out of Texas and California.

The hillbilly sound that had originated in the South was also part of the mix, but often it was more cultural than musical. The plain fact was that many of these young men and women who performed and recorded western music were country boys and girls—from the rural areas of America—and their roots showed.

Andy Parker is a good example. He was born in Mangum, Oklahoma, about thirty miles east of the Texas Panhandle, on March 17, 1913. Parker's debut on radio came on KGMP in Elk City, Oklahoma, when he was 16. He moved to San Francisco, where he achieved his initial fame as the singing cowboy on NBC's *Death Valley Days* (1937–1941). He also appeared on the popular barn dance program on KGO, *Dude Martin's Roundup*. During World War II Parker worked in a defense plant. In 1944 he moved to Los Angeles.

Andy Parker formed the Plainsmen as a trio in 1945; members included Charlie Morgan (brother of pop singer Jaye P. Morgan) and Hank Caldwell, who played bass. The trio obtained a recording contract with Coast Records, resulting in songs such as "Throw a Saddle on a Star," which featured Ocie Waters on lead vocal. The recording contract came after appearances in movies with Deuce Spriggins, Carolina Cotton, Ken Curtis and others. By this time (1946) the Plainsmen had expanded to include legendary steel guitarist Joaquin Murphy, fiddler Harry Simms and accordionist George Bamby; these three members had previously been with Spade Cooley's western swing group.

After the early years (1945–1948) when the group was called the Plainsmen, the group became Andy Parker and the Plainsmen when they began a series of eight westerns with Eddie Dean for PRC in 1947. That same year they signed with Capitol Records and achieved success with the Parker compositions "Trail Dust" and "A Calico Apron and a Gingham Gown." However, the sound of the group changed when, just before they started recording for Capitol, steel guitarist Joaquin Murphy went back to Spade Cooley's band; thus Harry Simms' fiddle became more prominent. The group remained on Capitol for five years and recorded over 200 transcriptions; they also served as a studio group, backing Tex Ritter.

Andy Parker and the Plainsmen gained national exposure through weekly network appearances on *Hollywood Barn Dance*, working with artists such as Jimmy Wakely, Merle

Travis, Cliffie Stone, Johnny Bond, Dusty King and others. At this point Hank Caldwell left the group and was replaced by bassist Paul "Clem" Smith. In 1950 George Bamby was replaced by Leroy Kruble.

During the first part of the 1950s the group appeared on television shows hosted by Dude Martin, Eddie Dean, Tex Ritter, Leo Carillo and others. They also appeared in films such as *The Beautiful Blonde from Bashful Bend*, released in 1949, which starred Betty Grable and Cesar Romero. They were on the soundtrack for the movie *River of No Return*, which starred Marilyn Monroe and Robert Mitchum.

Andy Parker and the Plainsmen were a popular group in Southern California, but they never really achieved national success on their own. In 1951, their contract with Capitol ended and during the early to mid–1950s, the public discovered rhythm and blues and early rock'n'roll. Suddenly, the sounds that had been so popular during the previous 20 years—songs from classic writers like Irving Berlin, the Gershwins, Rodgers and Hammerstein, and Hoagy Carmichael and sung by crooners like Bing Crosby, Perry Como, Frank Sinatra, Jo Stafford, Patti Page and others—were part of the past.

Group members dropped out of the Plainsmen and the group disbanded by 1956, although they made their final appearance in 1957. Andy Parker died in 1977, before the western music renaissance began, so he never saw the popularity of western music return. It is difficult—but not impossible—to find recordings by Andy Parker and the Plainsmen, but fans of western music are well-rewarded when they find the group on CD. The pictures of Andy Parker and the Plainsmen generally show a group dressed in western shirts and cowboy hats, but the sounds inside are jazzy and their pop-influenced tight harmonies are smooth and seamless. It is a sound that harks back to the 1940s and an era before the singing cowboys left the silver screen.

SOURCES:

Andy Parker and the Plainsmen. File at Frist Library and Archive, Country Music Foundation, Nashville, TN.

Green, Douglas B. *Singing in the Saddle: The History of the Singing Cowboy*. Nashville: Country Music Foundation Press and Vanderbilt University Press, 2002.

11

Foy Willing and the Riders of the Purple Sage

"Happy Trails" is one of the most popular, well-known songs in western music. It was the theme song for Roy Rogers and Dale Evans and songwriting credit for the song is given to Dale Evans. Evans always claimed that the *Grand Canyon Suite* was a major inspiration for that song. However, another songwriter, Foy Willing, wrote a song called "Happy Trails" the year before Evans wrote her "Happy Trails," and the opening of the two songs sounds eerily similar.

Dale Evans certainly knew Foy Willing and had heard his song; she and Roy Rogers sang Willing's song in the movie *Spoilers of the Plains*, released in February 1951. Evans wrote her song in 1952. By this time, Foy Willing had been in eleven movies with Roy Rogers, provided musical background on his radio show and toured with him on his personal appearances. The Riders of the Purple Sage was one of the top singing groups in western movies.

Foy Lopez Willingham was born May 14, 1914, in Iredell, Texas. The family moved to Belton, about 40 miles southwest of Waco, when Foy was a child. In high school, he sang on a 15-minute show on WACO sponsored by Cameron Lumber Company. After high school, he attended the Stamps-Baxter School of shaped note gospel singing in Dallas and then obtained a job on WOW in Omaha, Nebraska, singing with "The Tall Guys" on a show sponsored by Georgie Porgie breakfast cereal.

The group moved to Columbus, Ohio, before landing in New York in 1933, where they replaced Carson Robison on a show sponsored by Crazy Water Crystals. In New York, Foy performed on a 30-minute show on WNEW and then a 15-minute show on WMCA. He also did three one-hour shows a week for the NBC network, singing mostly folk songs such as "Put Your Little Shoes Away, Little Joe," "The Tie That Binds," "Little Rosewood Casket," "In the Baggage Coach Ahead" and "Get Along Home, Cindy." New York during the 1930s was a thriving spot for what later became known as "country" music. Also on the radio in New York were Tex Ritter, Texas Ruby, Rufe Davis, Ray Whitley, Patsy Montana, the Canova Family, Frank Luther and Vernon Dalhart.

In late 1935 or early 1936 Foy Willingham moved back to Texas and enrolled in Tyler Commercial College while he worked in sales for KGKB. In Palestine, Texas, Willingham worked as a radio announcer as well as in radio sales. In 1939 he finished college and went to work for Elliott Roosevelt, son of President Franklin D. Roosevelt, who was putting together the Texas State Radio Network.

Willingham was the sales manager for a radio station in San Angelo before he moved to Fort Worth to join a singing group, Men of the Range, comprising of Lew Preston, Jake

Wright and Foy, who went by the name of Lopez Willingham at the time. This group had their first recording session in April 1940 for Columbia's Okeh label; on that session they recorded "There Ain't Gonna Be No Me to Welcome You" written by Dick Reinhart.

In July 1941, the group went to California and appeared in a Charles Starrett film, *Prairie Stranger*, under the name "Lew Preston and His Ranch Hands." Willingham wrote "I'll Be a Cowboy Till I Die," which was used in that movie. In August the group appeared, without screen credit, in the Columbia film *Royal Mounted Patrol*. The Men of the Range group moved to

Foy Willing and the Riders of the Purple Sage (photograph courtesy of Packy Smith).

Los Angeles full time in 1943 and sang on a radio show sponsored by a dentist, Dr. Beauchamp. Willingham was then contacted by an old friend, Clark Fulks, who went by the name Cottonseed Clark, to join the *Hollywood Barn Dance* for CBS. Willingham recruited Jimmie Dean, brother of Eddie Dean, and Clark to form the group "Riders of the Purple Sage."

Riders of the Purple Sage was the title of a novel by Zane Grey, originally published in 1912. There were several singing groups named "Riders of the Purple Sage" before Willingham chose that name for his group, but none of the previous groups achieved national success under that name. There were several movies made from Grey's novel and Willingham claimed that he picked the name because he loved one of those movies.

The *Hollywood Barn Dance* was a successful radio show, created around 1932 and held at a dance hall next door to Grauman's Chinese Theater. By the 1940s the *Barn Dance* was broadcast from CBS' studio on Fairfax Avenue; this is when Foy Willing and the Riders of the Purple Sage joined and served as official hosts of the network show. Posters advertised Foy and the group but "Willingham" did not fit so Foy's name was shortened to "Willing" and so, from the time when the Riders of the Purple Sage were formed, he became "Foy Willing."

The *Barn Dance* was a hit show loaded with talent. The musical arrangements were done by Paul Sells, Johnny Bond did comedy, the bass player and emcee was Cliffie Stone, Kirby Grant sang western classics and Ken Curtis usually closed the show. Also on the show was Jimmy Wakely's trio and the Sunshine Girls—Vivian Earles, June Widener and Colleen

Summers (later known as Mary Ford of "Les Paul and Mary Ford"). Guest stars included Roy Rogers and Bob Nolan.

In December 1944, Foy Willing and the Riders of the Purple Sage were on a 30-minute show on ABC, *Eight to the Bar*, which changed its name to the *N Bar K Musical Showroom* when it was sponsored by Nash-Kelvinator. The group was offered a recording contract on Capitol Records and appeared in several movies. At this point, the Riders of the Purple Sage comprised Al Sloey, a friend of Willing's from Oklahoma who, with Foy, remained a key component of the group, Jimmie Dean, Fred Pugh or Paul Sells on accordion, bass player Cliffie Stone, Johnny Paul or Sammy Lehr on fiddle, clarinet by either Neely Plumb, Darol Rice or Maury Stein, and Jerry Vaughn on rhythm guitar. Their first Capitol recording was "Hang Your Head in Shame," b/w "Texas Blues."

In 1945 the group moved to Decca and then to Ben Selvin's Majestic Records where they recorded the classic song, "Have I Told You Lately That I Love You?" They also recorded one of Foy's songs, "No One to Cry To." After World War II, the group did *All-Star Western Theater*, a series of 30-minute western musical dramas, and played Las Vegas and Reno. Republic Pictures hired the group for a series of pictures starring Monte Hale. They backed Hale in six B westerns for two years, 1946 to 1948.

Roy Rogers was the biggest star for Republic during the late 1940s and had a network radio show sponsored by Quaker Oats. In late 1948, Foy Willing and the Riders of the Purple Sage replaced the Sons of the Pioneers in Roy's pictures. Rogers, as Len Slye, was a founding member of the Sons of the Pioneers and the group had been with him for a number of years, performing in many of his movies. But the Sons of the Pioneers had six members and received $2,000 per picture, which was scheduled to jump to $2,500 a picture when their next option came up. Republic's Herbert Yates was notoriously frugal and wanted cheaper talent; although Roy Rogers preferred the Sons of the Pioneers in his pictures, he had no say-so in that decision. Thus Foy Willing and the Riders of the Purple Sage—a four man group—began appearing in the movies of Roy Rogers, beginning with *Grand Canyon Trail* and *The Far Frontier* in 1948.

Foy and his group appeared in eleven Roy Rogers films over the next three years and also appeared with Rogers on his tours, performing at rodeos in Houston, San Antonio, Philadelphia, Boston and Madison Square Garden. The group had some successful recordings as well. "Anytime" reached the charts in 1948 and "Brush Those Tears from Your Eyes" reached the charts in early 1949.

The Roy Rogers Show, sponsored by Quaker Oats, was on the Mutual Network for two years on Sunday evenings. The musical group for the show was Foy Willing and the Riders of the Purple Sage." They were on during its entire run, from March 1948 until May 1951.

The group made six movies with Roy Rogers in 1950 but the following year made only two films, *Spoilers of the Plains* and *Heart of the Rockies*. *Spoilers of the Plains*, which contained Foy's song "Happy Trails," was released in 1951 and, according to Foy, "about 1952, Dale rewrote it and they used it for their television [show]. It's my copyright [but] I never did anything about it; they'll just have to live with it. I just wonder sometimes how they feel."* The big lingering question is what would have happened if Foy had brought a court case against Dale Evans for the copyright to "Happy Trails." Would he have won? Would Roy and Dale still have used it as a theme song? Would it have received the exposure that has allowed it to become one of the most recognizable songs in western music?

The split with Roy Rogers and Republic wasn't amicable. Foy Willing had a drinking problem and Rogers apparently wanted to keep the name of the group but use different per-

---

*Sharon Lee Willing, *No One to Cry To*, p. 80; see sources.

sonnel; however, Willing fought him in court and won the legal battle for the rights to the name.

The Riders of the Purple Sage had a number of members through the years. Foy Willing, Al Sloey and Scotty Harrell formed the core of the group; musicians who performed with them include Johnny Paul and Paul Girardi on fiddle, Jerry Vaughn on guitar, Bud Sievert on accordion, Freddy Taveres on steel guitar, Neely Plumb, Darol Rice and Maury Stein on clarinet and Irving Edelman and Cliffie Stone on bass. Willing disbanded the group in 1952 but hired Dale Warren just before the group quit. Warren joined the Sons of the Pioneers after leaving Riders of the Purple Sage, replacing Ken Curtis, and remained with that group for over 50 years.

Willing bounced around show business after the singing cowboy era ended. He worked in radio sales, appeared with Gene Autry during a tour in 1957 and recorded for a variety of labels. The group reunited for various recording projects and personal appearances but the era of western singing groups had passed by the mid–1960s. Foy Willing died on July 24, 1978.

SOURCES:

Sikes, O.J. "Foy Willing & The Riders of the Purple Sage." *The Western Way* (Spring 2005), 9–10.

Willing, Sharon Lee. *No One to Cry To: A Long, Hard Ride into the Sunset with Foy Willing of The Riders of the Purple Sage*. Tucson, AZ: Wheatmark, 2008.

12

Jimmy Wakely

Of all the singing cowboys, Jimmy Wakely was the most successful in terms of *Billboard* chart records after World War II. As a movie star, he never rivaled Gene Autry or Roy Rogers; and the Sons of the Pioneers, Autry and Rogers were certainly more influential to later country and western singers. But in terms of records on the *Billboard* charts, nobody beat Jimmy Wakely. The *Billboard* charts began in 1944 and the country charts were based on jukebox play. Jimmy Wakely had his first chart record in 1944 when "I'm Sending You Red Roses" reached number two.

Wakely began recording for Decca in 1940, when he did ten songs, including "Cimarron," "Maria Elena," "Too Late," "I Wonder Where You Are Tonight," and "Cattle Call." In 1941 he did 16 songs for the label, including "Be Honest with Me," "Gone and Left Me Blues," "Don't Bite the Hand That's Feeding You," and "Froggy Went A-Courtin'." In 1942 he recorded "There's a Star Spangled Banner Waving Somewhere" and three others; in 1943 he recorded four songs. Then, during the period 1944–1946 he recorded more sides for Decca.

In 1947 Wakely signed with Capitol Records and had a string of hits, beginning with "Signed, Sealed and Delivered" in 1948. That same year he had number one hits with "One Has My Name (The Other Has My Heart)," and "I Love You So Much It Hurts." His record of "Mine All Mine" was also on the charts in 1948.

In 1949 Wakely had "Forever More," "Till The End of the World," "I Wish I Had a Nickel," "Someday You'll Call My Name" and "Telling My Troubles to My Old Guitar" on the charts. But his biggest hits came with his duets with Margaret Whiting. "Slipping Around" reached number one on both the pop and country charts and stayed on the country charts for 28 weeks; the "B" side, "Wedding Bells," was also a crossover hit, as was the follow-up single, "I'll Never Slip Around Again."

In 1950 Wakely had solo success with "Peter Cottontail" and "Mona Lisa" as well as duet hits with Margaret Whiting on "Broken Down Merry-Go-Round," "The Gods Were Angry with Me," "Let's Go to Church (Next Sunday Morning)" and "A Bushel and a Peck." In 1951 Wakely and Whiting had crossover hits with "When You and I Were Young Maggie Blues" and "I Don't Want to Be Free," while Wakely had solo crossover hits on "My Heart Cries for You" and "Beautiful Brown Eyes."

Although Wakely was known as a "singing cowboy," his big hits were not "cowboy" songs. Indeed, his biggest hits were country and pop numbers and, although he retained a "cowboy" image for many people, Wakely increasingly performed a wide variety of music as he moved into the Las Vegas circuit in the 1960s.

Clarence Wakeley was born on February 16, 1914, in Mineola, Arkansas. As a young child he moved with his family to Octavia, then Ida, Oklahoma. He was influenced initially by Jimmie Rodgers and first sang on the radio in Elk City, Oklahoma, in 1932. Wakeley moved to Rosedale, Oklahoma, where he changed his first name from Clarence to James and changed the spelling of his last name from Wakeley to Wakely.

In Rosedale, Wakely became involved in gospel singing schools (shaped note singing) and learned to play the piano. In 1935 he began singing on KTOK in Stillwater, Oklahoma, after he won "Johnny Marvin's Discovery Night Contest"; Marvin began calling him "Jimmy" instead of "James." In December of that year he married Inez Miser.

In 1937 Wakely joined *Little Doc Roberts Traveling Medicine Show*, then formed the Bell Boys, who appeared on WKY on three 15-minute shows a week. This trio consisted of Scotty Harrell, Jack Cheney and Wakely, with staff guitarist Mel Osborne performing with the group. The group wore bellboy uniforms and pillbox caps and were sponsored by the Bell Clothing Stores.

Jimmy Wakely (photograph courtesy of Packy Smith).

In addition to Jimmie Rodgers, Wakley's other influences included Gene Austin, Bob Wills, the Light Crust Doughboys, Bing Crosby and Dick Powell. But his biggest influence was Gene Autry and "he is the reason [Wakley] chose to be a singing cowboy."

Because of Autry's influence, Wakely "wanted to wear western clothes and sing cowboy songs." He dropped Jack Cheney and Mel Osborne from his group and brought in Johnny Whitfield, who had a 15-minute show on KTOK, *Johnny Whitfield, the Lonesome Cowboy*.

The Bell Boys made their first trip to Hollywood in 1939; they also changed their name to Jimmy Wakely and the Rough Riders. In Hollywood, they made some transcriptions for Standard Radio and signed a contract to appear and sing in a Republic film, *Saga of Death Valley*, starring Roy Rogers. Failing to find more movie work, the group returned to Oklahoma. During this period, many singing cowboys toured to promote their latest movie release, performing songs in a movie theater before the feature was shown. Wakely's group opened shows for some of these Hollywood stars.

According to Wakely, in a memoir written by his daughter, Linda Lee, in 1940 the group was driving when lightning allowed them to see a poster of Gene Autry announcing his appearance in Okemah, Oklahoma. The trio—Wakely, Bond and Scotty—drove to Okemah and talked Bill Slepka, manager of the local theater, to let the trio sing on a radio broadcast from the theater. They also promised Slepka they'd get Autry to sing on the program.

In addition to an appearance at the theater, Autry was in a parade. Wakely's trio climbed up on an old store building as Gene passed. According to Wakely, "As he approached on his horse, Champion, we waved our cowboy hats. He spotted us and waved his white Stetson. 'Come on over to the hotel!' he shouted. I told Gene of my promise to my sponsor and he and Champion walked to the theater with us—with hundreds of fans following behind." Champion followed Gene into the elevator, then onto the stage, where he stood quietly at his side and listened to Gene sing, "South of the Border." After this performance, Autry invited the trio to come to Hollywood.

On May 29, 1940, Wakely, with his wife and two daughters, and Whitfield, with his wife, Dorothy, got in a Buick and headed to Hollywood, pulling a trailer which carried their instruments, luggage and household furnishings. During the drive out, Whitfield decided to change his name to Johnny Bond. In June, the group reached California. Autry was out of town at the time, so the group scrambled to get some work before their money ran out. Wakely managed to get a spot in a western series, *The Range Busters*, and his first movie was *Trailin' Trouble*.

When Autry came back into town he "arranged an audition for Jimmy's trio with his sponsor, Mr. Wrigley," according to Linda Lou Wakely in her book, *See Ya Up There*. "He told them if they were accepted and could get into the musician's union, he would put them on his radio show." The group "auditioned on closed circuit radio to Chicago for Mr. Wrigley's representatives," who turned them down. But "Gene said, 'Hell with it! I'm gonna put you on my show for two weeks. If Wrigley likes you, you can stay.'" That was the beginning of Wakely's group as regulars on Autry's CBS radio show, *Melody Ranch*.

By October 1940, Wakely had made a number of transcriptions, appeared in six movies, organized a western band to appear at the Aragon Ballroom, appeared regularly on "*Melody Ranch*" and worked with Autry on his personal appearances.

The musicians union fought the airplay of records on radio stations, so many stations subscribed to a "transcription" service, where an artist recorded a number of songs—or a whole show—for this service, which was then supplied to radio stations. Wakely, Bond and Dick Reinhart (who replaced Scotty Harrell in the group) did transcriptions for NBC as the Jimmy Wakely Trio, for World Transcriptions as Jimmy Wakely and the Rodeo Boys, and for Standard Transcriptions as Johnny Bond and His Red River Boys.

On October 9, Wakely's group opened for Autry, who wore a solid white cowboy outfit, at Madison Square Garden and "Gene fell off his horse and got some bad publicity," according to Wakely. During that same tour, Franklin Roosevelt was reelected to his third term as president and the group listened to election returns on Dick Reinhart's radio in Autry's dressing room.

On November 5, according to Wakely:

A wild bull broke out of the pen and took right out through the arena when Gene was introducing "South of the Border." It passed us then came right back after us. Gene was standing in the spotlight and could not see. It could see us though and ran full speed right at Gene. The crowd almost fell out of their seats. We all stood there behind Gene and when he finally saw the bull after him, he couldn't run as it was too late. He just let out a "Yippi!" and waved his hat. The bull turned a little and just missed him. Gene was quite a hero after that.

Wakely recalled other early days with Autry:

When we joined Gene in 1940 as his backup trio, we sang one song on every show, but we didn't do ballads; that was Gene's forte. Originally, I was his guitar player, but it developed that Bond took over this part when I became Gene's stand-in for the show. When Gene was on the road or rehearsing somewhere else, I would stand-in to sing and act his part to time the script and mark it for him. Then, when Gene came in, his script was exactly timed with all the edits, and all he had to do was just walk up to the microphone and go through it. I learned to work exactly like Gene and was one of the first radio stand-ins. One reason I resigned from his show was because I was beginning to work too much like him. I figured I'd never have anything on my own.

After two years on Autry's show, Wakely resigned and went out on his own. During World War II he toured as a member of Bing Crosby's group with John Scott Trotter's orchestra, Johnny Marvin, Johnny Bond (doing comedy), and Victor Borge, performing at military bases. Wakely also got a part in the Johnny Mack Brown-Tex Ritter series. In 1944 he changed the name of his group to "The Saddle Pals."

Wakely landed a plum spot in the western series for Columbia starring Charles Starrett. "It was in his movies that I started getting the solo parts that eventually led to my own pictures," remembered Wakely. He signed with Monogram and his first starring movie was *Song of the Range* in 1944, which was a remake of an old movie starring John Wayne and Ray Corrigan. That same year he bought a ranch in the San Fernando Valley.

Wakely's biggest success as a singing cowboy came in *Song of the Sierras*, released in 1946. His last starring movies were released in 1949: *Across the Rio Grande*, *Brand of Fear*, *Lawless Code* and *Roaring Westward*. In those movies he was teamed with Dub "Cannonball" Taylor as his sidekick.

The big band sound was the top selling sound of the 1940s and Wakely recorded with the bands of Bob Crosby, Hank DeVol, Les Baxter and Nelson Riddle. Beginning in 1949 he toured with Bob Hope and in 1950 hosted an ABC Radio show, *Wait for Wakely*.

In 1954 Wakely signed with Coral Records, then in the middle 1950s started his own label, Shasta. For Shasta, Wakely recorded himself as well as Johnny Bond, Eddie Dean and Tex Williams. When rock'n'roll hit in the mid–1950s, Jimmy Wakely was out of touch. His record sales fell and the music he loved dropped away, replaced by the sounds of rhythm and blues and rock'n'roll for young buyers. An era of TV cowboys began, but TV wanted new, young actors—not the older singing cowboys who had established the genre. Although Gene Autry and Roy Rogers had TV shows in the 1950s, by the end of that decade and the beginning of the next their shows had been replaced or eclipsed by shows like *Maverick*, *Cheyenne*, *Tales of Wells Fargo*, *Rawhide*, *Wanted: Dead or Alive*, *Life and Legend of Wyatt Earp*, *Wagon Train*, *The Rifleman*, *Gunsmoke*, *Bonanza* and *Have Gun, Will Travel*.

Beginning in 1959, Wakely toured the Las Vegas circuit. He formed a group with family members and played nightclubs, still drawing some old fans. He continued to perform for the rest of his life, but—like the other singing cowboys—the 1960s and 1970s were not kind to him. Wakely and others were relegated to being relics of the past until the western renaissance of the 1980s and 1990s gave them new respect. It all came a little too late for Jimmy Wakely, who died on September 23, 1982.

Jimmy Wakely was a difficult man, testy, opinionated and hard to get along with. His daughter wrote a loving memoir of him, *See Ya Up There*, published privately in 1992 and described her Dad as "an impatient man who possessed a quick temper that could be devastating" and as "old fashioned and chauvinistic." "There were times it was next to impossible to agree with my Daddy," she wrote.

Given all that, Jimmy Wakely must still be remembered as a pioneer in singing cowboy movies. He wasn't the first to ride the celluloid range, but during the 1940s, at the height of the popularity of the singing cowboys, he was an important player. Also, his success on the country and pop charts let the world know that the singing cowboys had talents and abilities that extended beyond western music.

Cowboys and western music have always had to fight for respect. Because of his successful recordings, Jimmy Wakely made sure they got it.

SOURCES:

Green, Douglas B. *Singing in the Saddle: The History of the Singing Cowboy*. Nashville: Country Music Foundation Press and Vanderbilt University Press, 2002.
Wakely, Linda Lee. *See Ya Up There, Baby: The Jimmy Wakely Story*. Canoga Park, CA: Shasta Records, 1992.

13

Johnny Bond

For years, Johnny Bond served as Gene Autry's right-hand man when it came to recording and performing. Although Autry was a good guitar player, he preferred to have Johnny Bond play guitar for him because (1) Bond was a better guitar player and (2) this allowed Autry not to have the burden of carrying a guitar around with him.

Cyrus Whitfield "Johnny" Bond was born on June 1, 1915, in Enville, Oklahoma, and grew up in that region. He learned to play the guitar and sang on local radio shows.

Jimmy Wakely formed the Bell Boys in 1937; the group appeared on WKY in Oklahoma City on three 15-minute shows a week. The original trio consisted of Wakely, Scotty Harrell and Jack Cheney with staff guitarist Mel Osborne performing with the group. The group wore bellboy uniforms and pillbox caps and were sponsored by the Bell Clothing Stores. On KTOK, "Johnny Whitfield, the Lonesome Cowboy" had a 15-minute show. Wakely soon dropped Jack Cheney and Mel Osborne from his group and added Whitfield. Whitfield (nee Bond) contributed the theme song to the group when he wrote "Cimarron" after noticing there was no song titled "Cimarron" although that had been the name of a popular western movie as well as a river in Oklahoma.

The first trip to Hollywood for the Bell Boys came in 1939; that same year they changed their name to Jimmy Wakely and the Rough Riders. The group recorded some transcriptions for Standard Radio and appeared in a Roy Rogers movie, *Saga of Death Valley*. However, when they were unable to find more movie work they returned to Oklahoma.

Bond was performing with Jimmy Wakely's group in Oklahoma in 1940 when Gene Autry was on tour promoting his latest movie, *Rancho Grande*. On April 22, Autry was in Okemah, Oklahoma, to celebrate "Pioneer Days" and the Jimmy Wakely Trio came over from WKY in Oklahoma City to perform.

Wakely's group discovered that Autry would be in Okemah when they saw a poster announcing the event. Wakely, Scotty Harrell and Johnny Whitfield, as he was known then, drove to Okemah and talked theater owner Bill Slepka into letting them sing on a radio broadcast from the theater, promising Slepka that Autry would also appear on the broadcast.

During a parade that featured Autry, Wakely's trio climbed on an old store building and as Gene approached on his horse the trio waved their cowboy hats. Autry, who had met the group previously, saw them and returned the greeting, inviting them over to his hotel. The Wakely trio told Autry of their promise to Slepka and Autry agreed to perform on the broadcast.

After performing with the group, Autry told them, "If you fellows should decide to come back out to California again, be sure and look me up!" That was good enough for the trio, who were, as Johnny Bond remembered, "young, ambitious and fearless." The group gave their notice to WKY that they were leaving, but group member Scotty Harrell chose to remain behind and was replaced by Dick Reinhart.

On May 29, 1940, Wakely, with his wife and two daughters, and Johnny Whitfield, with his wife, Dorothy, climbed in a Buick and headed to Hollywood, pulling a trailer which carried their instruments, luggage and household furnishings. During the drive out, Whitfield decided to change his name to "Johnny Bond." In June, the group reached California. Autry was out of town at the time, so the group scrambled to obtain some work before their money ran out. Wakely managed to acquire a spot in a western series, *The Range Busters* and his first movie was *Trailin' Trouble*.

When Autry arrived back into town he scheduled an audition for the trio with his radio sponsor, Mr. Wrigley, and told them that if Wrigley accepted them and they gained membership in the musicians union then he would put them on his *Melody Ranch* radio show, which had just started in January of that year.

Wrigley turned the group down but Autry decided to give the group a trial run on his radio show, telling them that if Mr. Wrigley did not object, they'd have a job on *Melody Ranch*. The only sticking point with Autry was that he preferred the trio with Scotty Harrell in it rather than the new trio with Reinhart. During a personal appearance with Autry at a rodeo in Duluth, Minnesota, the group stopped in Oklahoma and convinced Harrell to join them. Reinhart remained with the group, which meant that sometimes the trio was a quartet as Harrell and Reinhart alternated singing with the group during the next several years.

The Jimmy Wakely Trio joined Autry on the 30-minute *Melody Ranch* radio program in September 1940, singing their hit, "Cimarron." In addition to the radio show the group also toured with Autry, performing at the Madison Square Garden and Boston Gardens rodeos. In 1941 Bond signed a recording contract with Okeh/Columbia and recorded with his group, the Red River Valley Boys.

The *Melody Ranch* radio show was broadcast before a live audience, with free admission, in one of CBS' small studios at Columbia Square, located on the corner of Sunset Boulevard and Gower Street in Hollywood. By September, the show began with "Back in the Saddle Again," which became his theme song, replacing "Sing Me a Song of the Saddle." The Jimmy Wakely Trio generally performed a song by themselves on each show and sang with Autry on a "cowboy classic."

When Johnny Bond and his group joined Autry, they fell into Autry's social circle. Bond noted there were a lot of parties in homes. Gene and Ina Mae seldom arrived late, and when they did, Autry shook hands all around. Although Autry was usually in one of his cowboy outfits, it was "just plain old visiting like ordinary folks." A jam session usually followed, which might last until midnight. "We learned that Autry loved to sing whether on stage or off," remembered Bond. "He would begin with some of the older, more familiar favorites, followed by some new songs that he and others were working on. In this manner we all learned the new songs, sometimes even helping him revise certain parts of them."

Bond remembered that his "new boss would always suggest that each of us come forward with new compositions so, naturally, we began writing." Smiley Burnette generally wasn't there—he might be out on the road with his own show or he just might not come. The Burnettes were teetotalers and there was usually some drinking at these parties. However, the Burnettes sometimes hosted huge outdoor backyard parties at their home in Studio City, not far from Autry's home.

In October 1940, Gene Autry made his first appearance at the big Madison Square Garden Rodeo in New York. The group played before 25,000 in the Garden each night for six weeks—seven nights a week with four matinees. On the show, announcer Abe Lefton first introduced Jimmy Wakely and the *Melody Ranch* Gang, who ran to the center of the arena and performed four or five up-tempo songs. Then came the Grand Entry, with every cowboy and cowgirl connected to the event riding on horses and dressed in colorful costumes and carrying flags as they circled the arena.

Following this spectacle there were rodeo contests: bareback bronc riding, calf roping, and women's saddle bronc riding. After about 45 minutes of rodeo contests, Autry made his entrance on Champion, who jumped through a large hoop covered with paper with Autry's picture on it. Another trick was even more difficult. A baby grand piano, with the top down, was covered with a rubber mat. Champion came in on a gallop, jumped on the piano and stopped as Autry waved to the crowd from his back. Autry then put Champion through his series of steps, tricks and dances and this section ended with Autry and Champion in an "End of the Trail" pose.

Johnny Bond (photograph courtesy of Packy Smith).

Then it was back to more rodeo contests—bulldogging, trick riding and specialty acts—then Gene Autry and Champion rode into the center of the ring and the Wakely group joined them. Autry performed for about 15 minutes; he usually sang "Back in the Saddle Again," "Mexicali Rose," "Be Honest with Me," "South of the Border," "Tumbling Tumbleweeds," "Cool Water," "Empty Saddles," and "The Last Roundup." After these musical performances, Autry circled the arena on Champion, then rode out and the rodeo contests continued.

The first time the Wakely Trio backed Gene Autry on a recording session was on June 18, 1941, when Autry recorded two songs by Jimmie Davis, "You Are My Sunshine" and "It Makes No Difference Now" as well as two others. On July 28 they returned to the studio and recorded "Under Fiesta Stars" and three other numbers, then two days later they recorded four songs, including "Don't Bite the Hand That's Feeding You." On August 1 they recorded four numbers, ten days later they recorded another four songs and on the 27 they recorded three songs, including "Blue Eyed Elaine," the first hit from a young singer in Texas, Ernest Tubb.

On July 4 Autry and his troupe performed in a rodeo at Soldier Field in Chicago and the next day, with media in tow, he went to the recruiting station and enlisted in the Army Air Corps, although he was sworn in during a broadcast of *Melody Ranch* later that month.

When Autry entered the army the Jimmy Wakely Trio split. Dick Reinhart moved back to Texas, Wakely pursued a solo career in the movies and Johnny Bond stuck with Autry.

After Autry completed basic training, he was notified by the J. Walter Thompson Agency of arrangements between the military and Phil Wrigley to send him on a tour of bases, where he performed daily shows for servicemen and servicewomen. Performing with Autry were

Johnny Bond, Eddie and Jimmy Dean, and Carl Cotner on fiddle as well as an orchestra director for the radio programs. CBS arranged for staff musicians and radio engineers to travel from Chicago to wherever Autry performed for the radio broadcasts of *Melody Ranch*, the title of which became *Sgt. Autry* during World War II.

In 1947 Johnny Bond had three chart records: "Divorce Me C.O.D." and "So Round, So Firm, So Fully Packed," both written by Merle Travis, and "The Daughter of Jole Blon," written by Fred Rose. In addition to his appearances on *Melody Ranch*, Bond also appeared regularly on *Hollywood Barn Dance*. Since Bond had a small studio in his home—a disc cutting machine, actually—and was a talented singer and guitarist, he played a role in the creation of the Christmas standard "Here Comes Santa Claus."

Art Satherley wanted Autry to record a Christmas song, "An Old Fashioned Tree," and they needed a "B" side for the record. Autry had been grand marshall of the Christmas parade in Hollywood in 1946 and remembered the children shouting "here comes Santa Claus" so he gave that title to Oakley Haldeman, who headed his publishing company. Haldeman, Satherley and several others went to a home in the Hollywood Hills on a hot, August night and composed the song. The next evening, Satherley and Haldeman went over to Johnny Bond's house to have the song recorded as a demo. Since Gene Autry could not read or write music, he needed to learn songs from a recording. Bond recorded the demo that evening and on August 28, Gene Autry recorded "Here Comes Santa Claus," which became a big hit during both the 1947 and 1948 Christmas seasons.

The success of "Here Comes Santa Claus" led to Autry recording his biggest hit, "Rudolph, the Red Nosed Reindeer." Johnny Bond played guitar on that session too, which was held June 27, 1949, and remembered that Autry and his new producer, Hecky Krasnow, were not getting along well during the recording of the Christmas songs. Bond recalled they spent a great deal of time recording the selections: "We thought they would never get the takes to his satisfaction, but they did." During the 1949 appearances at Madison Square Garden, Gene Autry introduced "Rudolph," with Frankie Marvin dressed as Rudolph, complete with a flashing red nose.

Beginning in 1948, Gene Autry toured twice a year, generally playing a matinee and evening show every single day for about six weeks. Johnny Bond was in the cast, which also included Pat Buttram, Carl Cotner, Frankie Marvin and the Cass County Boys. The show boasted a number of other performers, who varied from year to year. In 1948 Autry began the first tour in January and the second in August. During the March through July period he usually filmed six movies.

By the end of the 1940s, Autry's *Melody Ranch* program was heard on CBS at 6:30 P.M. on the East Coast. It featured musical selections as well as a "Western Tale" of the day, a ten-minute fictional story with sound effects that often featured Hollywood actors. The show was heard in Los Angeles over KNX.

The show had become a much bigger production than in its earliest years and personnel had changed since Autry resumed the show after World War II. By the end of the forties, regulars in addition to Johnny Bond included Pat Buttram as Autry's comic sidekick; Jim Boles, Wally Maher and Tyler McVey in various supporting roles; musical performers Cass County Boys, the Pinafores, the Gene Autry Blue Genes, Alvino Ray, Carl Cotner's *Melody Ranch* 6, the King Sisters (Donna, Alice, Yvonne, and Louise) and Mary Ford.

The years 1950 through 1953 saw Gene Autry at the peak of his performing career. During his tours, he stayed in hotels, telling Johnny Bond, "You stay at someone's home, you're his prisoner for the day and night. You can't make a move without his knowledge or permission and his time is your time. That's why I always turn down such invitations regardless of who it is that might ask, even a close friend. Now, that's when you're working. If you're on vacation and have no deadlines, that's something else." Bond agreed, but noted that he "never knew Gene Autry to take a vacation!"

In November 1951 Autry did a tour of Canada. During the tour, traveling from Edmonton to Saskatoon, the group faced a snowstorm. Some members managed to fly ahead, including Johnny Bond. But Bond forgot to bring his guitar—his job was to go with Autry on visits during the day to hospitals, orphanages, and luncheons and if someone wanted a song, Bond would play while Autry sang. The incident brought out a rare display of anger from Autry, who chastised Bond, saying, "Listen Bond. If it ever gets to the point where it looks like the show might be delayed—if YOU can get here, bring your damned guitar. At least you and I can start it and keep them entertained until the rest of the crew gets here. Have you got that straight?" Johnny Bond learned his lesson. (Autry was fond of nicknames. He called Johnny Bond "Jonathan Q," Pat Buttram was "Big Butt," and Carl Cotner was "Flutter Tongue.")

In June, 1953, Johnny Bond told Gene Autry that he was resigning to move to Dallas. According to Bond, Autry said to him, "Hate to see you go. But, there comes a time in every man's life when he has to take that giant step. Tell you what. If things don't work out to your satisfaction, you can always come back. You job'll still be here, waiting."

Before the end of the year, Bond came back and rejoined Autry. According to Bond, "Not once did he ask me to explain or go into any form of detail as to what had happened both here and in Dallas, or to otherwise explain my actions or what was going on inside my feeble brain. While some of the gang were digging me deeply, not Gene. This, to me, was the sign of a big, big man."

Beginning in 1953, Johnny Bond and Tex Ritter both performed on *Town Hall Party* over the NBC Radio network and stayed with that show until it closed in 1961. In 1953, Autry filmed his last feature film, *Last of the Pony Riders*. The last episode of *The Gene Autry Show* was shown on its regularly scheduled Saturday night slot at the end of 1955 and in 1956 his CBS radio program, *Melody Ranch*, ended.

Johnny Bond wrote an unpublished biography of Gene Autry and noted in that work that he "began to get the impression that the Boss had lost interest in the radio show." "What with movie production already shut down, the TV films on their way out, maybe he felt that his radio years had had it." Bond also noted that Autry's drinking had caused him to miss a number of shows and that some old, recorded shows had to be programmed at the last minute because Autry was unable to perform. This raised the ire of the Wrigley company, which wanted Autry to perform the shows live and in good shape.

On the last show only Carl Cotner, Pat Buttram, Johnny Bond and the other regulars appeared; Autry was not in the studio. There was a message from the sponsor that Autry "was always welcome back whenever he chose to return." Bond remembered Autry saying about the cancellation, "Well, that's the way the old ball bounces." After Autry's radio show ended, Johnny Bond decided to quit touring so he could perform on *Town Hall Party*. Bond and Ritter also formed a publishing company. Autry hired Johnny Western to replace Bond on the tours.

In 1959 Gene Autry appeared in a number of small towns at county fairs before a grandstand crowd. Johnny Bond, who traveled with Autry, noted "these are the hardest to play. The performers are stationed on a temporarily constructed stage in the center of a race track. The audience is so far away that the echo of the singer's voice bounces back from the loud speakers five or six seconds after the words have been sung or spoken. Plus there are outdoor noises. One finds himself in the middle of much confusion. We tried to do our comedy bit, but out there in the open, we found ourselves in competition with the peanut and popcorn salesmen, barkers, merry-go-round Calliopes."

Bond remembered other incidents from these days:

> In order to offset the fact that we now were playing places beneath our dignity, we stopped off in New York City for a few days visiting with old business acquaintances just to get the feeling that we were still in the big time. We didn't have a full crew; it was Autry, Merle Travis, Carl Cotner, and me with a local band we'd hire, plus a few circus type acts brought in from other sources. It was mostly an outdoor affair, giving us all the feeling that we were now in a Carnival, sometimes considered to be a second rate class of show business. This smaller show coupled with the smaller crowds made it obvious to all that the end of the line was in sight.

In Albany, New York, they performed August 21 and 22 in a baseball park on a crude stage built over the pitcher's mound. The only people who turned out were a few of Autry's fan club members who were still around, remembered Bond. Autry commented, "Looks like we have them outnumbered" and laughed it off. "It's all a part of touring," he said. "Win a few, lose a few." The show ended when a heavy rainstorm drenched everyone. Then it was on to Sedalia, Missouri, then Wichita. "Lots of people turned out for the Fair in those cities," said Bond, "but not everyone came into the Grandstand to see us."

In June 1960, Gene Autry called Johnny Bond to accompany him to Philadelphia for "The Soldier Field Thrill Show," scheduled over three days, which attracted a stadium full of people. In Philadelphia, Bond called some local musicians and put together a band; Autry did not bring his horse and the 53-year-old star performed only five songs, then went back to the hotel where he watched a baseball game on television.

According to Bond in his unpublished manuscript, by this point Autry was drinking heavily and Bond was assigned the task of keeping him sober, a task he was not quite up to. Autry had imbibed a bit too much before he met some mothers leading small boys wanting autographs in the hotel lobby and before he passed through admirers at the airport who stared in disbelief. It was all embarrassing and taxing for Bond, who incurred Autry's ire when they returned to Los Angeles and Bond called their wives while Autry preferred to avoid the wives as they hung out and imbibed further.

Later that year Bond was with Autry on the singer's last tour. The tour began in September in Knoxville at a fair and continued to Reading, Pennsylvania; Trenton, New Jersey; Columbia, South Carolina; and Shreveport. In addition to Bond, Autry was accompanied by Rufe Davis, Merle Travis and either Anita Bryant or Betty Johnson.

Johnny Bond remembered: "[G]one were the huge crowds of old. Business was not good on these final tours. It was disheartening to look at a grandstand full of empty seats where once there were thousands of cheering fans."

During the winter of 1961 and 1962, Gene Autry did his last recording sessions at the International Sound Studios in Hollywood for an RCA album. He recorded past hits for an album that was released in 1962 as *Gene Autry's Golden Hits*. During the four day session, Bond noted "it was obvious that he was out of practice. We noticed that he perspired a lot, tiring out easily during each song."

In 1964 *Melody Ranch* became a television program on KTLA—channel 5. Starring Carl Cotner, the Cass County Boys, Billy Mize and Johnny Bond, the one hour show featured music and skits. Although Autry did not appear on the program, he sometimes dropped by rehearsals to watch.

Johnny Bond performed a great favor for Gene Autry in 1969 when Autry was nominated for the Country Music Hall of Fame. At that time, the five final nominees for the Hall of Fame sat in the audience at the CMA's televised awards show until the end, when the newest member of the Hall of Fame was announced. Autry was a bit miffed because a number of people he had helped—and who came after him—had already been inducted into the Hall of Fame, such as Hank Williams, Fred Rose, Roy Acuff and Eddy Arnold. Autry did not want to sit in that audience again, with the TV cameras panning him, while someone else's name was called. On the other hand, he did not want to be absent if he was the newest inductee.

Since the name of the new inductee was always kept secret until the show, Johnny Bond was faced with the challenge of finding out who that inductee was without having anyone tell him. He solved the problem by finding out the name of the person who engraved the Hall of Fame plaque and visiting their shop. During the visit Bond managed to sneak a peak under the blanket covering the plaque and saw that the new inductee was Gene Autry. Bond relayed this to Autry, who flew to Nashville where, on October 12, 1969, as time was running out on the show, Tennessee Ernie Ford interrupted host Tex Ritter and announced Gene Autry as the newest Hall of Fame inductee. Autry walked to the microphone and told the audience, "I don't deserve this. But then, I have arthritis, and I don't deserve that either."

During his career, Johnny Bond composed about 300 songs, including the classic "I Wonder Where You Are Tonight." In addition to the three chart records in 1947 previously mentioned, Bond had chart recordings on "Oklahoma Waltz" (1948); "Till the End of the World" and "Tennessee Saturday Night" (both in 1949); "Love Song in 32 Bars" (1950); "Sick Sober and Sorry" (1951); "Three Sheets in The Wind" (1963) and his biggest country hit, "10 Little Bottles" which he wrote and which reached number two on the country charts and remained in that position for four weeks in 1965. His biggest pop hit came in 1960 with "Hot Rod Lincoln," recorded for Autry's Republic Records.

Bond was also an author, writing his own autobiography as well as a biography of Tex Ritter and an unpublished biography of Gene Autry. As a music publisher, in partnership with Tex Ritter, they published "I Wonder Where You Are Tonight," "Your Old Love Letters," "The Fool's Paradise," "Cimarron" and "Tomorrow Never Comes."

SOURCES:

Bond, Johnny. Gene Autry: "Champion." Manuscript in the Country Music Foundation Archives.
_____. Interview at Country Music Foundation, Oral History Music Project.
_____. *Reflections: The Autobiography of Johnny Bond*. Los Angeles: John Edwards Memorial Foundation, 1976.
Green, Douglas B. *Singing in the Saddle: The History of the Singing Cowboy*. Nashville: Country Music Foundation Press and Vanderbilt University Press, 2002.

14

Rosalie Allen

When it came to yodeling ladies, it was hard to beat Rosalie Allen. In 1939 she won a yodeling contest that dubbed her "Queen of the Yodelers," a moniker she used throughout her career. Although Rosalie Allen was a great singer and cowgirl yodeler, she was also an important, influential disc jockey during and after World War II.

Born Julie Marlene Bedra on June 27, 1924, in Old Forge, Pennsylvania, Rosalie came from a large family. During the Great Depression she worked as a dishwasher at age nine. Later she learned to play her brother's guitar. Her first radio job was in Wilkes-Barre, Pennsylvania, then on WORK in York, Pennsylvania, as a vocalist with Shorty Fincher's Prairie Pals.

In 1943 Allen moved to New York City where she began working with Denver Darling's group, the Swing Billies; later she worked with Zeke Manners and her a duet partner, Elton Britt. She recorded a number of duets with Britt, including "Beyond the Sunset," "Quicksilver" (both chart hits), "Mocking Bird Hill," "Tennessee Yodel Polka," and "It Is No Secret (What God Can Do)."

She signed with RCA Victor in 1945 and had a hit record with Patsy Montana's "I Want to Be a Cowboy's Sweetheart" and "Guitar Polka." Backed by the Black River Riders, her other hits included "Hitler Lives," "Rose of the Alamo," "He Taught Me How to Yodel" and "Station L-O-V-E Signing Off."

Allen was the deejay on *Prairie Stars* on WOV from 1944 to 1946, appeared in the movie *Village Barn* in 1949, and then had her own TV show in New York—the first country show in that city—from 1949 to 1953. She also opened the first country record store in that city, Rosalie Allen's Hillbilly Music Center. During the late 1940s and early 1950s she wrote columns for the publications *National Jamboree*, *Country Song Roundup* and *Hoedown*.

Rosalie Allen performed mainly in the New York-Pennsylvania area during her career. Later in life, she retired to Alabama, then moved to California. She died on September 24, 2003, at the age of 79.

SOURCES:

Allen, Rosalie. File in Frist Library and Archive, Country Music Foundation, Nashville, TN.
Green, Douglas B. *Singing in the Saddle: The History of the Singing Cowboy*. Nashville: Country Music Foundation Press and Vanderbilt University Press, 2002.
McCusker, Kristine M. *Lonesome Cowgirls and Honky-Tonk Angels: The Women of Barn Dance Radio*. Urbana: University of Illinois Press, 2008.

15

Cindy Walker

If you love songs like "Blue Canadian Rockies" and "Silver Spurs" recorded by Gene Autry; "Dusty Skies," "Miss Molly," "Cherokee Maiden," "Don't Be Ashamed of Your Age," "Bubbles in My Beer," and "You're from Texas" recorded by Bob Wills; or "Warm Red Wine," "Two Glasses Joe" and "Hey Mr. Bluebird" recorded by Ernest Tubb, then you love songs from the pen of Cindy Walker.

Cindy Walker wrote classic songs in the western, western swing and country fields; some of those songs were also hits in the rock and roll and rhythm and blues fields. In addition to the songs just mentioned, Walker wrote "Dream Baby" (Roy Orbison); "In the Misty Moonlight" (Jerry Wallace, Dean Martin and George Morgan); "Jim, I Wore a Tie Today" (Eddy Arnold, The Highwaymen); "Distant Drums" (Jim Reeves); "Triflin' Gal" (Al Dexter); "China Doll" (Ames Brothers); "The Gold Rush Is Over" and "The Next Voice You Hear" (Hank Snow); "I Don't Care" (Webb Pierce); "Heaven Says Hello" (Sonny James) and "You Are My Treasure" (Jack Greene).

Perhaps her most popular song was "You Don't Know Me," which was a hit for Eddy Arnold (1956), Ray Charles (1962), and Mickey Gilley (1981). In addition, it was recorded by Ray Charles and Diana Krall (on Charles' duets album *Genius Loves Company*), Elvis, Van Morrison, Patti Page, Roy Orbison, Kenny Rogers and Emmylou Harris.

Eddy Arnold was the cowriter of "You Don't Know Me" and he remembers running into Cindy Walker at the Andrew Jackson Hotel in Nashville during DJ Week in October in the mid–1950s. Arnold was sitting with Steve Sholes, head of RCA's country division, and called Walker over and told her about an idea he had for a song "about a young man who is so shy he can't tell the girl his feelings and that he loves her. The title is 'You Don't Know Me.'" Walker called Arnold about two weeks after that encounter and told him, "I've hooked it!" Then she played the song for him over the telephone and he soon recorded it.

Cindy Walker was born July 20, 1918, on a farm near Mart, Texas, with songwriting in her blood. Her grandfather, F.L. Eiland, was a hymn writer whose most famous work is "Hold to God's Unchanging Hand." Her mother, Oree, was an accomplished pianist. Cindy began writing songs when she was 12 years old, composing on her Martin guitar.

In 1940 Cindy and her parents went to Hollywood, where she knocked on the door of Bing Crosby's office and played a song she had written, "Lone Star Trail," for Bing's brother. Bing recorded it. The next year she was a recording artist for Decca, singing a song she did not write, "Seven Beers with the Wrong Man" (an answer to "Seven Years with the Wrong Woman"). During the 1942–1944 period she wrote 39 songs for Bob Wills' western movies; her first top ten country hit was "You're from Texas" by Bob Wills in 1944. Also in 1944 she recorded another song she did not write, "When My Blue Moon Turns to Gold Again," which was her only chart success, reaching number five on the country chart.

Cindy Walker (photograph courtesy of Packy Smith).

Walker loved songwriting more than being a recording artist and performer so she concentrated her energies on writing. In 1954 she moved back to Texas, settling in Mexia in a three bedroom house with her mother. She developed a routine for writing: she rose at dawn, made herself a pot of coffee, then went upstairs where she wrote on her typewriter. Writing songs is only part of being a songwriter; the other part is getting them recorded. Cindy Walker, along with her mom, developed the habit of coming to Nashville and staying in an apartment for several months, playing her songs for artists and producers in order to get them recorded.

Cindy had an early marriage, which she sometimes acknowledged, but had no children and spent her life living with her mother in Mexia, about 40 miles east of Waco and about 90 miles south of Dallas. She won a number of awards—which she kept under her bed—and her peers acknowledged her genius when she was voted into the Nashville Songwriters Hall of Fame in 1970. In 1990, Cindy Walker was elected to the Western Music Hall of Fame, along with Eddie Dean, Johnny Bond and Elton Britt.

In 1991 Cindy's mother, Oree Walker, died, which made Cindy's induction into the Country Music Hall of Fame in 1997 somewhat bittersweet. Accepting the honor, she said that her mother had told her she should wear the dress she was wearing that night when she was inducted into the Country Music Hall of Fame. Cindy kept that promise to her mother.

Cindy Walker died on Thursday, March 23, 2006, at her home in Mexia; she was 87 years old. The funeral was held on Monday, March 27, at the First Presbyterian Church in Mexia with over 200 people attending.

SOURCES:

Green, Douglas B. *Singing in the Saddle: The History of the Singing Cowboy.* Nashville: Country Music Foundation Press and Vanderbilt University Press, 2002.
McCusker, Kristine M. *Lonesome Cowgirls and Honky-Tonk Angels: The Women of Barn Dance Radio.* Urbana: University of Illinois Press, 2008.
Walker, Cindy. File at Frist Library and Archive, Country Music Foundation, Nashville, TN.

16

Marilyn Tuttle

One of the joys of a Western Music Association Festival is seeing Marilyn Tuttle, the Grand Lady of the WMA, and hearing her sing harmony. "I love to sing," said Marilyn. "But the only time I get to sing is at church when we sing the hymns. That's why I love the Festival so much—I get to sing!"

Marilyn Myers was born September 3, 1925, in Montebello, California, just east of Los Angeles. Her mother was a pianist who played for silent movies and Marilyn was one of the Meglin Kiddies. "Ethel Meglin had a series of dance schools," remembered Marilyn. "And I attended one of those and studied singing and dancing. Those schools furnished kids for movies and that's how I got into the movies."

Her first movie was *Maytime*, starring Jeanette MacDonald and Nelson Eddy, which was released in 1937. Marilyn was in two Shirley Temple movies: *Little Miss Broadway* and *The Littlest Rebel* (the latter movie is where the great Bill "Bojangles" Robinson danced). "We weren't really acting, we were just extras," said Marilyn. "In *The Littlest Rebel* I can't even see myself but I know I was there in the cotillion. In *Little Miss Broadway* I was one of the kids in the orphanage and we sang to Shirley Temple. Then she ran away from the orphanage and we tied some sheets together for that."

"I was in some other movies but my scenes ended up on the cutting room floor," said Marilyn, laughing. "I know I was in a movie starring Jane Russell. The last movie I worked in was *Down Missouri Way* starring Eddie Dean. I was in a trio and we sang on a hayride and then did some singing on the front porch of a house. But I never pursued movie work because I didn't like it. Too much hurry up and wait." Marilyn remembers that the children in movies had tutors for their schoolwork but "the stars had a little schoolhouse. This was back when Mickey Rooney, Judy Garland and I believe Lana Turner were all going to school on the movie lot." After she graduated from high school in 1942—when she was 16—she worked briefly for Sears then landed a job as a song plugger "for a really awful publisher—you had to pay to have your songs published." She had moved out of her home and gotten an apartment in Hollywood by this time. "I don't remember how I got that job or who sent me," said Marilyn. "But it was a really good experience. It's a wonder I got through it though; I believe the Lord was watching out for me. Almost everyone was quite nice although a few guys chased me around the table a couple of times."

She first met Wesley Tuttle while she was working as a song plugger, although it was a very brief meeting. "I went to play some songs for Stuart Hamblen," said Marilyn. "I said, 'Mr. Hamblen I have these wonderful songs.' He said 'See my boys—Wesley Tuttle and Cliffie Stone.' Wesley never remembered that meeting, although they were nice to me."

Marilyn then obtained a job working as an elevator operator at CBS. Foy Willing and the Riders of the Purple Sage had "either a 15 or 30 minute show on CBS Radio at the time and they went on vacation for about a month," said Marilyn. "Wes, Merle Travis and Jimmy Dean (Eddie's brother) had a trio 'The Trail Riders' on CBS Radio while Foy and his group were on vacation. This must have been in 1943 or 1944."

During her time at CBS she was promoted from elevator operator to "script girl." She met a number of people. When Colleen Summers (later known as Mary Ford after she married Les Paul) left *The Sunshine Girls*, the backup group for Jimmy Wakely, Wes recommended Marilyn to Jimmy, who hired her as Colleen's replacement. Marilyn remembers she sang "at the Casablanca nightclub in Culver City and some radio shows" during her time with Wakely. She sang with the Sunshine Girls until Colleen returned to the group and then Marilyn joined the Tailormaids, who sang at the Carroll Theater.

"Earl Carroll was like a Florenz Ziegfeld," remembered Marilyn. "Carroll's Theater was right across from CBS and we sang at his theatre. There were showgirls there but we didn't have to be as bare as the showgirls. The shows started at 8 P.M. so we had to be there at 6 or 6:30. Earl Carroll decided we had to wear an 'up do'—putting our hair on top of our head—and we all wore body whitening because he wanted all the girls to have the same color skin. Also, white absorbs the light." The shows ended at one in the morning "and then we'd go to get something to eat," said Marilyn. "Then we'd go home and soak in the tub to get the body whitening off before we went to bed."

Marilyn started with the Tailormaids when she was "around 18, so this must have been around 1943 or 1944." The audience was filled "with Las Vegas types," remembered Marilyn. "Guys like Bugsy Siegel. In fact I dated a guy for awhile who I was sure was part of the Mafia, although I never really saw any of that. I saw his legitimate business but I knew the guys he hung out with."

Marilyn was a big fan of Stan Kenton and "wherever he played, I would go and watch him," she said. "He played those great jazz chords—very progressive stuff." During her time at Earl Carroll's she was thrilled to do some film "shorts" with Kenton and his group.

Meanwhile, Wes Tuttle had married Marie Cox in 1939 and they had a daughter; in late 1945 or early 1946 the couple divorced. Marie moved back to Kentucky, where she had family, and Wes returned to California, where his family lived. Shortly after he returned he called Marilyn. "We were never apart after that," she said.

Marilyn remained with the Tailormaids for a while, then went on tour with Wes in 1946. "He had a pick-up band," she said. "We didn't have a band as such but picked up musicians wherever we went. I worked as a solo singer, which I didn't like at all. I love singing in a group—not solo." In 1947, Wesley and Marilyn were married.

After their marriage, Wesley and Marilyn Tuttle were a "team." They recorded several duets together, including "Never," which was a chart record for them on Capitol. Wesley was signed to Capitol Records and so was Marilyn. In addition to her work with Wes, she also recorded duets with Buddy Dooley under the pseudonym "Kitty Holmes" for a different label.

During the early 1950s Wes and Marilyn were on *The Foreman Phillips Show* on ABC radio. "We did five shows a week, three hours a day, and then a two hour show on Sunday," said Marilyn. "We had a good size cast—including Merle Travis, Joe and Rose Lee Maphis. They didn't allow us to do the same song more than once a month. It just killed us."

At the end of 1951 "Bill Wagnon, a producer, wanted to start a show in Compton called 'Town Hall Party.' It was on KFI radio, then moved to TV—the radio show was on one night and the TV show was on Saturday night. We had somewhat the same cast on both shows— Eddie Dean, Les 'Carrot Top' Anderson, Johnny Bond, Wesley Tuttle. They had four or five headliners at the beginning but Eddie Dean didn't stay. It was a really fine show. Wesley and Johnny Bond wrote it and Wesley directed it."

The *Town Hall Party* show was on radio, while the TV show was called *Ranch Party*. "Most of what you see today on tape is the 'Ranch Party' shows," said Marilyn. "Most of the 'Town Hall Party' shows weren't taped. Tex Ritter emceed the 'Ranch Party' shows, which were done without an audience. It sounded like an audience was there when you watched the show because they had a canned audience."

During the time they were on *Town Hall Party* and *Ranch Party* she "had started going back to church," said Marilyn. "I had been a Christian when I was a teenager but left it because life was too much fun. But when you have children you think about giving them the foundation they need so I started taking them to church. Wes would have none of it. But then he started going a little bit and when our daughter drowned, that changed his outlook." Their four-year-old daughter drowned in the swimming pool at their home. "Rosie (Rose Lee Maphis) and I had gone to the doctor and Wes was home when she drowned," said Marilyn. "It was very hard on him."

"In 1955 or so we left Town Hall Party," said Marilyn. "We didn't know what we were going to do but a church in the neighborhood called us to do a concert so that was the beginning of us going into the ministry. Wes wanted to go to seminary, a Bible college and I started a Christian bookstore in San Fernando where we lived. As soon as the churches found out we had left 'Town Hall Party' they started calling for concerts. We had no idea this would happen—didn't even know that church concerts existed. So Wes only went to Bible college for a couple of years because he became so involved in song evangelism."

The Tuttles signed with Sacred Records and did a series of albums, including a solo album by Marilyn, *Sacred Hymns*. She also did studio work, singing backup with Lu Dinning and Rose Lee Maphis on one of Bob Nolan's album and also sang backup in the movie *Harvey Girls*. During the summer the family traveled and performed together. "Wesley, Jr. played piano on most of our albums," said Marilyn. "He also played piano for our concerts while our other son, Matt, sang."

The Sylmar earthquake on February 9, 1971, ended her involvement with the Christian bookstore. "It was swallowed up in the earthquake," said Marilyn. "Wes was in Texas at the time and I was home with Matt, our youngest son. I remember the piano came out in the middle of the room, then went back and made a hole in the wall. It was very frightening."

After the bookstore ended Marilyn became district manager for a direct sales company where she managed 150 people. She did that "for 13 or 14 years" then went back to college and studied agriculture, "beef and dairy courses. I just always wanted to be a cowgirl," said Marilyn: and continued:

> I went to a fair and saw a Charolais bull and just fell in love with that animal. Then one night we were at Stuart and Suze Hamblen's home and for some reason I showed them a picture of that bull and said "this is what I want." I didn't know this but Stuart's brother raised beef and had a registered Charloais bull. His brother gave me that bull and I bought two heifers and was going to start raising a registered Charloais herd. The problem was that both of the heifers calved bulls. That venture cost me money so we sold them off to a wealthy lawyer in Santa Paula. We took that money and went to Europe; took a Mediterranean cruise that started in Lisbon, then carried us to Greece.

Back in California, Marilyn worked as a school librarian and then a computer operator before she began work for a mortuary. "For eight years before Wesley died, I worked at a mortuary," said Marilyn. "Then I quit about a year before he died because I couldn't leave him anymore." After Wes passed away, Marilyn received a call from another mortuary, asking her to come work for them. "I do office work and work with families, praying with them," said Marilyn. "It helps to have an older person if you're an older person. I've been through it a few times so it helps to comfort them in their grief."

She stays active, teaching a Bible class in her home every Thursday evening. She is the program chairman of the Southern California chapter of the Western Music Association and works with the Autry Museum, setting up programs there.

Although she doesn't sing much, she has had the opportunity to do some studio work with contemporary western artists. While Wes was still alive they sang backup on Belinda Gail's gospel album. "That was very difficult," remembered Marilyn. "Because Wes couldn't remember the words." She also provided some backup vocals on an album by the Los Canyon Rangers.

These days her singing is mostly confined to the annual Western Music Association festival. "That's why I enjoy the festival so much," said Marilyn. "I get to sing and I love to sing!" She also loves the WMA and said, "I appreciate the WMA and the family values they embody and the way they promote the involvement of youth." The WMA loves Marilyn as much as she loves the WMA. She is a treasure and one of the highlights of attending a WMA Festival is getting to see and talk with Marilyn Tuttle.

Marilyn is an active senior who has packed a lot of living in her years. "I thank the Lord for a wonderful life," she says. Those who know her thank *her* for the joy she brings to every life she touches.

SOURCE:

Tuttle, Marilyn. Phone interview with the author, November 29 and November 30, 2006.

17
Smiley Burnette

Smiley Burnette was a comic genius who became famous as Gene Autry's sidekick, Frog Millhouse, but his comedy often overshadowed his tremendous talent as a musician and composer.

The only child of ministers George and Almira Burnette, Lester Alvin Burnette was born in Summum, Illinois, on March 18, 1911. When Lester was ten the Burnette family lived next door to part-time orchestra leaders Bill and Maude Baird in Concord, Illinois, and the Bairds loaned the youngster musical instruments to learn to play. Burnette was a fast learner and extremely talented. According to Jon Guyot Smith, "By the time he entered high school, Burnette had mastered several dozen instruments." He achieved some popularity when he sang at local functions, which led a furniture store in Champaign-Urbana to hire 19-year-old "Buzz" Burnette (as he was then nicknamed) to sing on WDZ in Tuscola.

In the spring of 1930, James and Edith Bush, who owned station WDZ, hired him as a staff announcer and entertainer. Buzz acquired the name "Smiley" from a children's show he hosted. In 1931 Burnette needed a character's name so he took "Mr. Smiley" from the Mark Twain story, "The Celebrated Jumping Frog of Calaveras County." "Mr. Smiley" soon became "Smiley" and "Buzz" was dropped.

In late 1933, Gene Autry, then living in Chicago, needed an accordion player for his band. Autry appeared regularly on *National Barn Dance* as well as daily shows on WLS and toured extensively in the area. Somehow he learned about Smiley Burnette in nearby Tuscola (either through his booking agent, J.L. Frank, or a theater owner) and called him on December 19. Autry offered the 22-year-old Burnette a job and the two first met on December 22. Since the Burnettes were teetotalers, Autry and J.L. Frank had to assure Smiley's parents that their son would not be booked into any place that served liquor or any other "disreputable" joint. After their meeting, Autry and Frank took Smiley over to a Sears store in Champaign and obtained a suit for him. The first time Gene Autry and Smiley Burnette performed together publicly was on Christmas Eve 1933 when they played a Sunday night performance at the Eighth Street Theater, home of *National Barn Dance*. This partnership proved fateful for 26-year-old Gene Autry.

In Chicago on March 26, 1934, Gene Autry recorded, for the first time, a song written by Smiley Burnette: "The Round-Up in Cheyenne." At the end of May, Autry took Smiley with him to New York for a recording session. On May 29, Smiley made his first recordings for the American Record Corporation, doing "Mama Don't 'Low No Music," "He Was a Traveling Man" and "The Lone Cowboy." On Thursday, May 31, Smiley recorded "Peg Leg Jack" and "Matilda Higgins."

In the summer of 1934 Gene Autry went to Hollywood to appear in his first movie, *In Old Santa Fe*, and Smiley Burnette went with him. During the drive out, with Gene and Ina Mae Autry in the front seat, Smiley sat in the back seat and composed "Ridin' Down the Canyon," selling Autry the copyright for $5.

During the 10 minute music scene filmed for *In Old Santa Fe*, Smiley Burnette performed "Mama Don't 'Low No Music"—the song he recorded earlier that year for ARC—and played all the instruments. In terms of sheer talent, Smiley Burnette proved he had it in abundance, but Gene Autry looked like a star and Smiley fit the role of a sidekick. In the serial *Mystery Mountain*, starring Ken Maynard, Autry and Smiley played wagon drivers; but Smiley had a larger role in *The Phantom Empire*, where he wrote a number of the songs ("Uncle Noah's Ark" and "I'm Oscar, I'm Pete") and provided comic relief.

In 1935 Autry starred in his first feature, *Tumbling Tumbleweeds* and Smiley was there with him. During the 1934–1942 period, before Gene Autry joined the Army Air Corps, Smiley Burnette appeared in every single film Gene made except two: *Melody Ranch* and *Shooting High*. During the Autry films, Smiley, playing the character "Frog Millhouse," became almost as famous as Autry. Burnette's horse, "Black Eyed Nellie" (also called "Ringeye") was a white horse with a black circle around his eye (painted on with shoe polish).

During World War II, Smiley Burnette worked as a sidekick with a number of other singing cowboys, including Roy Rogers, Eddie Dew, Bob Livingston and Sunset Carson. Smiley starred in his own series for Republic under the Smiley Burnette Productions logo. In this series Smiley performed one of his best known songs, "It's My Lazy Day," in *Bordertown Trails* (1944); but, by and large, the nine low-budget films were not memorable. When this series ended Mitch Hamilburg, who managed Gene Autry as well as Smiley Burnette, negotiated a deal with Columbia Pictures where Smiley costarred with Charles Starrett in 56 films in the "Durango Kid" series. For that reason, Smiley was not available to serve as Gene Autry's sidekick in the pictures made right after Gene Autry finished his tour of duty with the army. Instead, Autry hired Sterling Holloway.

Smiley Burnette (photograph from the author's collection).

Gene Autry worked with Pat Buttram as his sidekick on his films in the late 1940s and early 1950s and on his television series, *The Gene Autry Show*, until Buttram was seriously injured in an accident while filming one of the television shows. For that reason, Smiley Burnette reunited with Gene Autry for Autry's last films: *Whirlwind, Winning of the West, On Top of Old Smoky, Goldtown Ghost Riders, Pack Train, Saginaw Trail* and *Last of the Pony Riders*.

When Gene Autry finished *Last of the Pony Riders*, his final feature in 1953, it effectively marked the end of Smiley Burnette's movie career as well. Smiley was 42 years old and, to make ends meet, went on a series of personal appearances where he was quite popular with children. However, as the years passed and fewer and fewer children knew who Smiley Burnette—or Frog Millhouse—was because he was no longer in the public eye, it became more and more difficult to make a living.

By this time, Smiley had written over 300 songs, including "Ridin' Down the Canyon," "Song of the Range," "It's My Lazy Day," "Wagon Train," "The Old Covered Wagon," "Someday in Wyoming," "End of the Trail," "Let's Go Roaming Around the Range," "Hold On, Little Dogies, Hold On," "On the Strings of My Lonesome Guitar," "Fetch Me Down My Trusty .45," "Ridin' All Day," "It's Indian Summer" and "I'll Go Ridin Down That Texas Trail."

By the 1960s, Burnette's personal appearances in the South were largely confined to shopping centers, where he tried to entertain a new generation of children unfamiliar with his film work. In 1962 he recorded an album for Starday that was soon deleted from their catalog. He moved to Missouri for a while and became acquainted with Paul Henning, producer of *The Beverly Hillbillies* television show. Henning was planning a TV series, *Petticoat Junction*, and cast Smiley as train engineer Charley Pratt.

In December 1966, Burnette, in his fourth season as Charley Pratt, was unwell, often short of breath. In February, he required oxygen between his scenes. Few knew it, but Smiley was suffering from acute leukemia.

Burnette completed his last scene for *Petticoat Junction* on February 8, 1967; he was taken immediately to West Valley Hospital in Encino, where he died on February 17. He was 55 years old.

Smiley Burnette was elected to the Western Music Association Hall of Fame in 1998.

SOURCES:

Cusic, Don. *Gene Autry: His Life and Career*. Jefferson, NC: McFarland, 2007.
George-Warren, Holly. *Public Cowboy No. 1: The Life and Times of Gene Autry*. New York: Oxford University Press, 2007.
Green, Douglas B. *Singing in the Saddle: The History of the Singing Cowboy*. Nashville: Country Music Foundation Press and Vanderbilt University Press, 2002.
Smith, Jon Guyot. "Smiley Burnette: Gentle Genius Who Was Gene Autry's Pal." Originally published in "Gene Autry's Friends" and copied for the author.
Smith, Jonathan Guyot. "Smiley Burnette: It's Nice to Be Important, but More Important to Be Nice." *DISCoveries*, April 1994. pp 26–30.

18

Stuart Hamblen

There were singers dressed as cowboys—and singing cowboy songs—from the earliest days of radio and recordings. Carl Sprague recorded "When the Work's All Done This Fall" and other cowboy songs for Victor in 1925, and Jules Verne Allen was singing cowboy songs on radio in Texas during the 1920s. But it was the singing cowboys who came out of Hollywood that really set the image for western and country music.

The popularity of Gene Autry, after he began starring in movies in 1935, was key to numerous country singers dressing like cowboys all across the United States. However, when Autry arrived in Hollywood in 1934 there were already a number of singing cowboys on the radio. The Sons of the Pioneers had recorded "Tumbling Tumbleweeds" earlier that year and appeared in Autry's first starring western, named after that popular song.

Before Autry and the Pioneers were in California, dressed like cowboys and singing, there was Stuart Hamblen. He was the first radio star in California to dress in cowboy clothes; because of his success, he influenced the Sons of the Pioneers, Gene Autry, and all the other singing cowboys of the movies. How and why did Stuart Hamblen begin dressing like a cowboy?

Born in Kelleyville, Texas, on October 20, 1908, Hamblen first appeared on radio in Dallas and Fort Worth in 1925 as "Cowboy Joe." But the song that brought him his first popularity was "The Johnstown Flood," certainly not a cowboy song. His first recordings, in Camden, New Jersey, in 1929, were "The Boy in Blue," "Drifting Back to Dixie," "When the Moon Shines Down on the Mountain" and "Big Rock Candy Mountain No. 2." None of them were "cowboy" or "western" songs. He didn't dress like a cowboy either.

The music that Hamblen sang at that time was called "old fashioned," "folk," and "old home" music by the recording companies, and the dominant image was that of a hillbilly. At the time, Stuart fit that image in his stage dress and performances.

From New York, Hamblen went to California, where he joined the Beverly Hill Billies; however, he was fired from that group when he had to have his appendix removed and missed three weeks of shows.

Determined to keep his singing career going, Hamblen formed a group in 1930 and played on KMIC in Inglewood. During that year he began writing songs and recorded six that year—none of them "western." The following year he recorded four more songs, including "My Brown Eyed Texas Rose" and "My Mary," which was a hit for W. Leo Daniel and the Light Crust Doughboys.

In 1931 he began appearing on KMTR (now KLAC). In 1932 the station manager, Lyman Peters, decided Hamblen's group should wear cowboy clothing and sent them to

Western Costuming, where they were outfitted as cowboys. Part of the reason for doing this may have been because Peters wanted to attract the Lucky Star Outfitting company as a sponsor. Also, the group looked better in western outfits during their personal appearances. Although the singing cowboys had not yet arrived, cowboy movies were popular at that time.

Working for Peters at KMTR at that time was Veeva Ellen Daniels, who later married Stuart Hamblen. "Suzy," as she was known, recalled that Peters "was very creative. It was his idea—he didn't have a western store or anything. He was manager of the station—that was the only thing he did. He had an office in the studio. He was the one who brought them up from hillbillies and made western singers out of them." According to Suzy, Peters was "a real estate man—a developer. He went belly up when the Big Depression hit. He was the first one to develop bungalows, little motels where travelers could stop. Then the Depression hit."

Stuart Hamblen (photograph courtesy of Packy Smith).

The station approached the Star Outfitting Company about sponsoring Hamblen's program, and Stuart went into Sam Hoffman's office at the company and promptly announced, "The greatest salesman who ever stepped over your threshold just now came into your office." According to Suzy, when Stuart said that to Hoffman, Sam thought "Well, at least he's got a lot of self-confidence. And he just may be."

Stuart Hamblen never lacked self-confidence. Those who admired him noted his self-assurance, his charisma and the fact that he "filled up any room" he entered. Those who didn't admire Stuart called him "arrogant," "conceited," and "overbearing." However, everyone admitted he was talented, larger than life and a force to be reckoned with.

Stuart Hamblen appeared on the *Covered Wagon Jubilee* on KMTR from 7:00 to 9:00 each morning and his *Lucky Stars* radio show, sponsored by the Star Outfitting Company, on KFWB from 5:00 P.M. to 6:00 P.M. for twenty-one years. Later he was "King Cowboy and His Woolly West Review" on KNX.

Hamblen's first "western" recordings came in 1934 when he signed with the newly formed Decca Records. During that year he recorded "Poor Unlucky Cowboy," "Texas Plains," "Riding Old Paint Leading Old Bald," "Little Rag Doll" and "Lopez the Bandit." Hamblen was the most successful western radio performer in southern California, influencing a whole generation of singing cowboys, including the Sons of the Pioneers, who used to listen to his show regularly to learn new songs.

Individualistic and independent, Hamblen never had a manager or agent. According to Suzy, he was offered the role as a singing cowboy at Republic Pictures when Gene Autry walked off the set in 1938—but he turned it down. The contract was for seven years and would have given him $200 a week—much less than what he was making in radio. Republic eventually offered it to a member of the Sons of the Pioneers—Leonard Slye. Then they changed his name to Roy Rogers. Hamblen apparently never regretted his decision, he preferred to remain in radio, where he was a major star in Los Angeles.

Hamblen never achieved national recognition, except as a songwriter, until after World War II. His first national hit was "I Won't Go Huntin' with You Jake (But I'll Go Chasin' Women)" in 1949 and his second hit was "(Remember Me) I'm the One Who Loves You" in 1950. His two biggest hits, "It Is No Secret" and "This Ole House," were in 1951 and 1954 respectively. Those four songs, along with "Texas Plains," all of which he wrote, are his enduring legacy.

"Stuart wrote by inspiration," said Suzy. "If he ever spent more than an hour on a song he got very depressed. Thought he'd lost his gift—the Lord had taken it from him and he'd never be able to write again. He didn't sit down and labor over the words or the music. 'It Is No Secret' took him 17 minutes to write."

"Stuart was an inspired writer and a very versatile writer," continued Suzy:

> Some people, you can tell by a tune who wrote it because they always wrote a variation of the tune. But you could not tell that with Stuart's music. Ever. Either words or tunes. He would sing the melody to me and I would put it down. I would go to the organ and he would hum the tune and I would play it. Then he'd go to the typewriter on his desk and it would be almost like looking at a crystal ball, not really seeing me. And I'd play the melody and he'd write the words. We kept an organ in our bedroom and many times he'd wake me up in the middle of the night saying "I've got an idea for a song" and I'd turn the organ on. He knew not a note of music—couldn't read a note. But I could take it by dictation.

Another enduring legacy of Stuart Hamblen is his conversion in 1949 at a Billy Graham Crusade in Los Angeles. Hamblen's conversion was a turning point in Graham's career as well as in Hamblen's. Before his conversion, Stuart consistently lost the battle with the bottle. His drinking caused problems in his marriage, his family, his friendships and his career. After his conversion, he stopped drinking and, in 1952, ran for president on the Prohibition ticket. There's no truer believer than a convert.

Stuart Hamblen did most of his recordings after his conversion. During the 1950s he recorded a number of songs—gospel as well as country. He remained on radio with *The Cowboy Church*, a show he began before his conversion when the Star Outfitting Company wanted a Sunday show. And he toured throughout the United States, preaching and performing.

Before his conversion, Hamblen didn't tour; instead he made personal appearances in and around Los Angeles in order to keep his radio programs going. Elected to the Western Music Association's Hall of Fame in 1999, Stuart Hamblen added that honor to a long list of achievements, including election to the Nashville Songwriter's Hall of Fame in 1970, the Pioneer Award from the Academy of Country and Western Music in 1972, a star on the Hollywood Walk of Fame in 1976 and the Golden Boot award in 1988.

Many of the stars of radio have been forgotten; that medium has not lent itself to enduring legacies. As time has passed, Stuart Hamblen's star has dimmed because later generations never heard him on the medium where his star shone brightest. But those who know the history of western music know the importance of Stuart Hamblen. For them, he will always be remembered as one of the greatest cowboy singers of all time.

SOURCES:

Cusic, Don. *Gene Autry: His Life and Career*. Jefferson, NC: McFarland, 2007.
Green, Douglas B. *Singing in the Saddle: The History of the Singing Cowboy*. Nashville: Country Music Foundation Press and Vanderbilt University Press, 2002.

19

Tex Ritter

Tex Ritter was a Southwestern gentleman; strong but not afraid to be polite and kind. These personal traits, along with his distinctive, rustic, "cowboy" voice endeared him to fans and colleagues alike. Born Woodward Maurice Ritter in Panola County, Texas, on January 12, 1905, he came of age in the Jazz Age of the 1920s and knew the Great Depression firsthand.

Ritter was well educated and pursued a law degree at the University of Texas and, later, at Northwestern University, but he dropped out to join an operetta touring company. While at the University of Texas, his musical interests led him to collect a vast array of traditional cowboy songs, which became an important part of his repertoire in his early screen work and recording. Ritter's theatrical interests took him to New York in 1928, where he worked on radio and on Broadway. In New York, he landed a role in the musical *Green Grow the Lilacs*, which evolved into *Oklahoma*. He obtained a spot on radio station WOR with "The Lone Star Rangers," as well as a children's program, *Cowboy Tom's Roundup*. Later, he moved to WHN and had *Tex Ritter's Campfire*; in 1934 he was a featured performer on the *WHN Barn Dance*. It was in New York that he acquired the nickname of "Tex."

Ritter made his first recording, "The Cowboy's Christmas Ball" (which was unissued), for the American Record Corporation on October 31, 1932. His first releases were "Goodbye Old Paint" and "Rye Whiskey, Rye Whiskey," recorded on March 15, 1933, and "A-Ridin' Old Paint" and "Everyday in the Saddle," recorded on April 14, 1933. Ritter next recorded for Decca, on January 21, 1935, and stayed with that label throughout the 1930s, doing songs such as "Sam Hall," "Get Along Little Dogies," "I'm a Do-Right Cowboy," "Boots and Saddle," "The Hills of Old Wyoming," "We'll Rest at the End of the Trail," "Out on the Lone Prairie," "I'm a Natural Born Cowboy," "Sing, Cowboy, Sing" and "When It's Lamp Lighting Time in the Valley."

Tex Ritter starred in 58 singing cowboy movies between 1936 and 1945—more than any other actor in that genre except Gene Autry and Roy Rogers. His first singing cowboy movie, *Song of the Gringo*, came out a few months after Gene Autry's first feature film. Decca released "'A Melody from the Sky," "The Hills of Old Wyomin'" and "We'll Rest at the End of the Trail" at the same time.

In the early 1940s Ritter changed film companies and was teamed with "Wild Bill" Elliott in a popular series of Westerns. He was also the first western artist signed to Capitol; his first recordings for that label, on June 11, 1942, were "Jingle, Jangle, Jingle," "Someone," "Goodbye, My Little Cherokee" and "I've Done the Best I Could." On his sessions, Ritter was accompanied by guitarists Merle Travis, Johnny Bond and Wesley Tuttle.

Ritter's career was at a standstill in the early 1950s when he was called to record the theme song for the movie *High Noon*. This recording, made for Capitol on May 14, 1952, won an Academy Award for 1952 and revitalized his career. He continued to record and appeared frequently on the *Town Hall Party* television show in Los Angles. He toured extensively, often with Wesley Tuttle, and hosted his own syndicated TV show, *Tex Ritter's Ranch Party*, in the 1957–58 season. He was elected to the Country Music Hall of Fame in 1964 and joined the Grand Ole Opry in 1965, the same year he moved from California to Nashville.

The move had a moment of foreboding. When Tex moved to Nashville, he lived at the Andrew Jackson Hotel, where he kept his performing costumes, briefcases, favorite guitar and some hunting rifles. In late October, Tex's wife, Dorothy, came to Nashville to go house hunting for a new home for the couple. She attended the annual Country Music Association convention, where Tex, as outgoing president, delivered a speech.

Tex Ritter (photograph courtesy of Packy Smith).

Tex and Dorothy returned to the hotel around noon on October 22, 1965, and noticed the front of the hotel was blocked by fire trucks. The firemen were fighting a fire at the hotel. Looking up, Tex realized that smoke was coming out of his hotel room window. The damage to the hotel was limited to Tex's room, but he lost everything he had in it. Dorothy lost several suitcases of clothing, including an evening gown she planned to wear at the CMA banquet and a full-length mink coat.

Tex Ritter disliked the 1960s counterculture and the protests against the Vietnam War. In both 1969 and 1979 Tex went to Vietnam to entertain the troops. He was in South Vietnam for two weeks, following performances in Japan, Taiwan and Okinawa.

Tex decided to run for the United States Senate in the 1970 election. The incumbent, Albert Gore, had served Tennessee for eighteen years; but his opposition to the Vietnam War and support of civil rights legislation had put him out of favor with his constituents. Congressman Dan Kuykendall from Memphis had originally planned to run, but backed out. Things looked promising for a Republican; although the South was dominated by the Democratic Party, Howard Baker had won a senate seat in 1966, the first Republican to be elected to that office from the South since 1920. Republican leaders approached Ritter, who had appeared before the Senate Judiciary Committee to lobby for airplay royalties for recording artists.

Tex and Dorothy campaigned across the state; their son Tom worked as assistant to the campaign manager, Mark Brown. The Citizens for Tex committee was headed by Roy Acuff, who had run for the United States Senate in 1948. However, Republican congressman William Brock, who had been a member of the House since 1961, decided to throw his hat in the ring. Brock was a multimillionaire from Chattanooga who ran a well-financed campaign. Tex ran on his own money, although some supporters promised financial aid. Ritter was attacked for being a carpetbagger—not a true Tennessean—and this led to his defeat.

Bill Brock went on to win that senate seat and later served in the cabinet of President Ronald Reagan.

Tex Ritter went to the Nashville jail on January 2, 1974, to help arrange for one of his musicians to get out on bail. While there he collapsed with a heart attack and died.

SOURCES:

Green, Douglas B. *Singing in the Saddle: The History of the Singing Cowboy*. Nashville: Country Music Foundation Press and Vanderbilt University Press, 2002.

O'Neal, Bill. *Tex Ritter: America's Most Beloved Cowboy*. Austin: Eakin Press, 1998.

20
Wesley Tuttle

In a bright yellow house at the north end of the San Fernando Valley in Los Angeles, California, lived an elderly couple. Few who drove past the house, or who saw them out somewhere, knew these two people were integral parts of the history of country music in California. Legends in their time, Wesley and Marilyn Tuttle were part of the cornerstone of California country music. Their story went back to the days when the Beverly Hill Billies, Stuart Hamblen, Sons of the Pioneers, Gene Autry, Roy Rogers, Cliffie Stone and others were just beginning. Wesley and Marilyn Tuttle were silent legends, unknown to those who knew Gene Autry and Roy Rogers as household names. Still, their story formed an integral part of the heyday of Hollywood in country music.

Wesley Tuttle was born in Lamar, Colorado, on December 13, 1917. His parents worked in a restaurant; his mother was a waitress and his father was a cook. In 1922, when Wesley was four, they moved to the San Fernando Valley in California because his father had relatives there.

In California, Tuttle's father had a butcher shop. Around 1924, when Wesley was six and in the first grade, his father "let me go to the shop—which was always a great treat to me." He described what happened:

> This particular time was Valentine's Day. It was just a one-man meat market and we were putting up signs on the store which gave the price of turkeys and hamburgers. He'd started to grind some hamburger and told me "you stay away from that meat grinder" cause he wanted to go outside and paint some signs on the windows. "Oh, sure, Dad," I said. Well, the minute he got outside painting the signs, I got up on that counter, turned that hamburger grinder on and took the meat he'd cut up to put through it—you're supposed to put it through with a stomper or mallet—and I stuffed my hand in there and boom, there it went.

The meat grinder took three fingers off his left hand, leaving only the thumb and pinkie.

The Tuttles were a musical family, both parents sang and, with Wesley, they'd do three part harmony. "It was just in the genes, I guess," said Wesley. He remembers that back in Colorado there was a Victrola with a record of "The Missouri Waltz" and he sang along with it—before he could talk. Before the accident, Wesley played the ukulele and had sung at the Elks club and at a little church in Chatsworth, where he played and sang "Yes, Sir, That's My Baby."

After the accident, Wes picked up the ukulele again and learned to chord with his two fingers; then he received a tenor guitar and also learned to chord with two fingers. But later his father bought him a guitar, turned the strings around to make it a left-handed instrument, and Wes learned to chord with his right hand and strum with his left. He used a thumb pick, because he couldn't hold a flat pick, and learned to play rhythm guitar.

Stuart Hamblen first appeared on radio in Los Angeles in 1925; in late 1929 he began on station KFI as "Cowboy Joe," then joined the Beverly Hill Billies in 1930. He began his *Lucky Stars* program on KFWB in Los Angeles in 1932. Wes Tuttle used to listen to Hamblen's program and was a big fan, "so mother took me down to Stuart's radio show to sing and play for him—I wanted to audition. I got there before the band did and set my guitar up. The guys came in and were hung over and one of the guys had left his guitar, so he asked to play it. It was left-handed—so he put it down pretty quick! Well, my mother told Stuart I'd like to audition and after I did he asked me if I wanted to sing. So I sang 'The Yodeling Cowboy.' I was about 14 or 15 at the time."

Wesley Tuttle's heroes were Stuart Hamblen and the Sons of the Pioneers—he wanted to play with both. Ironically, he did. First, he was with a group, Jimmy LeFevre and His Saddle Pals. There were problems with the Sons of the Pioneers. "Tim Spencer didn't get along with the rest," he said. "I knew them all and knew their parts. So the Sons asked me to come in and take Tim's place."

When Leonard Slye left the Sons of the Pioneers and became Roy Rogers, Tuttle again filled in "until they got Pat Brady. But Pat couldn't do those parts, so they got somebody else—I think it was Lloyd Perryman." Brady remained with the Pioneers playing bass and doing comedy.

Tuttle "would work with the Pioneers when somebody got sick" and "did the same with the Beverly Hill Billies." Then he got his dream job—working with Stuart Hamblen. By the middle of 1934 Tuttle was in Hamblen's band. That's when he met Gene Autry. "We were doing a radio show when this guy walks in with a fat guy and an accordion," remembers Tuttle. "He said 'My name is Gene Autry and I'd like to sing on your radio show.' Stuart said, 'Sure, why not?' He had just come out to L.A.—it was just him and Smiley Burnette." Tuttle admits that Hamblen "must have known about Gene Autry from Chicago. He was big back there. That's probably why he said 'Sure, do a song.' But I'd never heard of him then." Autry didn't play on any more of Hamblen's shows and Tuttle said that soon Autry "went past Stuart so fast you couldn't see him."

Wesley Tuttle achieved lasting fame when he did the yodelling on "Silly Song" in Walt Disney's movie *Snow White and the Seven Dwarfs*. They needed people to yodel for the yodeling sequence, said Tuttle. "So they did a cattle call. There were seven or eight of us—Texas Ruby was there. It just happened that I had the little part they were looking for. We spent two or three days in the studio working on that."

"They didn't have an echo chamber back then," remembers Wes. "So they used a four inch in diameter pipe from an old wood stove. It was about ten feet long and at one end was a big balloon tied to it. The girl sang 'I'm Wishing for the One I Love' in that and that's how they got that effect."

In 1939 Wesley Tuttle left Los Angeles and moved to Cincinnati. He spoke of the move years later:

> At that time I was a fool. But I wanted to see what was on the other side of the mountain. I was working with Stuart Hamblen and the Sons of Pioneers. But a guy from back east—Rennie Dailey—was working with Stuart on his morning program. He was offered the job as Program Manager in Dayton, Ohio. He talked me into leaving Stuart—was going to make me the head of his music department at the radio station in Dayton. I had a brand new Studebaker—was making payments on it. We drove to Dayton but when we get there, I found out he didn't have the authority to hire me as his music director. The boss at the radio station wouldn't allow that.
>
> We got a room in a boarding house and I would just lay around all day—I was lucky if I could get lunch anywhere cause I didn't have any money and Rennie didn't have any money. I was hungry, out of money, and had a new Studebaker.
>
> They had big Fairs and radio acts came out and entertained so Rennie said we should go out to

hear the folks from WLW. Rennie Dailey introduced me to the people. Said I'd done singing in *Snow White and the Seven Dwarfs* and in Los Angeles so I was invited to sing. And that's where I heard the damndest guitar player I'd ever heard in my life. Merle Travis was playing with the group.

I sang my head off—I was a good yodeler. Travis said "You've got to come down to Cincinnati." I said "where's that?" And he told me. He was with WLW, which had 50,000 watts. I got my guitar and put it in the trunk of my car, hocked my watch to get enough money for gas, and drove down to WLW, went up the elevator and asked for Merle Travis. He introduced me to the Program Director and I sang and yodeled for him. They put me right on staff on the station.

On the station when Wesley arrived were Hank Penny, Tex Owen, Curly Fox, Texas Ruby, Merle Travis and Lulu Belle & Scotty—an all star lineup. But, Tuttle said, he grew disenchanged with Cincinnati: "I was homesick—it was cold there. So I wrote a letter to Stuart Hamblen, asking if I could come back. He answered me right back, said 'get your tail back here.' So I went back with Stuart around 1941." It was a full-time job with Stuart Hamblen. He had 2 major shows, one in the morning and the other in the evening. Then there were two 15 minute programs during the week.

Tuttle was with Hamblen on December 7, 1941, when news came about the bombing of Pearl Harbor. "Stuart used to book his show in once a year at the Million Dollar Theater at 3rd and Broadway in Los Angeles," said Tuttle. "He did live shows of 'Lucky Star Program' for a couple of weeks. This was a Sunday, and Saturday night we'd played a dance, so we didn't get to bed until around one o'clock in the morning. We were shot. I got in the car and the radio was talking about what all was happening and the bombing at Pearl Harbor. I parked the Buick and went in to the theater, but there wasn't much going on there."

In April 1942, Capitol Records was formed in Hollywood and one of the first acts signed was Tex Ritter. "Johnny Bond had always played guitar on Tex's recording sessions," said Wesley. "But he was out of town with Gene Autry doing shows so he told Lee Gillette, the guy producing the session to 'get Wesley.' That's how come I got called for 'You Two Timed Me One Time Too Often.' After that I played on all Tex's sessions, unless I was out of town, then Johnny Bond played." "Tex had a problem with rhythm," said Wesley. "So I had to sit right across from him by the microphone to cue him on when to come in. That's what led me to go on the road with Tex, who became a very dear and close friend."

The Ritter sessions led to Tuttle's being signed to Capitol. "I was a big fan of the Merry Macs and Lee Gillette and I were talking and he said 'you know their stuff?' He was impressed I knew and liked them. So he signed me to Capitol. My first record was 'Raining on the Mountain,' written by the Delmores, backed with 'I Dreamed That My Daddy Come Home' which was written by me and Merle Travis. The next record was 'With Tears in My Eyes' and that really shot to the top. I remember that on the charts I was number one and Tex Ritter was number two. That was a switch!"

On the road, Wesley Tuttle and His Texas Stars opened the show, then backed Tex Ritter. Travelling with Tex Ritter brought some memorable moments:

> On Ritter's trips we had two station wagons. One of them was Dub Taylor's and Ritter always rode with him. Dub had a xylophone and they carried it in back of his Ford station wagon—he didn't break it down, just tied it down. We'd finished a show just outside of New York and we were going to Worcester, Massachusetts. We came through New York at 4 o'clock in the morning and stopped because Ritter had a cousin who lived there and wanted to visit. So after that we headed north with no sleep. We got to the show but Ritter and Dub were not there. We had to start the show and after we started, here come these guys. Their clothes were tore up, mud all over them, stuff in their hair. Ritter and Cannonball were the worst drivers in the world and they'd had a few drinks. They turned the car over and the xylophone was all over the place. They weren't hurt bad. But when they got on the bandstand they were a mess and there was mud all over the xylophone.

Wesley Tuttle just shakes his head and chuckles as he tells that story.

Tuttle did not get royalties from Capitol. "I got $100 a side rather than royalties," he said. "All I got on 'Detour' one of my biggest hits, was about $800. I thought that was pretty good back there. But I was a sap. Was screwed a couple of times. Lee Gillette was supposed to be my real good friend. But he worked for Capitol."

In 1949 Tuttle left Capitol briefly. "Jimmy Wakely and I were in Nashville doing a session with Red Foley," said Tuttle. "We were singing on a couple of Red's songs. Paul Cohen was the head of Decca's country division and said to me 'if you ever leave Capitol, I'd like to have you on Decca.' Well, I left Capitol so he sent me a contract. But it was for Coral, a subsidiary. I did four records for them—eight songs. And then Lee Gillette took me back at Capitol."

During World War II Los Angeles was a hub of activities with the defense plants—especially building airplanes—and a million people moved to L.A. during the War. That meant there was a demand for round-the-clock entertainment. "Foreman Phillips organized these big dances," said Wesley. "There were three shifts a day—graveyard, swing shift and morning shift. People could go to a dance any time of the day they wanted to." But Wesley didn't play for any of those dances. Instead, he stayed active recording in L.A. and appeared on radio and in the movies. He also met his wife, Marilyn, but they met several times before they clicked.

In 1947 the Tuttles got married. They recorded several successful duets, including "Never." They began playing and singing together but faced some hard times. "We played on the road and Dick Wiley was our business manager. He took all the money we made, said he was sending it home and paying the bills. We even bought a new car. He was also managing Merle Travis and Andy Parker and the Plainsmen. When we got home, we had nothing. He was slick. We didn't have any money to show for our work."

During the 1940s Wesley appeared in a number of cowboy movies. "I was in three or four with Charles Starrett, 'The Durango Kid,' for Columbia," he said. "Then three or four with Jimmy Wakely and one each with Tex Ritter and Russell Haden. I always got billing. In *Song of the Sierra* I played myself, had some lines. That was my biggest part." Tuttle got these parts through his friendships with Johnny Bond, who worked with Gene Autry, and Jimmy Wakely, who starred in a number of singing westerns.

As the 1950s began, Wes and Marilyn Tuttle were on *The Foreman Phillips Show* on ABC. "We did for five shows a week, three shows a day, and then a two hour show on Sunday," said Marilyn Tuttle. "We had a good size cast—Merle Travis, Joe and Rose Lee Maphis, some girl singers. You couldn't do the same song more than once a month. It just killed us."

At the end of 1951 Bill Wagnon, a producer, wanted to start a dance in Compton called *Town Hall Party*. The show got on KFI radio, then moved to TV—the radio show was on one night and the TV show was on Saturday night. "I'd set the whole show up," said Wes. "I'd decide who sang what and when. Then I sat in the wings and stage managed. Back then they didn't have teleprompters and Merle Travis would write up something the size of newsprint—for every program. No way we could learn all this stuff."

The Tuttles stayed on *Town Hall Party* for about three years. "We left Town Hall Party because it was becoming rock'n'roll," said Marilyn. "Another thing," added Wesley. "Tex Ritter was booked for London or somewhere so they wanted to have a party and wanted me to take a drink. And I wouldn't do it. And that's when I decided to get out of the business." "It was just time for us to leave," said Marilyn. "So we just decided we would give our lives to the Lord and see where He would take us."

The catalyst was the death of their four-year-old daughter, who died in the Tuttle's swimming pool while Wesley was home with her one day. This shook them and tested their faith and brought about a major life change. "We didn't know what we were going to do," said Marilyn. But a church in the neighborhood called us to do a concert so that was the beginning of going into gospel."

Capitol would not let them do gospel recordings, so they signed with Sacred Records. "I took Bible college for about a year," said Wesley. "But I got so busy on the road doing concerts and revivals that I had to quit. I would do music for revivals, lead the singing. Sometimes I'd preach but usually there was a preacher for the revival. Marilyn stayed home and had a Christian bookstore."

That lasted until around 1974, when Wesley decided he wanted to get off the road and stay home. "A fellow had a car dealership in the San Fernando Valley," said Wesley. "And he asked if I would sell cars for awhile. I did that for a few months—did real well. But one morning I woke up and I was blind—couldn't see." "And that was the end of working," added Marilyn. Wesley Tuttle is legally blind, although he can see a little. "I can't read anything," he said. "But it could be worse."

The Tuttles live with a house full of memories. Wesley remembers Bob Nolan, one of the founding members of the Sons of the Pioneers and probably the best western songwriter of all time and the composer of "Tumbling Tumbleweeds" and "Cool Water." "I was very close with Nolan for many, many years," remembers Wes. "He wasn't that easy to get to know, but he took to me at the same time I took to him. That was in 1934, I guess. He had finished his lifeguard job at Santa Monica. I was doing a radio show and at an apartment house was Bob Nolan. He didn't like people to come to see him but he liked me coming by. He had just bought one of those home recorder things—so we got to fiddling around with that and I got with some friends—and we'd make records on that. But through the years they'd deteriorate."

One of the last times the Tuttles saw Nolan was at Ray Whitley's memorial service at the Sportsman's Lodge. "I asked if he was still writing," said Marilyn. "And he said 'every day.' He said the songs were in the garage." There's lots of songs, recordings, pictures and memories in the Tuttles "garage" as well. Their home is crowded with the history of California country. That bright yellow house fits the personalities of the Tuttles, who continue to be bright sunshine in a sunshine state.

Wesley Tuttle died on September 29, 2003.

SOURCES:

Green, Douglas B. *Singing in the Saddle: The History of the Singing Cowboy*. Nashville: Country Music Foundation Press and Vanderbilt University Press, 2002.
Tuttle, Wesley. Personal interview with the author, January 3, 2001, in Los Angeles, California.

21

Monte Hale

His hair is a beautiful silver and his face is strikingly handsome. Monte Hale hasn't been in a movie for about thirty years, but he still looks like a movie star.

Monte's family lived in San Angelo, Texas, and various bios list it as his place of birth; however, for the record that honor goes to Ada, Oklahoma. His father was a pitcher on the St. Louis Cardinals Farm League and was playing baseball in Ada, "so that's how I came to be born there," Hale said. "Actually, I did grow up in San Angelo."

Monte laughs as he shares some memories in his home in Los Angeles, surrounded by mementos and western artifacts. On a railing is a beautiful saddle with "Gene Autry" embossed on it. "I bought that from the Cowboy Hall of Fame in Oklahoma City in 1981," said Monte. "Gene had many of these Madison Square Saddles made and gave several to the Cowboy Hall of Fame. They eventually sold them and I bought one." He also has some cowboy boots with "Gene Autry" on them and one of Autry's white hats. "Jackie (Gene's widow) gave those to me after Gene passed away," he said. "Gene was my best friend."

Monte met Gene Autry back in Houston, while playing at the Ranch Club. Autry came to Houston for the big Fat Stock Show and Rodeo, which is still held annually. That led to a lifelong friendship.

Monte Hale first sang in church, where his father was a preacher. Later he began singing in clubs around Houston. To buy his first guitar—which cost $8.50—he picked cotton in Texas for a month. By the age of 18 he was playing professionally.

On Pearl Harbor Sunday, Monte Hale was at a hotel in Houston; he was performing at the Ranch Club during this time. During World War II, there were a number of bond drives and Houston theater owner Phil Isley was chairman of the Stars Over Texas Bond Drive. Isley hired Hale to play guitar for Lasses White as well as sing on a 30-day bond drive that raised about $60 million in bonds.

After the bond drive, Isley wired Ray Johnston at Monogram and Herbert Yates at Republic Pictures about Hale; Yates wired back and told Hale that if he could get to Hollywood, he'd receive a screen test. A good friend in Houston gave Hale the money to fly to Los Angeles for his Republic Studios test. With his good looks, talent, and charisma, Monte passed the screen test with flying colors and was signed to a seven-year contract in 1944.

Republic was the home of the singing cowboys—but Gene Autry had joined the armed services in 1942. Republic wanted to extend Gene's contract to include the years he would be in the service, but Gene refused to go along with that and decided he wanted out. Republic had been promoting Roy Rogers as "King of the Cowboys" while Autry was serving in the war, but there was concern that Rogers might not be able to keep his draft deferment.

In 1945, Republic was going to star Hale in *Don't Fence Me In* because they thought

Rogers would be lost to the service. However, Rogers got his deferment and wanted to star in the movie, so the Republic writers wrote *Home on the Range* in Magnacolor for Hale, his first starring picture, in 1946. The Sons of the Pioneers, as well as little Robert Blake, were featured in this movie. In all, Hale starred in 19 westerns for Republic, nine of them made in Trucolor. When a movie was released, Monte Hale hit the road, performing at theaters all over the country, singing and promoting the picture. He remembers that he once performed at 16 different theaters in Baltimore over a three-day period.

Although Hale sang in his movies, he generally had fewer songs than Rogers and Autry did in their movies. He recorded six sides for Bel-Tone and eight sides for MGM but never had a big hit, although he cowrote "Statue in the Bay," which Gene Autry recorded.

Hale's biggest musical influence was Jimmie Rodgers, and he remembers buying records from the Blue Yodeler. He

Monte Hale (photograph from the author's collection).

also admired Gene Autry, Roy Acuff and Eddy Arnold. His family had listened to the *Grand Ole Opry* as well as other barn dances during his youth, which influenced him.

When asked why he didn't pursue a recording career, Monte answers modestly, "I guess I just didn't have it." This isn't quite true—those who have heard Hale's records judge him "pretty good." Monte freely admitted that he would "rather entertain in person than record" and that he loved the live shows, being in front of people and feeling the excitement and energy of the crowds much more than recording. After his movie contract with Republic ended in 1950, Hale toured extensively, performing with Ray Whitley and others.

Perhaps another major reason Hale never developed a recording career was because he "never had a manager." He had an agent for seven months, but "then the agent passed away." So Hale had to book everything himself or depend on friends. Spike Lee got him the recording contract with MGM, and friends from his movie days called for him to appear in *Yukon Vengeance* in 1954, starring Kirby Grant; the 1956 classic *Giant* starring James Dean; and his last film role in 1973, *The Chase*.

After his movie days, Monte Hale attended a few western movie festivals. He said he "loved the people but didn't like to travel." His wife, Joanne, said, "Monte is a white knuckled traveler!"

Monte and Joanne played a major role in the last years of Gene Autry's life. Autry had a long-standing dream to establish a museum, which he originally wanted to house at his ranch in Newhall. But a fire destroyed much of the property and his memorabilia plans were put on hold. During a dinner in Palm Springs Monte brought up the subject again. As Jackie (Gene's wife) and Gene, Monte and Joanne enjoyed the meal, Monte said, "Gene, you remember you used to talk about building a western museum sometime back. When are you going to get the ball rolling on it?" Four or five days later, the Hales received a call from Jackie and Gene saying they were ready to put the plan into action—if Joanne and Monte would pull up stakes from Montecito and move to Los Angeles to pitch in. Joanne and Jackie Autry looked through warehouses of memorabilia, hauled artifacts around, cleaned, scrubbed and dusted things Autry had collected, and thus started the core collection for the Autry Museum.

Joanne also became the first executive director, working with Jackie Autry to find a location. She worked with city hall to get the museum built and then established it as one of the finest museums in the world. The focus of the Autry Museum of Western Heritage isn't a museum of Gene Autry—although he has a prominent place there. It serves as an educational and historical window into the history and culture of the American West, and the diversity of the people whose contributions built America. It is a fitting legacy to Gene Autry, a remarkable man as well as a great singing cowboy star.

It's also a great legacy to Monte Hale, who admits riding in a car with Gene behind a truck driven by "the girls," laughing at their dirty overalls and messy hands while they hauled things around. He played an important behind-the-scenes supportive role while the museum was getting established. From its inception he served on the board of directors and, along with Gene, in the late 1990s vas voted in as director emeritus.

Monte Hale spends his days in retirement, enjoying the large collection of western artifacts in his home. He proudly shows a rifle with "Monte Hale" engraved on the side, created by America Remembers in Virginia, a respected company that manufactured and marketed collector's editions of rifles embossed in 24 karat gold with famous movie cowboys. He also has one from John Wayne.

Monte Hale sits in a leather recliner now rather than a leather saddle. He looks fit and healthy and laughs easily in an open, friendly manner. It is obvious he loves people and still has that entertainer's desire to give himself to an audience. He has trouble remembering a lot of things from the past, "senior moments" block some memories. He was always an easy-going man, not as driven or as ambitious as Autry or Roy Rogers, and his career reflects that. Monte enjoyed his time in the spotlight, but it was never an obsession with him.

On many questions he was asked, Monte simply shook his head, chuckled, and said "That was so long ago—I just can't remember!" He makes it clear, though, that he loved Gene Autry, that Autry was his "best friend" and the two shared treasured moments together.

His wife, Joanne, is no longer executive director of the Autry Museum, but she stays actively involved on the board of directors and serves as its president. That gives them plenty of time to enjoy each other's company, and clearly they do. It's a great way to enjoy a sunset.

Monte Hale died on March 29, 2009.

SOURCES:

Hale, Monte. Personal interview with the author, March 25, 2001, in Los Angeles, California.
Green, Douglas B. *Singing in the Saddle: The History of the Singing Cowboy*. Nashville: Country Music Foundation Press and Vanderbilt University Press, 2002.

22

Rex Allen

The question of who was the best singer of all the singing cowboys can be endlessly debated—and has been—but no one can disagree that Rex Allen had the best talking voice. It was a voice that snuggled up beside you and enveloped you until you were captured and drawn into whatever it was he was narrating. A tall handsome man who filmed what is considered the last singing cowboy movie, Rex Allen was a legendary figure during his lifetime who made his mark on radio, television and recordings in addition to his movies.

Rex Elvie Allen was born on a ranch in Mud Springs Canyon, about 40 miles from Willcox, Arizona, to Horace and Faye Allen. After Rex's older brother died from a rattlesnake bite and his younger sister died from a childhood disease, the family moved to a ranch about four miles outside Willcox and about 85 miles east of Tucson. Shortly after moving to Willcox, Rex's mom, Faye Clark Allen, died of blood poisoning. Rex himself had a detached retina but the local Rotary Club raised the money so he could get medical help. Horace Allen struggled to hold the family together; he married Myrtle Crawford and they had two daughters.

The early years of the Great Depression in Willcox were tough. "It didn't rain a drop around Willcox for 20 months," remembered Rex. "Not a drop. Cattle all were dying. Ranchers going broke. People were sick." Sometime around 1934 Horace Allen quit the cattle business and went into the plastering trade. He was also a fiddler who played for dances in and around Willcox. He bought Rex a guitar from Sears when the youngster was 11 years old; the idea was for Rex to accompany his father's fiddling but soon the boy began to sing. "I was interested in singing since I was a little boy," remembered Rex in an interview with A.J. Flick. "I sang in the Baptist choir. And later, the choir in the Methodist church for the second service. I'd sing anywhere they'd let me."

He was encouraged by his high school music teacher. "Bernice McDaniels cheered me on," said Allen, but "she didn't want me to sing Western music. She wanted me to sing grand opera." After finishing high school, Rex moved to Phoenix where he worked for his father as a plasterer; then he landed a job at KOY in 1934. Also working at the station was a young comedian/actor, Steve Allen, who wouldn't speak to him because Rex sang cowboy music. "He's a jazz pianist," remembered Rex. A brief foray into riding in rodeos ended when a spill from a bull sent him back on stage singing.

The major influences on Rex Allen during the time he was learning to play guitar and earning his spurs as a performer were the early recordings of Jimmie Rodgers, Gene Autry, Carson Robison and the Carter Family.

In 1943 Rex moved to Trenton, New Jersey, where he performed on WTTM; then he joined WCAU in Philadelphia where he played fiddle and sang harmony with the Sleepy Hollow Gang. In the summer of 1946, Lulu Belle and Scotty—major stars on WLS in Chicago—heard Rex on WCAU and encouraged him to audition for WLS. He did and wound up performing at WLS and on *National Barn Dance* for four and a half years.

In Chicago, Rex married Bonnie Linder in 1946; their first son, Rex Allen Jr., was born the following year on August 23. Also in 1946 Rex signed with Mercury Records, a label started and based in Chicago. His first chart record, "Afraid," was on that label and charted in 1949 after several unsuccessful releases.

Meanwhile, out in Hollywood at Republic Studios the company was still making singing cowboy movies. Their newest star, Monte Hale, had done some features but did not have the "star appeal" of Gene Autry or Roy Rogers. Autry left the studio in 1947 and it looked like Rogers would soon leave (he left in 1951) so Republic was hunting for the next singing cowboy star. And what better place to look than WLS in Chicago, the station that had given the world Gene Autry, Patsy Montana, Max Terhune, Pat Buttram and Louise Massey and the Westerners.

In 1949, Rex Allen left Chicago for Hollywood, where he signed as a contract player—for $300 a week—to Republic. His first film, *The Arizona Cowboy*, was released in 1950 and Rex wrote the theme song for the movie, "Too Lee Rollum (I'm an Arizona Cowboy)." Over the next four years, Rex starred in 19 singing cowboy movies with Republic; sidekicks in his films included Slim Pickens, Buddy Ebsen and Fuzzy Knight.

When he began starring in singing cowboy movies for Republic, Rex bought Koko, "The Miracle Horse of the Movies." In an interview with A.J. Flick, Rex stated, "I bought him when I first went out there (to California). I furnished my own horse, my own wardrobe. Roy Rogers said, 'You furnish everything you need to make movies or else they'll have you wearin' my old wardrobe.'"

Unlike other movie cowboys, Rex wore his guns backwards. "I just wanted to be different than everyone else," he said. "I wanted to have a different colored horse, vest different, blocked my hat differently. Everything I could so nobody could say I was a copy of anybody else."

In addition to his movies, Rex told interviewer A.J. Flick that he "worked in a lot of rodeos, theaters, and auditoriums, nearly every summer. I'd go back for eight days and do a film and go back on the road. Take the horse and load 'em up and grab a few musicians."

Rex Allen's career at Republic ended with *The Phantom Stallion*, which was released in 1954 and was generally acknowledged to be the last singing cowboy movie ever made. Thus the glorious days of the singing cowboy in Hollywood rode off into the sunset. Or make that television, where Gene Autry and Roy Rogers both developed shows. Rex also developed a show, *Frontier Doctor*, where he played Dr. Bill Baxter for 39 episodes in the syndicated series. During 1961 he starred in *Five Star Jubilee* on NBC, which was a country music variety television show that originated from Springfield, Missouri.

The deep, resonant, authoritative voice of Rex Allen was perfect for narration and Rex narrated for a number of Walt Disney films: *The Legend of Lobo* (1962), *The Incredible Journey* (1963) and *Charlie the Lonesome Cougar* (1967). In addition, Rex was the voice for Country Coyote, Wildcat Bobcat, Greta the Misfit Greyhound, Nosey the Sweetest Skunk and Stud the Best Cowdog in the West in other Disney films. He was the voice behind the Purina Chow commercials.

In addition to his movie work, Rex continued his recording career. During his time as a singing cowboy with Republic he had hits with "Sparrow in the Tree Top" for Mercury in 1951 and "Crying in the Chapel" for Decca in 1953, both of which were chart records in the country and pop fields. In 1961 he charted with "Marines Let's Go" for Mercury. Then, in

1961, he had his biggest hit, "Don't Go Near the Indians," on Mercury, which was a top five hit in the country field and a pop crossover. His last two chart records were "Tear After Tear" (1964) and "Tiny Bubbles" (1968).

During the 1970s Rex recorded for Disneyland, Buena Vista and JMI. In 1983 he was inducted into the Western Performers Hall of Fame at the National Cowboy and Western Heritage Museum in Oklahoma City and his biography, *Rex Allen: My Life Sunrise to Sunset—The Arizona Cowboy*, written by Paula Simpson-Witt and Snuff Garrett, was published in 1989.

During the period 1976–1994 Rex toured with the Reinsmen, always singing what had become his signature song, "Streets of Laredo." He was elected to the Western Music Hall of Fame in 1989 and in 1995 recorded a Western album, *The Singing Cowboys*, with his son, Rex Allen Jr. It was not the first time this duo sang about the singing cowboys; in 1982 the two recorded "Last of the Silver Screen Cowboys" (with Roy Rogers) for Warner Brothers. In 1999 his duet album with Don Edwards, *A Pair to Draw To*, was released.

Rex Allen (photograph from the author's collection).

Rex Allen died on December 17, 1999, after his caretaker accidentally ran over him with a car. Rex was 78 years old, just two weeks shy of his 79th birthday. At the time of his death he was living just outside Tucson with his third wife, Virginia.

For a number of years, Rex had appeared at the annual Rex Allen Days in Willcox, where there is a Rex Allen Museum with much of his memorabilia on display. After his death Rex was cremated and his ashes were scattered near the Rex Allen Museum and Willcox Cowboy Hall of Fame.

SOURCES:

Allen, Rex. *My Life: Sunrise to Sunset*. As told to Paula Simpson Witt and Snuff Garrett. Scottsdale, AZ: RexGarRus Press, 1989.
Green, Douglas B. *Singing in the Saddle: The History of the Singing Cowboy*. Nashville: Country Music Foundation Press and Vanderbilt University Press, 2002.

23

John Wayne

John Wayne couldn't sing a lick. And he knew it. But, boy, he sure could talk and that voice still resonates today. Although John Wayne wasn't "musical," there was a lot of music in his movies. And he even tried to sing now and then.

In *Riders of Destiny*, his first film for Monogram, he was cast as gunfighter "Singin' Sandy" Sanders who sang when he got riled. This movie was released in 1933, two years before Gene Autry made his debut for Republic in 1935. Autry is acknowledged and celebrated as the "first" singing cowboy—but John Wayne got there first. If only he could sing.

John Wayne's voice was dubbed in, probably by Jack Kirk or perhaps by Bill Bradbury, the son of director Robert North Bradbury and brother of future singing cowboy Bob Steel. This embarrassed Wayne, who said a number of years later, "I was just so [expletive deleted] embarrassed by it all, strumming a guitar I couldn't play and miming to a voice which was provided by a real singer made me feel like a (same expletive) pansy. After that experience I refused to be Singin' Sandy again."*

John Wayne and Gene Autry used to kid each other about their respective abilities in singing and acting but it is interesting to note that in *Westward Ho!*, the first movie by John Wayne for Republic, there was plenty of singing, although it was done by "The Singing Rangers." Still, it came out before Autry's picture for that same movie company, so it is obvious that Republic had decided it would make westerns with singing in them. They just had to find the right person to sing and act in those movies.

Although John Wayne was never a singing cowboy, he became the quintessential cowboy hero in movies during the twentieth century. He starred in 150 movies; about half of them were westerns and in those movies he portrayed a man's man, unapologetically masculine. As he became a star leading man whose films attracted large audiences, he chose the roles he played and how he played them. Wayne stated, "I want to play a real man in all my films. and I define manhood simply: men should be tough, fair, and courageous, never petty, never looking for a fight, but never backing down from one either…. I don't want ever to appear in a film that would embarrass a viewer. A man can take his wife, mother, and his daughter to one of my movies and never be ashamed or embarrassed for going"†

The man who became known to the world as John Wayne was born Marion Robert Morrison on May 26, 1907, in Winterset, Iowa, the son of a pharmacist. His mother, Molly, called him "Bobby" until his brother, Bobby, was born in 1912.

---

*Bann, liner notes, *John Wayne's West*; see sources.
†Roberts and Olson, *John Wayne*, p. 604; see sources.

Wayne's father, Clyde Leonard Morrison, played football at Simpson College and graduated from the Highland Park College of Pharmacy in Des Moines, Iowa. After Clyde's graduation, the Morrisons moved to Winterset, Iowa, about 35 miles from Des Moines, where their first son was born. The family moved to Brooklyn, then Earlham, Iowa, and struggled to make a living; they declared bankruptcy at the end of 1911 and moved to Keokuk, Iowa.

Meanwhile, Clyde's father moved to Los Angeles in 1909 and entered the real estate business; when he died, he left an 80-acre farm in Southern California to his son. This led the Morrisons to move west to California in 1914 when John Wayne was seven. Clyde planted corn and wheat but did not know how to farm; in 1916 the family moved to Glendale where Clyde worked at the Glendale Pharmacy.

Wayne hated the name "Marion" so he insisted his friends call him "Morrison." He obtained the nickname "Duke" because the family had an Airedale named "Duke" that followed him to school each day. The dog waited at the fire department station every day for the boy, which led the firemen to call Marion "Little Duke" or "Duke." Marion liked that name.

The Morrison family moved around in Los Angeles and Duke joined the Boy Scouts when he was 12, where he obtained the rank of First Class. At Glendale Union High School he was president of his senior class, salutatorian and a football star on the line. He applied to the United States Naval Academy but was not accepted; however, USC offered him a football scholarship and he entered that university in the fall of 1925. In the classroom he studied to be a lawyer and on the football field he was moved from guard to tackle.

Duke always loved watching movies, and during his freshman year he earned money as an "extra" in some movies, especially football films. Western star Tom Mix put some USC football players on the Fox Studio payroll during the summer of 1926 so he could have a personal box at USC home games and Duke earned $35 a week for this. He took a screen test for MGM but didn't pass.

Duke did the props—"a glorified furniture mover"—at Fox during the summer of 1926 and at the end of the summer, just before summer football workouts, broke his collarbone and separated his right shoulder while surfing in the ocean. That ended his career as a football player and the following year he dropped out of USC after obtaining a job with director John Ford.

Under Ford, Duke worked as a general gofer and assistant property man; in this role, he also worked as a stuntman and an extra in crowd scenes and did whatever else needed doing on and around the movie set. In the 1929 film *Cheer Up and Smile*, directed by John Ford, Wayne worked with the props and was noticed by director Raoul Walsh as he carried the furniture back to the property warehouse. Walsh ordered a screen test for the young man and signed him to a contract. For his first starring role, Duke was cast in *The Big Trail*, directed by Winifred "Winnie" Sheehan.

Sheehan did not like the name Duke Morrison so he and Walsh decided to change Duke's name. Walsh suggested "Anthony Wayne" after the Revolutionary War hero but Sheehan countered that "Tony Wayne" sounded like a girl's name. When someone suggested "John Wayne," Sheehan agreed and Duke Morrison became John Wayne, even though he wasn't at the meeting and had no input into the decision. Duke hated the name John Wayne and grew accustomed to it only years later. To his friends and family he was always Duke or Marion and, as the years rolled by, he became known as John Wayne but never John.

John Wayne took lessons to learn how to ride, rope, shoot and act from real life cowboys and stuntmen. Director John Ford advised him to copy Harry Carey's mannerisms and Wayne did; the Harry Carey way of talking and walking became the John Wayne way of talking and walking.

On October 24, 1930, *The Big Trail* premiered at Grauman's Chinese Theater. The film was a commercial flop. Wayne did two more films for Fox in 1931 then the studio dropped his contract. He signed on with Columbia and appeared in several films, including the westerns *Range Feud*, *Texas Cyclone* and *Two Fisted Law*, before he took supporting roles in westerns by Buck Jones and Tim McCoy.

After these films, Wayne's agent, Al Kingston, obtained a contract for him with Nat Levine and Mascot Pictures, where he was signed to do three serials—none of them westerns. From Mascot, Wayne went to Warner Brothers, which had purchased First National Pictures where Ken Maynard had starred in a series of silent westerns. Warner Brothers decided to recycle the Maynard films and update them for sound; the studio believed Wayne looked enough like Maynard to sign him for six low-budget pictures. During the mid–1932 to mid–1933 period Wayne made *Ride Him Cowboy*, *The Big Stampede*, *Haunted Gold*, *The Telegraph Trail*, *Somewhere in Sonora* and *The Man from Monterey*; he played a character whose first name was John in each of these films. Wayne was in four movies for Warner in 1933—none westerns—and at the end of the year Warner released him.

John Wayne (photograph from the author's collection).

The film studio Monogram had series starring the Bowery Boys, Charlie Chan, the Shadow, and the Cisco Kid and had Tex Ritter, Johnny Mack Brown, Ray "Crash" Corrigan, Ken Maynard, Tim McCoy, Hoot Gibson, Buck Jones and Bob Steel on their roster. Duke Wayne signed with them in 1933 and Trem Carr, head of the film company, cast him as a western hero in 16 pictures over the next two years. The first film was *Riders of Destiny*, released in October, in which Wayne played "Singin' Sandy Saunders." In 1934 Monogram released nine low budget films starring Wayne: *Sagebrush Trail*, *The Lucky Texan*, *West of the Divide*, *Blue Steel*, *The Man from Utah*, *Randy Rides Alone*, *The Star Packer*, *The Trail Beyond* and *The Lawless Frontier*. In 1935 Wayne starred in '*Neath the Arizona Skies*, *Texas Terror*, *Rainbow Valley*, *The Desert Trail*, *The Dawn Rider* and *Paradise Canyon*. The films were done cheaply, on a budget of $10,000–12,000 per picture, and generally had five major characters.

Wayne states, according to Roberts and Olson in their book *John Wayne's America* (p. 131), "I made up my mind that I was going to play a real man to the best of my ability. I felt many of the Western stars of the twenties and thirties were too goddamn perfect. They never drank nor smoked. They never wanted to go to bed with a beautiful girl. They never had a fight.... They were too goddamn sweet and pure to be dirty fighters.... I was trying to play a man who gets dirty, who sweats sometimes, who enjoys kissing a gal he likes, who gets angry, who fights clean whenever possible but will fight dirty if he has to. I made the Western hero a roughneck."

Roberts and Olson (pp. 137–8) note, "Before the end of his first eight-picture deal with Monogram, the basic screen persona of John Wayne was in place.... [T]he cowboy hero is a lean, tough loner, impatient with small talk and small matters, willing to implement justice and protect the weak. The physical mannerisms of John Wayne were also in place. The familiar rolling walk, the mid-sentence pauses, the double take after being floored by a powerful punch, the economical use of his hands to emphasize a particularly crucial point, the cold, dead stare when he was mad—all the movements and gestures."

Republic Pictures was created out of Monogram and Mascot because both owed money to their film processor, Consolidated Film Industries, owned by Herbert J. Yates. Early in 1935 Yates proposed that Republic Productions be formed by merging their production and distribution operations with the processing laboratories of Consolidated, along with investment capital from Consolidated. The merged companies bought out Liberty, Majestic and Chesterfield Pictures. W. Ray Johnston, founder of Monogram, was named president and headed distribution, while Nat Levine, founder of Mascot, and Trem Carr, head of Monogram, handled production. Herbert Yates was chairman of the board.

Republic acquired the old Mack Sennett Studios on Ventura Boulevard through Nat Levine, who had a lease with an option to buy the facility; however, Levine spent money on film production instead of the production facility. Levine had Gene Autry and Ann Rutherford signed to Mascot; Johnston and Carr had Ray Bradbury and John Wayne signed to Monogram. By the fall of 1935, Republic was ready to release its first film, *Westward Ho!*, starring John Wayne—as a singing cowboy. Their next film was *Tumbling Tumbleweeds* starring Gene Autry—as a singing cowboy.

Gene Autry established the role of the singing cowboy in his movies. John Wayne could never be a singing cowboy, although the studio tried one more time in his second Republic film, *The Lawless Range*. In that film, Glen Strange sang for Wayne. But from 1935 on, Republic was the home to the singing cowboy and John Wayne soon left after filming *The Lawless Nineties*, *King of the Pecos*, *The Lonely Trail* and *Winds of the Wasteland*, all in 1936.

In 1936 Trem Carr left Republic and Yates after the financier bought out Carr's and Johnston's stock for $1 million. Carr then went to Universal, where he gave Wayne a six-film contract, none of them westerns. At the end of his contract, Universal dropped Wayne. In 1937 John Wayne signed with Paramount and, along with Johnny Mack Brown, starred in *Born to the West*, which was released in December. Then Wayne went back to Herbert Yates and Republic, where he signed a five-year deal which obligated him to eight westerns a year. First he replaced Robert Livingston as Stony Brooke in the Three Mesquiteer series; in that role Wayne starred in *Pals of the Saddle*, *Overland Stage Raiders*, *Santa Fe Stampede* and *Red River Range*.

John Wayne's big break as an actor came when he was cast as The Ringo Kid in *Stagecoach*, directed by John Ford. Ford had purchased the film rights to the short story. "Stage to Lordsburg" by Ernest Haycox, which was published in *Collier's* magazine in April 1937. Ford signed Wayne as the male lead but paid him only $3,000 for the film. Claire Trevor, the female lead, received $15,000 and the other main characters in the film, Thomas Mitchell, Andy Devine, Louise Platt, George Bancroft, Donald Meek, Tim Holt, Berton Churchill and John Carradine all received more than Wayne, who was "loaned out" by Republic for $600 a week. At the end of October 1938, filming began on *Stagecoach*; it finished filming on December 23. Many of the exteriors were shot in Monument Valley, a favorite location of Ford's along the Utah and Arizona border. Other locations included the Kern River at Kernville, Victorville, Newhall, Chatsworth and Calabasas, California. The interior scenes were all done on a studio lot.

Although John Wayne did not sing in his movies—and was not a musician—many of his movies are known for their songs and musical scores. There was a lot of music in the score to *Stagecoach*; the songs "Jeannie with the Light Brown Hair," "Shall We Gather at the River," "Gentle Annie," "The Union Forever," "My Lulu, "The Trail to Mexico," "Ten Thousand Cattle" and "Bury Me Not on the Lone Prairie" were all in the film, which was previewed on February 2, 1939, and released nationally a month later.

The year 1939 was a great one for movies. In addition to *Stagecoach,* the films *Mr. Smith Goes to Washington, The Hunchback of Notre Dame, Destry Rides Again, Gunga Din, Goodbye, Mr. Chips, The Wizard of Oz, Wuthering Heights, Drums Along the Mohawk, Young Mr. Lincoln* and *Gone with the Wind* were all released that year.

Stagecoach held its own in that illustrious company; it was nominated for seven Academy Awards: Best Picture, Best Director, Best Supporting Actor, Best Cinematography, Best Score, Editing and Interior Decoration. It won two Oscars, for Best Score and Thomas Mitchell for Best Supporting Actor. The New York Critics awarded John Ford the Best Director award, but John Wayne did not win a single award for the film. Instead, he established his career as a movie star with it. From this point forward, John Wayne was no longer a "B" actor; after *Stagecoach* he was considered an "A" actor for "A" movies.

After *Stagecoach,* Wayne returned to Republic and starred as Stony Brooke in three Mesquiteers films, *Texas Steers, Wyoming Outlaw* and *New Frontier,* but it was obvious to Herbert Yates that he could make more money with Wayne as a star rather than as a sidekick. His last "B" film was *Allegheny Uprising,* released in November 1939. Republic attempted to make an "A" picture with *The Dark Command,* directed by Raoul Walsh and released in 1940, which starred John Wayne and featured Roy Rogers. It was a profitable film for Republic.

Although John Wayne later became a super patriot he never served in the armed forces, particularly during World War II when 75 percent of the men his age did serve and a number of Hollywood actors—including Gene Autry—served. Instead, Herbert Yates and Republic Pictures arranged for Wayne to star in movies during World War II, which boosted Wayne's career enormously. In 1942 Wayne starred in *The Spoilers, In Old California* and his first World War II film, *Flying Tigers.* This last film became one of the top box office draws for 1942.

After *Flying Tigers* Wayne starred in *Reunion in France* and *Pittsburgh* so he had five movies filmed and released in 1942. Two other films, *Lady for the Night* and *Reap the Wild Wind,* were filmed the previous year but released in 1942. Wayne also starred in a radio series, *Three Sheets to the Wind,* as an alcoholic detective. In 1943 Wayne starred in *In Old Oklahoma,* which had "Put Your Arms Around Me Honey," sung by Dale Evans. That same year he starred in *The Fighting Seabees.* In 1944 he starred in *Tall in the Saddle* and *Flame of the Barbary Coast*; in 1944 he filmed *Back to Bataan,* which was released the following year. Also in 1945 Wayne starred in *They Were Expendable,* another war movie, then he starred in *Dakota.*

Because of his value as a leading film star during World War II, John Wayne moved away from Republic and Herbert Yates. In 1946 he starred in *Angel and the Badman* and formed his own production company, Argosy Productions, with John Ford and Merian Cooper. Wayne's first film for his company was *Fort Apache,* based on the James Warner story "Massacre," which was published in the *Saturday Evening Post.* In *Fort Apache,* former singing cowboy Dick Foran sang "Sweet Genevieve." Another story in the *Saturday Evening Post,* "The Chisholm Trail" by Borden Chase, became *Red River,* a classic western that featured Montgomery Clift in the costarring role. In 1949 there were five films released starring John Wayne: *Three Godfathers, Wake of the Red Witch, She Wore a Yellow Ribbon, The Fighting Kentuckian* and *Sands of Iwo Jima.*

In 1950 *Rio Grande* was released and, according to Roberts and Olson in *John Wayne, American* (p. 325), "the politics of "Rio Grande" had become Wayne's politics. In 1948, when he began his rise to the top of his profession, he had been one of the more politically inactive stars in Hollywood, remaining distant from the debate that consumed the industry. But by the end of 1950 he was in the middle of the fight, "searching for enemies, naming names, and taking stands." The Sons of the Pioneers sang "Yellow Stripes," "I'll Take You Home

Again, Kathleen," "Cattle Call," "The Erie Canal," "My Gal Is Purple," and "Down by the Glenside" in *Rio Grande*. In 1950 and 1951 John Wayne was the top box office attraction in Hollywood.

In *The Quiet Man*, released in 1952, Wayne finished his contractual obligation to Republic. The film was nominated for Oscars in seven categories, including Picture of the Year. But Wayne was not nominated for any award although the film earned an Academy Award for John Ford in the director category and for cinematographers Winton Hoch and Archie Stout. In addition to *The Quiet Man*, Wayne starred in *Big Jim McClain*, *Trouble Along the Way*, and *Island in the Sky* in 1952. In the summer of 1953 Wayne filmed *Hondo* in Mexico, which was released in November. The hit western movie that year was *Shane*, starring Alan Ladd.

In 1954 John Wayne formed a new movie production company, Batjak; during that summer he filmed *The Conqueror* and *The Sea Chase*. In 1955 Batjac released *Blood Alley*; that same year Wayne filmed the classic western *The Searchers* in Monument Valley. The film, considered by many to be the greatest western ever made, came at a time when the western was riding tall in the saddle; at that point, there were 35 westerns on TV and the western novels of Louis L'Amour were selling in large numbers. For John Wayne, the character of Ethan Edwards in *The Searchers* is often considered his greatest performance. That movie was released in March 1956. In the film, the Sons of the Pioneers sang "The Searchers" and "We Will Gather at the River," while Ken Curtis, a former member of the Sons of the Pioneers, sang "Skip to My Lou/Yellow Rose of Texas."

Rio Bravo, directed by Howard Hawks, was John Wayne's answer to *High Noon* and *3:10 to Yuma*. *High Noon* showed a town afraid to confront three killers; *Yuma* was also a town filled with fear. John Wayne thought the films portrayed a town without a backbone, not truly representative of America and Americans. He set out to correct that with a film of his own. Singers Dean Martin and Ricky Nelson both had roles in *Rio Bravo,* and the duo did "My Rifle, My Pony and Me." Martin did "Rio Bravo" and Nelson and Walter Brennan sang "Cindy" in that film.

In October 1958, shooting began on *The Horse Soldiers*, Wayne's movie about Civil War calvary. The film died at the box office; Wayne was clearly overweight in the picture. In *The Horse Soldiers*, a male chorus sang "I Left My Love," "Bonnie Blue Flag," "The Girl I Left Behind Me" and "Tenting Tonight." During that year John Wayne turned 51.

In August 1959, Wayne began work on *The Alamo* in San Antonio, Texas. He had long wanted to do a picture on the Alamo. In 1955, *Davy Crockett*, a series on Walt Disney's Sunday night television show, created a huge craze of coonskin hats, in 1956 Republic had filmed *The Last Command* about the Alamo.

John Wayne spent a good part of his life—and a lot of his money—filming *The Alamo*, a story that allowed him to say things that he wanted to say about the West, America and himself. Music was an important part of the film and Wayne recruited top talent to sing in that film. Marty Robbins sang "Ballad of the Alamo"; The Brothers Four sang "The Green Leaves of Summer"; and Frankie Avalon sang "Tennessee Babe," "The Green Leaves of Summer," "Here's to the Ladies" and "The Ballad of the Alamo."

Filming began in September and ended in December. The premier was scheduled for the end of October 1960 to coincide with the presidential election. The film was 206 minutes long at the premier in San Antonio; after the premier Wayne spent four days cutting 30 minutes from the film and released it nationally the following weekend. *The Alamo* received six Oscar nominations: Best Sound, Best Song, Best Cinematography, Best Score, Best Supporting Actor (Chill Wells) and Best Movie; the only Oscar it received was given to Dmitri Tiomkin for Best Score.

In November 1960, *North to Alaska* was released. In that film Johnny Horton sang "North to Alaska," which became a number one song on the country charts in 1959. In that same movie Fabian sang "If You Knew." In October 1961 *The Comancheros* premiered. Claude King recorded "The Comancheros," a song "inspired" by the movie and that song was a top ten on the country chart in early 1962. In *The Man Who Shot Liberty Valance*, released in 1962, Gene Pitney recorded the song "(The Man Who Shot) Liberty Valance," but it was not included in that movie. However, the record was a top five pop hit for Pitney in 1962.

In 1962 Wayne appeared in a cameo role in *How the West Was Won* as General William T. Sherman. *How the West Was Won* was filled with songs and singing. The Ken Darby Singers did a number of songs, as did the Whiskeyhill Singers. Dave Guard of the Kingston Trio did "Wanderin'" and "Poor Wayfarin' Stranger," and Debbie Reynolds sang "What Was Your Name in the States," "Raise a Ruckus Tonight," and "A Home in the Meadow." Wayne made another cameo appearance in *The Longest Day*, also released in 1962. Late that year he filmed *McClintock* for Batjac Productions.

In August 1965, *The Sons of Katie Elder* premiered. The film featured a song by that same title sung by Johnny Cash, which was a top ten country hit in 1965. *El Dorado*, costarring Robert Mitchum, was released in 1966, and *The War Wagon*, based on the novel *Badman* by Clair Huffaker, was released the following year. In that film Ed Ames sang "Ballad of the War Wagon." In 1968 John Wayne starred in *The Green Berets*, a pro-Vietnam movie based on the book by Robin Moore. A few years earlier, "The Ballad of the Green Beret" had been a number one pop song for SSgt. Barry Sadler.

True Grit opened in July 1969. Based on the novel by Charles Portis, Wayne played Rooster Cogburn, a man with an eye patch, and that film led to Wayne's only Oscar for acting. It was a joyous occasion for him, and he noted that if he'd known he'd receive an Oscar playing a man wearing an eye patch he would have worn one years earlier. Also in *True Grit* was Glen Campbell, who sang the title song, a top ten country song and one also on the pop chart in 1969.

In May 1970, *Chisum* was released, which featured Merle Haggard singing "Ballad of John Chisum" and "Turn Me Around." Wayne shot *Chisum* in Durango, Mexico, where filming was much cheaper than in Hollywood. He also filmed *Big Jake*, *The Train Robbers* and *Cahill, U.S. Marshal* in Durango. Charlie Rich sang "A Man Gets to Thinking" in *Cahill, U.S. Marshal*.

During the 1970s John Wayne recorded a patriotic album in Nashville, *America, Why I Love Her*. The album featured Wayne doing ten recitations: "Why I Love Her," "The Pledge of Allegiance," "The Hyphen," "Mis Raices Estan Aqui," "The People," "An American Boy Grows Up," "Face the Flag," "The Good Things," "Why Are You Marching, Son?" and "Taps." On the recordings, Wayne is backed by an orchestra and chorus for his dramatic readings. "Why I Love Her" was a favorite poem of Wayne's, which he recited at the 1964 Republican convention in San Francisco. The album was recorded in 1973 and released that same year. It entered the country chart on March 24 and rose to number 13, remaining on the country chart for 13 weeks. This was during the time the Watergate hearings were underway and the Vietnam War was winding down.

Duke Wayne's final film was a western, *The Shootist*, based on the novel by Glendon Swarthout. Wayne played J.B. Books, a man with prostate and rectal cancer whose time on earth is quickly coming to an end. In real life, John Wayne was suffering from terminal cancer. The film, costarring Lauren Bacall, James Stewart, Richard Boone and Ron Howard, was released in 1976 and was nominated for an Academy Award in the Best Art Direction-Set Decoration category, but it did not win. *The Shootist* was the perfect ending for John Wayne's career: a western gunfighter who chose to go out with his guns blazing. In the film he makes comments about impending death that resonated in his own life.

John Wayne's actual death was much less dramatic, although no less tragic. He was in and out of the hospital with stomach cancer in 1978 and 1979, increasingly emaciated, and died on June 11, 1979. He is buried at Pacific View Memorial Park in Newport Beach, California. As an individual he "was a simple, complex man, both more and less than he seemed.... Hollywood was his home, film his identity ... a soldier who never served, a cowboy who lived on the beach, a man of violence who longed for peace," according to the biography by Randy Roberts and James S. Olson (p. 646). But to fans of westerns he was the man they wished to be, a man who was fearless and firm in his convictions, a man who rode tall in the saddle and was proud to be an American.

John Wayne's closest connection to country music was his album, *America, Why I Love Her*, which was recorded in Nashville and reached the country album chart. But John Wayne, cowboys and country music are connected because he was the quintessential western film hero and the country audience identified with him. If a fan sat in a movie theater watching a John Wayne western, there was a pretty good chance that the people sitting there with them also liked country music.

SOURCES:

Bann, Richard W. "John Wayne's West" liner notes in *John Wayne's West in Music and Poster Art*, Bear Family Records, BCD 16739 SE, Hamburg, Germany, 2009.
Davis, Ronald L. *Duke: The Life and Times of John Wayne*. Norman: University of Oklahoma Press, 2001.
Roberts, Randy, and James S. Olson. *John Wayne: American*. New York: Free Press, 1995.
Shepherd, Donald, and Robert Slatzer. *Duke: The Life and Times of John Wayne*. With Dave Grayson. New York: Doubleday, 1985.

24

Bob Wills, King of Western Swing

Western Swing is the marriage of old time Texas fiddle music with Big Band Swing. It was created by rural musicians who were enthralled with the music of the Jazz Age and Swing Era.

Bob Wills is given credit for being the father of western swing; in truth he's more like the big brother in a large royal family who refined the music and brought it to the forefront of American music. And, as the elder brother, he became King of Western Swing in his time.

Bob Wills grew up in West Texas, where he and his father, who played fiddle, performed at "ranch dances." These ranch dances were all night social gatherings held at someone's ranch house. When radio developed in the 1920s, Bob Wills began to perform on that medium.

Some of the fiddle tunes Wills played can be traced back to British folk songs. But fiddlers were always altering tunes or making up new ones or perhaps even adding some lyrics to an old tune. The audience for Wills' early performances were westerners—ranchers, cowboys and those connected to the cattle trade. And the purpose of the music was dancing. That's why a social gathering hired a fiddler!

Wills moved to Fort Worth early in 1929 and, with two other musicians, obtained a spot on WBAP. However, the group didn't have a sponsor and so, to earn money, Wills began playing in a medicine show. In the fall of 1929, he made his first recordings, "Gulf Coast Blues" (a Bessie Smith number) and "Wills Breakdown" for Brunswick.

Wills had teamed with guitarist Herman Arnspiger and in 1930 they began performing on KTAT in Fort Worth as well as at house parties. During a house party the Wills Fiddle Band doubled in size when singer Milton Brown and his brother, guitarist Durwood Brown, joined the group. The group was successful in and around Fort Worth, and in the fall of 1930 they began a show on WBAP sponsored by the Aladdin Lamp Company. The group became the Aladdin Laddies and, in addition to their radio performances, began performing at dances at Crystal Springs, a dance pavilion in Fort Worth.

In January 1931, Wills and his group were on KFJZ, sponsored by Light Crust Flour, a product of the Burrus Mill and Elevator Company. The band became known as the "Light Crust Doughboys" and soon a Burrus Mill executive, W. Lee O'Daniel was announcing for the band. O'Daniel, who had fired the group because he didn't like their music, was persuaded to hire them for a salary but the musicians had to spend forty hours a week at the mill. They therefore practiced eight hours a day to earn their salaries.

The show thrived but personal differences led Milton Brown to quit in 1932 and form his own group—Milton Brown and His Musical Brownies. Wills hired Tommy Duncan to replace him. In 1933, Wills left the group, taking many of the musicians with him, moved to Waco, Texas, and formed the Texas Playboys. The original group consisted of Wills on fiddle; Tommy Duncan, piano and vocals; Kermit Whalin, steel guitar and bass; Johnnie Lee Wills, tenor banjo; and June Whalin, rhythm guitar.

In early 1934 Wills and his group moved to Oklahoma, first to Oklahoma City, then to Tulsa, where they began performing on KVOO. Here the group and the music both blossomed, as Wills added more musicians to his group and moved their sound closer to the Big Band music that was heard on network radio.

Bob Wills and the Texas Playboys recorded first in 1935 for Brunswick in Dallas. Brunswick was later purchased by Columbia, which was later purchased by the American Record Corporation. The records that Wills made sold extremely well and soon he had a major reputation in the Southwest. This reputation was enhanced by the broadcasts and dances at Cain's Ballroom in Tulsa. Wills went to Hollywood in the summer of 1940 with his Texas Playboys to appear in a movie, *Take Me Back to Oklahoma*, starring Tex Ritter. This was followed by *Go West Young Lady*, starring Glenn Ford. But he returned to Tulsa and continued performing at Cain's and on KVOO.

Bob Wills (photograph from the author's collection).

When World War II began in December 1941, Wills lost a number of musicians to the draft. This trimmed his band, which had grown to 17 members. At the end of 1942 he was back in Hollywood, filming more movies and playing at the Venice Pier to large crowds. Then he returned to Tulsa, where he joined the army. Bob Wills didn't last long in the army. He was three months short of 38 when he was drafted; he was discharged about six months later. Since almost every member of his old band had either joined the service or left Tulsa, he decided to move to California which he did in September 1943.

Wills and his new band began performing on KMTR in Los Angeles and played at the Mission Beach Ballroom in San Diego. Wills was soon making movies again and signed with MCA, the major talent agency for big bands, in 1944.

In 1944 Wills put together his biggest band—22 instrumentalists and two vocalists. Unfortunately, this group never had a recording session in the six to seven months it played. Musically, the sound of Wills' music changed during World War II. The horns were essential to the Big Band sound, but during the war the fiddle began to emerge as the dominant sound in the group. The guitar and steel guitar also assumed major importance.

In January 1945, Wills had his first recording session since July 1942. The term "western swing" had emerged by this time to describe the music that he played. The "look" of the group was "western" by this time as well—a result of Wills appearing in singing cowboy movies. It was also a product of the fact that Wills came from Texas and Oklahoma, where it was usual for men to wear cowboy hats and boots.

In June 1945, Wills moved to Fresno, California, and made radio transcriptions for

Tiffany Music in Oakland. These Tiffany Transcriptions, which were sold to radio stations across the nation, include over 220 different songs. Many consider these recordings to be the best example of Bob Wills and the Texas Playboys. They may also be considered the canon for Western Swing.

In 1947 Wills ended his association with Columbia and began recording for MGM. That same year he purchased the Aragon Ballroom near Sacramento, changed the name to Wills Point, and began performing there. In September 1948, Tommy Duncan ended his 16-year association with Wills and formed his own band.

In 1949 Wills moved back to Oklahoma City then, in 1950, moved to Dallas. By this time, he was in financial trouble from back taxes he owed. He sold his music company—including the rights to "San Antonio Rose." Wills continued to record and tour and moved back to California in 1952. But the Big Band era was over—and so was the era of Western Swing. In 1953 Wills moved to Amarillo, then back to California in 1954. He had a TV show in Los Angeles in 1955 and signed with Decca. In 1957 he moved to Abilene, then returned to Tulsa before moving to Las Vegas in 1958.

The rock 'n' roll era had come and Wills could not make a living with his music, except in Vegas. But the Vegas crowds were there to listen—not to dance—and Wills never enjoyed being there, although that was his base of operations until 1961.

In 1960 Wills and Tommy Duncan reunited and made a number of recordings for Liberty. They toured together until 1962; at this point, Wills moved back to Tulsa.

During the last ten years of Bob Wills' life he had major heart attacks (in 1962 and 1964), toured, recorded for Liberty, and moved to Fort Worth (in October 1963). After 1964, he never had a band of his own; instead, he would front for other bands. He continued to record—and made almost 100 recordings between 1963 and 1969—mostly for Kapp Records.

Bob Wills never really cared for the "country" music that developed in the 1930s and 1940s. First, he did not like the term "hillbilly" applied to himself or his music. It was a derogatory term and Wills resented it. The country music that developed during his time came out of the South and had the mountaineer image. It was not made for dancing; the Bible Belt prohibition against dancing led that branch of country to develop the story song.

After World War II, country music was increasingly centered in Nashville, and Wills did not like recording in Nashville. He felt the musicians didn't understand his music. The country music that came out of Nashville was not like the swing band dance music spiced with liberal doses of jazz that Wills loved and played. And so he held a certain disdain for Nashville and the music that came out of that city. Finally, Wills was a product of the Jazz Age and the swing era. His music was sophisticated—and he wanted himself and his band to be hip and "cool." Country—or "hillbilly"—was not hip or cool.

It is ironic that Bob Wills was elected to the Country Music Hall of Fame in 1968 in a ceremony held in Nashville. Although he never felt part of the country music community and his musical influences—outside the early fiddle tunes—were never country, Bob Wills had a major impact on country music because of his influence on the musicians who played and sang country. Many of those performers grew up listening to Bob Wills, and his music had a major impact on their lives, even though the country music that evolved did not sound much like the Western swing that Wills pioneered. A bigger honor, in Wills' eyes, occurred two months after the CMA induction when the Cowboy Hall of Fame in Oklahoma City honored him for his "contribution to America's Western music lore."

Bob Wills' final recording session occurred in February 1969. About two months later he suffered a major stroke at his home in Fort Worth. On May 30—just before his stroke—Wills made his last public appearance. He never fully recovered from these strokes. Although he lived until 1975, his legacy would have to be carried on by other musicians. The first to do so was Merle Haggard, whose album *A Tribute to the Best Damn Fiddle Player in the World* came out in 1970. In the fall of 1971 Haggard brought Wills and ten former members of the Texas Playboys to his home in Bakersfield, California, for a historic recording session for Capitol.

Tommy Allsup organized a recording session in Dallas for United Artists in December 1973; right after this session Wills suffered another major stroke. He remained in a coma for nearly 18 months before dying on May 13, 1975; he is buried in Tulsa, Oklahoma.

Bob Wills put the "western" in swing music, and the swing in "western." Every musician and singer in the fields of western, country or contemporary western swing has been influenced by the music of Bob Wills. To honor Bob Wills for his tremendous influence, the Western Music Association inducted him into their Hall of Fame in 1995.

SOURCES:

Cusic, Don. *Discovering Country Music*. Westport, CT: Praeger, 2008.
Green, Douglas B. *Singing in the Saddle: The History of the Singing Cowboy*. Nashville: Country Music Foundation Press and Vanderbilt University Press, 2002.
Townsend, Charles R. *San Antonio Rose: The Life and Music of Bob Wills*. Urbana: University of Illinois Press, 1986.

25

Bing Crosby and Country Music

In January 1944, *Billboard* published its first chart on country music; on that chart was Bing Crosby's recording of "Pistol Packin' Mama." The song was a remake, or "cover," of the Al Dexter hit song which Crosby recorded with the Andrews Sisters for Decca Records. Dexter's hit was on Capitol and was a huge hit during World War II; in the tradition of those times, it was not unusual for a pop artist to cover a recording originally released in the country market. The record labels have always segmented the market for their releases and it was generally felt that the pop and country audiences were two different audiences.

This was not the first time Bing Crosby had a hit with a country recording. In fact, Crosby's second major hit—following "Sweet Leilani" in 1937—was "New San Antonio Rose," a song written and originally recorded by Bob Wills and the Texas Playboys. "San Antonio Rose" was originally an instrumental, recorded by Wills and his group in Dallas in 1938; it was the closest thing they had to a really big hit. The song came to the attention of Fred Kramer with the publishing company Irving Berlin, Inc., in New York. Kramer called Wills about the song because, although it had been recorded and was a hit, it had never been published. Kramer flew to Tulsa where Wills was based and agreed to give Wills a $300 advance if Wills provided some lyrics for the song. Wills agreed and—with the help of several of his musicians, including Sleepy Johnson, Everett Stover and Tommy Duncan—wrote lyrics and renamed the song "New San Antonio Rose." Wills then recorded "New San Antonio Rose" on April 16, 1940, for Vocalion, a subsidiary of Brunswick Records. This version, recorded with a big band sound of winds and horns, came to the attention of Crosby, who recorded the song December 16, 1940, for Decca using the same basic arrangement that Wills used. Crosby's "New San Antonio Rose" was released at the end of January 1941 and sold a lot of copies. This recording eventually sold over one and a half million copies, only the second million seller for Crosby.

Bing Crosby was a pop singer interested in making commercial records, and he was not adverse to looking at the country field (Wills' recordings were listed as "folk" by his record company) for material. In fact, Crosby recorded a number of other songs from the country field during the 1930s, although most were actually songs written by pop songwriters for cowboy movies or traditional songs from the western tradition. In 1933 he recorded "The Last Roundup," "Home on the Range," and "After Sundown"; in 1935 he recorded "Take Me Back to My Boots and Saddle"; in 1936 he recorded two songs written by Fred Rose, who later founded Acuff-Rose publishing in Nashville, "A Roundup Lullaby" and "We'll Rest at the End of the Trail," as well as a Johnny Mercer song, "I'm an Old Cowhand (From the Rio Grande)" and two other cowboy songs, "Empty Saddles (In the Old Corral)" and

"Twilight on the Trail." Obviously, these recordings reflected the popularity of the singing cowboys in the movies, led by Gene Autry, Roy Rogers and Tex Ritter.

In 1938 Crosby recorded "Silver on the Sage" and "When the Bloom Is on the Sage,"; in 1939 he recorded "El Rancho Grande (My Ranch)"; in 1940 he recorded "Along the Santa Fe Trail," "The Singing Hills," and the Sons of the Pioneers classic written by Bob Nolan, "Tumbling Tumbleweeds." In 1941 Crosby recorded a version of the old classic "Clementine," as well as two Gene Autry hits, "Goodbye, Little Darlin', Goodbye" and "Ridin' Down the Canyon." In 1942 he recorded "Deep in the Heart of Texas" and in 1943 "San Fernando Valley," written by Fred Rose under the name Floyd Jenkins.

The significance of Bing Crosby's recordings of these songs are two-fold: (1) he gave a "legitimacy" to the country music field by showing these songs could appeal to the pop sophisticate as well as the rural audience and (2) he did them with integrity instead of as "hokum" and looking down his nose on this music. For this reason, Bing Crosby played a major role in the popular acceptance of songs written originally for the country field.

Although Bing Crosby did a lot for country music in the 1930s and 1940s—especially during World War II—the reverse is also true: country music helped Bing Crosby quite a bit as well. Until Frank Sinatra emerged as the bobby-sox teen idol in pop music in 1943, Crosby was the most popular singer in America. He kept that honor by recording top songs, and some of those songs originated in the field of what later became known as country music.

Bing Crosby (photograph courtesy of Packy Smith).

The connection between Bing Crosby and country music also involved the link between big band and country music. Crosby recorded with a big band behind him. His country recordings were backed by bands such as the orchestras led by Vic Schoen, Lennie Hayton, Jimmy Dorsey, Victor Young, John Scott Trotter, Bob Crosby, and Woody Herman. It was during this same period when Crosby recorded these previously named songs—the 1930s and early 1940s—that big band influenced country music to the extent that western swing was the best-selling segment of country music.

Big band was dance music and so was western swing. The roots grow in two different directions: to the radio network shows of bands such as Benny Goodman, the Dorsey Brothers and Glenn Miller, and to Texas, where bands such as the Light Crust Doughboys, Milton Brown and his Brownies, and Bob Wills and the Texas Playboys originated.

SOURCES:

Cusic, Don. *Gene Autry: His Life and Career*. Jefferson, NC: McFarland, 2007.
Giddens, Gary. *Bing Crosby: A Pocketful of Dreams: The Early Years 1903–1940*. Boston: Little, Brown, 2001.

26

Riders in the Sky

Riders in the Sky have never had a hit song on the radio, never headlined a major arena tour, and don't have a gold or platinum album hanging on their wall. And yet the Riders are one of the most influential groups in the history of country or western music in the twentieth century.

Before the Riders were formed at the end of 1977, western music was basically dead. The Sons of the Pioneers were still performing, but they did not have a major label recording contract and were viewed more as a nostalgia act than as a current, vibrant part of the music industry.

Seminal figures in western music like Bob Nolan, Eddie Dean, Jimmy Wakely, Ray Whitley and others were living in retirement or semiretirement in California, all but forgotten. Some of the early performers like Tex Ritter, Tim Spencer, Lloyd Perryman and Johnny Bond had passed away. Roy Rogers and Dale Evans were still somewhat active in the entertainment field but Gene Autry was more involved in running a baseball team and his business empire than in being a singing cowboy.

There were no western festivals featuring western music, no circuit for a performer to tour, and no recognition for western music from any trade organizations. The Western Music Association did not exist. A tiny spark of western music was kept alive by the chuck wagon groups and dude ranches that invited guests for a few days or a week or so and during the visit might serenade them with some western songs by a campfire.

The "outlaw" movement—Waylon Jennings, Willie Nelson and the boys—dominated that era in country music. Their idea of being a cowboy was that of a fiercely independent cuss doing as he pleased (and they wore black hats). There were some songs that mentioned cowboys—the most famous being "Mamas Don't Let Your Babies Grow Up to Be Cowboys" by Waylon and Willie—but the cowboy who wore a white hat, fancy clothes, and sang of the beauty and romance of the West wasn't around.

The members of Riders in the Sky seemed like an unlikely source to lead a revival of western music; the three original members all grew up in Michigan far from the cactus and sage of the West. Two newer members grew up in Tennessee and North Carolina and the three core members who became Riders in the Sky were steeped heavily in folk, bluegrass and old time country music. Their newest member grew up in Chicago saturated with polka music. If you were going to bet on who would lead the revival of western music in America, it's doubtful you would have laid your money down on these guys.

The beginning was rather inauspicious as well: a thrown together group of three musicians on a Monday night in a little bar in Nashville to substitute for another singer who'd come down sick. That performance—a small step for entertainment, an even smaller step for western music—occurred on November 11, 1977, at Herr Harry's Phranks 'n' Steins. The three musicians were Doug Green, Fred LaBour and Bill Collins.

At the time, LaBour and Collins were working on the road in Dickie Lee's band and Green was a researcher and historian for the Country Music Foundation. "Windy Bill" Collins soon dropped out and was replaced by "Tumbleweed Tommy" Goldsmith on guitar; Paul Chrisman—known as "Woody Paul"—joined on fiddle.

Douglas Green still played bluegrass but had come to love and cherish western music with a passion. Fred LaBour, who had only been vaguely aware of the Sons of the Pioneers before he moved to Nashville, first heard a Bob Nolan song when Green performed it. Woody Paul was a fiddler whose taste ran off in a number of directions—none of them towards western music—while he was earning a PhD in physics. Joey Miskulin, who became a fourth Rider about eleven years later, performed polka music with Frank Yankovic.

Riders in the Sky (photograph by Jim McGuire, courtesy of Riders in the Sky).

That first performance by the group that came to be known as Riders in the Sky (they got their name about a month later off a Sons of the Pioneers album named after that Stan Jones' song) was like putting a match to a gas cloud for Douglas and Fred. Green felt like a dream had come true and he was ready to charge ahead with more western music performances, while Fred thought, *America will pay to see this.*

The group began playing at a small club in Nashville, Wind in the Willows, on Tuesday nights and they soon developed a cult-like following along with their stage show. Here they did their first radio drama—written by Tumbleweed Tommy—worked on their between-songs repartee and honed their harmonies.

Although there were immense financial struggles during their first couple of years, good things kept happening. They recorded their first album for Rounder, *Three on the Trail*, which was released in 1980. At an appearance in Austin, Texas, Terry Likona, from *Austin City Limits* saw them and decided to book them on that show. In January 1981, the appearance was broadcast, giving them their first national exposure.

In June 1982, they became members of the Grand Ole Opry—after appearing 26 times on that program. In March 1983, they began their TV show on TNN, *Tumbleweed Theater*, which ran for five years (although the Riders taped the program for only three years). After the TV show ended, they began a radio show for National Public Radio (NPR), *Riders Radio*

Theater. With the introduction of that show, they received a major label recording deal with MCA. The Riders taped their radio show from 1988 until 1995, then began taping *Riders Radio Theater* TV specials for TNN. They also did a number of *specials* for TNN, including several Christmas shows.

During the 1991–1992 TV season, their kid's show, *Saturday Morning with Riders in the Sky*, appeared on CBS. The show was not renewed, but brought them more attention as well as an appearance at the Macy's Parade on Thanksgiving, which was televised. For about 15 years (1983–1998) they appeared regularly on TNN in their own shows, Rider's specials, or shows like *Nashville Now, Star Search, Tennessee Outdoors,* and *Country Cooking*.

The Riders continue recording and touring (they have done around 200 appearances a year since around 1980) and have released over 25 albums. It is difficult to have a long-term career in the music business; those who have long careers are the exception, not the rule. But the Riders have been at the top of their game for over 30 years—and counting.

You can be "western" by birth, by location, or by choice. The Riders in the Sky members weren't born in the West and have never lived in the West, but they are western by choice. They might not be "authentic" westerners, but they are certainly authentic entertainers. They have taken the West and dressed it up in colorful costumes, put it on stage, and sung songs by, about and for it. More than any other group in the past 25 years, their name has become synonymous with western music.

Along the way, Riders in the Sky put together a pretty impressive team to help them do what they do. Paul Lohr has played a key role in the careers of the Riders, first as their booking agent, then as their manager and agent. When he began booking them, he decided to pursue performing arts centers instead of clubs. As a result, the Riders are now a concert act for small venues. Although those who book them into a venue often want them back soon, Lohr tries to have 12 to 16 months between dates in a market so the market isn't overplayed. Through the years this strategy has worked, so the Riders have been able to grow their audience and increase their price.

In the past, Lohr booked them as an opening act but, he says, "The Riders never really blossomed as an opening act—country artists want something contemporary—so they never rode the coattails of anyone else." "The comedy aspect is the common thread for creating their broad fan base. Everybody loves to laugh and Riders make them laugh," continued Paul. "Then they sneak in this classic music and it touches a spot." At this point, Lohr sells four different shows on the Riders: their regular show, a kiddie show, a show with a symphony, and their Christmas show. This has managed to keep them fresh for audiences as well as for themselves—they're not doing the same show over and over again, which can burn out an act.

Too Slim is quick to acknowledge his wife, Roberta LaBour "who advances the dates for us and oversees the mercantile and is always there to plug holes. She's helped design the look of our stage shows, helped design the clothes. She won an Emmy for the clothes she designed on our kids show in 1991. She's got an artistic sense and a great comedic sense and that has helped give us a look as well as providing the nuts and bolts of keeping Riders in the Sky on the road." He continues:

"When I try to sum up Riders in the Sky, I think that one thing we've done that separates us from other groups is that there were precious few people doing what we did when we started. We've made it fun for people. I think that with our show, with the good time we have playing the music, that it's a fun experience for people to come and hear us. It's entertainment and it happens to be western music. We can rope 'em in the door and then they realize there's this whole body of great western music which they will then go and check out. We've had so many people say, 'I heard you guys and then I heard some records by the Sons of the Pioneers—have you heard those?' And we say, 'Yes we have.' So people have become aware of this whole cowboy music renaissance that's going on."

Woody also talked about their performances: "A whole lot of our material is developed on stage—the seed will be thrown and then it germinates until you get really sick of it so you get something else. One of the bad things about the kinds of shows we do, most of the time they're only an hour or an hour and ten minutes long, so you try to do your most tried and true material even though it's not always the best. I used to always, between every couple of songs, try to come up with something—stupid or off the wall—to get Slim or Doug going so they could create something."

Slim reflected: "Part of our appeal is that we're accessible." "We're enough of a show biz traditionalist so that we get people in and entertain 'em and expose them to this wonderful heritage of western music. Then, hopefully, they'll continue this heritage and kick it down the trail a couple of more feet. We stand on the shoulders of the giants of the past like Bob Nolan and Tim Spencer and Roy Rogers and the Farr Brothers and Foy Willing and Andy Parker and all the great musicians who have worked in this genre as well as those who continue to work in it today—like the Sons of the San Joaquin and Don Edwards. We owe a great debt to these folks from the past. Patsy Montana, Gene Autry—the list goes on and on. Those are the people who invented what we do and made it possible for us to go on and do what we love to do."

Joey added his thoughts: "What most impresses me about each of the Riders is that each one is not only a fine musician but also a fine stylist. Too Slim has developed a style of bass playing that's all his own. Ranger Doug has developed a style of playing rhythm guitar that is all his own. Woody Paul has a bluegrassy-bebop style of playing fiddle, his banjo-esque fiddle solos are wonderful. The amazing thing is that the end result is what's on everybody's mind—how does this work? Not how does it work for Woody or Joey or Doug or Slim—but how does it work for Riders in the Sky? Everyone is looking out for the whole. When a new piece of material is brought in, the question is always "how does this work with the band?"

Slim took up the thread again: "Joey has become an integral part of the band and has helped us tremendously with his musicality and with his production know-how. He's produced our last records and knows us intimately, probably far more than he would ever need to or care to. He knows what we can do and is never satisfied with what we do—he always wants us to do better and tries to pull out the best performances. Plus he's great on the road. He's dependable to the nth degree and always goes the extra mile. When we thought that three was it, we had not met Joey. Joey knows where to step out, where to stay back, where to add the pad, where to put the dramatic fill and he's just a great musician and it's great to learn from him and play with him every night and learn about music from him."

As for their outfits, "we've all worn so much different stuff," said Woody. "That's part of the fun of having a band that dresses up to play. I didn't realize it at first but then all of a sudden it was like a door opened and I could see where all these guys who were in professional bands wore flashy clothes. Now I'm in a band where I can wear clothes as flashy as I want. That's part of the fun. There's a lot of people who play music just so they can wear those kinds of clothes." Woody continued: "Ever since practically day one with the Riders I've felt that we were successful. To me, those things that happened—like the TV shows and Riders Radio Theater and the Grammy—are just icing on the cake. I always knew that we could entertain and we were good musically and had fun on stage. I've always been very positive and felt successful from the first day with the group."

"After all these years of performing on the road, I've had more than enough applause to last a lifetime," said Ranger Doug: "My ego has long been gratified and if I never perform again I wouldn't miss the applause. But I would miss the music. What drove that 21-year-old guy so hard—well that's hard to remember. I guess, as I try to reconstruct the past, that I was eager to prove that I could more or less do the impossible and found a place I could shine, a place so unlikely and so completely different from my sheltered suburban upbringing that it was like stepping into another world. To take on this other world and succeed in it seems like the grandest twist of fate I could ever pull off. It still seems like a great scam to have pulled off. To have been successful as a cowboy singer given my raising and my limits as a singer and a musician. I couldn't ever have been happier if I had done anything else."

Joey sums it up for all the Riders when he says, "There's no finer and no more satisfying feeling than standing up there with three of your friends and playing the music that you love for people that you love."

The Riders continue to tour extensively. Most nights on stage are high moments as they entertain full houses of fans who have come to see them; many times, these are long-time fans. That can be attributed to the fact that the Riders don't put on a bad show—they perform as hard for 150 as they do for 1,500 or 15,000. That's because first and foremost the Riders are entertainers. To entertain is their love, their passion and their life. The fact that they play western music in their show and promote "the cowboy way" makes them ambassadors of the West and all things western.

For a number of years, the cowboy fell out of favor with American popular culture. There were still cowboys in the West—through their work or through their dress—but the cowboy in the world of entertainment was hard to find. And the singing cowboy was impossible to find. Not that there weren't people dressed up as cowboys singing. Country music singers regularly wear cowboy hats, boots and jeans, although country singers before Waylon and Willie tended to dress in sports coats, slacks and even tuxedoes. But there's a difference between singers dressed as cowboys, cowboys who sing, and the singing cowboys. There are a lot of singers dressed as cowboys and a good number of cowboys who sing. But the singing cowboys in their fancy flashy clothes singing songs of the beauty and romance of the West were gone from the American musical landscape until Riders in the Sky came along.

America owes a big debt to Riders in the Sky. After America had made cowboys antiheroes in the movies—lonesome, ornery and mean cusses in song and relegated to the dust bins of history in everyday life—the Riders walked onstage in white hats and made the cowboy hero come alive again. Their success rejuvenated interest in western music and helped inspired Bill Wiley to begin the Western Music Association in Las Vegas in 1988.

Before Riders in the Sky came along, America had forgotten all about her singing cowboys. Riders in the Sky brought them back and reminded Americans what a source of joy, hope, inspiration, humor, and beauty the singing cowboys and their songs can be. Thanks to Riders in the Sky, western music is now alive and well and the singing cowboy is a hero once again.

SOURCE:

Cusic, Don. *The Cowboy Way: The Amazing True Adventures of Riders in the Sky.* Lexington: University Press of Kentucky, 2003.

27

Flying W Wranglers

Russ Wolfe married a rancher's daughter from Kansas. After Russ came out of the armed services in World War II, he moved to Colorado Springs, where his father-in-law had bought another cattle ranch. Russ cowboyed for his father-in-law, then in 1953 he decided to get a string of horses, invite people out to the ranch, and serve them dinner. For after-dinner entertainment, he hired some local musicians to perform western songs. That was the beginning of the Flying W Chuck Wagon, which celebrated its 50th year in 2002. And that's why the Flying W Wranglers advertise themselves as "the second oldest western singing group" (the Sons of the Pioneers being the oldest).

At the end of the 1953 season, Russ got rid of his horses and concentrated on building his chuck wagon and entertainment. Along the way he constructed some buildings, until a whole western town with museums was in place at the Flying W. Today, during the summer season, about 1,400 people come each night seven nights a week to have dinner and be entertained by western music.

Those first musicians who played "were mostly folk musicians," said Vern Thompson, who's been a Flying W Wrangler for twenty-five years. "Then Russ hired Cy Scarborough, Babe Humphrey, Chuck Camp and Buck Teeter, and they're the real 'originals' for the Flying W Wranglers." These were all musicians dedicated to western music and who lived and breathed the cowboy life. After those men left, they each formed a chuck wagon of their own: Cy Scarborough formed the Bar D in Durango, Colorado, Babe Humphrey formed the Bar J in Jackson Hole, Wyoming, and Chuck Camp formed the Triple C. That's not to say that there's been much turnover at the Flying W. "In 50 years, we've only had 22 members," states Thompson. "And in the 25 years I've been here, we've only had to replace two guys."

Vern Thompson grew up in Texas and left home at 16 to play music. By 22 he'd had enough of the traveling. He'd been in rock 'n' roll and country bands and was friends with Denny Peter, the bass player with the Flying W Wranglers at the time. Denny invited him to join the group when there was an opening and Vern did. Denny wasn't a front man, so when he left Vern took over leadership of the group.

The Flying W Wranglers consist of Vern on guitar and drums, fronting half the show; Scott Vaughn also plays guitar and drums and halfway through the show switches with Vern and fronts the show; the fiddle player is Joe Stephenson; Ronnie Cook plays lead guitar, mandolin, banjo and dobro; and Wes English plays bass. Everybody sings.

"We'll play 330 to 350 shows a year," said Vern. "During the summer season, we play every evening. That season runs from the middle of May until the end of September. Then in the Winter—October, November and December—we'll play two shows each on Friday and Saturday nights. Colorado Springs is a convention town, so sometimes we'll get the convention out to the Flying W and do a show. We do the same thing in the March-April-May time." The group is hard working and rock steady. "In 25 years, I've only missed one show," said Vern. "Scott has only missed two shows, and that's because his son, who played linebacker for Colorado State University, was playing in bowl games."

Although western music had some lean years, the Flying W Chuck Wagon never really did. "I think what really kept us going was that we did family entertainment," said Vern. "More than anything else, I think people want good, clean entertainment and that's what we've always done. We're all Christians and we believe in family entertainment."

The group has done albums for 50 years, which they sell at their performances. They signed with Brentwood Records in Nashville and released a gospel album on that label but continued to produce albums in their studio at the Flying W to release on their own label.

The Flying W Wranglers love what they do. "We've gotten pretty corporate," said Thompson. "We have profit sharing and a retirement account and we play for good crowds every night." The only drawback, said Vern, is that "most people still come here expecting to hear a country band playing. We spend the first 20 minutes of each show convincing folks that we're the real deal and that western music is worth listening to."

The Flying W Wranglers may spend the first 20 minutes winning over the crowd, but at the end of their show there's no doubt they're singing to an audience of converts to western music.

SOURCES:

Green, Douglas B. *Singing in the Saddle: The History of the Singing Cowboy*. Nashville: Country Music Foundation Press and Vanderbilt University Press, 2002.
Thompson, Vern. Phone interview with the author, December 2002.

28

Michael Martin Murphey

"I sorta see myself as C.S. Lewis with a cowboy hat and guitar," said Michael Martin Murphey. "I'm a missionary for the western lifestyle."

He dresses western, he lives western, and he performs western music. In fact, since his *Cowboy Songs* album was released in 1990, Murphey's performances have been overwhelmingly western, in both the songs he sings and the places where he sings them. He has become a spokesman for western music, the western lifestyle and issues affecting the American West. He is bright, well-informed and willing to talk for hours about western music and the West. He is a man who does not give short answers.

The roots of this missionary work of Michael Martin Murphey go back a long way—to Dallas, Texas, when he was six and received a small, plastic ukulele from his grandfather for Christmas. When Michael was 13, his grandfather gave him a Martin guitar; he still has that D-28.

He first performed publicly in the Baptist church but doesn't remember it, although his mother does. However, when he was 11 or 12 he "started playing in junior high school at public assemblies. Then when I was 17, a guy came to me and said he wanted to start a folk music club and wanted me to be the marquee name on it." Murphey agreed and from that came a television show called *Hometown Hootenanny*, broadcast over Channel 8 in Dallas one summer. "They actually paid me to do that," remembers Murphey.

His first "paying gig" was at the Sky Ranch in Lewisville, Texas, where he was a counselor: "I worked as a horse wrangler, taught kids how to ride and entertained on the weekends" playing songs around the campfire, doing "a combination of old cowboy songs and gospel music" like "Do Lord" and "Kum Ba Yah." "I'm still to this day sort of a camp counselor," said Murphey with a smile.

Murphey was deeply involved in his church when he was young. "I was a lay preacher when I was in high school and college," he said. "I would go around and give messages to youth groups and sometimes preach to a regular church group. I didn't think of myself as preacher but I guess that made me a preacher. I considered myself a speaker and I would usually bring my guitar, so my speaking was usually accompanied by my singing. Once in a while I would do something just as a preacher. And that's kinda continued in my life."

After high school, he enrolled at North Texas State University where he had a double major, speech and drama along with English. However, he became convinced he needed a change: "I decided I didn't want to just read the great writers, as much as I wanted to write myself and study them so I could learn to write." This desire to study creative writing led him to move to Los Angeles and enroll at UCLA. "I was really interested in the classical world—Greek and Latin—because, wanting to be a songwriter I understood that the troubadour tradition was one thing you could study to learn to be a better troubadour songwriter," said Murphey. "When I went to UCLA I put together my own major and it was sort of a creative writing focus but designed around songwriting and so I went back to the ancient history stuff and I studied a lot of that too."

Michael Martin Murphey's professional music career began in Los Angeles while he was a student at UCLA. The musical seeds planted back in Dallas, singing folk songs, also took root in California. "It was an era when there were a lot of coffee houses and folk music venues and there was a whole scene of acoustic music and singer-songwriters," said Murphey. "And I gravitated towards that. I didn't gravitate towards rock and pop music, like what was playing at the Whisky a Go-Go on Sunset Strip. I preferred a little club down on Santa Monica called the Troubadour." Murphey was in an early version of the Nitty Gritty Dirt Band as well as the New Christy Minstrels. He also hung out with Michael Nesmith and Mickey Dolenz. "We were all sitting around rehearsing—we were in a band called the New Survivors," remembers Murphey. "Everybody was reading the trades and *Variety* when Mickey Dolenz said, 'Hey, look at this—they're taking auditions for people to be in a TV series with musicians in it.'" Nesmith and Dolenz decided to go but "the rest of us said, 'We don't want to be on some dumb TV show. We want to be Bob Dylan or somebody cool.'"

Out of those auditions, Dolenz and Nesmith both became members of "The Monkees." The Monkees were developed by Screen Gems, and Murphey ended up writing songs for their publishing company. One of his songs, "What Am I Doin' Hangin' 'Round" was recorded by the Monkees and was Murphey's first major success as a songwriter. "What Am I Doin' Hangin' 'Round" was a bluegrass song that Mike [Nesmith] just liked and he talked them into letting the Monkees do a few country songs," said Murphey. "And, boy, they were against it—they were really, really against it. But they went ahead and did it because the guys had a lot of power at that time because they were such big stars. Nobody wanted them to throw a tantrum and walk out of the recording studio!"

Later, the company "tried to put together a western version of the Monkees called 'The Kowboys.' We made the pilot. I was in the four," said Murphey. "It was a copy of the Monkees, only in the Old West and it was cowboy music and country-rock music. We made a pilot and they took it to the networks, who said 'That's the worst thing we've ever seen in our life.' It was pretty God-awful," admitted Murphey.

After the TV show fell through, Don Kirchener, the man behind the Monkees, teamed Murphey with Boomer Castleman to form "The Lewis and Clark Expedition." They had to change their names. "I was Travis Lewis," said Murphey. "We had a couple of albums, toured and had some minor hits. We were kind of a country-rock band—one of the early ones. We had some pop hits." Among those hits from the Lewis and Clark Expedition were "I Feel Good, I Feel Bad," which made the charts in 1967 and "Chain Around the Flowers," which didn't make the charts.

"That whole thing kinda came apart and Boomer and I did a duo for a while and then I just went back to songwriting," said Murphey. "I started going back to Texas once or twice a year and playing some of the coffee houses. I moved up into the San Gabriel Mountains in San Bernardino and fell in love with the mountain lifestyle and determined I never wanted to leave the mountains, no matter where I went. Then in 1970 I broke that rule when an earthquake struck. I had a one-year-old child and I said, 'I'm not going to live somewhere where your house can fall down on your kid.' So I packed up everything, sold my house and moved to Texas."

Murphey said he "picked Austin because I had a little bit of stuff going on there playing a few funky coffee houses. It really wasn't much. But at least you could play your own material there. One night I was playing in the Rubaiyat, a little coffee house that held about 150 people. Bob Livingston played bass for me. A guy walked in, saw the show and said 'Listen, I'm Bob Johnston, Bob Dylan's producer, and here's my card. If you're interested, give me a call.' I said, 'I don't have to give you a call! I'm interested right now.' Then I said, 'Well, what should we do next?' and he said, 'Come to Nashville and we'll make an album.' So that night I went and borrowed my Dad's Buick, and we drove to Nashville and knocked on Bob Johnston's door the next morning. He wasn't home yet so I told his wife that Bob told us to come to Nashville, so here we are! He landed that same afternoon. He had a good laugh because he said he'd never seen anybody act on anything so fast in his whole life."

Johnston took them into Columbia's Studio B and said, "'Let's make a demo with you and your bass player,'" remembered Murphey: "So we sat down and played like 35 or 40 songs in a row, because I'd been doing all this live performing and picking in that format. After I'd finished I said, 'Listen to these and tell me when you want to pick some songs for an album.' Then I asked, 'When do you think that'll happen?' And he said, 'I'll tell you what, I'll do what you just did to me. You've made the album.' I said, 'What do you mean?' He said, 'Well, it's multitrack recording so we'll just overdub everything else. I liked the way you played, I liked the way you sang so we'll just add everything else on the record.' And he did. That was the *Geronimo's Cadillac* songs." In 1972, the single "Geronimo's Cadillac" reached number 37 on the pop charts. The second album was *Cosmic Cowboy* and the third was called simply *Michael Murphey*, all from the Austin days.

Michael Martin Murphey (photograph by Vaughn Wilson from *Tell Me About That Horse*, courtesy of Michael Martin Murphey).

Looking back on his time in Austin, Murphey admits he never quite fit in: I think it was because I'd been in Los Angeles and Southern California and worked with people like Don Kirchener and been around the Monkees and I knew what it was all about to try and get your songs cut. [Also,] I wasn't in the drug thing. I woke up in the morning pretty lucid and could get around. I wasn't any kind of a business genius but I wasn't completely blasted all day long. I was very isolated, very much a man to myself and they used to always kid me and say that maybe I was really a narc and all this stuff."

"Austin started to try and imitate the West Coast as soon as the music scene took off there and that's why I left. I just wouldn't get involved. I got so tired of all that, so I just decided to up and leave and move into the mountains. That's why I left Austin and moved to Colorado."

Murphey's fourth album, *Blue Sky/Night Thunder*, came after he'd moved to Colorado. The album was recorded at the Caribou Ranch and contained the hit single "Wildfire." Murphey had this to say about that song:

"I wrote that back in the late 60s when I was a college student at UCLA. I was writing songs with another guy for a Kenny Rogers project called *The Ballad of Calico*, which was kind of a country-rock opera about a ghost town in the Mojave Desert and—I know this sounds really strange—but I was kind of channeling this ghost town. I lived close to there in California and there was something about that place that got to me. Well, all through the night I was trying to write songs about the West and then this image came to me and it had nothing to do with the town of Calico or this project, but I had a dream and I woke up and I wrote it all down on a yellow pad by my sleeping bag. I was staying with my songwriting partner, Larry Cansler. I went up to his bedroom, knocked on the door—woke up him and his wife—she wasn't too happy about that, but she lived with a songwriter! He got up, came down and sat down at the piano and we spent about another hour writing it. It all sorta came out in one night."

By the time he recorded the *Blue Sky/Night Thunder* album, "I was kinda in a position that a lot of guys get into in this industry. I thought maybe I was on my last album," he said. "CBS was thinking about dropping me as an artist 'cause the previous album hadn't done very well. So I decided I would put on this album songs that down deep I felt good about. I was encouraged to do that by George Briner, who was a product manager with CBS at the time. He said, 'You know, if you're going to go out, go out in flames. Put everything on there that you've ever wanted to do that you never got to do.' So I went to my producer and I played him all these songs and he said, 'Of all those songs the one song I don't feel like you should do is 'Wildfire.'" I said, 'Bob, just compromise with me on this. Let me put this one song on the album and I'll do all the rest of my songs that you pick.' So he picked 'em all and I got to do that one." Radio stations began playing the album cut until it became so popular Columbia released it as a single. It reached number three on the *Billboard* pop charts in 1975.

Beginning in 1976, Murphey became a regular presence on the country music charts, with some occasional crossovers into the pop charts. "A Mansion on the Hill" was his first country chart record (#36), then in 1977 he had "Cherokee Fiddle" (#58). In 1979 he reached #93 with a remake of the old Sam Cooke hit, "Chain Gang," followed by "Backslider's Wine" that same year. He reached #83 in 1981 with "Take It as It Comes," a duet with Katy Moffatt. After this he left the CBS organization and signed with Liberty.

His first releases for Liberty, in 1982, were "The Two-Step Is Easy," which reached #44. This was followed by his first number one record, "What's Forever For?" followed by "Still Taking Chances," which reached number three that same year. In 1983 he had "Love Affairs" (#11) and "Don't Count the Rainy Days" (#9); in 1984 he had "Will It Be Love By Morning?" (#7), "Disenchanted (#12), and "Radio Land" (#84). He switched over to EMI America in 1984 and had two top ten hits, "What She Wants" (#8) and "Carolina in the Pines" (#9). Then he signed with Warner Brothers.

His first single for Warner, in 1986, was "Tonight We Ride" (#26), followed in 1987 by "Rollin' Nowhere (#86), "Fiddlin' Man" (#40) and "A Face in the Crowd," which was a duet with Holly Dunn (#4); then came a number one single, "A Long Line of Love," and "I'm Gonna Miss You, Girl" (#3). The next year, 1988, Murphey had a duet with his son Ryan on "Talkin' to the Wrong Man," which went to number four. This was followed by "Pilgrims on the Way (Matthew's Song) (#29) and "From the Word Go" (#3).

In 1989 Murphey had his last country single that reached the top forty, "Never Givin' Up On Love" (#9), which came from the movie *Pink Cadillac* starring Clint Eastwood. At this point, Murphey was at a crossroads.

The "Class of '89," as it was called, introduced Garth Brooks, Clint Black, Travis Tritt, and—the following year—Alan Jackson to the country audience. Randy Travis was still going strong and Ricky Van Shelton was coming on strong. Alabama, Reba McEntire and George Strait were all doing well—with lots of airplay and selling lots of recordings.

Murphey wasn't in that group. In fact, he wasn't selling many records, and his singles, even those in the top ten of the charts, did not have the impact of songs by Garth, Reba, Alan and others, so he decided to step out and follow his heart. It was a 180-degree turn from where country music was. But it was the right direction for him. "Most of the good moves I've made have come from going back to my instincts, musically, about something that moves me, something I'm passionate about, sticking with it," he said. "The story of my career has been people telling me I shouldn't do things that I really felt in my gut that I should do, going against the grain and then that turning out to be a success. But it's always a battle to get there."

"When I decided to make an album of cowboy songs that I loved, I took that to my record company and they said, 'you gotta be crazy. It'll ruin your career. Nobody wants that anymore.' I told them that my experience playing around the country at fairs and rodeos and honky-tonks where people listened to country music showed they were wearing cowboy hats and were into the cowboy thing. And yet our songs didn't directly address that. So I wanted to go back to the roots and have a cowboy album."

"*Cowboy Songs Volume 1* was my most popular album, best sales of any album I ever put out. Warner Brothers dropped me for a short space until they finally called me up on Christmas and said, 'O.K., we'll make a little concession here. We'll put the cowboy album out and then you go back to being your real self.' And I was kinda playing a little game with them. I said, 'O.K.' They said, 'We're not going to market this thing. It's up to you—you have to get this thing rolling. So I rolled up my sleeves and I dug up every single contact that had anything to do with the West, from *American Quarter Horse* magazine to *Western Horseman* to the western buff magazines like *Wild West*. Everything I could come up with. And I sent a 117-point letter to my manager saying, 'These are the things we should pursue.' He wrote me back and said, 'There's no way we can do half this stuff.' I said, 'Well, just start with point number one and let's just go down the list.'"

"I ended up having a great ally in Ralph Emery," Murphey continued. "He liked Marty Robbins and missed him. I went to him and said, 'This is what I'm doing.' He said, 'You remind me of Marty. I'll tell you what I'm going to do. I'm going to do the first theme show I've ever done on *Nashville Now*. We're going to build a completely different backdrop and set and I'm gonna come out dressed in a western Doc Holliday outfit and we're going to do all cowboy music on the show. And that was how the album took off. We ran an 800 number and the album started selling over the phone. Warner Brothers called me up and said 'We better release a single. And we're going to make a video.' It was *Cowboy Logic*. It just kept on building."

This led to the formation of Warner Western, which introduced artists like the Sons of the San Joaquin, Don Edwards and Waddie Mitchell to a wider public. The idea was Murphey's, but by the time Warner Brothers formed the sub-label he "decided it was not a good idea" because "segregating western music was like putting it in a corner and then it would be ignored by mainstream radio." Murphey's first two *Cowboy Songs* albums received some radio airplay, "but by the time *Cowboy Songs III* came out we had compartmentalized ourselves and radio was ignoring it. I then found myself arguing against something that was my idea."

Musically, Michael Martin Murphey has been influenced from a number of different directions. "When I was a little kid," he said, "I loved all the singing cowboy stuff—Gene

Autry, Roy Rogers, Tex Ritter, Tex Williams and Bob Wills and the Texas Playboys. Flatt and Scruggs—I liked a lot of bluegrass music. Woody Guthrie had a lot of influence. When I was a kid, my uncle gave me a whole bunch of old 78 records that he had in his attic. There was Jimmie Rodgers, Carl T. Sprague, Vernon Dalhart. All this really old stuff. At home we listened to the *Grand Ole Opry* a lot. So I was really influenced by that kind of music. Songs you could play with a guitar and sing. You know, 'The Ballad of Floyd Collins' and all those great old tunes. All those great Jimmie Rodgers songs. All you had to have was a guitar and the ability to yodel a little bit."

Another song that had a major impact on him was Marty Robbins' "El Paso." "Back when I was a kid trying to learn the guitar and looking at maybe trying to write a song, I thought that was a great masterpiece of a song," said Murphey. "And I still do. I like the story songs. I like songs that in a three- to five-minute, seven-minute time period give you a little haiku of life that you can relate to."

Murphey wasn't a big fan of Elvis or the Beatles when they first came out. In fact, he didn't really care much for the pop music that excited his fellow teens and caused them to scream and shout.

When the Beatles first hit America, "I thought they were really, really, really weird," he said. "These guys had kinda girlish looking long hair and there were girls screaming. I was into folk music and Bob Dylan and things that I considered to be socially meaningful. And this was nothing but a teenager teeny-bopper deal like that. That has always turned me off more than it's turned me on. I mean, looking back, I realize that Elvis was a great vocalist and there were some great songs that he was singing, but as far as the phenomena goes, it didn't make me want to go out and buy tight pants and a black leather jacket and swing my hips around on stage. I wanted to sing songs that meant something to somebody. And I guess I'm still the same way.

"The kinds of music I liked were folk music and I was also a big jazz fan. I liked cowboy music, you know, and bluegrass. Roots music, blues. I listed to a lot of Sonny Terry and Brownie McGhee. I liked the thinking man's music, but I also liked the real roots, gutsy deep down kind of emotional music too. But real stripped down. I just loved Lightnin' Hopkins and those kinds of guys. I liked jazz, but I liked small ensembles. I liked Dave Brubeck and a few guys backing him up. I wasn't into the big band jazz. I liked the very cool three or four piece jazz where you could really lock into an individual's ability to take off on a theme and play incredible stuff and it was different every time. Once in awhile they'd capture a magic performance. I listened to all these guys when I was a kid. Charlie Parker, Thelonious Monk."

Since Murphey started WestFest in 1986, he's been a leader in the western revival. There have been high points in the "movement": the publication of the novel *Lonesome Dove*, which won a Pulitzer, the release of the movie *Dances With Wolves*, which won several Academy Awards. And there have been some low points. Murphey looks at it philosophically:

"It goes through cycles," he said. "I think right now it's going back up again dramatically. It seems to be dependent on whether the country wants to adapt a cowboy attitude or not. And right now people are trying to be all-American and they're very conservative again. I was starting to see this before 911. And I think when they're like that, the cowboy logic makes sense. The cowboy way of thinking, which is a simple thing like a man's handshake is as good as a contract. Get a job and do it. If you don't like the job then ride off in the sunset but don't sue your employer for wrongful discharge or employee abuse. When people start thinking like individuals and less like committees, they buy into a philosophy that plays right into the cowboy thing, something they admire.

"This goes back to medieval and ancient things that are deep inside of us and it's almost union, in a sense. There are things deep inside our brains that will not change about territorialism. Once you've crossed over and violated my territory and my standards, I'm going to have to stand up. When people feel like wimps, they don't really do anything about the cowboy thing. But whenever they decide they want to take a stand, all of a sudden that's viewed very much as a cowboy thing. And that's part of the myth. Regardless of whether that's true about the Old West or not, that's part of the western myth and that's how I see the cycle going up and down. Right now it's very strong."

In answer to the question about others following his lead in organizing events similar to WestFest, Murphey answered as follows, "I welcome competition. There has to be a 'scene.' The reason I started Westfest was I like western stuff and I like cowboy music and western art and anything that has to do with the whole western lifestyle. And that really requires there be some kind of a scene. I always saw the western thing not as a fad but as a culture. It's a part of our culture. And it'll always be there—will always be a part of our history whether we want to address it or whether we don't.

"I don't see an end to the growth of it, although it'll always go up and down in cycles. But I think we'll always come back and address our frontier history because we are a frontier nation. We think in terms of frontiers. Whether that frontier is Afghanistan or whether that frontier is space, we are always seeing ourselves as an exploring nation because that's how we started. As far as the competition goes, the more the merrier."

Although Murphey did not grow up on a ranch, he did have cowboy roots that went beyond his love for the singing cowboys. Those roots led him to plant himself in rural areas when he is not performing on the road. "I grew up in suburbia, the middle class, but all my grandfathers and uncles and relatives outside my immediate family were all ranchers and farmers," said Murphey. "And my Dad, being an accountant, often got called in to try and save those guys with some numbers thinking. When tax time came around, you definitely got invited out to the ranches. And my Dad used to ship me and my little brother off to stay at the different ranches in the family every summer. We'd spend all summer. And that's how I fell in love with the rural lifestyle.

"I always knew I was going back. I had to go through living in West Hollywood and all that but once I got something going I moved to the mountains in California and after that, when I moved to Austin, I lived way outside of town on a lake in a rural area. Then I moved to Colorado where it was almost like living in Alaska. There were guys with big beards and axes and chain saws who basically didn't want to talk to anybody. Just wanted to go huntin.' I lived around that and then I moved to New Mexico and I was back around more agricultural rural people and a minority group—Hispanic. Cattle ranchers, sheep ranchers, farmers—almost ninety percent Hispanic and very few Anglo whites down there. I got along with them because I admired their ability to kinda survive off the land and that's what I wanted to do and I just stuck with it because I love it.

"Right now, I live in a log cabin in Red River, New Mexico. I have five neighbors in about a four-mile radius. I'm still kind of an isolationist. I like to live in a rural area. I love farming and agriculture and I love rural people.

"I'm only in one business, continued Murphey. "I'm in the cowboy and western way of life missionary business. There's different ways you can express it. I have a magazine, called *American West* magazine, that I publish with a partner. I have the Westfest events that I do and I have my own record label and I'm the only artist on it and I don't intend to sign anyone else. It's just a thing I'm doing by myself. And I have the Singing Cowboy ranch concept that I started last year and I'm looking at putting that into several different locations. Changing the Red River venue into a Singing Cowboy ranch that adds trail riding and chuck wagon events. These are basically places that are right there in my region. I can tour in a little circuit, because certain times of the year I don't want to get too far from my house and summertime is one of those times. Summertime in the Rockies is just a time when you don't want to leave. You just don't want to leave the high country.

"I have several working ranch operations. The ones in Wisconsin, Red River and Colorado are all horse operations. The one in Kansas is cattle—no horses there."

Can you make a profit with a working ranch these days? Murphey answers a resounding "yes," then explains, "Number one, the next best thing to making money in the cattle and horse business is losing money in the cattle and horse business. In other words, you have to be a romantic. You gotta love it. I've never seen a romantic lose money in the business. I've seen a lot of hard-nosed guys who really thought they were smart lose. 'Cause they're always trying to outsmart somebody and what that really means is, the guys that'll stay in it for a lifestyle because they love it will generally, over the long haul, do pretty well. 'Cause they will work, will hold onto a good animal for a breeding line, they'll do all the right things you should do to be successful.

We live in a fast-moving world where you think Internet on anything and get it done quick. And it's all Chicago Board of Trade and cattle futures and all that stuff. Forget all that! Just get yourself some great animals, put 'em out on great grass, and hold on for 15 years and you'll make money. Everything's fine. Even if a disease comes through and wipes out all your animals, there's protection now. The federal government will come in and compensate you for that. So I really believe that's the key—it's long-term romanticism. The other thing is don't get in over your head. Don't go borrow so much money that, even if you're doing great, you can never pay it all back. That means a lot of times don't buy the land, lease the land. When you lease the land you don't have taxes. It's a one hundred percent write-off on the lease."

Murphey also manages to get involved in other business activities, such as organizing trail rides. "I started a thing last year up in Colorado called the Singing Cowboy Ranch and we take people on trail rides and we take them on overnight camping trips and we play guitar around the campfire at night," said Murphey. "I love that. What we found is that our base audience is adults who want to be kids again. So now I'm looking at doing that in several different locations because it was a real big hit in Colorado. I don't go on every one of these trail rides but it's sorta my operation."

He continues: "For about eight or ten years now I've been outfitting with a couple of different partners in the Rockies, taking people to the Grand Canyon, Yellowstone National Park, Zion Canyon, on different trail rides. I even do one in West Virginia. Because, just personally, I like to get out there. You know, I don't like to just sing about being out there, I like to sing while I'm out there and write about it while I'm out there."

Talking about the future, Murphey said, "We're all gonna end up old and it depends on what you define as broke. I decided that if I have land and I have animals and I have enough capital to be able to grow food, then I'm not broke."

He added this: "I've been up and down in my career. I've invested some money that I've made off of different projects and some things that lost money. But they were always things that had to do with what I love. I've always believed in investing in something that you love."

Murphey concludes: "The best moves I've ever made in my life have been things like that where you just go back to the core of who you really are and you fight for it. And you gotta realize that puts a lot of stress on you. You can really wear yourself out fighting those kinds of battles. But the longer it takes and the harder it is, the bigger the victory."

SOURCE:

Murphy, Michael Martin. Personal interview with the author, February 19, 2002, in Nashville, Tennessee.

29

Ray Price

At the end of World War II, western swing was the popular type of country music, with bands led by Bob Wills and Spade Cooley dominating the juke boxes. But as the Big Band era ended at the end of the 1940s, the era of western swing ended as well—except in Texas, where they kept dancing. During the 1950s Ray Price and his Cherokee Cowboys played those Texas dance halls, mixing western swing with the honky-tonk sound that kept people on the dance floor. Ray and the group embraced the western image, although a bit differently than other acts: the group performed in Indian outfits wearing full headdress during some sets.

Ray Price is a talented, creative man who loved western swing but yearned to grow musically. As the 1960s progressed, Ray embraced the Nashville Sound and moved towards pop oriented arrangements on his recordings. But he never forgot his western swing roots and today Ray Price, in his 80s, performs a mixture of western swing, honky-tonk and "countrypolitan"—he's had big hits in all facets of country music—during his concerts.

On December 7, 1941, 15-year-old Ray Price was an usher at the Majestic Theater in Dallas, Texas, when the news came that the Japanese had bombed Pearl Harbor. "That whole theater came alive," remembered Ray, who wanted to enlist but was too young. Ray's brother, who was in the National Guard, had been activated in 1938 and was sent to the Pacific theater. Ray turned 16 about a month later but needed his mother's consent to join the armed forces, and she wouldn't hear of it. Ray quit school when he was 16. "Like a lot of kids, I thought I was real smart and didn't need to know anymore," he reminisced. Finally, in 1943, when Ray was 17, his mother gave her permission for him to join the Marine Corps. In the meantime, he landed a job at Dallas Aviation learning how to be an aviation mechanic.

In August 1943, Ray went to Marine Corps boot camp at Camp Pendleton in San Diego and took basic training. After basic, Ray was assigned to a naval base in Norman, Oklahoma, where he was in training to become a machinest mate. But on the obstacle course, Ray had an accident. "I fell about 25 feet and landed just flat on my back," he remembers. "I spent about a year in the naval hospital in Oklahoma but they never could find out what was wrong. They didn't know anything about your back at the time, they just knew it was holding your head up. Turns out it was the rings in my spine that was injured."

Ray spent three years in the Marine Corps during World War II but never left the United States. "I went back to active duty twice but my back was killing me," he said. "The way the bunks were in the Marine Corps it was just a wire with springs on it and when you laid down your back just bulged down and my back just couldn't handle it." Most of Price's squadron were sent overseas and "only three of us in my division made it through the war.

The rest didn't. I hated it because I wasn't up front with the rest of them. But as I got older, I was glad I survived. But I have mixed feelings about it." Still, Price admits, "I'm proud that I was a Marine. It taught me to pay attention."

In February 1946, Ray Price was discharged from the Marine Corps and went to work in a steel mill in Dallas as a lathe operator. The Germans had been defeated in May 1945 and the Japanese surrendered in August, which meant the end of World War II. It took a while for war production to wind down but the government soon cancelled the orders for 9 mm shells—Price was part of the group making those—and he was transferred over to the machine shop.

"After working the machine shop all day, you came home and you looked like a coal digger—just black all over," remembered Ray. "I didn't like it so I thought I might for once do something smart and instead of quitting school I'd go back to school." Ray enrolled in Dallas High School with about 20 other vets and after about three months the principal, Mr. Allen, informed them of a new test devised by the United States Armed Forces Institute which allowed students who passed that test to receive a high school diploma. This was the General Education Development Testing Service, later known as the GED, which at that time was limited to veterans but since 1963 has been available to anyone.

Ray passed the test and then enrolled at North Texas Agricultural College in Arlington (now the University of Texas, Arlington) and studied veterinary medicine on the GI Bill. He lived in an empty naval barracks about ten miles away as the Government allowed vets to stay free of charge at the facility, which wasn't being used, and in that group of former servicemen were some musicians. This encounter with those musicians changed the life of Ray Price.

Noble Ray Price was born on January 12, 1926, in Peach, Texas, a community that no longer exists. Peach was in Wood County, which also had Perryville, with a population in the twenties in 1930.

In 1930, when Ray was four years old, his parents divorced; his mother could not take living out on a ranch and moved to Dallas, where she landed a job designing jackets and coats for Niemen-Marcus. Ray's Dad stayed in Perryville, raising cotton, corn and some livestock. During the school year, Ray lived in Dallas with his mom; during the summer months he lived on the 190 acre ranch with his Dad, working in the fields and with the animals.

Ray's mom married an Italian who was in the garment business. During Ray's early years they moved to Forrest City, Arkansas, and opened a clothing factory, but in the late 1930s the factory burned down. Ray's stepfather loved opera and during their time in Arkansas, Ray remembers attending several operas in Memphis with his parents. Ray always had a good singing voice and his stepfather insisted he take classical singing lessons. In fact, the first record Ray Price ever owned was an opera aria.

While he was in college, Ray Price and his buddies had been going to Roy's House Cafe in Dallas. Roy was "an old showman," remembered Price, "and he had a lot of buddies he'd worked with who were in a band or who would stop by and get onstage. He'd call people up out of the audience to sing. It was a fantastic show." Ray sang at Roy's, boosted by friends who'd heard him sing around the barracks. He performed songs like "Nobody's Darling but Mine," which was popularized by Gene Autry, and Hoagy Carmichael's "Stardust."

In 1950, Dick Gregory, a guitar player, had written some songs and one day he asked Ray if he would sing them for a publisher. Ray agreed. "I don't know why he asked that 'cause I don't know if I sang in front of him or not," said Price. The first publisher they visited "wasn't really interested in any newcomers so he sent us to another publisher," said Ray. That second publisher was Jim Beck, who owned a recording studio in Dallas on Ross Avenue:

They were recording some radio shows for Jim Jeffries, who was very popular in radio at that time, [said Ray] and they was taking a break so he said, "Go ahead and sing a song." So I sang the songs and Hank Thompson was there—he was doing some radio shows with Jim Jeffries for the Texas Radio Network—and everybody was listening to me. Then Jim Beck, who owned the studio, said, "Look, we gotta go back in and make these radio shows and we don't have any time to talk with you today so come back tomorrow." The guitar player got real excited and I said "sure," so we went back the next day and before I sang they introduced me to a fellow named Arthur Ganong from Bullet Records and he had a contract for me. That's how I got in the music business.

That was in January 1950, and Ray recorded two songs, "Jealous Lies" and "Your Wedding Corsage," which were released on Bullet Records. They didn't chart, but they did get Ray some attention in and around the Dallas area and led to him performing on the *Big D Jamboree*.

The *Big D Jamboree* began as *The Texas State Barn Dance* in 1946; it was formed by radio personality Uncle Gus Foster and Slim McDonald, a Dallas club owner. They held the Jamboree at the Sportatorium, a wrestling arena owned by Ed McLemore, who served as a coproducer on the radio show. The show was broadcast over KLIF and hosted first by disc jockey Big Al Turner, then by John Harper. In late 1947, the show was broadcast over WFAA and rechristened *The Lone Star Jamboree*. When the show switched to KRLD in the fall of 1948, it was renamed the *Big D Jamboree*. Johnny Hicks of KRLK was the original host and coproduced the show. The Light Crust Doughboys, the group originally formed by W. Lee "Pappy" O'Daniel whose original members included Milton Brown and Bob Wills, served as the house band for a number of years. The Doughboys were billed as the Country Gentlemen when they were the house band.

The studio where Ray Price first recorded was located at 1101 Ross Avenue in Dallas. It was owned by Jim Beck, who was born in Marshall, Texas, on August 11, 1916, and had apparently learned electronics on his own. Don Law, who signed Ray Price and produced him for about twenty-five years, used Beck's studio in the early 1950s, recording more sessions there than in Nashville and New York.

During World War II, Beck served in the army and gained experience with broadcasting and recording techniques. After he returned to Dallas in 1945, he built his first recording studio, which did contract work for the army. Beck joined KRLD as an announcer and through their connection with the *Big D Jamboree* he began to appreciate country music.

Beck borrowed money to open his studio on Ross Avenue, where Lefty Frizzell made his first demo recordings. Frizzell recorded his early hits at Beck's studio, which brought Beck and the studio to the attention of Don Law, head of A&R for Columbia. Beck had an excellent studio and recorded sessions for Bullet, King, Imperial and Decca as well as Columbia. In addition to Lefty Frizzell, Fats Domino recorded there. Because of the quality of the studio and Beck's expertise, it seemed likely that Dallas might become the center for recording country music in the early 1950s.

Troy Martin worked for the publisher Peer International, whose catalogue included all the Jimmie Rogers songs as well as the songs from the Carter Family, like "Will the Circle Be Unbroken." Troy heard Ray on the *Big D Jamboree*, was impressed with his talent and lobbied Don Law, head of A&R for Columbia Records, to sign him. Law resisted, according to Ray, about 21 times before Troy made his final pitch.

"Don, I want to talk to you about Ray Price," said Martin, and Law replied, "Troy, if you don't stop pitching that man to me I'm going to throw you out of this damned hotel room." Troy asked, "You sure?" and Don replied, "Yeah." Then Troy said:

> Well I just want you to know because Paul Cohen is coming to Dallas tomorrow to sign Ray to a record deal with Decca." [With that statement, Law] picked his head up a little bit, and the next

day he was in Dallas and they called me in and said, "we're going to do a session" and signed me to a contract. At the session the next day I was setting in the studio playing the guitar—I never was very good at it—but I was playing the guitar and singing a song and this nice fellow walked in and never said a word, just asked, "You're Ray Price, aren't you?" and I said, "Yes, sir" and he said "I'm Paul Cohen and I'm with Decca Records and I've come to sign you to a contract." I said, "Gee, Paul, I don't know what to tell you—but I've just recorded for Columbia Records." And he went through the ceiling. Then he went out and signed 17 acts, if I remember right, so Don couldn't get any more of them because he didn't want to lose any more acts to Columbia.

Ray Price recorded his first songs for Columbia, produced by Don Law at the Jim Beck Studio in Dallas on March 15, 1951. On that date he recorded four songs: "If You're Ever Lonely Darling," written by Lefty Frizzell; "I Saw My Castles Fall Today," written by Rex Griffin; "You've Got My Troubles Now," written by Ray; and "I Get the Short End Every Time," written by Elsie Johnson. The last song was never released by Columbia.

In May, Price was back in the Beck studio and recorded one song, "Hey La La," written by Leonard McBride; McBride's wife sang harmony on the songs. That was actually a thrown together "fooling around" session that was recorded, even though no session had been planned at that time. On August 6, Price went into the Dallas studio and recorded two Rex Griffin songs, "The Answer to 'The Last Letter'" and "Beyond the Last Mile," a song written by Stu Davis, "Until Death Do Us Part" and "Heart Aching Blues," credited to Price, Jimmy Fields and Ray Pulley.

In fall 1951, Troy Martin brought Ray to Nashville to appear on the *Friday Night Frolics*, which were held in WSM's Studio C. The show was sponsored by Duckhead Overalls and starred Hank Williams that evening. Ray walked into the radio studio, was introduced to Hank and, as they shook hands, "It was an instant liking of each other," according to Ray. Hank insisted Ray go with him the next day to Evansville, Indiana, where Hank had a show.

The next day, Hank brought Ray over to his house to meet his wife, Audrey, "and of course he and his wife were fussing and that embarrassed him" but then they set out driving to Evansville. On the drive up Hank told Ray that he needed a hit song and he would write him one. The two bounced ideas back and forth as they drove but nothing clicked until Ray suggested the title "Weary Blues." That lit a spark and Ray and Hank wrote that song in the car, although only Hank's name appears as a writer "because of publishing complications," said Ray. When they got to Evansville, Hank called Ray up onstage to sing "Weary Blues." "I didn't even remember the words," said Ray. "He made me start it about five times—I'd stop it and then start it—we was just having a ball."

When they got back to Nashville, Ray had to return to Texas where he was appearing at a club in Kilgore. Back in Dallas, Ray entered the Beck studio on October 16 and recorded "Weary Blues (From Waiting)" and three other songs: "I Made a Mistake and I'm Sorry," "We Crossed Our Heart" and a song written by Carl Smith, "Your Heart Is Too Crowded."

Red Foley was the host of the "Prince Albert" segment of the *Grand Ole Opry*, which was broadcast over the NBC network. Foley's wife died in November 1951, and Hank Williams was scheduled to host the show in Foley's absence. Hank called Ray in Texas and reached him on a Thursday; the show was scheduled for Saturday night but there was a rehearsal on Saturday morning. Hank wanted Ray to be his guest on the show, but Ray had to play that night in Kilgore and then had only one day to get to Nashville for the rehearsal. "I didn't have a hit, I only had one record out," said Ray. "So the idea of being on a network show scared me. But I went up there and broke every traffic law to get there. I threw the rubber off four tires getting to Nashville and I don't mean that figuratively."

The *Grand Ole Opry* was the biggest and best country music show on radio in the early 1950s; it was a star-maker where new acts played and became nationally known. Ray Price still has the tape of Hank Williams introducing him on the *Grand Ole Opry*. Ray's success on the Opry that night in November 1951 and his connection with Hank Williams convinced him to move to Nashville in January 1952.

Ray and his wife moved into a house on Natchez Trace in Nashville. They lived upstairs and Hank, who was going through his divorce with Audrey, lived downstairs. Ray remembers that Nashville "was heated by coal then." The city sits in an area surrounded by hills, like a bowl, and "if you came in to town from the hills you couldn't even see the town—smoke was all you could see." In Texas, the heat came from natural gas, so Nashville looked "kinda spooky" in the winter when Ray arrived.

About a month after he moved to Nashville—on February 8, 1952—Ray Price recorded his first Nashville session at the Castle Studio in the Tulane Hotel. Castle was Nashville's first major recording studio. It was started by three engineers from WSM—Aaron Shelton, Carl Jenkins and George Reynolds—in 1946. The studio, named from WSM's logo, "Air Castle of the South," was a key to the growth of Nashville as a recording center. The engineers first began recording sessions at a studio at WSM, whose offices were located at Seventh Avenue North and Union Street in the old National Life Building. The increase in demand for the studio's services led the engineers to move to the Tulane Hotel on Church Street between Seventh Avenue and Eighth Avenue North where the engineers set up in a dining room.

Before Ray Price recorded there, the studio had recorded "Chattanoogie Shoeshine Boy," a hit for Red Foley in 1950, and "You Win Again," a hit by Hank Williams in 1952. On the Ray Price session, which featured Hank's Drifting Cowboys members Don Helms on steel, Howard "Cedric Rainwater" Watts on bass, Jerry Rivers on fiddle, along with Sammy Pruett and Chet Atkins on guitars, and Ray Price, who played the guitar while he sang. The four songs they recorded were "Talk to Your Heart," "I Know I'll Never Win Your Love Again," "I Lost the Only Love I Knew," and "The Road of No Return."

"Talk to Your Heart" was written by Ray and C.M. Bradley, but because of "publishing complications" the cowriter with Bradley was listed as Louise Ulrich, which was Price's mother. He recorded another Hank Williams song, "I Lost the Only Love I Knew" (cowritten with Don Helms) and a song he cowrote with Helms, "I Know I'll Never Win Your Love Again." "The Road of No Return" was credited to C.M. Bradley alone.

Six days later, on Valentine's Day, Price was in the Castle Studio again with the same lineup except that Owen Bradley on piano replaced guitarist Chet Atkins. Three of the songs, "Talk to Your Heart," "I Know I'll Never Win Your Love Again" and "The Road of No Return" were repeats from the previous session, indicating the label was not satisfied with the takes. The fourth song, credited to C.M. Bradley and Louise Ulrich, was "I've Got to Hurry, Hurry, Hurry."

Ray Price and Hank Williams lived in the Natchez Trace house for about six months before Ray moved out. Williams' divorce was "tearing him up" and Hank, who was not drinking when Ray and his wife moved in, was soon drinking heavily. "I couldn't take it any more," said Ray. The last time Ray saw Hank was when Ray was driving into Nashville and saw Hank at a service station "standing out there beside his Cadillac," Ray remembered: "He threw up his hand and I pulled in. He asked me where I was going and then I asked him, 'Where are you going?' 'Back to Shreveport,' he said and he kinda laughed when he said it. 'You wanna come?' And I said, 'Naw, I better not.'"

In July, Ray Price was in the Castle Studio and recorded four songs, "You're Under Arrest (For Stealing My Heart)," "Move On in and Stay," "Won't You Please Be Mine (Just for Today," which was written by Buddy Killen, and a Hank Williams song, "I Can't Escape from You." On September 16, Ray recorded the Slim Willett song, "Don't Let the Stars Get in Your Eyes" and "My Old Scrapbook" at the Castle Studio.

Just before Christmas, Hank Williams called Ray and asked about his plans for Christmas. Ray told him he was going to spend that time with his mother in Dallas and invited Hank to come. Hank agreed, but later decided to spend Christmas with his mother in Alabama. During that conversation, the two singers discovered they would both be performing in Ohio on New Year's Day, about 50 miles apart, and they agreed to meet for lunch. That lunch never happened. Sometime between about 10 o'clock on New Year's Eve and the morning of January 1 and somewhere between Knoxville, Tennessee, and Oak Hill, West Virginia, Hank Williams died in the back of his Cadillac while his driver drove towards Akron, Ohio.

After Hank died, Ray spent almost two years touring with Hank's old band, the Drifting Cowboys, as his backup group. And then one night in Grand Junction, Colorado, Ray said, "This fellow came up to me and he was very complimentary. He said 'Ray, I want you to know that you sound more like Hank every day.'" That compliment struck a disturbing chord deep inside Ray Price: "When you play with Hank's band, that's how you are going to sound." On the drive back to Nashville, Ray told steel guitarist Don Helms and fiddler Jerry Rivers, "Boys, I love all of you but I can't do this. It isn't any good sounding like Hank because I want to sound like me." The band members "all agreed and we split friends," said Ray. But then he had to find another band.

Ray had worked a couple of dates with a group in Houston, the Western Cherokees, who played western swing. Ray brought them to Nashville to be his backup group. The group got its name, The Cherokee Cowboys, when Ray brought them to the *Grand Ole Opry* for the first time. George D. Hay, known as the "Solemn Old Judge," was the founder and announcer of the Opry. As he and Ray stood in the wings, with Hay ready to introduce the group, he asked Ray their name. Ray replied they didn't have one and Hay countered that they needed one and "you'd better hurry—you've got five minutes" before the introduction. "So I combined the last two names—the Drifting Cowboys and the Western Cherokees and came up with Cherokee Cowboys," said Ray. "And it stuck."

In August 1954 there was an announcement in the *Pickin' and Singin' News* that Ray Price's new band, the Cherokee Cowboys, comprised Bernie Annett, piano; Bob Heppler, fiddle; Jimmy Bigger, steel guitar; Jimmy Dennis, drums; Pete Wade, guitar, and Tommy Hill, rhythm guitar, front man and master of ceremonies. A picture of the new group in an issue two weeks later showed the band dressed as Indians with full headdress; Ray was dressed in a western outfit—the shirt had fringe—and wore a cowboy hat.

Tommy Hill soon left the Cherokee Cowboys and Blackie Crawford replaced him, then in the fall of 1954, Blackie Crawford left and Price hired Van Howard (real name Howard Vandevender) to sing tenor harmony and play guitar. Howard, born March 1, 1929, in Grady, New Mexico, began singing on KICA in Clovis, New Mexico, when he was a teenager. In 1951 he went to Jim Beck's studio and met Beck and Tillman Franks, who got him a spot on the *Louisiana Hayride* in Shreveport, playing guitar and singing harmony. Howard also worked for the First National Bank in Shreveport (back in New Mexico he had worked as a bank teller). Howard recorded some sides for Imperial Records, a result of his success as a harmony singer on Slim Whitman's records for that label, but none hit.

In the fall of 1954, Lefty Frizzell was looking for a road band when he appeared on the *Louisiana Hayride*. Howard and some of the Hayride musicians—pianist Floyd Cramer, steel guitarist Jimmy Day, drummer D.J. Fontana, fiddler Bill Peters and bassist Chuck Wiginton—joined Frizzell on a tour of the West Coast. As soon as Frizzell's tour ended, Lefty's manager, Al Flores, left and went to work for Price. Van Howard was booked for two weeks in Tucson, Arizona, and during that booking Flores called Van Howard and told the singer that Blackie Crawford, who fronted Ray's shows, had left and asked if Howard wanted to join the Cherokee Cowboys, starting with a job in San Antonio.

Van Howard joined Price's group and fronted the show as well as emceed. The harmony vocals came around after Price and Howard sang together in impromptu sessions. Howard was a great harmony singer, his tenor ringing out on the choruses of Ray's songs, which led to the first recording session when Van Howard sang harmony with Ray Price for the first time. The session, held at Jim Beck's Studio in Dallas on April 27, 1955, and produced by Don Law, produced five songs: "Sweet Little Miss Blue Eyes," "The Way She Got Away," "Let Me Talk to You," "Call the Lord and He'll Be There," which was written by Van Howard, and "A Man Called Peter." The last two songs, both gospel numbers, were recorded because Ray felt he needed some gospel songs for his audiences when he played in the South.

In 1956, there was a great deal of turmoil in the country music industry. In August 1955, a directive had come from Jack DeWitt, president of WSM, that WSM employees who had outside business had to either relinquish their business in order to stay with WSM or leave WSM for their outside business. The three WSM engineers who owned Castle Studio decided to give up their studio and stick with WSM. The Tulane Hotel, where the studio was housed, was razed and Owen Bradley built a studio in a house on 16th Avenue South—which later became known as "Music Row"—and constructed a Quonset hut in the rear, where the bulk of the country recording was done for Decca, Columbia and Mercury in the coming years. Bradley's business was helped by the fact that Jim Beck died on May 3, 1956, which meant that Dallas no longer competed for country recording business after that time.

In January, Elvis Presley, a new artist just signed to RCA, went into a Nashville studio and recorded "Heartbreak Hotel" and several other numbers. "Heartbreak Hotel" would be number one on the pop charts for eight straight weeks. During that year Elvis became a musical as well as cultural phenomenon; he sold ten million records, appeared on the TV shows of Jimmy and Tommy Dorsey, Milton Berle, Steve Allen and Ed Sullivan, toured constantly and starred in his first movie, *Love Me Tender*.

In Nashville on Thursday, March 1, Ray Price went into the Bradley Recording Studio and recorded three songs: "Crazy Arms," "You Done Me Wrong," and "Wild and Wicked World." The first song on that session, "Crazy Arms," written by steel guitar great Ralph Mooney in 1949, would be a life and career changer for Ray Price. According to Price, Bob Martin, a disc jockey in Tampa, Florida, gave him a record of "Crazy Arms" by a female singer and told him he thought the song would be good for him. Ray took the song into the studio and recorded it with a "shuffle beat," the beginning of the "Ray Price sound."

Although Don Law is listed as producer on that session, Price notes "Don was in England and Troy Martin of Peer International Music and I did the album." Martin served as Price's manager at that time. On guitars were Jack Pruett, Pete Wade, Van Howard and Price. Jimmy Day was on steel guitar, Buddy Killen played bass, Tommy Jackson was on fiddle and Floyd Cramer played piano. Putting a 4/4 beat to the record was "absolutely, my idea," said Price, who added he was "playing a lot of dances and the 4/4 beat was perfect for that; that's why I did it." The "sound" of that record defined the Ray Price sound for a number of years. "All I was trying to do was find my own sound," said Price. "And I found it on that cut." "Crazy Arms" entered the *Billboard* country chart on May 26, 1956, and landed in the number one spot on June 23, bumping Elvis out of the top spot. The song stayed number one for 20 consecutive weeks and on the charts for an amazing 45 weeks.

The year 1956 marked the start of a series of years when country music suffered at the hands of rock 'n' roll. Radio stations axed their Saturday night barn dances, and disc jockeys increasingly played rock 'n' roll records; so country music had trouble getting on radio. Lack of exposure on radio meant a decline in demand for live appearances for country acts, who saw their incomes go down as fewer people wanted to see their shows.

But the rock 'n' roll juggernut never really affected Ray Price like it did other country acts. First, his bookings were primarily for Texas dances and the Texans kept dancing during the rock 'n' roll craze. "I had been playing dances in Texas all along," said Ray. "And I knew I could work and that's what we did—we played dances. At that time, that was most of our bookings." Ray kept getting played on jukeboxes and had hits with "My Shoes Keep Walking Back to You" (number one for four weeks), "City Lights" (number one for 13 weeks) and "The Same Old Me" in the 1950s.

For the next seven years—until around 1963—Ray Price and the Cherokee Cowboys was one of the best, most consistent acts in country music. The musicians were all top-notch, the band was tight, and they had a cocky self-confidence knowing they were the best in the business. Their shuffle sound was perfect for the Texas dance halls, and that's where they primarily played. If they played in the East, the audience generally sat and watched, but out west, they cut loose with dance music, playing song after song after song, varying between Texas two-step numbers and waltzes.

The Cherokee Cowboys attracted some of the best musicians in country music, although simple companionship and the ability to put up with the crazies of life on the road seemed to be part of their hiring criteria as well. Van Howard, who was Price's harmony singer, left in 1958. According to Ray Price, "Van married the niece of Webb Pierce and when we did 'Crazy Arms' Van sang tenor and his wife said, 'Honey, you're the one that made that record.' So Van came to me and he wanted half credit on my records. I said, 'I'll tell you what I'll do. If you want half of the credit, then you find the song, you pay the musicians, and you tell me for sure it's gonna be a hit, then I'll give you half.' He said, 'I can't do that' and I said, 'Well, don't let the door knob hit you in the butt.' And so he left. And I did all the tenor singing after that."

The departure of Van Howard meant there was an opening in Price's band for a guitar player and harmony singer who sang tenor. And that led Price to meet a young fireman in Amarillo, Texas, named Roger Miller and audition him for the job. Ray remembers: "Somebody said 'there's a guy who plays fiddle and sings at the Fire Department.' So we got hold of him and he came out to audition and I liked him right away. But he made a mistake—he wanted to play fiddle right off the bat and when he got through he said, 'How'd I sound to you?' and I was trying to keep from laughing—he wasn't a great fiddle player—so I said, 'Can you sing and play guitar?'" Roger made light of the situation—"Well, I messed that up" or something along those lines—and then played the guitar and sang for Price, who hired him. Price recorded Roger's song, "Invitation to the Blues," which was a top three country hit in 1958.

When Johnny Paycheck decided to leave the group to pursue a solo career, Price asked Willie Nelson, who was writing for his publishing company, if he could play bass. Nelson replied that he did, remembered Price, "and somehow or other he got into Paycheck's uniform—it was a little tight—but he did it. We went out for 10 or 12 days and when we came back Willie said, 'I bet you didn't know that I couldn't play bass' and I answered, 'The first night!' But then we became friends and he worked for me a long time."

"Crazy Arms" was not only a professional shot in the arm for the career of Ray Price—a career-defining recording—but it also led him into a successful business venture with music publishing. The song was published by Pamper, a small company in California that was owned by Claude Caviness, whose wife was the first to record "Crazy Arms." After Price recorded the song, Caviness "came to Nashville and wanted to know if [Price would] be interested in going in with him in a publishing company." Price countered that if Caviness allowed Ray to pick someone to run the company, and give him a third, then he would become a partner.

The man Ray had in mind was Hal Smith, who played fiddle in Carl Smith's band. Hal's wife, Velma, was an excellent guitar player who did recording sessions in Nashville. "I saw potential in him as a manager of a business," said Ray, "and I thought I could be partners with him. Claude Caviness lived in California and I thought California was too far away for a partner so I went to Hal and said, 'If you'll come with me, I'll give you a third of the publishing company.' He thought about it, agreed and we started with 'Crazy Arms.'"

For eight years, Pamper was the Cinderella company among Nashville publishers. Its office was in Goodlettsville, about 20 miles from Music Row, which Price considered "an advantage because you didn't have all the street traffic. It was a little too far out and hard to find. If you want to do business, then they're going to come to you and they're serious." It was also close to Price's home in Hendersonville near Lake Hickory.

The company hired Hank Cochran to write and pitch songs. Cochran found a young Texas songwriter named Willie Nelson and signed him to the company. Harlan Howard brought songs to the company too and Pamper became known for their stable of hit songwriters. After eight years, Price was forced to sell the publishing company because "we kinda had a misunderstanding. I was president of the company and they got mad at me because I did one of Paycheck's songs and I told 'em when we formed the publishing company 'I'm not going to do songs just because they're in our publishing company if they're not worth a damn.' So they agreed to that. Well, when I did Paycheck's song, things got crossways and it was just a misunderstanding."

The end result was that Pamper was sold to Tree Publishing, which was a huge break for that company. Tree had published "Heartbreak Hotel," "Green Green Grass of Home," by Curly Putman, and Roger Miller was signed to them. Miller hit with "Dang Me," "King of the Road" and a batch of hits in 1964 and 1965. But Pamper Music was the first major acquisition of a rival publishing company.

In 1960, Price recorded an album of western swing as a tribute to Bob Wills. The following year he recorded the *Night Life* sessions, which featured Willie Nelson's song. "Night Life," a jazzy blues piece on an album that leaned more towards the audience that frequented an uptown dinner club rather than a Texas honky-tonk.

Ray Price had always loved the lush sound of an orchestra and used a 17-piece string section on his *Faith* album, a collection of gospel songs released in 1957. "That got me on a track that people liked strings," said Price. "So I began adding strings down through the years to certain songs. I was experimenting until I did 'Danny Boy.' That's when I went all out, and that's when it all hit the fan." Actually, he had recorded another lush ballad, "Make the World Go Away," which was a hit on the country charts in 1963. The song, written by Hank Cochran, came out before "Night Life" later that year. In 1965 Eddy Arnold—who said he'd never heard Ray Price's version—recorded "Make the World Go Away" and it was an international hit.

This was the era of the "Nashville Sound," where violins replaced fiddles, the piano replaced the steel guitar, and the country music establishment sought respect by appealing to the American middle class. Country music was the counter to the counterculture in the 1960s and yearned for respectability as a music that could be enjoyed by the country club set. Country artists got rid of their rhinestone outfits and wore sports coats, suits or tuxedos.

In 1965 the FCC issued an edict that required radio station owners who owned both an AM and an FM station to program each outlet differently; prior to this time, station owners would simulcast on both stations. Radio was dominated by AM programming, which increasingly meant that pop/rock was broadcast. There were few FM radios and FM stations had long been ignored. However, with demands from entrepreneurs to open up new stations, the government elected to open up the FM spectrum.

In the late 1950s and into most of the 1960s, country music had to depend on "crossovers" to achieve big success and big sales. That meant that a record had to get played on pop/rock radio in order to be successful. However, as pop/rock increasingly moved over to FM, the AM stations programmed country as an alternative. As the number of radio stations that played country music grew, it became easier for a country record to remain in the country format in order to become a major hit. But that was not the case back in the mid–1960s. Country performers often felt like second-class citizens during the 1960s. They were not considered "cultured" or "sophisticated" to the country club set and weren't "hip" to the youngsters who loved rock 'n' roll. Many Americans looked down their noses at country music and country performers. The music was considered "white trash" and the performers themselves were seen as hicks, rubes and hillbillies. It is no wonder that so many country performers fought back by putting on a tuxedo and singing with an orchestra; they had to prove they were as talented as pop artists and as worthy of respect as any other artist in any other genre. I hated how they used to talk about us," Ray said. "How they said we all sang through our noses and that kind of bullshit."

Ray Price had a series of great steel guitar players in his band. Don Helms came from the Drifting Cowboys, then Jimmy Day and Buddy Emmons joined. Emmons remembers that "Danny Boy" was a favorite song for steel guitar players to perform and that he had played it a number of times during the opening segment before Ray Price took the stage.

Price remembers that each year at the Disc Jockey Convention, held in October in Nashville when the record labels put on a big bash for radio DJs and booking agents, he used to close the Columbia Records show. He did "San Antonio Rose" for several years, then one year he decided to close with "Danny Boy" "and they went wild." "For three years I did that," said Price, "and everyone was telling me 'you've got to record Danny Boy.' So I took 'em at their word." He first recorded "Danny Boy" on February 22, 1966, at the Columbia studios with his basic rhythm section but was dissatisfied with the result, so that session was shelved. On April 14 he recorded it again—again as the last song on the session—but that version, was not released either.

Price recorded five more sessions before he tackled "Danny Boy" again, this time on November 8. Just prior to that session, Price met with Clive Davis, president of the label, who was down from New York for the DJ convention, and spoke to him about "Danny Boy," saying, "If you let me record it the way I want to record it, I promise you a number one song.'" And he looked at me like I was crazy but I was so successful he could hardly deny me. So he said, 'Go ahead and do it.'" "I talked to Grady Martin and Don Law and I told Don, 'I want to use a lot of strings,' said Price. "I'd done it on a *Faith* album years before with Anita Kerr and it seemed to have worked well so Don said, 'Anything you want to do.' That was the great thing about him. So I talked to Grady Martin, who I always had as leader for my sessions because he was really fantastic and I said, 'Do you know anybody who can write charts?' He said, 'Yeah, I've got a young fellow who just wrote something for Brenda Lee that I think you'll like.' He said 'I'll bring him up to the office tomorrow and so you can meet him,' and that's how I met Cam Mullins."

Price gave Mullins free rein to "write charts like [he] always wanted to write them but wasn't allowed to," although Price admits he wondered why Mullins said that. Mullins came back with a full orchestration for "Danny Boy" and the musicians filled Columbia's Studio A for that session, which was cut "live," the strings playing along with the rhythm section as Ray Price sang the song. On March 25, 1967, "Danny Boy" by Ray Price entered the country chart and climbed to number nine; it entered the pop chart the same time and rose to number 60. It was a groundbreaking song that broke Ray Price's heart and almost broke his career. He was accused of selling out by the country fans, and Texas audiences hissed and booed when he played that song.

"They really raked me over the coals," said Ray. "I'll never really understand it because nobody reacted that way when Eddy Arnold, Marty Robbins and Glen Campbell went outside the country sphere. But they landed on ole Ray. I was convinced then that the music had reached a point where it had to go off in a new direction. Thank goodness it finally went the way it did. Now, you can play country music in Las Vegas, New York, or Hollywood and nobody thinks anything about it. But it wasn't that way back then. And I'm convinced they never would have been able to do that with the old sound."

In 1968, Price left Nashville and moved back to Texas. He was going through a divorce, his father was gravely ill, he was sick of the criticism and controversy over "Danny Boy" and "all my work was out west," he said. He had a bitter taste about how he had been treated as a member of the *Grand Ole Opry* as well. That bitterness went back to 1956, when Jim Denny, manager of the Opry, was fired for having an outside company (Cedarwood Publishing). However, Denny had booked a major tour of Opry acts with the folks who were marketing Marlboro cigarettes and the Marlboro executives elected to remain with Denny after he had been fired. This caused the Opry to have a showdown with the acts scheduled to perform on that tour: stick with the Opry or get fired.

The Opry told Price that if an act went with Denny on his Marlboro tour, they'd never be with the Opry again. Price believed them and gave up the tour—and a substantial amount of money. But a year or so later, some of those acts returned to the Opry lineup. Price felt that he had been betrayed. "That's when I discovered what WSM meant," said Price. "Wrong Side of the Mississippi!"

Ray Price sold his house in Nashville and bought a ranch in Perryville, about 100 miles east of Dallas and about 25 miles from his Dad. He raised thoroughbreds, fighting cocks, and racing pigeons and he invested in some real estate. He continued to record an album a year for Columbia but stayed off the road for about seven years. He said of Texas, "It's my home and I always wanted to come home. It cost me money to do it and it almost ruined my health, not to mention my career. But I woke up one day and said, 'I just don't have to live in Nashville.... I'm going home and that's the way it's going to be.' I got tired of letting other people run my life."

In 1973 he established his own management and booking agency in Dallas; his wife, Janie Mae, ran the organization. As the years rolled by, he realized how much he missed performing, the applause, hanging out with musicians, playing music and singing for crowds. And so he went back out on the road, but this time he wore a pinstripe suit and toured with a 16-piece orchestra. He remembered that Tony Bennett had made pop hits out of Hank Williams songs and reflected that country music "was shutting out a lot of people. I thought country music was good enough for anybody and I wanted to go after a much broader base of people." He felt that way back in the 1960s when he recorded "Danny Boy" and he still felt that way. And he also had some big hits under his belt by this time to prove his point.

It was probably in late 1969 and Ray was working a gig at the Starlit Club in Odessa, Texas, when he received a tape of a song Fred Foster sent him. Foster owned Monument Records and Combine Publishing and produced the big hits of Roy Orbison. The tape was given to a musician who handed it to Ray. Between sets, Ray listened to the song on an old Wollensack reel-to-reel tape player and invited his band to listen to it after they finished their second set. The song was "For the Good Times" and it was written by Kris Kristofferson, a struggling songwriter in Nashville. Price reportedly told the band after playing the song for them, "This is the best song I'll ever record and the biggest one I'll ever do. And they listened to it real polite like, but musicians are funny. They didn't know whether they liked it or not."

The song had originally been recorded by Bill Nash for Mercury Records. Jerry Kennedy had produced the record and Cam Mullins had written the orchestration. When he found out that Price was going to record the song, Mullins asked Kennedy if he could use the same arrangements for Price that he used for the Nash session. Kennedy agreed because the Nash song was stuck in the can and it didn't look like Mercury was going to release it.

"The strangest thing about that record was that I had the biggest fight because Columbia was promoting the other side of the record," remembered Price. "They were pushing 'Grazing in Greener Pastures' while that great song was laying on the back of it. It took me six months to get them to turn it around. And then somebody helped me—some cat put on the back page of *Billboard* magazine 'Wayne Newton has the pop hit on "For the Good Times." Ask anybody at Columbia and, when he saw that, Clive Davis went through the roof, told 'em to turn the record over and bring it home." "For the Good Times" by Ray Price entered the *Billboard* country chart on June 27, 1970, and reached number one; it entered the *Billboard* pop chart about two months later—on August 29—and reached number 11.

Ray Price had apparently met Kris Kristofferson when the songwriter worked as a janitor at Columbia Studio, where Ray recorded, but Ray did not remember him. But he certainly remembered "For the Good Times" and he wanted to hear more Kristofferson songs. That led him to record a complete album of Kristofferson songs. On that album was "Help Me Make It Through the Night," which Price wanted as his next single; however, he had to wait until "For the Good Times" ran its course and that song stayed on the country chart for six months. During that time, Sammi Smith released "Help Me Make It Through The Night," which became a huge hit for her.

Price released "I Won't Mention It Again," written by Cam Mullins (which was number one for three weeks on the country chart), before he released Kristofferson's "I'd Rather Be Sorry," which reached number two on the country chart. He continued to record smooth, urban countrypolitan music after that; "She's Got to Be a Saint' and "You're the Best Thing That Ever Happened to Me" were number one songs in 1972 and 1973, respectively.

Ray Price continued to record and tour. In July 2009 he had an operation to remove a large part of his intestine because of colon cancer. But he went back on the road several months later and, although he was frail and a bit weak physically, his voice was still strong. In concerts he performs with a Cherokee Cowboy lineup supplemented by a seven-piece string section. Today he walks slowly to the middle of the stage and stands there and sings; he doesn't move much physically but his vocals move the audience.

He has few regrets, although he still carries a few memories from back in the days when things weren't so good. He still looks for songs that "fall on the real side. That's the side where there's something there, it's a real story, well put together and not something that's just put up there to flash but instead is something that makes me think of something in my life. And if I like it, I do it. I've been lucky, finding 'em. So I keep trying. It's just hard now with current talent like it is. I think it's the worst case of age discrimination from radio; they won't play the older artists." Great songs and great performers are timeless but radio is for the here and now. Fortunately, people don't need a radio to hear Ray Price. All they have to do is find a CD, a download or go to one of his concerts. For 50 years, the voice and music of Ray Price have been an American treasure that is timeless. There is no doubt that as the ages roll by the legacy of Ray Price will endure.

SOURCES:

Ayres, Tom. "Ray Price Remembers Hank Williams, or, How Old Hungry Gave Ray Price His Start." *Country Music*. 5, no. 12 (September 1977): 41–44, 56.

Copper, Daniel. "Being Ray Price Means Never Having to Say You're Sorry. *Journal of Country Music*. 14, no. 3 (1992) 22–31.

Hickey, Dave. "Hillbilly Heaven: The Solution According to Ray Price." *Country Music*. 5, no. 6 (March, 1976): 40–43, 61–64.

McCall, Michael. "Don't Let the Stars Get in Your Eyes: Ray Price's Singular, Six-Decade Journey Forsakes Shine for Substance. "*Journal of Country Music* 25, no. 2, 30–43.

Morthland, John. "Ray Price: Back on the Road." *Country Music*. 8, no. 7 (April 1980): 44–46.

Price, Deborah Evans. "Ray Price Remembers Good Times with Hank Williams." *Close Up*, August/September 2009, 38–39.

Price, Ray. Personal Interview with the author, October 2, 2009, in Nashville, Tennessee.

"Ray Price Signs Up 'Cherokee Cowboys' of Houston, Texas." *Pickin' and Singin' News*, August 14, 1954, p. 1.

"Ray Price's New Band, Picture of Cherokee Cowboys." *Pickin' and Singin' News*, August 31, 1954, p. 1.

30

Marty Robbins

There are three trails leading into the town called "Western Music." The first is that of the songs of the old-time cowboys from the 1800s, which were mostly derived from British folk songs; the second is the songs for the singing cowboys in the movies, like Gene Autry and Roy Rogers, which were mostly pop songs with lyrics about the West written by the pop songwriters who wrote for Broadway and the movies; and the third trail is that of country music, which has used the cowboy and the West to define a visual image of a country singer as well as reflect the fact that it was once known as "country and western" music.

The music of Marty Robbins reflects all three of those trails. He grew up in the West and that heritage was deep inside him. His first musical hero was Gene Autry, and the singing cowboys had a huge influence on his life. He spent his life in country music with a career based out of Nashville.

Martin David Robinson and his twin sister, Mamie, were born near Glendale, Arizona, on September 26, 1925. The Robinson family of nine children lived in poverty. When Martin was 12 years old, his parents divorced; he saw his father only twice after this and, after he left Arizona and moved to Nashville, lost track of him completely and never tried to find out anything about him.

Robinson was a rowdy kid who disliked school. In the eleventh grade, he dropped out and joined the navy; there wasn't much else for him to do. It was 1943, the middle of World War II, and the Service needed young men. Robinson knew that if he joined the army, he'd probably see a lot of action and get shot at, so he chose the navy and served in the South Pacific. At this point, the man who would later change his last name to Robbins had no idea what he wanted to do with his life; but the seeds had already been planted for him to sing western songs, although he didn't realize it at the time.

"My grandfather was my first audience," Robbins told reporter Joan Dew. "He was a great old character—Texas Bob Heckle—and he could tell the best stories and biggest lies of any man I ever knew. He was a real medicine man. Had his own show. They ran him out of Texas for stealing horses. He told me he was a Texas Ranger; that was just one of his big lies. But they were all great stories. So we had a deal. He'd tell me a tale of the Old West, and I'd sing him a song. I did that from the time I was three or four until he died when I was six."

Texas Bob Heckle "wasn't educated, except by life, but he was pretty wise, and I could tell by the words he used that he was a pretty intelligent man," said Robbins. "The stories he told me were cowboy stories that he had heard around the campfire. That's how the stories were related back in the early days of the American West. I guess one rider would take it from one camp to another. But when my grandfather would tell me these stories, he would make me believe that I was really there."

"My grandfather could write," continued Robbins. "But he could not write melodies, so my brother would write melodies about my grandfather's stories. In reality, my grandfather inspired me to be a cowboy." Texas Bob died at the ripe old age of 86. Shortly after that, Robbins saw his first musical hero, someone who remained a major influence on the singer's career. "I ... started seeing Gene Autry in movies," said Robbins. "I thought, *What a perfect life—riding the open range, singing cowboy songs*. I didn't want to play the parts, I wanted to live them. But since I couldn't live those days, I've done the next best thing. I sing about them."

In the navy, Robbins was assigned to an amphibious landing craft as a deckhand; two years later he mustered out with the rank of seaman first class—not a lot of advancement for a young man. "I just enjoyed life," said Robbins, who joined the "52–20 Club" after his discharge, which meant that veterans received $20 a week for a year. When that source of income dried up, Robbins returned to Glendale and took a variety of jobs—working on a construction gang, driving a milk route, then an ice route, working as an electrician's helper and a mechanic's helper and on an oil rigger, all in a six-month period. "I couldn't find out what I wanted to do, except I knew I didn't much want to work," confessed Robbins.

Robbins learned to play the guitar in the navy but admits he "wasn't very good." However, there was a guitar player in a band in Phoenix who had an electric guitar and amplifier—something Robbins did not have—and who was "less good" that Robbins, so Marty took over his position. Talking about those early days with writer Bob Allen, Robbins stated, "I tried a lot of things and then I got a job playing music. I didn't sing at first, I got a job as a guitar player. But right then, I knew it was what I wanted because it fit my hours. I didn't have to go to work till 9 o'clock at night and then got off at one o'clock. That was great!"

"I just couldn't believe that a person could make a living doing that," continued Robbins. "I had never paid any attention to that. I knew people could make good money making motion pictures, but I didn't think or know that they could make any money singing, unless they were in motion pictures. I didn't know you could make a living singing in a club. But when I found that out, I knew that was what I wanted." Performing at the club, called Fred Cares, Robbins "did everything: western songs, songs by Perry Como, Johnnie Ray, Ernest Tubb, Roy Acuff, Eddy Arnold—everybody's songs." Robbins performed with a three-piece group in a club that "couldn't hold more than 100 people. But every night, for three years, it was packed."

He landed a radio show on KPHO in Phoenix, where the station manager was Harry Stone, who had just left WSM and the *Grand Ole Opry* to take the job in Arizona. Stone was also program director for the television station that had been launched in Phoenix. Harry Stone was a desperate man; he needed to fill the air time on the new TV station and he was 15 minutes short, so he approached Robbins.

"One day the program director said, how would you like to do some television?" remembered Robbins. "And I said, 'Oh, no, I don't want to do any television!' Because it scared me. He said he needed me that afternoon, that they had a fifteen-minute spot where they didn't have anything to run. I kept telling him I couldn't do it. He finally said, 'Well, if you want to keep your radio job, you'll do it.'"

The show featured just Robbins and his guitar on live television. "I didn't have any fancy clothes to wear on TV, just a cowboy shirt and Levis," said Robbins, who kept his early morning radio show (which he taped) and continued to perform each evening at clubs. "I had a list of songs in my shirt pocket, and all I could do was look in my pocket and say, 'and for my next song, I'd like to do.'" I must have done ten songs in fifteen minutes, because

I couldn't talk. But it went over big ... so he made me do fifteen minutes a week by myself from then on."

One day Little Jimmy Dickens came to Phoenix to play a show date and went on Robbins' show to plug the date. When Robbins performed, Dickens "just stood there and listened. There wasn't even an audience in the studio, just a little space in front of the camera," said Robbins. "At that time, I had a lot of confidence, but I didn't know how I was going to get on record, or become a recording star, but I never worried about it because I had found what I wanted and I didn't really see how I could fail. So I knew that it had to happen, that there could be no other way."

Dickens recommended Robbins to the executives at Columbia Records, who signed the young artist. Robbins then moved to Nashville and joined the *Grand Ole Opry* in early 1953. His first hit was "I'll Go on Alone," which reached number one in early 1953. Several chart records followed, and then in 1956 he hit with "Singing the Blues." The following year he hit with "A White Sport Coat (And a Pink Carnation)" and "The Story of My Life." This was the era of Elvis and early rock 'n' roll and Robbins found himself regarded as a teen idol.

But he could never settle for doing the same thing over and over. "Styles change, and new trends come along all the time in this business," Robbins told Laura Eipper of the *Nashville Tennessean*. "If you've got talent, you'll last. Do you know what talent really is? It's being able to please the people. What I do isn't anything great, but I have a good time and so does the audience. Knowing how to please people is the only secret for staying in the business. You've got to change, stay flexible, or you're gone. Some people record the same stuff over and over again. I can't do that. I have to do what I do, and that means all kinds of different material."

Robbins recorded Hawaiian songs for his second album, *Songs of the Islands*, then turned his eyes towards the West. "I never read about the West until I moved to the South," Robbins told interviewer Bob Allen. "It was all there and I never thought that much of it until I moved away from it. That's the reason I wrote a lot of the cowboy songs, because I wanted to be in the West, but Nashville was where I had to be." Robbins decided to do an album of western songs.

"The gunfighter ballads weren't inspired from motion pictures or other songs," Robbins told reporter Mark Dawidziak. "When I moved to Tennessee, I really missed the West, so I read a lot of western stories and early West books. I wrote songs on *Gunfighter Ballads* like "El Paso" and "Big Iron" because of that. And there was nothing like it on the market." The biggest hit off that album would be his song "El Paso."

"I had always wanted to write a song about El Paso," Robbins told Allen Le Grand for an article in *El Paso Today*, published in March 1975. "I was born and raised in the Southwest with Mexicans and Indians. The first time I ever heard 'El Paso,' I said to myself, *That must mean the pass.* Ever since then, I wanted to come here."

"I went through El Paso one Christmas and wanted to write a song ... but I never really had any ideas what I would write—until I wrote it," continued Robbins. "At that time, there were a lot of waltzes and pop songs going around. I thought about writing a song called the 'West Texas Waltz,' then the 'El Paso Waltz,' but nothing came of it. The third time he drove through El Paso, that song came to him. "I finally stumbled onto the song as I was driving and it just kept coming out, flowing like a nice easy river," said Robbins.

Robbins told interviewer Bob Allen that he wrote "El Paso" "in one day when I was driving through. I never even got it down on paper until I got to Phoenix the next day. But I couldn't forget it because it was like a movie and I didn't know how it was going to end. I must have been going 100 miles an hour when I ended it. It was so exciting. Once I got started, it just rolled out. I never changed a word"

The song was long—over four minutes—and Robbins' recording label did not want to release it as a single, although they consented to let him record it on his album *Gunfighter Ballads and Trail Songs*. It soon proved popular on radio and was released in 1959, where it reached number one on the *Billboard* charts and remained there for 26 weeks. The third Grammy for country music was awarded to "El Paso," written and sung by Marty Robbins. "If I never had another hit after 'El Paso,' it wouldn't have mattered," said Robbins. "That song made it for me."

Ironically, he wrote a follow-up to "El Paso" entitled "Felina," which he felt was "better than El Paso—it was sheer poetry." At first, he was unable to finish the song, so he decided to fly to El Paso for some inspiration. He checked into a hotel, looked out of his window at the mountains "and had the song finished in just a few minutes." The problem was that the song was eight minutes long, so it never received any radio play and was confined to an album cut.

In August 1969, Marty Robbins suffered a heart attack; he had bypass surgery in January 1970 when that procedure was still experimental. In 1975 he came close to death in three auto races that year and suffered his second heart attack, which led to his second open heart surgery and second bypass.

Although Robbins remained interested in the West and western music—he wrote a western novel and starred in several western movies—his attention increasingly turned towards NASCAR and auto racing. He competed in NASCAR races for a number of years and, at the end of his life, racing was his passion, although he continued to record, perform and tour. In 1976 Robbins had a hit with "El Paso City" and the following year a hit with "Adios Amigo."

In 1982, doctors convinced him to enter the hospital for another heart surgery before he had another heart attack, which they felt was imminent. The week after Thanksgiving, Robbins entered the hospital with surgery scheduled for December 6; however, while he was there he suffered a massive heart attack and died on December 8, 1982.

SOURCE:

Robbins, Marty. File, Frist Library and Archive, Country Music Foundation, Nashville, TN.

31

Johnny Cash

Johnny Cash's young son, John Carter, asked his Dad, "Who's Gene Autry?" when the name of the famous singing cowboy came up in the Cash home. This inspired Cash to write and record a song, "Who's Gene Autry?" in answer to his son's question. In that song Johnny Cash told of going to a Gene Autry movie and that when ole Gene was riding across the silver screen he rode along with the cowboy because ol' Gene was an inspiration to a poor boy from the country. Gene Autry and the singing cowboys were a huge influence on Johnny Cash during his growing up years but that song was not the first time Cash dealt with cowboys, Indians and the West in his songs and recordings.

Johnny Cash was born in Kingsland, Arkansas, on February 26, 1932, two years before Gene Autry went to Hollywood. The Cash family moved to the Dyess Colony in northeastern Arkansas, located on the Tyronza River, when young J.R., as he was known, was three years old. The Cash family grew cotton on their farm there for almost twenty years. This is where Johnny Cash lived for fifteen years, from 1935 until 1950.

Johnny Cash's mother, Carrie Cash, bought him his first guitar from Sears, Roebuck and tried to teach young J.R. to play; but he wasn't really interested and later sold it to another local boy. Instead, J.R. sat at the kitchen table every evening and listened to the radio. After he graduated from high school in 1950 Cash moved to Michigan, where he worked in an auto assembly line for two weeks. Then he worked in an oleomargarine factory back in Arkansas before he enlisted in the air force that summer.

Cash received his basic training at Lackland Air Force Base in San Antonio, Texas, then received training as a radio operator before he was sent to Landsberg, Germany, where he monitored air traffic. In the air force Cash began to play and sing country songs with some friends in the barracks who called themselves the Landsberg Barbarians. From this group, Cash was inspired to learn to play the guitar, so he bought a cheap German model for about $5 and a friend taught him chords. Soon, Cash began to play the songs of Hank Williams, Jimmie Rodgers, Ernest Tubb, Hank Snow, the Carter Family, Roy Acuff, and other country stars. He also began writing songs. After his discharge from the air force in the summer of 1954 Cash returned home, married Vivian Liberto, whom he had met in San Antonio during basic training, and moved to Memphis. He obtained a job with Home Equipment Service as an appliance salesman and enrolled in the Keegan School of Broadcasting on the GI Bill to learn how to be a radio announcer. Cash was never a very good salesman but the owner, George Bates, liked him and asked what he really wanted to do. Cash replied he wanted to be a singer and Bates agreed to sponsor a fifteen-minute radio show on Saturday afternoons over KWEM in Memphis. The show lasted two months.

By this time Cash had joined Luther Perkins and Marshall Grant, two mechanics who worked at a Chevrolet dealer, and they began practicing at Cash's home. John Cash had a burning ambition to hear himself singing on the radio and was aware of Sun Records in Memphis, which was owned by Sam Phillips. Cash dropped by Sun Records several times in hopes of meeting Phillips, but each time the owner was either out of the office or unavailable. Finally, Cash met Phillips and asked for an audition. Phillips invited him in and Cash sang a number of songs. Phillips may have recorded two songs with just Cash and his guitar, "Wide Open Road" and "You're My Baby" (sometimes known as "Little Woolly Booger") at this meeting. Later, Cash came back with Luther Perkins and Marshall Grant and they auditioned.

At this point the group viewed itself as a gospel group and Cash wanted to do gospel material. But Phillips was reluctant to record gospel because Sun couldn't sell it; the future for the record company was in what became known as rockabilly. Cash quickly realized this and during this audition, probably in early 1955, Sam Phillips recorded the group doing "Folsom Prison Blues," "Hey Porter," "Wide Open Road," "Two Timin' Woman," "Port of Lonely Hearts," and "My Treasure," all of which Cash had written, and "Goodnight Irene," which had been a big hit in 1950 for the Weavers. In February Cash, Grant and Perkins went back into the studio and recorded "Wide Open Road," "Cry, Cry, Cry" (which Cash had written since the last session), and "Hey Porter." The last two were the two sides of his first single release from Sun. "Cry, Cry, Cry" entered the *Billboard* country chart on November 26 and reached number 14.

Cash began performing in and around Memphis and recorded more songs for Sun. His second single for Sun, "Folsom Prison Blues," but it was his third single, "I Walk the Line," that catapulted him to stardom. The song was recorded on April 2, 1956, and released in May. It entered the *Billboard* charts the following month, moved to number one and stayed on the charts for 43 weeks, selling well over a million singles. In 1958 Cash left Sun and began recording for Columbia Records.

Johnny Cash's first session for Columbia was on July 24, 1958, and his second was two weeks later, on August 8. On his third session, August 13, he recorded "Lead Me Father," "I Still Miss Someone," "One More Ride," "Pickin' Time," and "Don't Take Your Guns to Town." The last two songs are interesting because on "Pickin' Time" Cash wrote about his childhood and life back on the farm. On "Don't Take Your Guns to Town," Cash wrote a western movie.

The whole country was crazy about TV westerns from the mid–1950s to the early 1960s and Johnny Cash was certainly part of this. Television westerns began to blossom in 1955 when *Gunsmoke* and *Life and Legend of Wyatt Earp* were introduced; they joined other westerns *The Lone Ranger*, *Sgt. Preston of the Yukon*, *Adventures of Rin Tin Tin* and *Gene Autry*—on regular network programming. In 1956 *Broken Arrow*, *Adventures of Jim Bowie*, *My Friend Flicka*, and *Dick Powell's Zane Grey Theatre* were added. The top western shows during the 1956–57 season were *Gunsmoke*, which finished at seven, and *Adventures of Wyatt Earp*, which finished at 18 in the overall TV ratings.

The beginning of the heyday for the network television westerns in prime time was 1957–58. During this season the overall TV ratings showed *Gunsmoke* at number one, *Tales of Wells Fargo* at three, *Have Gun, Will Travel* at four, *Life and Legend of Wyatt Earp* at six, *The Restless Gun* at eight; *Cheyenne* at 12, *Dick Powell's Zane Grey Theatre* at 21; and *Wagon Train* and *Sugarfoot* tied at number 23. Clearly, the western began to dominate TV during the 1957–58 season.

The success of television westerns continued during the 1958 season when, in the overall ratings, *Gunsmoke* was number one, *Wagon Train* was two; *Have Gun, Will Travel* was three;

The Rifleman was four; *Maverick* was six; *Tales of Wells Fargo* was seven; *Life and Legend of Wyatt Earp* was ten; *Dick Powell's Zane Grey Theatre* was 13; *The Texan* was 15; *Wanted: Dead or Alive* was 16; *Cheyenne* was 18; and *Sugarfoot* finished at number 21 in the overall ratings.

In 1959 westerns on the networks in prime time included *Colt .45, Maverick, The Lawman, The Rebel, The Alaskans, Riverboat, Cheyenne, The Texan, Tales of Wells Fargo, Sugarfoot/Bronco, Life and Legend of Wyatt Earp, The Rifleman, Laramie, Wagon Train, Johnny Ringo, Dick Powell's Zane Grey Theater, Law of the Plainsman, Bat Masterson, Black Saddle, Rawhide, Hotel de Paree, Wanted: Dead or Alive, Have Gun, Will Travel, Gunsmoke,* and *Bonanza.* During this 1959–60 TV seasons, in overall TV ratings *Gunsmoke* and *Wagon Train* were tied at two; *Have Gun, Will Travel* was three; *Wanted: Dead or Alive* was nine; *The Rifleman* was 13; *The Lawman* was 15; *Cheyenne* was 17; *Rawhide* was 18; *Wyatt Earp* was 20; and the *Zane Grey Theatre* was 21.

During the 1960–61 season and the 1961–62 season, western shows took the top three spots in the overall ratings: *Gunsmoke, Wagon Train* and *Have Gun, Will Travel* in 1960–61 and *Wagon Train, Bonanza* and *Rawhide* in 1962–63. In addition, *Rawhide* and *Bonanza* finished in the top twenty in 1960–61 and *Rawhide* finished in the top twenty in 1961–62. In the 1962–63 season no western finished in the top three, but *Bonanza* finished at four, *Gunsmoke* was 10, *Rawhide* was 22 and *Wagon Train* was 25. This is significant because the 1962–63 season marked the end of the heyday for the TV western, although a western (*Bonanza*) was consistently rated at number one or in the top ten throughout the 1960s.

The period 1955–1963 was the era of the TV western, but the network shows were only part of that. In addition to the network fare, there were syndicated shows such as *The Cisco Kid, Annie Oakley, Tales of the Texas Rangers, The Sheriff of Cochise, The Range Rider, Buffalo Bill, Jr., The Adventures of Champion, Pony Express, Union Pacific, Brave Eagle*, and numerous others. But perhaps the key to understanding the influence and success of TV westerns during this time period is to look at the westerns which appeared on Saturday morning TV. This list includes *Acrobat Ranch, Adventures of Champion, Adventures of Kit Carson, Rin Tin Tin, Annie Oakley, Broken Arrow, Buffalo Bill Jr., The Cisco Kid, Cowboy Theatre* (old western moves), *Fury, Gene Autry Show, Howdy Doody, Hopalong Cassidy, Junior Rodeo, Lash of the West, The Lone Ranger, Red Ryder, The Rough Riders, The Roy Rogers Show, Sergeant Preston of the Yukon, Steve Donovan, Western Ranger, Tales of the Texas Rangers, Tim McCoy, Wild Bill Hickok*, and *Yancy Derringer.*

Johnny Cash grew up watching "B" westerns and singing cowboys in Arkansas; one of his heroes was Gene Autry. "Don't Take Your Guns to Town" tells the story of a young man between grass and hay who strapped on some guns and headed to town; his mother warned him not to take his guns to town but the young man thought he was big enough to handle any situation. Well, the inevitable happened: he got into an argument with an experienced gunslinger and was shot down. That song was included on an album of folk-oriented songs that included "I Still Miss Someone," which was originally a poem written by Johnny's brother, Roy. "Frankie's Man, Johnny" is a rewrite of the old folk ballad "Frankie and Johnny," while "Run Softly, Blue River" is a rewrite of the Robert Burns classic, "Flow Gently, Sweet Afton."

On March 12, 1959, Cash recorded "I Got Stripes," "You Dreamer You," "Five Feet High and Rising," "The Man on the Hill," "Hank and Joe and Me," "The Caretaker," "Old Apache Squaw," "Don't Step on Mother's Roses," and his own arrangements of "I Want to Go Home," "The Great Speckled Bird," and "My Grandfather's Clock." This session perhaps sums up Johnny Cash and gives a preview of his entire career. "Five Feet High and Rising" is a story from his childhood based on the Mississippi flood of 1937, which occurred about a month before Cash's fifth birthday.

"Hank and Joe and Me" is a western song about men searching for gold in the desert; "Old Apache Squaw" shows his early interest in Indians; "I Got Stripes" shows his interest in prisons and prisoners; "My Grandfather's Clock" and "The Great Speckled Bird" are both old songs considered "folk," and "The Great Speckled Bird" is a gospel number. These songs came out on an album, *Songs of Our Soil*, which was his first "concept" album.

On Cash's album *Ride This Train*, recorded early in 1960, Cash developed the idea of a "concept" album further. On this album he composed "Dorraine of Ponchartrain," "Going to Memphis" (a rewrite of an old folk song) and "When Papa Played the Dobro." There were no hit singles from this album but it was a landmark album for Cash. The folk movement was a lyric-dominated music interested in issues and topics deeper than a hit song. Cash's concept album lent itself to this folk movement.

Johnny Cash (photograph courtesy of Packy Smith).

In the summer of 1962 Cash recorded another concept album, *Blood, Sweat, Toil and Tears*. He did not write any of these songs except "Legend of John Henry's Hammer," in which he took the basic folk song of "John Henry" and turned it into a dramatic eight-minute masterpiece that shifted tempos and brought this story vividly to life. The album also contained songs such as "Casey Jones," "Busted," "Another Man Done Gone" and the Jimmie Rodgers classic "Waiting for a Train."

In 1963 Johnny Cash began a string of top single hits for Columbia, beginning with "Ring of Fire," written by June Carter and Merle Kilgore, and "The Matador," written by Cash and June Carter, both that year; "Understand Your Man," "The Ballad of Ira Hayes" and "Bad News" in 1964; "Orange Blossom Special," "The Sons of Katie Elder" (the title track from the movie of the same name), and "Happy to Be with You" in 1965; and "The One on the Right Is on the Left" in 1966. His album *Ring of Fire* was a huge success, and it contained the TV theme song "The Rebel Johnny Yuma," which he did not write.

The widespread interest in cowboys may have spurred Cash's interest in Indians. He was part Cherokee, so there was a natural interest, but the 1950s and 1960s also saw Indians and the Old West reexamined through a number of movies. Johnny Cash had written "Old Apache Squaw" in 1957 while in Tucson on tour and recorded it in 1959. It was released on the album *Songs of Our Soil*. But Cash's interest in Indians was spurred further when he heard Indian songwriter Peter LaFarge performing in 1963 in Greenwich Village at the Gaslight Club. This is the same evening Cash first met Bob Dylan.

Back in Nashville, Columbia promotion man and Cash friend Gene Ferguson played him "The Ballad of Ira Hayes," written by LaFarge. This song tells the story of an Arizona

Pima Indian who was one of those who raised the flag at Iwo Jima, an incident immortalized in a photograph and monument at Arlington National Cemetery. But when Hayes returned home he faced discrimination, humiliation and poverty. An alcoholic, Hayes died a tragic death, drowned in a ditch.

On March 5, 1964, Cash went into the studio and recorded "The Ballad of Ira Hayes," a protest song in the era of protests. The song was released in July of that year and climbed to the number three position on the *Billboard* charts, spending 20 weeks there. On June 29 and 30 Cash was back in the studio recording the rest of the album that became *Bitter Tears*. During this same period of time, Peter LaFarge was in Nashville at the Race Relations Institute at Fisk University, where the subject of Indian injustice received attention. Johnny Cash landed in the midst of the civil rights movement by recording songs about Indians, although he also stood up for blacks and against the southern racism that was in the daily news during that time. Cash's reason for recording a concept album about Indians—indeed, it was an angry album as much about civil rights and protest as about Indians per se—were artistic as well as commercial.

In addition to "The Ballad of Ira Hayes," other songs on the album included "Custer," "Drums" and "White Girl," all by Peter LaFarge, "The Vanishing Race" by Johnny Horton, and four songs written by Cash: "Big Foot," "The Talking Leaves," "Apache Tears" and "Old Apache Squaw." "Big Foot" was written after Cash had visited Wounded Knee, South Dakota, site of the final Indian "fight." There, on December 29, 1890, the 7th Cavalry slaughtered a group of Indians who were led by Big Foot, a chief suffering from pneumonia at the time. Cash wrote this song in a car after leaving the Wounded Knee battlefield on his way to the Rapid City airport.

"The Talking Leaves" is the story of Sequoia, the Cherokee who developed a written language for his people. "Apache Tears" is the story of the eradication of the Apache who lived in the southern Arizona and New Mexico area and who were the last tribe subdued by the army. "Old Apache Squaw" is also the story of the Apaches, told from the very human side of a woman who has seen her family, tribe and heritage killed.

Johnny Cash's interest in the West and cowboys, which he originally expressed in songs like "Give My Love to Rose" and "Don't Take Your Guns to Town," led to a double album of cowboy songs, *Johnny Cash Sings the Ballads of the True West*, which he recorded in March 1965. This album includes a number of old cowboy classics, such as "The Streets of Laredo," "I Ride an Old Paint," "Bury Me Not on the Lone Prairie," and "Green Grow the Lilacs," as well as some original songs, "Hiawatha's Vision," "The Shifting, Whispering Sands," "Hardin Wouldn't Run," "Mean as Hell," and "Reflections."

In the liner notes to this album Cash states that the idea for the album came from his producer, Don Law, who also brought Cash some books about the West. Cash read the books as well as back issues of the magazine *True West* and talked about the West with people like Joe Austell Small, publisher of several western magazines. When Law called a few months later to ask about the western album, Cash began writing out ideas for songs, using some folk song collections and the advice of Tex Ritter. Cash also spent time in the desert with his jeep, absorbing the landscape of the West before he finished the album.

The album features narration by Cash between a number of songs, and the songs he wrote show the diversity of the West. In "Hiawatha's Vision" Cash used Longfellow's poem as a starting point to tell the story of the settling of the West by whites who displaced Indians. "Hardin Wouldn't Run," written after Cash had read a biography of the famous outlaw, is a narrative of John Wesley Hardin's life and death. "Mean as Hell" is a recitation about a pact the Devil made in order to settle the West. The poem is long and involved and endlessly fascinating. Obviously, Cash knew the violence of the West and the dangers of the desert; this is not an area for the squeamish. In "Reflections," the last song on the album, Cash again presents a recitation that captures the panoply of the West, the history of this vast, savage land and the tough, resilient people who came there. In addition to this western album, Cash sang the theme song to the movie *The Sons of Katie Elder*, which starred John Wayne. The song reached number ten on the charts in 1965.

After Columbia released the double album of *True West*, the album was edited down to a single album entitled *Mean as Hell* and it was released, too. And so 1965 ended with Johnny Cash's image firmly established as a folk singer about the mythical West. The West and western songs were an important part of Johnny Cash's life and recordings, but he could never be fenced in by anything. A lot of people saw him as larger than life; he probably saw himself the same way. In his songs, albums and life he always projected a sense of vision, a sense of "calling" and a higher purpose to his life and work. He had never been just another artist looking for the next hit or a singer just trying to get to the next gig.

If Johnny Cash achieved the status of a great man it was because he had aspired to become a great man. He set high standards for himself—in his life and in his work—and worked hard to fulfill them. Although he may have fallen short of greatness at times in his life and work, his vision was always there and he was able to continue his journey having learned his lessons. Few people carry the ambition and resolve to become a great man in their life; Johnny Cash was one of them.

On June 7, 1969, *The Johnny Cash Show* became a weekly show on ABC-TV. The hour-long program was originally a summer series, broadcast on Saturday nights. In the fall of 1969 it was moved to Wednesday evenings, where it continued its run until May 1971. (It was briefly revived as a summer series in 1976). This popular television program brought Johnny Cash into American homes each week and multiplied his fame. Again he used this platform to do more than entertain. He had a "Ride This Train" segment which combined history and geography, he featured gospel music, and he introduced performers such as Bob Dylan and Kris Kristofferson. With this TV show, Johnny Cash went from being a superstar in country music to an American icon/figure in country music of almost mythic proportions.

Johnny Cash never recorded another album comprised solely of western songs after his 1960s album but he often reached back to the West for songs. The 1980s began on a high note for him. In October he was elected to the Country Music Hall of Fame. But during the 1980s Johnny Cash left Columbia Records and recorded for a variety of labels and sang on a number of other artists' recordings. He continued to tour, appeared in several TV movies and on some TV series (such as *Dr. Quinn, Medicine Woman*). Perhaps the most satisfying work for Cash during the early 1980s was his double album of gospel songs, *A Believer Sings the Truth*, recorded for the Cachet label. On this album Cash was able to express the many dimensions of his faith. There is an old hymn ("Oh Come, Angel Band"), an old southern gospel favorite ("Gospel Boogie"), some spirited black gospel ("There Are Strange Things Happening Everyday") and a spiritual ("Children Go Where I Send Thee"). He also wrote a number of songs for the album.

In his gospel songs Cash's early work shows him repeating themes he'd heard in church or retelling biblical stories. But by the time of this album he was trying to apply the gospel message to the contemporary world and find new insights into biblical messages. "Wings in the Morning" is reminiscent of his early work as he sings about life after death. "When He Comes" tells of the Second Coming. "I'm a Newborn Man" was cowritten with his young son, John Carter, and came from a phrase the young boy was singing. "I'm Gonna Try to Be That Way" was recorded previously and talks of his commitment to be like Jesus. "What On Earth (Will You Do for Heaven's Sake)" is an admonishment to believers to live the Christian life here on earth, while "Over the Next Hill" is about the coming end times.

The most interesting song on the album is "The Greatest Cowboy of Them All," in which he compares Jesus to his cowboy heroes and uses cowboy imagery to point out that Jesus loves every critter and helps them all, even the mavericks who stray. This album seems to sum up Cash's spiritual life and spiritual journey better than any other. If he had never made another gospel album, this one would stand as an excellent summation of Cash's Christian beliefs.

In 1994 he released an album, *Cash: American Recordings*, on the new American Recordings label produced by alternative producer Rick Rubin. The album was done with just Cash and his guitar and summed up Cash's career pretty well. The first song, "Delia's Gone," was originally recorded by Cash in 1961. There were folk songs ("Tennessee Stud" and "Delia's Gone"), a humorous song ("The Man Who Couldn't Cry"), a cowboy song ("Oh Bury Me Not"), a gospel song ("Why Me, Lord"), songs with a haunting personal vision ("The Beast in Me" and "Bird on a Wire") and four songs he wrote. The self-penned songs tell stories and encompass Cash's spiritual vision. There was nothing new on this album except the audience; young people suddenly discovered Johnny Cash and found him both profound and "cool." It was a surprising rebirth for a man whose audiences and fans now included people younger than some of his grandchildren.

"Let the Train Whistle Blow" is yet another song with the imagery of a train, this time to carry his memory when he's gone. "Drive On" is a song looking back at the wounds of Vietnam, and "Redemption" is a straightforward gospel song about the old time religion and a sinner washed in the blood. "Like a Soldier" is the best of Cash's songs on the album. In this song he looks back over his life and sees a wild young man who is lucky to be alive and is thankful that God and a good woman have seen him through. Although the song tells of regrets from the past, in the end Cash is convinced the past was necessary for him to arrive at where he landed. These "American" albums validated Cash's status and stature as an American icon and gained him a new, young audience. After the first album, three others followed.

His final album, *The Man Comes Around*, contains fifteen songs. It begins with the Cash-penned title song that carries the gospel message. But there's a double meaning—"the man" could also be read as Johnny Cash giving his final message while he is alive.

The song "Hurt" from Nine Inch Nails was filmed as a video and won a number of awards from both MTV and the Country Music Association, which tells you a whole lot about the timeless appeal of Johnny Cash. Also on this final album, he recorded one of his old songs, "Give My Love to Rose"; a Hank Williams song, "I'm So Lonesome I Could Cry"; the old western song "Streets of Laredo"; a Beatles song, "In My Life"; a Simon and Garfunkel song, "Bridge Over Troubled Waters"; and the Roberta Flack song "The First Time Ever I Saw Your Face."

In May 2003, June Carter Cash went into the hospital for heart surgery and fell into a coma; she died on May 15, a devastating loss to Johnny Cash. Within a week after her death, Cash contacted some friends because he wanted to record more songs. During the four months between her death and his, Cash recorded about 50 songs. In September he was set to fly to Los Angeles to record songs with Rick Rubin but failing health forced him to enter the hospital, where he died on September 12.

It took a long hard life to write the songs Johnny Cash wrote, and a good, sweet life to sing them. Johnny Cash lived both. The songs he wrote reflect both the hardness and the sweetness of his life, the sinner and the saint, the success and the failure, the strengths and weaknesses, all wrapped up in the greatness called Johnny Cash.

SOURCES:

Brooks, Tim, and Earle Marsh. *The Complete Directory to Prime Time Network TV Shows 1946-Present.* New York: Ballantin, 1988.

Cash, Johnny. *Cash: The Autobiography*. With Patrick Carr. Cash: The Autobiography. New York: HarperSanFrancisco, 1997.
_____. *Man in Black*. Grand Rapids, MI: Zondervan, 1975.
Cusic, Don. *Johnny Cash: The Songs*. New York: Thunder's Mouth, 2005.
Smith, John L. *The Johnny Cash Discography*. Westport, CT: Greenwood Press, 1985.
Whitburn, Joel. *Top Country Singles 1944–1988*. Menomonee Falls, WI: Record Research, 1989.
Wren, Christopher S. *Winners Got Scars Too: The Life and Legends of Johnny Cash*. New York: Dial Press, 1971.

32

Johnny Western

With a name like "Johnny Western," how could you be anything but a western singer? "Roy Rogers told me once that it was the greatest name that you could ever have," remembered Western. "'I would have given anything to have your name' he told me. 'Don't ever change it—it's the best calling card you'll ever have.'" He's kept it.

Born in Two Harbors, Minnesota, on the edge of Lake Superior northeast of Duluth on October 28, 1934, Johnny Westerlund saw a Gene Autry movie, *Guns and Guitars*, on his fifth birthday, and from that moment on a singing cowboy was "all [he] ever wanted to be." This was during the Great Depression when Westerlund's father worked at one of President Franklin Roosevelt's Civilian Conservation Corps (CCC) camps; the movie was shown at an officers' club.

Westerlund grew up in Northfield, about 25 miles south of Minneapolis-St. Paul where his father was a high school coach and head of the physical education department. At nearby Carlton College, a three-member band saw 13-year-old Westerlund sing in a Rotary Club show and invited him to join their group. The group then recorded a demo tape for radio station KDHL, about 13 miles away, but by the time the radio station offered them a job, the others "had bailed," said Johnny.

"The guy at the radio station said, 'We liked your song best' and offered me a job, a 15-minute program on Saturdays," said Western. "That soon developed into three shows on Saturdays and then a show every day from noon to one P.M. on the Farm and Home Hour. I would take off from school for the lunch hour but I was always late getting back."

Because all of those shows demanded a lot of songs, young Johnny became a disc jockey as well as a singer. "The first record I sang on the air was 'Ghost Riders in the Sky' and the first record I played on the air as a disc jockey was 'Ghost Riders in the Sky' by Vaughn Monroe," remembered Western. "I had to play records because I ran out of songs."

Johnny Westerlund became Johnny Western when Ralph Hafstad, who ran the radio station, thought "Westerlund" was "too much of a mouthful" and started searching for another name. A calendar from the Great Western Salvage Company was hanging on the wall of the radio station and so, in a matter of moments in that summer of 1949, a 14-year-old boy was introduced as Johnny Western, disc jockey and entertainer. "Western was close to Westerlund," recalled Johnny, many years later. "I had to legalize it later, but no one ever questioned my name during my entire career. Dad was pretty well known in Northfield so I was still Johnny Westerlund there, but the rest of the world knew me as Johnny Western, although I didn't legalize it until later."

When he was 16—the summer before his senior year in high school—Johnny Western toured the Midwest with the Sons of the Pioneers. He had recorded for Joco Records (which was an abbreviation of Johnson Olson Company). His first single was "The Violet and the Rose," followed by "Give Me More, More, More," "Let Old Mother Nature Have Her Way" and "Little Buffalo Bill." The record company had distribution in five states, and his records had done well in the region when the Sons decided to tour that area. Because Western's success in that market gave them an extra edge, the Sons booked him to open their shows.

After high school, Johnny Western moved to Austin, Minnesota, about ten miles north of the Iowa state line in the southernmost part of Minnesota where he hosted a kiddie TV show, *Circle 6 Ranch Time*. "It was a 45-minute show," said Western. "We'd show a western movie every day—half of the movie one day and the other half the next. A lot of western stars came through there and I got to interview them and open their shows when they performed." That's how Johnny Western came to meet Roy Rogers, Dale Evans, Gene Autry, Rex Allen and Tex Ritter.

"Everyone who came by offered to help," said Western. "But you know what that's like—that's something most people say but when you turn up later, they don't really mean it. The difference was that all those big stars really meant it. Nudie the Rodeo Tailor really helped a lot—he'd made costumes for me when I was on the TV show. Tex Ritter had me over to his house and fed me and my family."

Western married when he was 19 and moved to Hollywood, in 1954, where he got a job in an ink factory testing ink cartridges. For the next two years he made the rounds at movie studios, hoping for an audition, but every time someone asked about previous film work Western had to tell them he had no experience—and the interview ended.

Western was performing whenever and wherever he could—a few paying gigs here and there—when a stroke of luck hit. "I became friends with Dick Jones when I arrived," said Western. "He was working for Gene Autry—was in the 'Buffalo Bill' TV series. One day he asked if I could come by and sing for a Hollywood Christian group. I had no idea that Roy Rogers, Dale Evans, Susan Hayward and Gene and Ina Autry would be there."

That was the first time Autry heard Johnny Western sing. It was 1956, the year when Autry's *Melody Ranch* radio show ended and his TV show stopped production, although the shows continued to be shown for several more years. Johnny Bond, Autry's longtime guitar player, decided to quit touring so he could perform on *Town Hall Party*, a weekly TV show that he cohosted with Tex Ritter. Bond and Ritter had also formed a publishing company. This meant that Autry needed a guitar player. Western, a longtime fan of Autry, knew all of Johnny Bond's guitar parts, was handsome and could sing well. A few weeks after that fateful meeting, Autry asked Dick Jones to call Western and arrange an audition.

On July 4, 1956, Johnny Western began performing with Gene Autry. Their first performance was in Pueblo, Colorado, at the Colorado State Fair. "We had 12,000 people a show for three days," said Western. "It was hot but we still had to do 'Rudolph.'" Also on the show were Merle Travis, Gail Davis ("Annie Oakley"), and the Cass County Boys.

From Colorado, the Autry troupe went to Toronto. "We played before three million people over 14 days," said Western. "Every show was a sell-out. It was an incredible way to start a professional career in Hollywood!" Western's featured song on the show was "Blue Shadows on the Trail," a Roy Rogers song. (Johnny Bond had been performing "Oklahoma Hills," a song about his native state.)

"Gene Autry was the biggest thing in the world then," remembered Western. "His image was so overwhelming. It was Gene Autry and then everybody else." Being with Autry for the next two years opened a lot of doors for Western. First, Autry placed him with his agent, Mitchell Hamilburg. Hamilburg was known for his work with merchandising; he handled Autry's merchandise as well as that for the shows *Range Rider*, *Buffalo Bill* and *Annie Oakley*. Western recalled the situation:

> Gene had established a good relationship with Mitch through the years. So he put all his people with Mitch—Dick Jones, Smiley Burnette, all those guys had Mitch as their agent. Bill Begg worked for Mitch and he was my direct agent. Mitch asked me what I wanted to do before he put me with Bill. And then he told me that if I ever had any problems to "call Uncle Mitch." That was a key connection because Mitch Hamilburg had a lot of prestige. He really got things done—whenever he placed a call to one of the big shots in Hollywood, that call would be either taken or returned.
>
> It was fun to watch Autry work. To drive him around and listen to him talk—just me and him. He loved to laugh, loved jokes. And he gave me a lot of advice, like "watch out for the shady characters." He also told me that when you get applause from a crowd, "Let it go to your heart—but don't let it go to your head." He was the least self-important person I ever knew. He could have dinner with the president one day and the next have dinner with some hillbilly in a shack in Arkansas. He really was a man of the people and the people knew it.
>
> Gene had no kids, while Roy Rogers had nine. I was his kid. In fact, he called me "kid" but he wouldn't let anyone else call me "kid."
>
> Gene could always pick up a phone and call anyone in the world. That opened a lot of doors for me.

In fact, after working for Gene Autry for two years Johnny Western appeared in 37 feature films. Johnny Western did not pursue a recording contract after he landed the job with Autry; instead, he concentrated on acting in movies and TV shows and had steady work there from 1957 to 1963.

In one of his TV roles, Johnny Western became the lead trooper on the syndicated television series *Boots and Saddles*. That show was filmed in Kanabe, Utah, the same place where *Gunsmoke* was filmed. While there Western was approached by agent Peter Marcos about representing him. Bill Beggs had retired so Western agreed. He was booked to appear on *Have Gun, Will Travel*, with a script written by the show's founder, Sam Rolfe. The script featured a shoot-out with Paladin (Richard Boone) that was a big thrill for Western:

> There was no theme song written for Paladin. The only music was a little piece of orchestral music when Paladin drew his gun at the beginning of the show.
>
> My wife was pregnant at that time. We finished shooting at nine P.M. The baby was born at seven the next morning, on March 14, 1958, and by nine A.M. I had written the song "Paladin," which was just a "thank you" card for Richard Boone and Sam Rolfe. I called a guy in Hollywood who had a studio and owed me some studio time and went down and put the song down with my guitar. I got two acetates, took one to Boone and the other to Rolfe. That was on a Friday. Over the weekend, they called and wanted me to meet with Bill Dozier, the head of CBS. We met on Tuesday at two P.M. and they offered to buy the song from me for $500. There had already been 14 shows in that series shot without a theme song. It was mid-season.
>
> Peter fought with CBS, who told me, "You had no right to write this song. We own this show, we own this character" and blah blah blah. So they offered to use my tracks but no royalties and no screen credit. Then, Leo Leftcourt, the CBS attorney, went from an offer of $500 to $5,000 in about fifteen minutes. Peter thought if they were moving that fast then it must be worth a lot more.
>
> I wanted some money up front and then just a standard contract from the unions, but they didn't want to give me screen credit. Well, they were playing it in the office when Mitch Miller, the head of Columbia Records, called and heard it. So he signed me as a singer and songwriter right there.
>
> That song was a complete fluke. But it totally changed my life. It was written in about 20 minutes as a thank you card. I wasn't even thirty years old. After it got on the air someone in CBS publicity told me that 350 million people saw it [the TV show] each week—it was in 78 foreign countries. In those other countries, the voices were all dubbed—but they always left the song alone.

On Johnny Western's first road trip with Gene Autry, he met Johnny Cash when the troupe performed in Toronto. The meeting came about because Carl Cotner, Autry's music director, wanted to get out of the confines of the hotel, so he invited Western to tag along. They decided to see Cash, who was performing at the Casino Theatre, doing six shows a day. "He was at a movie theatre," remembered Western. "So it was movie, show, movie, show—all day long. John had the flu and felt horrible. We met briefly. I went back to watch his show after that but didn't bother him. I could tell he felt awful."

This was in 1956 when "I Walk the Line" was hitting; the song was Cash's first huge hit. In 1958, Cash had moved to Los Angeles (he bought Johnny Carson's house) and settled in there. Gordon Terry took Western by Cash's office and reintroduced him. By this time, the *Paladin* theme was on television and Western was recording for Columbia, the same label Cash recorded for.

Johnny Western (photograph courtesy of Johnny Western).

"He called and hired me to do three shows with him in California," said Western. "They were all sold out. A week after we got back he called and asked if I could do 16 shows with him in the Midwest. Thirty-nine years and eleven months later, I did my last show with Cash. It was on the outskirts of Wichita on October 14, 1997." Western has a lot of warm memories of Johnny Cash. "John was my musical mentor," said Western.

The last film Johnny Western did was *The Nightrider*, which starred Johnny Cash. Also in the movie were Eddie Dean, Merle Travis, Gordon Terry, Dick Jones and Wesley Tuttle, who played a preacher (Reverend Wesley Tuttle). The TV movie was released in 1962.

"My life has been ABC," said Western. "Autry, Boone and Cash." Being around those three guys—who were superstars and major celebrities—showed Western the price of fame. "I really lucked out being a second banana," chuckled Western. "The weight of the world was on those guys' shoulders. If that TV show flopped, Richard Boone was responsible. If an actor or script brought him down—he took the heat. That's why if a professional acted in an amateur way Boone was all over him. Everyone wants a piece of your time when you're at that level and there's not enough hours in a day. They can't even eat a meal in a restaurant without someone wanting their autograph. It's no wonder they succumb to drugs and booze to keep them going." Western admits he was lucky there: "I never drank because I'm allergic to alcohol. And I never got into grass because I didn't smoke. I was the one who stayed sober."

Although the demands on them were great, Western never saw Johnny Cash or Gene Autry "stiff anybody. They always signed autographs—no matter what. Richard Boone got to the point where he had his name signed to a Paladin card and he'd give those out. And John would keep walking while he was signing. But those guys always signed."

"The great era of westerns in movies and on TV changed when *Gunsmoke* came on in 1955," said Western. "That changed the complexion of the Westerns. After *Gunsmoke*, there were thirty adult westerns on every week on TV. Then, in 1962, James Bond came and changed everything. James Bond and the *Man from U.N.C.L.E.*, which was created by Sam Rolfe, left the cowboys behind. At the same time, country music almost died because of rock. Country artists who were playing for four or five thousand people a night found themselves playing to four or five hundred."

Johnny Western managed to weather that storm well. "I was lucky," he said. "I signed a contract at the end of the sixties for a minimum of eight weeks each year—sometimes it was more—at the Golden Nugget in Las Vegas. That led to dates in Reno and Tahoe, so I was doing fifteen weeks a year there. Hap Peebles booked me on one hundred fifty dates a year at nightclubs and fairs. So I made a very good living in the Midwest during that time."

In 1963 Johnny Western moved to Scottsdale, Arizona, then got divorced. He met his second wife through Waylon Jennings, who introduced them. Johnny and Waylon soon became fast friends. Then in January 1986, Johnny Western started a new career as a disc jockey on KFDI in Wichita. He still performed on weekends, but as the western music festival scene started to blossom he found himself in demand for a number of festivals.

"I'll never do the whole country thing again, with a big bus and a band," said Johnny. "But I love the role of the lone troubadour."

When he started at KFDI, he had heard of the Riders in the Sky but had never met them. That changed in February 1986, when Orrin Friesen, another DJ at KFDI, called him at home and invited him to come down to the Two Feathers Mexican Restaurant and meet the group. Johnny had already had dinner, but he jumped at the chance to drive down, meet the guys and have a few tacos.

Later, he performed at Carnegie Hall with the Riders and that was "the gas of all time." "Doug Green is such a brilliant guy," said Western. "He loves all the things that I do. And he really lives the part of the singing cowboy. Dresses the part and really knows the history."

Although the first Elko gathering in 1985 was a major turning point for many involved in western music, Johnny Western had this to say about it: "I really didn't care about Elko. They were trying to preserve cowboy poetry—the music came later. But the main reason is that Elko wasn't about the movie and TV cowboys. They want to dress like the 1880s, while I grew up with the cowboys who dressed to the nines—like Ranger Doug with the Riders. My purpose on earth is to continue the tradition of Gene Autry and Roy Rogers—the TV and movie cowboys. I want to keep the Saturday morning western going."

Johnny Western turned 73 in the fall of 2007, but he says he feels he's still forty-five or fifty inside. He still loves performing for audiences but, he says, "If the money isn't there, the situation doesn't feel right and I don't get a ticket for my wife—I ain't going. I owe this to my wife. For 17 years I was on the road while Jo raised the kids." Although he doesn't have the wealth of a Gene Autry, Western says, "If it ends tomorrow, I'll be O.K."

The bookings continue to come. "I played everywhere and people remember, so they call—they know how to find me," explained Johnny. "Also, an independent agent who worked for Hank Thompson books some dates for me."

He'd like to write a book about his life and experiences but admits he "just don't have that kind of dedication." He remembers a day in February 1988 when Johnny Cash gave him his guitar and asked, "When are you going to write the book? You're the only one sober during those days!" Waylon had also encouraged him to write a book and Johnny had jotted some notes. But when John Smith asked him to write a foreword to a biography of Waylon, Western said he spent a good deal of time "locked in on Waylon—and that wore [him] out." Since that time, he "hasn't had the drive to become an author."

"I do four hours on the radio every day and I've turned into a homebody," said Johnny. "I love to go home at night and have dinner with my wife. I've got seventeen grandkids and a great-grandson. That's where my life is now." It's been a good life, and well-rewarded with honors. In 2000, Johnny Western was inducted into the Country Music DJ Hall of Fame as well as the Old Time Country Music Hall of Fame in Avoca, Iowa. In November 2001, he was inducted into the Western Music Association's Hall of Fame. In March 2003, he received "The Cowboy Spirit of the West" award from the National Festival of the West in Scottsdale, Arizona.

The deaths of Waylon Jennings, Cash, Autry and Rex Allen took a toll on Western. "I miss 'em," he said. "I can't pick up the phone and call them any more. And that hurts." The death of Rex Allen especially hurt. "I stayed in touch with Rex Allen for over fifty years," said Western. "He really was a mentor to me. Gene gave me that first big break, but then he switched horses. Gene had two separate personas: the stage persona and the business persona. He was the sharpest businessman I ever knew. After he got the Angels, he just became the businessman. Roy Rogers stayed with show business longer but Rex never quit. So when I talked with Gene it was about old times. But with Rex, we talked about things happening now."

There are few regrets in Johnny Western's life. "I'm the luckiest guy in the world," said Western. "How many people get to work for their heroes? I did!"

Western became the first western act to play Carnegie Hall three times: in 1962 with Johnny Cash, in 2002 with the Sons of the San Joaquin and in 2003 with the Riders in the Sky. The latter two also featured the Prairie Rose Wranglers.

The big moments keep coming. In March 2006, Western went to China, with a troupe that included the Prairie Rose Wranglers, Rex Allen Jr., Joe Sullivan (who portrays Hopalong Cassidy) and Jeff Hildebrandt, and performed in Beijing and Shanghai.

Johnny Western is the last of the 1950s-era singing cowboys still performing. He dresses sharp—in black with a paladin logo on his chest—and he still sings well. That glorious voice sings classic cowboy songs and "Paladin," of course. As he sings he gives a running commentary on the songs and on his life, and holds the attention of the audience. Watching him, you see a pro in action—professional in every aspect. Johnny Western is a real performer on the stage and a real gentleman off the stage—honest, friendly, courteous, and talented.

SOURCES:

Green, Douglas B. *Singing in the Saddle: The History of the Singing Cowboy*. Nashville: Country Music Foundation Press and Vanderbilt University Press, 2002.
Western, Johnny. Phone interview with author, August 31, 2005.

33

Red Steagall

On the night in February 2005 when the Grammys were telecast, Red Steagall was sitting in front of his TV at home on his Texas ranch watching the broadcast. Nora Jones had recorded "Here We Go Again" with Ray Charles on that legend's last album, and she sang it on that show amidst the glitter and glitterati in Los Angeles. There were two Red Steagalls watching and listening at home: the Red Steagall who used to be and the Red Steagall who is now. "Here We Go Again" was written by Red and Don Lanier back in 1965 and recorded originally by Ray Charles, which meant a big songwriting check for $19,000 for a guy in L.A. who was struggling to get by. The struggle as a songwriter was not over with that check or that song. Each song a professional songwriter writes must have the potential to be commercial, must interest an artist who'll want to record it and must appeal to radio program directors in order to reach an audience who will, hopefully, like the song enough to want to hear it and buy it.

It's not what they've written in the past, it's what they've written today and will write tomorrow that drives professional songwriters. Red Steagall lived that life for a number of years, trying to come up with catchy tunes and lyrics that would connect to a fickle public. Chasing hits, day after day after day. And then it all changed with Elko.

Russell "Red" Steagall was born in Gainesville, Texas, just across the line from Oklahoma, almost due north from Fort Worth. He grew up in Sanford, in the Texas panhandle, north of Amarillo. He took guitar lessons when he was nine but it wasn't until he was 15, after he'd had a bout with polio, that he seriously began to play the guitar. That first guitar was a Guild. Red paid half the cost with money earned from a paper route and his Mom paid the other half. Red's still got that Guild guitar.

In college, at West Texas A&M where Red studied animal science and agronomy, he began performing. After college, he joined the Shamrock Oil and Gas Company in advertising, where his job was "to make sure their bathrooms were clean and the people who were selling gas knew what they were doing." Red had a big territory—Texas, Colorado, Utah, New Mexico—so his performing career gained a wider arc as he played local clubs and coffeehouses on his travels.

Buddy Knox, Jimmy Bowen and Donnie Lanier had a group called the Rhythm Orchids. The group had a two sided hit in 1957 with "Party Doll" on one side and "I'm Stickin' with You" on the other. Donnie Lanier and Red had gone to school together before Donnie moved to Dumas, Texas, where Bowen lived. After Buddy Knox was drafted, Lanier and Bowen called Steagall to join them in Los Angeles in 1965. From 1966 until 1968, Lanier and Red Steagall lived together, which is how they came to write "Here We Go Again" in 1966.

Red took the song to both Ray Price and Buck Owens, but neither would record it unless they could have the publishing. "And Don Lanier and I were not going to give up the publishing," said Red. Talking with Buck Owens in Buck's Bakersfield office, Red told him, "I think I'll pitch it to Ray Charles."

Red walked across the street from Buck's office and called the office of Ray Charles in Los Angeles and made an appointment for 10:00 A.M. the next morning with Mike Akavoff. Akavoff listened and told Red, "If you give us a one-year exclusive on this song [meaning it would not be played for any other artists to record] then we'll guarantee you the 'A' side of a single."

That was in August of 1966. In May 1967, Ray Charles released it as a single on ABC, and it reached number 15 on the pop charts and number five on the R&B charts. That opened the floodgates, as other artists, including Glen Campbell, Nancy Sinatra and George Strait, all eventually recorded "Here We Go Again."

Red Steagall (photograph courtesy of Red Steagall).

Red Steagall worked for United Artists Publishing before he and Jimmy Bowen started Amos Publishing. Warner Brothers executive Dick Glaser, a friend of Red's, invited him to record for Warner and Red did one single for that label and then was dropped. His next recordings came for Dot Records, when Joe Allison invited him to join the label. Allison and Steagall were both based in L.A. at the time, although the recordings were made in Nashville. ABC bought Dot Records and Jim Foglesong moved from New York to Nashville to head up that label. Red recorded only one record for Dot, then left and went to Capitol, where Joe Allison had taken over as head of that label in Nashville.

Steagall stayed with Capitol for five years, until he recorded his album *Lone Star Beer and Bob Wills Music*. Frank Jones had taken over as head of Capitol in Nashville by this time and refused to release the album because it had the name of a product in the title. Steagall took the tapes across the street to ABC/Dot, where Jim Foglesong agreed to release the album. He gave Steagall a check for the production costs of the album and Red walked back over to Frank Jones' office, handed him the check and got his release from Capitol. And that's why *Lone Star Beer and Bob Wills Music* was released on ABC/Dot.

That occurred in 1975, when Red was living in Nashville. In 1977 he moved back to Texas but remained as an artist on ABC/Dot until 1980, when MCA bought out ABC/Dot. MCA was headed by Red's old friend, Jimmy Bowen, who emerged on top in that merger. Later, Bowen headed up Elektra, where he signed Red to record an album for that label. Then it was back to MCA where he recorded again before joining Warner Western in 1990 for an album. Since that time, Red has left the major labels and worked with independents.

Red Steagall was successful in country music but not in the superstar range. He wrote over 200 songs recorded either by himself or others, had 23 singles on the *Billboard* country chart and released 20 albums. He's had songs in movies, performed an average of 200 dates a year, toured Germany, Spain, Australia, the Middle East, South America and the Far East, was a regular on the NBC series *Music Country USA* and even sang at the White House for President Reagan in 1983.

Then, in January 1985, the first Elko was held in Nevada. Red heard about it and went up to check it out, "seeing what it was all about." Not only did he find out what Elko is "all about," he also discovered what Red Steagall is "all about."

Red Steagall had been performing both "country" and "western" music for a number of years, but the western was in western swing. When he wrote a song he always looked at it as a professional songwriter: Is this commercial? Will someone find this appealing enough to record it? Could this be a hit?

After Elko, Red no longer thought that way. From then on, Red Steagall wrote songs that satisfied his inner muse. He decided to write the songs he felt like writing—commercial or not—and to record western music as an extension of his cowboy lifestyle. Granted, it might be stretching it a bit to call Red's home a working ranch when, he says, "You can't make a living with ten head of horses, two longhorns and two Buffalo cows." But at least he has a ranch. Since 1985 in Elko, Red Steagall has found a home on the range.

He had stayed in country music "until I couldn't compete anymore," he admits. "I just couldn't sing those songs." The western songs he began singing gave him a new lease on life, and it was richly rewarding in both a material and spiritual sense.

In 1991 he hosted the first Red Steagall Cowboy Gathering in the Stockyards National Historic District of Fort Worth, Texas; that gathering has been a major event on the cowboy calendar ever since. The Gathering came about when two county agents approached him with the idea; it is now in its 15th year.

In 1994, Steagall launched his syndicated radio show, *Cowboy Corner*, which has featured guest artists such as Reba McEntire, Charlie Daniels, Don Edwards, Waddie Mitchell, Baxter Black and the late Buck Ramsey. The idea for the radio show came about when he spoke to a Rotary Club luncheon and a friend in the advertising business, Max Churchill, asked afterward if Red would do a three-minute radio spot, sponsored by Churchill.

Red replied that he didn't have any three-minute poems. Stuart Balcom was then approached about helping put together a 30-minute radio show which would be syndicated. Mike Oatman heard it and said, "Make it an hour and I'll put it on my stations." So Red put together a one-hour show and contacted Ron Huntsman in Nashville, who marketed it to 154 radio stations. The radio show is now in its 12th year.

Elko rejuvenated an interest in cowboy poetry for Red. "From 1889 to 1937, there was cowboy poetry published," notes Steagall. "But then from 1937 until 1985 there was only a handful published. A lot of people were still writing it, but grandchildren would find it in a shoebox when grandpa passed away."

Red has made cowboy poetry an integral part of his concerts and recordings. He has published four books: *Ride for the Brand* in 1993, *The Fence That Me and Shorty Built* in 2001, *Born to This Land* in 2003 (which was done with photographer Skeeter Hagler) and *Cowboy Corner Conversations*, a collection of interviews from his *Cowboy Corner* radio show that was published in 2004. Along the way, Steagall collected a slew of honors and awards. The National Cowboy and Western Heritage Museum in Oklahoma City honored him with its Western Heritage Award for best album of the year in western music in 1993 (for *Born to This Land*), 1995 (for *Faith and Values: Red Steagall and the Boys in the Bunkhouse*), 1997 (for *Dear Mama, I'm a Cowboy*) and 1999 (for *Love of the West*). In 2002 his song "Wagon Tracks" won for best western song of the year.

Red was inducted into the Texas Trail of Fame in 1999, the Hall of Great Westerners at the National Cowboy and Western Heritage Museum in Oklahoma City in 2003 and the Texas Cowboy Hall of Fame in Ft. Worth in 2004. In 2005 he was named "Poet Laureate of Texas." "Most academics won't recognize poetry that rhymes," said Red. "So I was really honored to get this award."

Red currently does about 60 concerts a year. About ten of them are with a 10-piece western swing band and the rest are with "either two or three guys or by [him] self." He notes that he "related to country music twenty-five to thirty years ago. Back then there were millions of fans and no way to buy the product. Now that's the situation with western music, but with the Internet, that's changing. Western music has a niche audience that grows and the Internet has been great for it."

"My audience is anywhere people understand what I'm talking about," said Red. "I write from experience, which is why I only write about West Texas cowboys. I don't write about Montana cowboys. That makes a big difference."

Red used to play 35–40 rodeos a year, but he doesn't any more. "That's gone to young people," said Red. "The rodeo promoters couldn't afford talent with the big purses they now give, so they've gone to contract acts and novelty acts."

Young people like the music of the young, so that means "the rock sound" in rodeo arenas, and since promoters want to attract a young audience they feel they need to play rock. "There's some good in that because it introduces people to rodeo," said Red. "Some don't like it because they want to stick with the old ways, but this is progress and that's part of life."

When a man loves what he's doing, he doesn't work a day in his life. In that light, Red Steagall is an incredibly busy man who doesn't know what work is. And he intends to keep it that way. "In the future I'd like to keep doing what I'm doing," said Red. Looking back on his life, he says, "I can't think of one single thing I would change."

SOURCE:

Steagall, Red. Phone interview with the author, May 23, 2005.

34

Don Edwards

"For a number of years I sang by myself—a one man orchestra," said Don Edwards, talking about his years at the White Elephant in the Fort Worth Stockyards. "I really came from folk music—not country music—and western songs are part of the folk tradition. Then, on the weekends at the club, we'd play western swing dances."

"Those are really two distinct roles for a performer," said Don, comparing the solo performances to playing with a band. "I loved them both but it's hard to travel with a western swing group. It's easier and more economical to just travel with a guitar. But I can't say that I like one better than the other."

For his album *Saddle Songs II*, Don performed mostly with only his guitar. "I perform a lot with just my guitar," said Edwards. "And people seem to like it. To do those old songs, it seems most authentic to do them simply—not overproduced. And there's a lot of freedom just playing by yourself."

Don researches the old cowboy songs by "reading books," and listening to people "who know this stuff" rather than finding an old cowboy who knows the old songs. "I love doing the research, although I'm not an academic. It's not like the days when Jack Thorp and John Lomax were collecting cowboy songs," said Don. "You really can't find those old cowboys around anymore." The genesis of Don's research into the stories behind these old songs was at the White Elephant, where he sang solo and added anecdotes, telling the story behind the songs. "It would get real quiet," said Don, reflecting on those days. "The crowd would be raising hell and drinking beer, but when I'd tell these stories, they would really get quiet and listen." During his earliest years, Don Edwards felt that God had played a cruel joke on him. Fate handed him the fact that he was born in New Jersey and spent a good part of his growing up years in Massachusetts while yearning to live in the West. But destiny and fate are not sealed by where we are born; in America you can choose a destiny. In his heart of hearts, Don Edwards was a westerner. So that's what he became, and the West became a richer place because of that choice.

"I wasn't born into ranching or cowboydom, either one," states Edwards in the autobiographical essay in his book *Classic Cowboy Songs*. "It was an intentional effort on my part to at least experience the lifestyle firsthand. I have, and still do partake in cowboying in one capacity or another, but I don't claim to be no cowboy."

Edwards was born in Boonton, New Jersey, in 1939. His father was a vaudeville magician who left show business and got a "regular" job to support his growing family. Still, his father was an active record collector and Don remembers that his father's stack of old 78s included "everything from Bach to John Philip Sousa, from Glenn Miller to Jimmie Rodgers, and

Louis Armstrong to Gene Autry. He had Carter Family records and cowboy singers like Vernon Dalhart, Jules Verne Allen, Carson Robinson and Bill Bender. He even had some Bob Wills and the Sons of the Pioneers." Edwards' father also had a Silvertone radio and phonograph console that allowed him to record radio shows, and he recorded *The Gene Autry Melody Ranch* regularly.

The Edwards family moved to Milton, Massachusetts, when Don was young. However, "I never gave up putting the pressure on my dad for us to move out West," states Don. On Christmas 1948, Don received his first guitar—a Silvertone sunburst arch-top from Sears. That was a landmark Christmas for young Don Edwards; he also received his first Will James book, *Smoky the Cow Horse*, and a BB gun.

Don confesses that growing up he was "totally absorbed with Will James, Gene Autry, Tom Mix and the like. Most of my Saturday afternoons were spent at the local movie theater where, for twenty-five cents, you could spend the whole afternoon watching all the high-riding heroes." Don said that later in life his mother admitted she "hadn't given much

Don Edwards (photograph by Donald Kallaus, courtesy of Scott O'Malley Agency).

thought to my 'cowboy thing' when I was young; that was something every kid wanted to be when they were growing up. She just thought I'd outgrow it sooner or later." However, both Don's mother and father struggled to get him to remove his cowboy hat and boots to get "dressed up long enough to go to church on Sunday morning."

One advantage of living in Massachusetts was being able to go to the annual Boston Garden rodeo, which was held for two weeks every fall. In addition to the rodeo contests, there would be guest appearances from top singing cowboy stars. Don remembers that "Gene Autry, Roy Rogers, The Sons of the Pioneers, Ray Whitley and the Cass County Boys all played there." Don confesses he "bugged" every cowboy he managed to meet, peppering them with questions; and he fondly remembers that Ray Whitley, Karl and Hugh Farr and Casey Tibbs all treated him and his questions kindly.

Edwards quit school in the 11th grade, bound and determined to head to Dublin, Texas, where he hoped to land a job with the Lightning C Ranch. He packed his suitcase and guitar in his 1951 Ford and headed in that direction, but his car broke down and left him stranded in Dover, New Jersey, where he ended up playing in a beer joint. "This is where I learned my first lesson in survival and self-preservation: when a fight breaks out, keep on playing," writes Don. "If you're the intended target, protect your body and your instrument by getting the hell out of there." Edwards reluctantly concluded "Texas just wasn't part of the plan at the time."

In New Jersey, he met Elton Britt and opened shows for Ray Price, Hank Thompson, Carl Smith and Johnny Cash. He also met Herb Hooven, who became his close friend and mentor, and learned about performing for a crowd. Edwards states he "loved everything from old-time country to early jazz to folk blues and western swing" and played a wide variety of music in those early days. But he always wanted to get behind the songs, dig a little deeper into the music.

"I was always wanting to know who influenced whom, who wrote this or that song, where some old song came from," he states. "I became a self-taught historian of sorts. I'm still doing all that, except now they call me a musicologist." His biggest influence was Marty Robbins and Edwards states he admired Robbins because "his roots were deep in the western tradition, yet he recorded everything from country to pop to Hawaiian to Mexican ballads."

Finally, Don Edwards struck out towards the West again and, in the fall of 1959, arrived in Fort Worth. He took an assembly-line factory job and found he "couldn't stand being shut up in some building for eight hours." He lasted only half a day on that job: "I went to lunch and never went back."

Reading the newspaper want ads, he found that Six Flags Over Texas was looking for entertainers. He auditioned, singing "Cattle Call" and "Strawberry Roan," and landed a job in the park helping build the park's first steam locomotive. In the summer, he worked in the gunfighter shows, "Four skits every twenty minutes, twelve hours a day, seven days a week" earning $150 a week. During the off season he had a job hauling oil-field supplies for the Fort Worth Pipe and Supply Company.

Known as "The Young Ranger," Edwards released his first record in January 1964 on Ren Records, a label based in Dallas. He made the rounds at radio stations and jukeboxes promoting the record and saw some regional success. At the end of the 1964 season at Six Flags, he left the park and began performing in and around Fort Worth, playing at the Cowtown Jamboree as well as at Panther Hall, where he opened for Tex Ritter—a real highlight in his burgeoning career. At this point, Don Edwards' musical dreams were obstructed by financial reality. He had a wife and two small children. "My wife at that time wasn't very supportive of my show business career. She was always telling me to get a real job and forget all this guitar-playing foolishness," he said.

Don wasn't ready to give up his dream, so he made the trek to Nashville, where he met legendary steel guitar player Pete Drake, who recorded two records on him for Stop Records. Those records didn't go too far. Next, Don joined a troupe for a Canadian tour, which started out O.K. but soon turned into a mini-disaster and the group ended up in Las Vegas.

The late 1960s and mid-1970s "were years of uncertainty that were causing heartache and unhappiness to my family and people around me," remembers Edwards. "I was working so hard at such unrealistic goals that all I had left to show for my selfish quest for success was a cheap guitar and a failed marriage." He hit bottom when, after his divorce, his father died and then his youngest daughter, Dayle, was killed by a car in California. "These were the most heartbreaking and bleakest years of my life," he states.

After a visit back to his home in Massachusetts, Don headed back to Texas. But he was stopped and arrested for car theft, then locked up for 36 hours. The problem: the car he was driving had matched the description of a stolen car used in a robbery. A half-hearted apology from the police, who admitted they'd nabbed "the wrong guy," was all Edwards got from that escapade, although he did manage to find his way back to Texas.

Don Edwards found himself at a crossroads. He loved music but disliked the business that carried that music to the masses. "It was the 'business' of music that I disliked," relates Don in his songbook when talking about his experience in Nashville. "Music factories belching out overproduced, homogenized pablum for the unsuspecting masses. There's a world of difference between manufacturing music for money and creating art for love, but I also thought that having talent mattered."

Talent does matter and Don Edwards discovered that when he met Joe Dulle, owner of the White Elephant Saloon in the Fort Worth Stockyards: "[This was the] same place where, in 1908, John Lomax collected many of his cowboy songs. If I never believed in destiny, I do now." "How does one explain the mystic trails of life?" asked Don. "It's not just the trail itself or where it leads to. It has to do with how hard it is to travel."

Don Edwards spent 14 years performing at the Fort Worth Stockyards. In addition to blossoming musically, his personal life also blossomed when he met Kathy Jean Davis, whom he married on January 7, 1978.

In 1986, Don left the White Elephant to devote his full time and energies to touring, writing and recording. He still performed occasionally at the White Elephant. "[But] I wanted more time for study and research projects," he said. Today, the White Elephant is no more. While still at the White Elephant, performing each week, Don went to the Elko Gathering, an event that changed his life.

"I went to the second Elko Gathering," said Don, talking about the landmark event that began in 1985. "I had some friends who said, 'This is a place you need to be.'" In Elko, Don met Waddie Mitchell (whom he had heard of), Gary Morton and Hal Cannon. Ever since that 1985 Gathering, Don has been a regular at Elko.

At Elko, Edwards also met Michael Martin Murphey, who was pleased to discover there were other performers who wanted to do what he wanted to do, which was sing the old cowboy songs. After Murphey recorded his *Cowboy Songs* album for Warner Brothers and it became a surprise hit, Murphey's label, Warner Brothers, formed Warner Western and signed several acts—Waddie Mitchell, Sons of the San Joaquin and Don Edwards.

"I thought it would work with their deep pockets and resources," said Don. "But they had the usual mentality of trying to record something that was radio friendly. They threw it all in the mainstream and fans are going to look for what they know. If they had targeted the audience better, I believe it could've worked." Alas, that was a dream that did not come true. Still, it was another step in the growing popularity of western music.

"Elko was important, but then Murphey's WestFests really created a huge amount of interest," Don said. "He would mix western performers with top name country acts and it really drew the crowds." Edwards' career took off during this period as he went from a local act at the Fort Worth Stockyards to someone with a national reputation and national audience.

One of the most beautiful, moving albums in western music is the album Don and Waddie Mitchell did with the Fort Worth Symphony. The seeds for that album were planted back in 1982 when Paul McCallum of the Fort Worth Convention and Visitors Bureau came to Edwards in the Stockyards and presented the idea of "Cowboys and Culture."

It was partly a way to bring some attention to the Fort Worth Stockyards, but also a way to bring "high art and folk art together," according to Edwards: "They have mostly been kept apart. But the season ticket holders saw it and liked it and the idea brought in some cowboys and country fans who don't normally go to a symphony."

Usually, an artist has to achieve a certain stature before they can perform with symphonies, but a great idea works as well. Edwards embraced this great idea in Fort Worth and now performs regularly with symphonies, doing his cowboy songs and backed by some of the finest classical musicians in the country.

Patrick Markey was a fan of Don Edwards' music, although Don didn't even know the man. But Markey knew Robert Redford; in fact, Markey had produced the movie *A River Runs Through It* and was producing *The Horse Whisperer*, starring Redford. "He played one of my albums for Robert Redford and Redford said, 'That's what I'm looking for—that's what I want.' He had been pitched a lot of country acts, but he knew the difference between western and country music." That led to Edwards going to Santa Monica for an audition, where he sang a song, recited a poem, and talked about cowboy life. He landed the part of "Smokey," which was more significant in the uncut version than the one that made it into movie theaters. "I had a couple of really good scenes that were cut out," said Edwards. "The movie was over four hours at first, so the studio told Redford it had to be cut back—it wasn't an epic. There was one scene that we spent a week filming—and that was cut out. But it was a real thrill doing it and the money was good."

Edwards has a small ranch (although "you could really hardly call it a ranch," he says) and runs about 40 head of mixed breeds. He's taking part in a government program called "Equip," which attempts to bring back the native grasses to a region. He enjoys the cowboy life but makes sure that it doesn't get in the way of his singing, which is his real, honest true love. "I've been blessed these last 30 years," said Edwards. "I try to do an album a year, but I don't do it just because I have to. I do it when I have something to say."

For future projects, he's tapped into several things that are holding his interest. "I love the old Gene Austin songs, like 'My Blue Heaven' and the songs of Jimmie Rodgers," he said. "I'd love to do something along those lines"—this from a man who admits to listening to "everything from Blind Lemon Jefferson to big band music, from Jimmy Rodgers to Gene Autry to Gene Austin."

His other interest is in cowboy blues. "The poor lonesome cowboy singing is 'cowboy blues,'" said Edwards. "And if you look at the structure of a lot of old cowboy songs, like 'Old Chisholm Trail,' they're written in a blues format. I've been working on that idea for 14 years." The idea came when he went to Yale in 1986 at the invitation of Howard Lamar and Paul Stone to talk to Westerners International for the History Department. There, Jan Murry, an African-American lady from Mississippi, told him how much she loved cowboy music and that it is "so much like the blues." "That hit me in the head like a sledgehammer," said Edwards, who began his quest then for cowboy blues.

The question comes up: How does someone make a living in western music? "If somebody is good at what they do, and they perform a lot, then they can make a living," said Don, who cautioned that he meant "a living—not getting rich:

> I'm not talking about being a big star in mainstream country. But there are people out there looking for something with substance instead of what's hyped. Western music is so refreshing, it's almost like a spiritual experience. It's hard to find but you can hunt it up. I did and others who loved the music have done it.
>
> It's important not to try and pander to the Nashville community. We've got to keep it alive where it came from and then add something. You can't spend your life doing 'Tumbling Tumbleweeds,' but you can put songs like that in your performance, mix 'em in with some new things that sound like the old songs. That's actually what I write. The new songs I do actually sound like something old.

Western music could be at a turning point, according to Don. "The mainstream country fan doesn't really care about it," he said. "But some of the rock fans really love it, because they see the artistic value. The college crowd appreciates it because they tend to be an eclectic crowd, open to all kinds of things. But the audience we're missing is the bluegrass audience. Those folks are playing the same kind of acoustic music except we've got the western lyrics. I think if we started working with the bluegrass people, that's where we could see a bigger audience."

Edwards has already played several bluegrass festivals, including the giant MerleFest in North Carolina, where huge crowds saw him perform backed by a band that included legendary bluegrassers Tony Rice, Peter Rowan and Norman Blake. In fact, Edwards and Rowan have done an album together. "Our music is the same as the Appalachian and folk music," explained Don. "But nobody in western music has really recognized that so far." In terms of the singing cowboys from Hollywood, "that was really jazz, with jazz players," according to Don, referring to the Farr Brothers with the Sons of the Pioneers and others from the West Coast.

In the autobiographical essay in his songbook, Don relates the following: "Regrettably, as I look back, I never became a full-time participant in the cowboy life. I was only passing through. A wide-eyed, adventuresome kid with a war bag of dreams and a wore-out guitar." The essence of that statement is still true, although the guitar isn't worn out and the "kid" has put some miles on his years. But that same love of the West and the cowboy life still inhabits the hopes and dreams of Don Edwards, who found his calling in life when he followed his heart West.

SOURCE:

Edwards, Don. *Classic Cowboy Songs from the Minstrel of the Range.* Salt Lake City: Gibbs-Smith, 1994.
_____. Phone interview with the author, March 2, 2004.
_____. *Saddle Songs: A Cowboy Songbag.* Colorado Springs, CO: Sevenshoux, 2003.

35

Rex Allen Jr.

"During my entire career, it didn't make any difference if I was doing Paris, Texas, or Paris, France, I always did western music in my shows because that's my heritage," said Rex Allen Jr. "That's what I grew up with."

Indeed, Rex had hits with "Can You Hear Those Pioneers" (which featured his dad as well as the Sons of the Pioneers on background vocals) back in 1976 and "Last of the Silver Screen Cowboys" (with his dad and Roy Rogers) in 1982 when he was a country act on Warner Brothers. Other chart songs from Rex include "Cowboy in a Three Piece Business Suit," "Teardrops in My Heart" and "Ride Cowboy Ride." Although Rex made an effort to get western music back on the radio—and succeeded to an extent—western did not become a mainstream music.

This led Rex Allen Jr. to develop some definite ideas about the past and future of western music. "In order for western music to come back and be a mainstream music, it needs film or television like it had in the 1930s and 1940s," said Rex. "When my dad did his last film in 1954 it ended western music in film and, since that time, it seems that western music has developed almost like a cult following.

"For my father's generation, the great western songs were 'Ghost Riders in the Sky,' 'Tumbling Tumbleweeds,' 'Cool Water'—those songs. But for my generation, the greatest western song is 'Desperado' by the Eagles. Some of the old-line traditional western people will argue against that but it's an attitude towards western music that's at stake here. How those people think about it and whether they accept it will determine the future of western music. That's why on my newest album I have a duet with Johnny Western on 'Pancho and Lefty.' That's a western song!

"I think if more of us who are western artists are more open to the new generation of western songs, we'll go a long way towards pulling western music into the mainstream. But you've got to teach your audience. Western music did not end in 1954. There's some great western acts out there like the Sons of the San Joaquin and Riders in the Sky, but we should be giving the Entertainer of the Year award to acts like Garth Brooks. 'Beaches of Cheyenne' and 'Rodeo' are western songs."

When it was pointed out that the most popular country song during the 1990s—determined by airplay—was "Shoulda Been a Cowboy," Rex nodded his head and said, "But did Toby Keith win Song of the Year according to the Western Music Association? No!"

There is an uneasy alliance between those involved in country and western music. Country performers tend to embrace the image of the cowboy and the West and this connection to the West has long been an important part of country music. But those in western music have emphasized the differences between western and country music, wanting to keep a distance between the two worlds. Still, the biggest asset a western performer can have is a successful background in country music that includes some hit records.

"A country background pays off," noted Rex who, like several others, enjoyed success as a country artist before moving into western music. "Michael Martin Murphey and I do the same thing but he plays off the pop audience as much as he does the country audience. Murph had one of the greatest pop records of all time with 'Wildfire.' I've had almost fifty chart records and nineteen albums. I believe that Murph did everything he could to bring western music into the mainstream again and got very little support.

"I think the western music community was sometimes at odds with him about that just like they're at odds with me because I do western festivals and I do cowboy music but I also do my country hits, 'Lonely Street,' 'It's Over,' and 'Solitaire.' I've got an album full of cowboy songs but I find that people get pissed off if I don't do the country songs because they come to hear those too. It's the same with Murphey, but the western traditionalists don't like it when Michael and I do things like that. But that's part of what made us what we are."

Rex Allen Jr. was born on August 23, 1947, in Chicago during the time his father was appearing on *National Barn Dance* on WLS. Before Rex Jr. was two, the family moved to Hollywood, where Rex Allen became a singing cowboy in the movies. Rex Jr. grew up in Hollywood and from a very early age accompanied his father on the road.

"In high school I started out with a band playing folk music. When I was about fourteen I'd play folk music during the school year but when June came, I'd go out on the road and play rhythm guitar in my father's band—playing cowboy music," said Rex. "When the Beatles came along in the early sixties, they killed folk music, so my band added a set of drums and a microphone, did the same songs. But then we were a rock 'n' roll band. So during my high school years I had a rock 'n' roll band."

There was a generation gap that surfaced between Rex Sr. and Rex Jr. and Rex Jr. went through a period when he thought his father wasn't cool, and Rex Jr. wanted to keep a distance. "I wanted to grow my hair long and he wouldn't allow me to do that," said Rex. "Musically it was very interesting because Dad would say about the Beatles, 'I hate those long-haired hippies,' and kept telling me how bad their music was. According to him, it was terrible music. So one day my Dad and I were talking and he said 'Play me a song.' I played the Beatles song 'Help' but slowed it down and made it a ballad. Then I played another Beatles song, 'In My Life.' He said, 'Those are great songs. Did you write them?' And I said, 'No, they were written by those long-haired hippie Beatles that you hate so much.' That changed Dad's attitude toward them. For the rest of his years, until he died, I'd bring him different things, like Mark O'Connor. I turned Dad on to Mark O'Connor and he became a huge fan. The most wonderful thing about my father is that he gave me the freedom of expression. To a limit. I mean I wasn't allowed to have my hair long but musically he didn't suppress anything. He loved to experiment with music."

As a youngster, Rex Jr. socialized with others in the field of western entertainment. "My parents would have parties and Roy and Dale would be there, Bob Nolan would be there and they'd pass the guitar around," remembered Rex. "Slim Pickens did 'Strawberry Roan' and there's about eight billion different verses for 'Strawberry Roan' and the ones that Slim sang were the filthiest ones I'd ever heard. That's the kind of thing I grew up with. People like Hi Pockets Busse and the Frontiersmen were always around.

"You know, as a performer, there are times when I need to be 'Rex Allen Jr.' for a while. My Dad, Roy and Gene were like that too. They would put on the persona of the singing cowboy star, but I grew up with Dad and Slim Pickins going on hunting trips. The same with Roy Rogers. When I was a kid, I used to spend two weeks of the summer at the Rogers' house with Dusty, and then Dusty would spend two weeks of the summer at my house. Dale was the mom who said, 'No you can't have that.' They were just people to me.

Rex Allen Jr.

"After high school I went to college, even though I didn't want to, but to stay out of the draft. I ended up at the MGM Actor's Studio but I never did much acting. Then I got drafted and went in during the Vietnam War and had people spit on me when I entered the service. I remember those days; it was a horrible, horrible time. But the service was wonderful to me. I ended up in Special Services. My first record had just come out and didn't do a flip but I guess it played a part in me ending up in Special Services. I kept my nose clean and did over ninety variety shows for the troops. I performed at hospitals, was in some theatre productions. I got more education in the service when it came to performing than I ever did at college.

"When I got out of the service I moved back to California and started working in clubs. I worked every beer bar and skull orchard in Southern California, but I wasn't the only one doing them. Tex Williams and Jimmy Wakely did them too; Johnny Bond worked them occasionally. I had an agent—Marty Landau—who booked all of us hillbilly acts on the West Coast. Finally, I got my first record deal and moved to Nashville."

Rex Allen Jr. was signed to Warner Brothers records. His first chart record, "The Great Mail Robbery," came out at the end of 1973. The following year he had three chart records: "Goodbye," "Another Goodbye Song" and "Never Coming Back Again." His biggest hits were "Two Less Lonely People," "I'm Getting Good at Missing You (Solitaire)," "Lonely Street," "No, No, No (I'd Rather Be Free)," "With Love" and "Me and My Broken Heart," which were all top ten records during the 1976–1979 period.

Rex Jr. had a band, a bus and a big overhead on the road. He played regularly on the road but never broke through into the top echelon of hit acts and his last chart record came in 1987. Still, he made his mark in Nashville as a steady, reliable performer and someone whose records fit easily on country radio.

But it was after he moved from Nashville that he had his biggest impact in the country music industry. In 1983 The Nashville Network (TNN) was created and by the 1990s had programming that reached a large number of American homes.

In 1992 Rex Allen Jr. became a regular on *The Statler Brothers Show* on TNN. He had a regular slot in a segment titled "Yesteryear," where songs from a particular year were sung. This eventually spun off into a series of its own, *Yesteryear*, on September 30, 1994. In addition to Rex, the show starred Eddy Raven, Lisa Stewart and Kathy Ballie. Rex said "I have no idea how I got on the Statler Brothers Show. I had gotten a divorce and had to leave town so I moved to Tyler, Texas, which is where Deanna is from. I still had an agent, bus and band based in Nashville but I lived in Texas. One morning the phone rang and Deanna answered it and said, 'you probably want to take this call.' I said, 'Who is it?' She said, 'They claim it's the Statler Brothers.' Yeah, right, but I got on the phone and it was all four of the Statler Brothers on a conference call. They said, 'Rex, we're doing a television show and we'd like you to be on it.' I said, 'I'd love to. Do you want me to do one episode or two?' They said, 'No, we want you to be a regular.' To this day, I don't know how they got my phone number."

However, getting on the show may have had something to do with an old Rex Allen film. "The Statlers and I always had something in common because Don and Harold Reid and Lew DeWitt were big western film buffs," said Rex. "Back in the seventies, my fan club got me a copy of my Dad's first film, *Arizona Cowboy*. I made a copy and sent it to Harold and Don because I always wanted to be the opening act on a Statler Brothers tour. But the Statlers never hired a male, they always hired a female singer like Reba or Barbara Mandrell. Anyway, I sent them the film with a letter that said, 'Dear Stafford Brothers, I understand that you'uns folks like to watch these old western films.' Just a funny letter. I got a letter back from Harold, which started, 'Dear Tex Alvin Jr.' So we had a running gag for years."

During the show's run, the Reid brothers, Harold and Don, who wrote the show, "would throw songs at me every week that were obscure tunes for the 'Yesteryear' segment," said Rex. "Finally, one day Harold and Don walked up to me and they were smiling. I said, 'What's going on?' They said, 'Rex, for two years we have thrown every off-the-wall freak hit record at you and you've known every one of them. And we want to know how?

"I told them that my musical college was AM radio in Los Angeles and they played everything from Squeakin' Deacon to Hoagy Carmichael so I knew all that stuff.

"The Statler Brothers Show still holds the record for being the highest rated cable show on Saturday nights. It was a huge, huge audience. And record companies couldn't understand the audience—still don't. The only thing the record companies in Nashville know about TV is video. They don't understand the power of television or how to market to that audience. What it means for me when it comes to western festivals is that people are more apt to come and see me perform because it's not just the music but the TV exposure too.

"I had a great time with them and had a lot of fun. Those shows were a lot of work because the whole season was taped in about three weeks. That's like ninety songs in three weeks and there's no way you can memorize the lyrics to ninety songs, so everything was on cue cards. The hardest one I did was the old Hank Snow song 'I've Been Everywhere.' I was laughing through most of it because there are so many words to that song that cue cards were flying behind me."

In 1997 Rex Allen Jr. wrote, staged and starred in *Gone Country*, a major stage production in Las Vegas. But the show took a toll on him and almost marked the end of his performing career. "Before we staged *Gone Country*, I went to Las Vegas eight months ahead of time. I was still on the road but I commuted back and forth," said Rex. "I was vice president of entertainment for this resort and we built a theater from the ground up. They hired Deanna and me to do the first show at the resort, and I wrote the show and it lasted about eight months. I worked two shows a day six days a week. Deanna was dealing with the seventeen women on the show, and there were always problems to be dealt with there. Then there were the men, and one guy was always mad at some other guy. I was off Monday but Monday I had a corporate staff meeting at eight in the morning. I was also doing all the payrolls, so I worked seven days a week for two years. When I finished that show, I went to the house, put my guitar in the corner and told Deanna, 'I hope I never pick up a guitar again!

"It had been wonderful but I'd had enough, and it was only because of Johnny Western that I went back singing. John called one day and said, 'What are you doing?' I said, 'NOTHING!' He said, 'I want you to come to Gene Autry, Oklahoma,' and I said, 'I don't want to go to Gene Autry, Oklahoma.' He said 'Yeah, I know but you really need to come to Gene Autry.' I said, 'Why do I need to go to Gene Autry, Oklahoma? I don't even know where it is.' He said, 'Well, they're giving me an award and I want you to present the award.' So I said, 'O.K., for you I'll do that.' Then he said, 'By the way, bring your guitar.' I said, 'I don't play anymore.' He said, 'Yeah, I know. Bring your guitar anyway.' I said, 'John, I've had buses and bands for the past fifteen to twenty years and I've had enough.' He said, "Yeah, right. Bring your guitar and be prepared to sing a few songs.' So I said, 'All right.'

"So my wife and I climbed on a plane and went to Gene Autry, Oklahoma, and for the first time in twenty-five years I went out on a stage just me and a guitar and played—and had a great time! Part of the reason I had a wonderful time is that I got to do all those wonderful songs I could never do before. When you have a band you have a set show you have to do and I always did 'Tumbling Tumbleweeds,' 'Cool Water' and 'Streets of Laredo.' But I never got to do 'Ghost Riders in the Sky,' and if somebody wanted 'Ride, Cowboy, Ride' I had to say, 'Sorry, the band doesn't know it.' But there I got to go out on stage and do an hour and fifteen minutes with just the guitar and have a great time. The funny thing is that through all the bus and band years, the 'Gone Country' and Las Vegas years, my Dad would say, 'You need to get rid of that damn band. It's covering you up. Just do you and the guitar.'

"Out of the mouths of the old wise ones sometimes comes the most wonderful suggestions." [Rex smiled.] One of the highlights of my career was when I got to do my solo show for my Dad. I did it in Tucson. He came and saw the show and loved it. Because of that, about sixty percent of the dates I do now are just me and the guitar.

"People ask me about longevity. Dad certainly had it; he was around a long time. More than Roy or Gene, who both stopped performing. The key is that you have to continually reinvent yourself. My Dad taught me that. I remember when I was fifteen or sixteen years old, he handed me a Wallensack tape recorder and the *Los Angeles Times* and said, 'Son, if you're going to be in this business, you're going to have to know how to read.' I said, 'Dad, I already know how to read.' He said, 'No, you need to learn how to read copy.' He said, 'My business is changing. I've been in movies, television and performing but my business is moving and I'm doing more and more narrations and commercials. That's how my life is changing.' So I sat down with the *Los Angeles Times* and my Dad taught me how to read copy. Dad continually reinvented himself and by example he taught me to do the same thing.

"Lives and careers are like curves; there are peaks and valleys. We all have them. I had one of the valleys several years ago, right after the 'Gone Country' show closed in Vegas, where I sat down and was kicking myself in the butt, thinking, *I'm a failure*, so on and so forth, but I went back thanks to Johnny Western and started having fun with the music. Johnny taught me that what matters is the music—that's what really matters. Still, I found me kicking myself one day and going down and down until I realized, *Hey, you've had over fifty top fifty records, you've been on the most popular television show in cable history, you have a wonderful heritage, and you've entertained people all over the world. What a wonderful career! And it's not over yet!*

"I had one down period for almost two years when I was the director of the Media Department at Baptist Hospital in Nashville. "That was 1988 and 1989. I was off the road. I still worked occasionally but not very much. It was a great experience, a great education. But like my wife said, 'All you guys are basically hams at heart. Once you're in this business you basically never get out of it.'

"There's a lot of things I credit my Dad with—things that he taught me and things I try to teach my kids. My Dad treated everybody the same. It didn't make any difference to Dad if you were the president of General Motors or a cowhand building fences. He treated everyone the same—as genuine and as honest as he could. What he taught me was that everyone has something to give to you if you'll allow them to give it to you—a piece of themselves. I try to live my life that way."

"I live in Las Vegas because I love the West and it's very easy to commute out of there," said Rex. "My year runs from January through April when I generally perform in the Southwest. My country music buddies don't understand it because they say, 'What are you doing?' and I say 'I'm working big RV parks.' They say, 'Rex, that's horrible—you have to work RV parks!' I say, 'No, you don't understand. There's an RV park I work in Tucson that will not allow any RV in the park if their motor home is worth less than a million dollars. They book people like me, Glen Campbell and Willie Nelson.

"Those RV parks have wonderful stages and activities departments. So I work those and then I usually have a couple of months to do other things and then in June I start the fairs with a little band. I usually work with Leroy Van Dyke; we have a package called 'Country Gold.' I do probably ten to fifteen dates with them. Then, in the fall, I go back into concerts all over the United States.

"I've done some Western festivals, like Mary Brown's Festival of the West, but I try to limit those to a great extent. I bring a larger, different kind of audience to the festivals. I have the heritage of Rex Allen, and I've had hit songs on the radio like 'Can You Hear Those Pioneers' and 'Ride, Cowboy, Ride,' so I carry the western heritage. But I was also on television for eight years with the Statler Brothers."

Rex says there are "a lot of people in the western music business" that he admires: I think there are some unbelievably talented people coming into the western music business and it makes me sad that they are not getting the recognition they deserve."

"I think that I'm at the point in my career where I really care a lot about two things career-wise," Rex Allen Jr. continued. "One is the music. I want to take people on some kind of musical historical journey through my music. I'm not trying to educate people, I'm just trying to say, ... 'It's here, let's see it.' The second thing is that it's extremely important for me to try to remind people where our heritage comes from. I think the best way for me to do that is get people interested in the two hundred fifty to three hundred singing cowboy films. The Western channel has only four of my dad's films; they don't have any of Tex Ritter's.

"I think that eventually students will write doctoral theses on that genre of film and what it did for the morality of children. You know, Tom Brokaw wrote a wonderful book called *The Greatest Generation*, but I think Brokaw missed something when he talked about the morality of that generation. In my opinion, they got that morality from the films of Rex Allen, Roy Rogers and Gene Autry."

SOURCE:

Allen, Rex, Jr. Personal interview with the author, May 31, 2006, in Nashville, Tennessee.

36

Lynn Anderson

Before her songs were heard on the radio, Lynn Anderson was seen riding horses in rodeo arenas. And even when she was on top in the world of country music, her songs heard all over the radio, she was still in love with horses and riding in horse shows.

Lynn Rene Anderson is the granddaughter of Norwegian and Swedish immigrants who came to the United States to help build the Great Northern Railroad. She was born September 26, 1947, in Grand Forks, North Dakota, to Casey and Liz Anderson. In North Dakota, Lynn's grandparents founded a "saddle club" and Lynn says, "I could ride before I could walk—at least that's what they tell me." Laddie and Vego were the names of her grandparent's horses, and she remembers taking them on sleigh rides and skiing behind them.

When she was a young girl, the Andersons moved to San Jose, California, where it was warmer. Casey, Liz and Lynn lived in a subdivision. Lynn begged her parents to move to a ranch, so they bought a "ranch" that was two acres in Sacramento. "There were hundreds of acres surrounding it," remembered Lynn, when they moved. Her first horse was Apache, which was purchased for $75 and included a McClellan saddle and bridle. "We also adopted a mustang, then tried a Morgan," said Lynn. "But I learned to ride on Apache." When she was nine years old, Lynn won second place in the Western Horsemanship Championship held at the Cow Palace in San Francisco.

Then her grandparents came to California with two horses, a Tennessee Walking Horse named Dakota Thunderbird and a palomino named Dakota Chief. At home she was a tomboy. "I'd get up and feed the horses, maybe ride a little before I went to school," said Lynn. "Our school's team name was the Broncos, so Apache became the school mascot." As she grew into her high school years, Lynn's family had a series of horses, "all named after TV shows," according to Lynn. "There was Cheyenne, Sugarfoot and Maverick."

During high school, Lynn landed a job working for a radio station and then, after graduating, became the secretary to the general manager and recorded advertising spots. Meanwhile, she continued to enter horse shows.

While Lynn was in the show ring, practicing with her horses, her mom, Liz, was in the stands writing songs. She began sending those songs to Nashville and Los Angeles, trying to get producers and artists interested in recording them. Chet Atkins heard some demos and offered Liz a recording contract with RCA, which caused the Anderson family to move to Nashville. This was devastating for Lynn. "I had a boyfriend back in California," she remembers. "I thought I would die!"

Before they moved to Nashville, the Anderson family traveled to the Salinas Rodeo in California where Lynn competed in the contest for "Miss Rodeo Queen of California." During the car ride Liz was writing a song, "Ride, Ride, Ride." Lynn announced, "When you finish that, I want to record it." This was a surprise: Lynn had never shown any interest in being a singer or having a recording contract before this time.

Lynn Anderson did not win the "Miss Rodeo Queen of California" title. "There were three parts to the contest. I finished first in horsemanship, first in scholarship, but fourth in personality and appearance. So I finished third in that contest because I was rude and ugly!" laughs Lynn.

Beginning in 1966 Liz Anderson had 19 chart singles for RCA. Her biggest hits were "The Game of Triangles" (with Bobby Bare and Norma Jean) and "Mama Spank," which both finished in the top five on *Billboard*'s country charts. She also had a duet with Lynn, "Mother, May I."

Liz signed a publishing agreement with Slim Williamson, who also owned a small record label, Chart Records. Slim signed Lynn to his label in 1966. Her first session was a "split session," with Lynn recording "Ride, Ride, Ride" and "In Person" while another Chart artist, Jerry Lane, recorded two songs. "Ride, Ride, Ride" was released that year and rose to number 36 on the country charts. That and her next two chart releases were written by her mom: "If I Kiss You (Will You Go Away)" and "Keeping Up Appearances," a duet with Jerry Lane. There was a problem with recording for a small label. "I kept getting covered," said Lynn. "After I released 'Ride, Ride, Ride,' Brenda Lee covered it and had a pop hit."

Lynn had a series of chart records on Chart: "Too Much of You," "Promises Promises," "Not Another Time," "Big Girls Don't Cry," "Flattery Will Get You Everywhere," "Our House Is Not a Home," "That's a No No," "He'd Still Love Me," "I've Been Everywhere," "Rocky Top," and "It Wasn't God Who Made Honky-tonk Angels."

During the 1967 and 1968 television seasons, Lynn was a regular on the *Lawrence Welk Show*. That booking came because Larry Welk, Lawrence's son, saw Lynn's album cover and had a crush on the pretty girl sitting on a horse, wearing the outfit she wore for the Miss Rodeo Queen of California title. Larry also loved horses and begged his father to book Lynn on his show so they could meet. "Mom and Dad tried to get me married to Larry," said Lynn. "But it didn't work."

At first, Lynn sang songs like "Buttons and Bows" as well as songs with the Lennon Sisters and other group songs. "Country music was 'country and western' to the people in California, because the only thing they knew about country was Gene Autry, Roy Rogers and Bob Hope in *Paleface*," said Lynn. "So they dressed me up in high button shoes, gingham dresses, with a parasol, and put me beside a wagon wheel with a bale of hay. One day I told Mr. Welk that I wanted to quit because what I was singing was NOT country music. Mr. Welk was an incredible marketer and paid attention to what people liked and then he'd go with it. So he started letting me sing a country song every Saturday night, including my most recent release." The *Lawrence Welk Show* was an important step in Lynn Anderson's career. "The Welk Show allowed me to have crossover success," she said. "That show set up 'Rose Garden' and without the Welk show I don't believe that song would have been as big as it was."

While Lynn was having problems on the West Coast with people's perception of country music, she also had problems in Nashville being accepted in that world. "It took me a while to get accepted in Nashville," said Lynn. "I was seen as a kid from California on the Welk show—not a real country artist. There was a rift between California and Nashville country and I was somewhere in between. The West Coast was grounded in western music and I fought against that at the time. What gave me legitimacy in the country field in Nashville was my record of 'Rocky Top.'" "Rocky Top" was released in the spring of 1970 and reached number 17 on the country charts.

Lynn Anderson met Glenn Sutton through publisher Al Gallico at an awards dinner. During her time with the Welk show in California, "Mr. Welk and Mom and Dad tried to get me married to Larry," laughs Lynn. But Sutton, a producer for the CBS labels in Nashville, began to visit her in California because he was interested in producing her. A romance developed and the two married in 1968.

CBS then bought her contract from Slim Williamson at Chart Records and in 1970 she began recording for Epic, one of CBS's labels, produced by Sutton. Her first release was "Stay There 'Til I Get There," which was written by Sutton and became a top ten record. Her second Columbia release was "I Found You Just in Time," written by Sutton and his writing partner, Billy Sherrill.

"Glenn was very politically connected at Columbia and Epic [the two CBS labels]," said Lynn. "His writing partner was Billy Sherrill and their publisher was Al Gallico. Billy and Glenn wrote a lot of hits but Billy was Glenn's boss at CBS so Billy got the first choice on all their cowrites. Glenn would come home and play me a song they'd cowritten, like 'Your Good Girl's Gonna Go Bad' or 'I Don't Wanna Play House,' and I'd go, 'That's great—can I record it?' and he'd say, 'No, that goes to Tammy [Wynette].' So I had to find songs from other sources, which is why a lot of my songs were written by other people."

That's how she came to record "I Never Promised You a Rose Garden," a song written by Atlanta singer-songwriter Joe South. "Rose Garden" first hit the country chart in November 1970 and stayed in the number one position for five weeks. The *Rose Garden* album won a Grammy for Anderson for Best Female Country Vocal Performance and for Joe South as the songwriter. The album was an international hit and achieved platinum status in the United States.

Her next Columbia release, "You're My Man," stayed at number one for two weeks, and her third Columbia single, "How Can I Unlove You," remained in the number one spot on the country charts for three weeks. "How Can I Unlove You" was also written by Joe South, whose own recordings of "These Are Not My People," "Games People Play," "Don't It Make You Want to Go Home" and "Walk a Mile in My Shoes" were all pop hits. Lynn had a string of hits on Columbia, hitting the number one spot with "Keep Me in Mind" and "What a Man My Man Is," and reached the top five with "Cry," "Listen to a Country Song," "Fool Me," "Top of the World," and "Sing About Love."

It was a busy time for her, touring and doing personal appearances but she continued to enter horse shows. "I'd go sing at a concert, then fly to a horse show, then fly back the next night for a concert. I was real serious about showing horses!" said Lynn.

Anderson's last chart record for Columbia was "Even Cowgirls Get the Blues," in 1980. It could have been the title of the next chapter of her life.

Lynn and Glenn Sutton divorced in 1977. She then married Harold "Spook" Stream and moved to Louisiana. "I told CBS, 'I quit,' and they said, 'You can't.' Then I told them, 'I'm pregnant' and that didn't make them happy either," said Lynn. "I still did a little recording but it was never the same without Glenn as my musical liaison."

Lynn and Spook had two children, but that marriage also ended in divorce. So she moved back to Nashville, where she reconnected with Mentor Williams, whom she had met at an ASCAP Awards event when Mentor won an award for his song "Drift Away." When she moved back to Nashville, she was adrift as a recording artist. Lynn had never had a manager: "Dad mostly managed me at first and then I married Glenn and he managed me while I was at CBS. I never had to call the head of the label—Glenn did that." Since she did not have an outside manager, she did not have an advocate working on her career and knocking on doors for her. Lynn was at a low point in her life, filled with regrets. "I remember Bob Hope asked me to go to Vietnam with him for his Christmas tour but Glenn didn't want me to go," said Lynn. "I regretted that. I was also offered a part in the movie *W.W. and the Dixie Dance Kings* but Glenn didn't want me to do that, either. He didn't want to see me making out with Burt Reynolds in the backseat of a car!"

"Walking away from CBS like I did was a huge mistake," said Lynn. "I walked away from what a lot of people dream about. When I came back from Louisiana I tried to get my career going but I was a little afraid about whether I'd be accepted or not. It was awfully easy for me at the beginning because my recording career was almost an accident; it came from being Liz Anderson's daughter. I was there when she opened the door. There's no way I would ever have been lucky enough to become a star if not for Mom kicking those doors open. She's the one who worked for years and years to get her music to publishers and record labels. When that door squeaked open, I snuck in."

When Lynn returned to Nashville, she never even thought about calling CBS to try to get back on that label; she felt that door was permanently closed. However, she did sign with Bonnie Garner, a former CBS vice president,

Lynn Anderson (photograph courtesy of Packy Smith).

as a manager. Still, she was in no place to resume her career where it had left off as a hit recording artist. Those days were behind her.

After all those years on top—and a shelf filled with awards from the country music industry—Lynn and Mentor lived in Nashville for several years before they decided to move to Taos, New Mexico. "Mentor was originally from New Mexico and wanted to get back," said Lynn. "And I fell in love with Taos."

The pace was slower and peace came haltingly. She loved the western way of life. "I wear the boots and hat every day," said Lynn. "It's not just for show." Liz Anderson increasingly wrote western songs and recorded western music. This stirred fond memories of Roy Rogers and Dale Evans in Lynn.

"You had to pick a favorite—Gene Autry or Roy Rogers—and I picked Roy and Dale. You had to be faithful to your hero and I was," said Lynn, who came to know Roy and Dale from working with them. "I rode a horse into a rodeo arena, just like Roy and Dale did. I was the only country singer who could do that because I grew up riding horses. I saw several rodeos with them and we sometimes traded dates. I would be on one night and they would be on the next night. I actually worked more with Dale, who was my hero. I remember sitting in dressing rooms, just swapping stories with Dale." There was another connection. "I've always called my parents 'Roy and Dale' because they're very much the same kind of people as the real Roy Rogers and Dale Evans," said Lynn. "They are similar because they epitomize the cowboy way."

As Lynn talked with her parents and listened to her mom's western songs, she began to feel an urge to record them. "I wanted to make Mom and Dad happy," said Lynn. "I hadn't recorded anything for a while and the combination of Mom having cancer and my respect for her and her music made me realize that this was something I needed to do."

The result is her album *Cowgirl*, which contains a song she cowrote with her mother, "Full Moon in Baghdad." "Singing was always easier for me," said Lynn. "Besides, I was always around a writer—first Mom, then Glenn and now Mentor—and so I had made it a point of not writing. But on this song, I wrote down all the ideas I wanted to say and took them to Mother. And that's how that song came."

Lynn resumed performing. "I don't want to die in the back of a Silver Eagle," said Lynn. Then she tells the story of Fern Sawyer, who ran the New Mexico State Fair for years. "Fern rode a horse leading the Grand Entry at the New Mexico State Fair, then after the Entry, when the horse stopped, she fell off. That's probably a good way to go."

Life certainly has its ups and downs, and Lynn has known her share of both. But she is now happy, active in her career and enjoying her work with a number of charities. "I helped found Special Riders in Franklin, Tennessee, and was on their board for several years," said Lynn. "That program started when my daughter had a birthday party and we had horses there for the kids to ride. There was one boy on crutches who wanted to ride so we got him in the saddle, put someone on each side of him and had someone else lead the horse. Later that evening his mom called back and said he couldn't stop talking about that horse ride. She said, 'Can we keep this going?' So that's how we started."

In Fort Worth there is the Rocky Top Riders. "I didn't found it," said Lynn. "But they named it after my song." She has been on the board of the National Autistic Treatment Center in Dallas and does an annual fund-raiser for them. She's also involved in Canine Search and Rescue. "We started fund-raising for 'all things that are creatures,'" said Lynn. "It is animals working with people. My special love is working with kids and horses."

Lynn conducts Rodeo Queen clinics, helping young girls learn "how to get ready for those contests. All the little stuff, from grooming your horse to grooming yourself. How to present your horse and yourself," said Lynn. "We have clinics on everything from how to wear your hair under your hat to matching your outfit with your horse." Lynn has also been involved in the American Cancer Society through the National Cutting Horse Association. "We use horses to raise money for cancer care," said Lynn. "My special contribution is wearing a pink cowboy hat for cancer awareness."

Lynn Anderson found a new home in western music. "I do it because I love this music," she said. "Having walked away from Nashville and the country music business, I still want to sing because I love it and I love hearing the applause of an audience."

SOURCE:

Anderson, Liz. Phone interview with the author, May 9 and May 11, 2007.

37

Ian Tyson

When he was in his 40s Ian Tyson fell in love with the English language. He read a lot and wrote a lot, and out of that has come his western songs. Those songs happened at the right time, because it was during that period the Elko Cowboy Poetry Gathering began. This event, started in 1985 by folklorist Hal Cannon and cowboy poet Waddie Mitchell, was a seminal event in the resurgence of "cowboy culture" in the United States and revived a genre that had been forgotten: western music.

The early years were years of stumbling for Tyson. He stumbled into being a musician, and he stumbled to his success in folk music. Then he stumbled out of the folk era and out of his marriage to his singing partner, Sylvia. And then he stumbled into the West. But, as Tyson notes, "When you stumble into something, you have to do something about it." Tyson did that, developing a strong career on the folk circuit for about ten years before hosting a popular TV show in Toronto, then moving to Alberta where he found a home in western music.

Ian Tyson's father, George Dawson Tyson, grew up in Liverpool, England, and left in 1906 for Canada. The British Tysons (Ian's grandfather) were well off and George Tyson always expected to inherit a good deal of money.

Arriving in Canada, George Tyson worked as a ranch hand near Calgary, served in World War I, then sold insurance. He married Margaret Campbell and the family lived on Vancouver Island, where Ian Dawson Tyson was born on September 25, 1933. Margaret's inheritance assured a private education for young Ian, who grew up loving cowboys through reading books by Will James. This led to his entering some rodeos, but the cowboy life was just one influence of many on young Ian.

After high school, Tyson went to the Vancouver School of Art and studied impressionism as well as commercial art. He had not been terribly influenced by music until he found himself in a hospital in Calgary with a broken ankle after being tossed from a bronc in a rodeo. The year was 1956 and Elvis was exploding. Sun Records, the label that launched Elvis, had released "I Walk the Line" by Johnny Cash. This was the first song Tyson, then in his 20s, tried to play as he learned the guitar. That guitar came from a patient in the bed next to Tyson. "It took a long time to learn how to play," said Tyson. "I'm not a natural musician, but I'm sure glad I stuck with it."

Tyson was in his third year at art school when he learned to play the guitar; he soon got with a rockabilly band, The Sensational Stripes, and started playing dances. "Rockabilly was something that I loved and I could play," said Tyson. "It only had three chords." Another appealing aspect was that Elvis had demonstrated that a guy with a guitar could get girls.

Tyson fell in love with a beautiful young lady of Greek descent and followed her to Los Angeles. The stay was brief—she soon sent him packing—but that experience was later immortalized in his song "Four Strong Winds."

In 1958, Ian Tyson graduated from the Vancouver School of Art and, having read Jack Kerouac's *On the Road*, decided to hit the road himself. Hitchhiking south, he was picked up near Seattle and driven to Chicago. From Chicago, Tyson went to Toronto, where he landed a job with an advertising agency and bought a guitar.

The folk craze hit America in 1958 when the Kingston Trio's "Tom Dooley" reached number one on the pop charts. Soon, almost everyone was playing a guitar and singing folk songs, and Tyson joined the crowd. He formed a duet with Don Francks and quickly established himself on the Toronto folk music scene.

In his biography, *I Never Sold My Saddle*, Tyson remembers he "became an instant folk musician. I'd sing those songs in the coffeehouses.... Soon I was working every night in a different coffeehouse, so I gave up my day job." Tyson also says that, at that time, "I had no plans or ambitions about anything. I had no focus, no goals. No high expectations. I just tried to be good at what I did."

Ian Tyson (photograph courtesy of Packy Smith).

In 1959 he met Sylvia Fricker while he was still working with the ad agency. She sang to him over the phone, wanting help to break into the folk circles in Toronto, and they met soon afterwards. Sylvia, from Chatham, Ontario, about 30 miles east of Detroit, was seven years younger than Tyson and came from a musical family.

Ian and Sylvia began performing together in 1959 after she had moved to Toronto in the fall of that year. They put together an impressive repertoire of blues, spirituals, English and Scottish ballads and American folk songs and practiced their act. In the summer of 1961 they performed at the first Mariposa Folk Festival and acquired a manager, Edgar Cowan, who was involved with Mariposa.

Ian & Sylvia had gone as far as they could go in Toronto, so they set their sights on New York, the mecca for folk singers. Cowan sent letters to a number of agents and set up a few appointments in New York. Joe Taylor, a newspaperman, drove them down and they went to Gerde's Folk City, where they performed. This caught the ear of legendary manager Albert Grossman, who managed Odetta at the time and was putting together the group that became Peter, Paul and Mary. Grossman signed them to a management contract, got them a record contract with Vanguard, and booked them into the Gate O'Horn in Chicago for six weeks. They played the college circuit and performed on the TV show *Hootenanny*.

In 1961 they had a real breakthrough when they performed on the main stage at the Newport Folk Festival and their performance was reviewed by Robert Shelton in the *New York Times*. Soon afterward, they played a concert at town hall in New York and that show was also reviewed by the *New York Times*.

Ian & Sylvia recorded their first two albums, *Northern Journey* and *Early Morning Rain*. At this point, Ian Tyson had all but forgotten about his love for the West and cowboys. He was a successful folk singer, making good money and performing in concert. Ian & Sylvia sold out Carnegie Hall twice.

Inspired by Bob Dylan, who had begun writing songs, Ian tried his hand at writing. His first attempt produced the classic "Four Strong Winds," which Ian and Sylvia recorded on their second album. The song came easily to Ian on a rainy fall day as he sat in Albert Grossman's New York apartment. It was an autobiographical song, written about that Greek girlfriend from his art school days, although Tyson later admitted he "didn't know what the four strong winds were." A later song, "Someday Soon," which was a originally a big hit for Judy Collins, "was completely made up. I don't know where it came from, but I made it up," said Tyson. At this point, Ian & Sylvia were a professional couple. In 1963, they got "personal," and then they got married on June 26, 1964. The following year their son, Clay Dawson Tyson, was born and the couple bought a house in the upscale Rosedale area of Toronto. It was a marriage that was born from their professional relationship, but on the personal level Ian and Sylvia were already headed in different directions when not on the stage.

When Ian got his first big check for "Four Strong Winds" in 1963, he bought a cattle farm in Newtonville, Ontario, east of Toronto. Then, in 1969, when the big check came from Judy Collins' version of his song "Someday Soon," he bought the adjoining farm and stocked it with Hereford cattle and started breeding quarter horses. Sylvia was not interested in life on the farm; she was made for the city.

The best years for Ian & Sylvia were from mid–1962 until mid–1964, when they toured heavily and sold a good number of albums for Vanguard. But in 1964 the Beatles hit and began the era of the British Invasion. "The Beatles shut us down," said Tyson in his autobiography, *I Never Sold My Saddle*. "It was over. OVER! We didn't know how to play with electric instruments. We didn't know how to use drums. We didn't know how to EQ. Then California guys like Jefferson Airplane and the Grateful Dead came up and they had several months on us. They'd been playing badly with amps, but at least they'd been doing it. All us folkies were just standing there with egg on our faces. The only one who had the guts to challenge the rock 'n' roll guys on their own terms was Dylan. He just jumped in."

Ian & Sylvia were already out of step with the folk movement by this time. The early and mid–1960s were a time when folk music became heavily political, addressing issues like civil rights and the Vietnam War. But Ian Tyson was not political—he just wasn't tuned into all that. There was pressure to write and perform political songs but Ian & Sylvia missed that boat and, as a result, they found themselves not quite fitting in with where the folk movement was headed. "We outlived our usefulness, I guess," said Tyson of those days.

Ian Tyson did not have to worry about the draft; he was classified 4-F because of his rodeo injury, a shattered ankle that had pins in it. "I just had no concept of what Vietnam was until I went to Japan and saw these servicemen, saw on their faces that they'd been through hell," remembered Tyson.

Ian & Sylvia tried to join the folk-rock movement with a country rock band, The Great Speckled Bird, named after the Roy Acuff song that got him on the *Grand Ole Opry* in 1938. The folk music world had shunned country music during the 1960s because country music represented the conservative movement in America, while the folkies were liberals. Ian Tyson had grown up loving country music in Canada and did not have that prejudice. Roy Acuff's song "Wreck on the Highway" was a song he'd heard in his youth and always remembered. So the group went to Nashville and recorded *Nashville*, their last album for Vanguard.

Still, the duo had to contend with audiences who came to see and hear the Ian & Sylvia of old, not a reinvented country-rock group. Success had trapped them and they felt locked in, unable to change. "We should have changed our music," said Tyson. "But we still had one foot in the Ian & Sylvia thing. We got what we deserved, I guess, which was nothing."

One thing that saved them was their songwriting. Ian had written "Four Strong Winds" and "Someday Soon" and those songs were recorded by numerous artists, giving him some income, although that eventually dried up. Sylvia had written "You Were On My Mind," which was a number three pop hit for We Five in 1965.

In 1969 the Great Speckled Bird's first album was released, produced by Todd Rundgren for Albert Grossman's Bearsville Records. It was leased to the Ampex label, where it died. The group then parted company with Albert Grossman; their new manager was Bert Block, a former associate of Grossman who managed Kris Kristofferson. Grossman had put most of his energies behind Bob Dylan, whom he started managing as the singer began his career.

Ian Tyson then became host of *Nashville North* in 1969. The following season it became *The Ian Tyson Show*, which was broadcast on CFTO, Toronto's flagship station on the Canadian Television Network, CTV. Sylvia appeared on only half of the shows; this was Ian's show and he performed Nashville-style country music. His rival was *The Tommy Hunter Show*, a popular program on the CBC network.

Tyson was, by his own admission, "pretty messed up during that time," smoking a lot of marijuana and frustrated with the demands of stardom and the music industry. Whenever possible, he slipped away from Toronto and headed out to his 300-acre farm.

Beginning with the TV show, Ian became a solo act and was doing quite well when suddenly, in 1975, he quit the show, recorded an album for A&M, *Ol' Eon*, and headed out as a solo act. Things did not go well and by the fall of 1976 his life was falling apart, both personally and professionally. On the personal side, Ian was still married to Sylvia, but he was not happy and the two were headed in opposite directions. He wanted to sing with a country band and she wanted to stay home and be a mom.

Tyson wanted to move to Nashville but couldn't because a 1971 marijuana bust in Toronto meant he could not obtain a green card. Still, in the fall of 1976, he came to Nashville where he had a manager, Melva Matthews, and where the Outlaw Movement, led by Waylon and Willie, was in full swing. Ian Tyson thought he fit in with the Outlaw Movement. "[B]ut I never could get anything going in Nashville," he said. He discovered that he really didn't fit in with the country music establishment in Nashville—and the Outlaw Movement was actually part of that establishment, albeit a renegade version of it. "I never got a shot because I never could schmooze," remembered Tyson. "That's held me back more than anything else over the years. I've got great friends, but I could never do the industry schmooze."

Tyson went back to Toronto and formed a band, but his heart wasn't in it. He wanted to move to Texas but the drug bust prevented it. "I'm sure glad that didn't work out," said Tyson. "Texas has changed a lot; it's not cowboy anymore." He was booked in Alberta for a couple of dates and, while there, took a look at the Rocky Mountains. He decided he'd rather starve beside the Rockies than live comfortably in Toronto.

Tyson sold his farm in Toronto, divorced Sylvia, and moved to Alberta, where he worked on a ranch in Pincher Creek where the foreman was an old buddy, Alan Young. Tyson lived in a cabin on that ranch for two years, writing only a couple of songs. "I just shut her down," said Tyson. "I couldn't care less about music. I just wasn't interested. I was interested in riding wild horses and chasing wild cattle. I had the middle-aged crazies."

Tyson still performed occasionally and in 1977 began singing with a band, Northwest Rebellion, that did a Canadian tour. The songwriting royalties were no longer coming in, so Tyson's income came from being a cowboy and a weekend singer at a honky-tonk. Then, in 1979, Neil Young released "Four Strong Winds" on his album *Comes a Time* and the money from that song allowed Tyson to make a down payment on the T-Bar-Y Ranch. In October of that year he released his first album in four years, *One Jump Ahead of the Devil*, on Boot Records, an indie label out of Toronto.

The touring life did not suit Tyson, who settled into a regular gig at Ranchman's, a club in Calgary that paid him well to perform about eight weeks a year. There Tyson sang country music songs made famous by George Strait, Bob Wills and Merle Haggard. At the Ranchman's, Tyson met a teenage waitress, Twylla Biblow, who helped him at the ranch. Their daughter was born at the beginning of 1986; in July, the couple wed.

Shortly after the birth of his daughter, Ian Tyson went to Elko, Nevada, to perform at the Cowboy Poetry Gathering. In 1983, Ian had released *Old Corrals and Sagebrush*, an album of western songs for Columbia Records. The album was recorded in his home and was inspired by an old friend who shod horses and encouraged Tyson to sing some old songs with just his guitar. That led to Ian's writing songs and recording the album. That album led to his appearance at the first Elko gathering. "There's no way to minimize the power of Elko to our sub-culture," said Tyson. "Waddie Mitchell and Hal Cannon didn't know it when they started it, but it was something that was waiting to happen. It created a small industry."

It was through recording this album, and then his appearance at Elko, that Ian Tyson finally found his voice. "It's like it was preordained," he said. "It's like I was selected by something, somebody to do this. I know how changeable and difficult the journey was. When I finally got here, it was like waking up and realizing that this was the work I was always meant to do. It's scary, but it's also wonderful. Cowboy music is much freer than the folk stuff. You're not expected to do a certain song a certain way every night. There are no rules like that. It's just 'Tell me a story.'"

The performance at Elko was an epiphany for Ian Tyson. There, he connected with the audience, and the audience connected with him. The heart and soul of cowboy life was gathered at Elko for the Poetry Gathering and Tyson's songs were a communal experience for those gathered there. This is the kind of experience that most performers only dream about. Prior to Elko, Tyson had no knowledge of or experience with western music. He wasn't aware of Riders in the Sky, although he did know Don Edwards: "I used to go to Fort Worth with my cutting horses and heard Don at the White Elephant. We couldn't believe that someone else was into this music; we were glad to find each other."

Tyson's next album, *Ian Tyson*, was also on Columbia but did not sell well and he left the label. Then he was back on TV, cohosting a show with Dick Caldwell in Edmonton, *Sun Country*. A new album was being born, but Tyson did not have the money, or label support, to record it. The songs were written in an isolated cabin and Tyson set out to record them. He contacted car dealer Einar Brasso and rancher Dan Lifkin, who bankrolled the album for $37,000. Adrian Chornowol, a classical pianist, produced it. "He was totally on top of everything. He was a genius. He had a complete vision. Arrangements. Everything. It's like he was chosen—and whoever chose him turned it off for him," said Tyson. (After producing the album, Chornowol had a sex change operation and changed his name to Toby Dancer.) *Cowboyography* was pressed up on Eastern Slope Records, Ian's own label, with the Edmonton-based Stony Plain label handling Canadian distribution. A song on that album, "Navajo Rug," a song Tyson cowrote with Tom Russell, was a hit on radio, gaining considerable airplay.

But it was the album that established Ian Tyson as a voice for the West. Some of the songs on the album were old ones. "Old Cheyenne" came from the *You Were on My Mind* album of 1972, and "Summer Wages" was on two Ian & Sylvia albums, *So Much for Dreaming* (1967) and *Ian and Sylvia* (1971). The album sold over 100,000 copies and led to Tyson receiving his first awards. "I'm singing subculture music for an audience that's gotten much bigger than the subculture," said Tyson. "I just wanted to be the voice of the cowboys, the working cowboys, because those guys can't relate to the Nashville urban cowboys. I just wanted to speak for them. I didn't know it was going to get out of hand."

In 1988, Tyson released *I Outgrew the Wagon*, then five more albums followed: *And Stood There Amazed* (1991), *Eighteen Inches of Rain* (1994), *All the Good'uns* (1996), *Lost Herd* (1999) and *Live at Longview* (2002). Each of those albums solidified Tyson's reputation as a voice of the West, from the West, for the West.

In November 2003, Ian Tyson went into a studio in Toronto and recorded *Songs from the Gravel Road*. The title came from a gravel road, about a mile long, that Tyson walked to get to his cabin, where he writes songs. He recorded with studio musicians who were not "country" or "western." "They said, 'we don't know anything about this cowboy stuff,'" said Tyson. "I told them to not worry about the cowboy—I would supply that—I just wanted them to play big. And they caught on pretty quick."

Most of the songs were brand new; Tyson worked on them during the summer at his home and recorded demos with his band. They'd never been performed live. "There was no opportunity," said Tyson. "But I wasn't going to worry about that. I wanted a sound and I got a sound." Things ran smoothly in the studio. "After two days, I knew it was special. That's why I went to Toronto. It's so much easier to sing the songs with those professional studio musicians," said Tyson. "We worked with a great producer, Danny Greenspoon, who had done part of the *Lost Herd* album. The only problem was that you've got to be careful about what key you pick to sing. Those guys can play anything so if you pick the wrong key, then off you go!"

"Silver Bell" had been written previously and was a song for his daughter, who is a barrel racer. "I wanted to surprise her with that song." "One Morning in May" was a song he'd heard on Jim Rooney's album and decided to record. Tyson was going through a difficult divorce at the time he was putting those songs together, and "Love Without End" and "So No More" both came out of that experience.

Tyson spoke of the last two songs on the album, "Moisture" and "Casey": "I didn't know what to do with [them]," said Tyson. "Neither did the producer." The songs had been recorded live at East Longview Hall, and Tyson wanted them on the album but wasn't sure how they would fit. Then, he said, "[a] one day I was driving in my truck and listening to a Dido album, which I love. At the end of the CD, I didn't turn it off and put another one in. I just let it stay and after a minute or so there was another song or two. That's the first I knew about 'bonus tracks.' So we decided to do that with 'Moisture' and 'Casey.'"

Ian Tyson is unique among western singers because he wasn't strongly influenced by the singing cowboys, those like Gene Autry and Roy Rogers although he saw their movies: "I distinctly remember seeing Tex Ritter and the Sons of the Pioneers perform when I was a kid." Recently, Tyson sang "Cool Water" and "Tumbling Tumbleweeds" with a female backup group for the Canadian Songwriters Hall of Fame, which inducted Bob Nolan.

"I'm a rancher," said Tyson. "Music has given me an opportunity to have a ranch. I never thought about doing music at this point in my life when I was younger and, in fact, I tried to quit several times. But I always came back to it." The audience keeps coming back to Ian Tyson, too. His tour of Canada and some western states in the U.S. was a series of sold-out shows. But it was the tickets that sold, not Ian Tyson—he's not selling out, just pushing the envelope with his music, staying on the cutting edge with his songs from the foot of the Rockies.

SOURCES:

Tyson, Ian. *I Never Sold My Saddle*. With Colin Escott. Vancouver, B.C.: Douglas, 1994.
_____. Phone interview with the author, March 2, 2005.

38

Sons of the San Joaquin

Lon Hannah hit hard times during the Great Depression and left southwest Missouri, where he lost his small subsistence dairy farm and came to California looking for work in 1934. He worked for two years in California, landing a job on a ranch near Elderwood, then sent for his wife and sons, Joe and Jack, both born in Missouri in 1933 and 1934 respectively. They moved West in 1937.

Lon Hannah found a job as a ranch foreman and laborer; his wife, Melba, worked in a packing house. Dad and mom loved music and both Jack and Joe remember growing up with music in the home, especially classical music. "Mom played the piano and she played classical music," remembered Jack. "Dad played the guitar and loved the Sons of the Pioneers." Jack and Joe Hannah have a musical past steeped richly in classical, opera, show tunes, pop and western music and both commented, "Home was work and music."

"Our family was people who worked hard and had a happy home," said Jack. "Our home was very classical but I loved the big bands of Harry James, Ralph Flanigan and Glenn Miller. Caruso was very real in our lives and I also loved singers like Perry Como, the Ames Brothers, Tony Martin, Bing Crosby and Frank Sinatra."

Although the Hannahs came from southwest Missouri, and Dad Hannah had a great voice, "he didn't sing country or have a hillbilly voice," said Joe. "Our mother hated country music. Both my parents insisted we perform with good diction." That is evident in their western recordings, which sound more "pop" than "country." It is obvious the Hannahs have trained voices, a result of years of Jack singing Broadway songs and Joe singing opera.

Dad Hannah was a deeply religious man but their home "was not some somber place where he cracked the whip," remembered Jack. "He always said, 'There's nothing secular in a Christian life—do it all for the glory of God.' He believed that your daily life was a witness. He provided a beautiful example of what is real in life. He was a very kind and gentle man." The parents did not allow the boys to see many movies, but singing cowboy movies—especially those starring Roy Rogers—were O.K.

Jack and Joe Hannah inherited two important genes from their Dad: the talent to sing and the talent to play baseball. "Dad was a great baseball player in the Ozarks," said Jack, and both he and Joe followed their father's footsteps into baseball.

After high school Jack enrolled in Fresno State in 1952 where he played football and baseball; then in 1955 he signed with the Milwaukee Braves organization as a pitcher. "If I had realized it then, I would not have signed with the Braves," said Jack. "They had Warren Spahn, Lew Burdette and a roster of great pitchers."

Jack's earliest ambition was to pitch in the major leagues well enough to be inducted

Sons of the San Joaquin (photograph courtesy of Scott O'Malley Agency).

into the Baseball Hall of Fame in Cooperstown. Unfortunately, he only made it to Triple A, although he was invited to spring training twice.

During the baseball season, Jack pitched but in the off season he took classes at Fresno State until 1958, when he graduated. Jack felt like his future was coaching and so he had studied physical education, obtaining a degree which allowed him to teach most subjects. In 1963, after eight years in organized baseball, Jack hung up his spikes and started teaching at a high school in Visalia, California, as well as coaching the football and baseball teams. After he started teaching, Jack continued his education and received a masters' in counseling. "My 30 years in education was the richest experience I ever had, dealing with young people and helping them find their way and reach their potential," said Jack. "I really loved that and had a great rapport with the kids."

Joe Hannah signed as a catcher to play with the Chicago Cubs organization the night of his graduation. "We went to a dance after the graduation," remembered Joe, "then to the Johnson Hotel. Dad met me there and I signed with the Cubs."

Joe played for a number of clubs; the Visalia Cubs while in high school, then Janesville, Wisconsin, and Topeka, Kansas, where he was drafted with two weeks left in the season. He was sent to Fort Ord, where he played baseball on a team organized there, then to Korea where he "climbed over mountains with the 5th Regimental Combat Team" until the cease-fire. When a baseball team was formed Joe played baseball for the army in Korea.

After his discharge from the service, Joe joined the Pacific Coast League Los Angeles Angels during the last two weeks of the season, then went to Macon, Georgia, to play for that club. In 1956 he platooned as catcher for the Angels, who won the Pacific Coast League championship. Second baseman Gene Mauch, later a major league manager (including a stint as manager of Gene Autry's American League Angels), considered that club "the greatest minor league baseball team of all time." In addition to the Angels, Joe played for the Memphis Chicks and the Fort Worth Cats. In 1958 he was sold to the Havana ball club, which traded him to the Toronto Maple Leafs, where he played for a few years. "I wasn't a very good hitter," admits Joe. "Plus, I had five children, so my wife and I decided I should quit in 1963."

With a smile, Joe stresses that he quit, not retired. You've got to play in the majors in order to retire." So at the end of 12 years on the baseball diamond, Joe hung up his catcher's gear and went to barber school, then worked as a barber for "four or five years" before he enrolled in college at Fresno State, where he studied vocal music and earned his accreditation to teach.

Joe always loved to sing; during his baseball days he remembers singing on buses going from town to town and in clubhouses. He played under manager Pepper Martin, member of the legendary Gashouse Gang from St. Louis, and Martin loved singing. "A guy named Jake Jacobs played guitar and sang country music—Hank Williams songs—and I would harmonize when he sang. Pepper loved that and was adamant that we sing at baseball games. We didn't want to sing but he pushed us out there between doubleheaders, where we'd sing songs."

Joe Hannah was 39 years old when he started his teaching career. He spent the next 21 years teaching at a junior high school in Visalia. He developed some excellent boys' choruses and, in his last two years, worked at the high school, where he molded some excellent young men choruses. Joe also found time to work with the Fresno Opera Company, performing one of the leads in *La Bohème* and having the main lead in *The Barber of Seville*.

Jack Hannah had performed in Broadway musicals produced locally in Visalia and had recorded two albums of gospel songs—most of which he wrote—before the Sons of the San Joaquin were formed. Jack's songwriting goes back a long way; he wrote his first song when he was four years old, a western song entitled "The West." "My mother thought it was cute," said Jack. "But I've written songs ever since. I've written a lot of poetry, then folk and then gospel music."

So how did two men, trained and schooled in classical, show tunes, big band and pop music end up as western singers? The creation of the Sons of the San Joaquin was really a fluke engineered by Joe's son, Lon Hannah (named after his grandfather). In 1987 Joe and Jack and their families the elder Lon's gathered in backyard to celebrate his 85th birthday. These gatherings for birthdays and other special events almost always included singing—and Dad, Jack and Joe loved to harmonize on Sons of the Pioneers songs. This particular year Lon, then in his mid-20s, asked if he could join on "Blue Prairie." Jack replied, "But you don't know this stuff." Lon countered, "I've been listening to you guys for 20 years!"

Lon had this to say: "I'd always loved music and grew up singing and hearing it in the house. I always wanted to sing with my dad and Jack—I had sung in the school choir and the jazz band—and I sorta felt like I had some musical ability. So I asked if I could sing with them and they said, 'You don't know this stuff.' But I'd heard them sing a couple of those songs for years. Even they liked it—it was a good blend."

Lon added tenor harmony to Joe's lead and Jack's bass and all agreed that it sounded great. A month later, Jack got a call from Lon informing him the family group was booked to perform cowboy songs for the Lions Club in Ivanhoe. "We taught Lon about five songs for that appearance," remembered Jack. "We had to encore so we did one song over again."

A year later, Jack received a phone call from someone wanting the group to sing some cowboy songs at a cowboy Bible study in Bakersfield. "I figured it would be a small group," said Jack, who was surprised to find himself singing before approximately 200 people. "We had taught Lonnie 10 or 11 songs and the show went over well. Somebody taped the show and at the end gave me a cassette of us singing. I didn't want it so I gave it to Lonnie, who then gave it to Doc Denning, who played fiddle for the Sons of the Pioneers. Doc added lead guitar, bass and fiddle and gave it back to Lonnie, who gave it to me to play. I played it in my truck and loved it. 'Who are those guys?' I asked? Well, it was us."

Doc Denning was giving Lon Hannah guitar lessons at the time. Doc, an accomplished jazz guitarist and fiddler who filled in on fiddle for the Sons of the Pioneers a time or two, added bass, another rhythm (to boost Jack's guitar) and fiddle to the group's performance. Then he made some cassette copies for Lon.

In the summer of 1987, while Joe was in Europe with a choral workshop and Jack was rafting on the Colorado River, Lon went to Las Vegas for a Sons of the Pioneers reunion, at the gathering that laid the groundwork for the Western Music Association. Doc went with him.

In Las Vegas, the Reinsmen performed and Lon managed to sing, impressing the crowd. He gave a tape of the trio singing at the Lion's Club to Gary McMahon, who took it home but forgot about it until one day he was bucking some hay and decided to listen to something. Rummaging through his glove compartment—where there were 25 or 30 cassettes—he came across the tape Lon had given him. Thinking that perhaps Ranger Doug of Riders in the Sky had sent it to him, he popped it into the cassette player. He must have liked what he heard because he called Lon. McMahon also called Hal Cannon in Salt Lake City. Hal, one of the founders of Elko, was pulling together the Gathering for January 1989 and Gary told him about the group on the tape.

Hal told him not to send the tape—he already had a bunch and none of them were good so he wasn't inclined to listen. But Gary sent it anyway and Hal managed to listen. This prompted a phone call from Cannon to the Hannahs, inviting them to Elko for the session on harmony singing, led by Gary McMahon. This performance at Elko by the Sons of the San Joaquin was their first appearance outside the area where they lived.

After hearing them perform, Hal Cannon asked the trio to stay and perform on the Saturday night show. They did and met Michael Martin Murphey in the greenroom before the show. Lon introduced himself and talked about "Long Line of Love," one of Murphey's hits. Lon loved the song and had taught the chorus to Joe and Jack on a pack trip into the mountains. Lon then asked Murphey if he would sing "Long Line of Love" with him. "I'd never do that now," he said, but Murphey agreed, got out his guitar and when the two sang the chorus, Joe and Jack came over and added harmonies.

"This is like a religious experience," said Murphey. "I want you guys on my cowboy record." Murphey had finally gotten the go-ahead from Warner Brothers to do a record of cowboy songs and extended an invitation to the Hannahs to join. "Sure," they said, not expecting much to come out of that. The reason Murphey had been so agreeable to singing with Lon as well as inviting them to perform on his album was because he had heard them sing during the harmony workshop and loved their blend of voices.

The invitation to Elko caught the group unaware. Jack didn't want to go—he'd never heard of Elko, Riders in the Sky, Michael Martin Murphey or any of "names" in western music. The group wasn't very good on their instruments except for Jack, who played the guitar well. The group needed a name "because people wanted to know who we were," so since they came from the San Joaquin Valley they called themselves Sons of the San Joaquin, an echo of Sons of the Pioneers, whose songs they performed. They had worked up five songs and after the first one, "Timber," received a standing ovation. "We thought somebody was putting us on," remembered Jack. "The sound was a little thin and I looked at Lon and the pick was two or three inches above his guitar strings."

Three months after Elko they received a message to be in Nashville for a recording session. Along with the message come plane tickets to take them there. The trio knew only about five Sons of the Pioneers songs, but the folks at Warner Brothers—who were starting a Warner Western label—wanted to sign them as soon as they heard them harmonize. And that's how they received a recording contract, which led to the group releasing five albums on the Warner Western label.

The original idea after signing with Warner Western was to keep their day jobs and sing part time, but that soon proved to be untenable. Joe was ready to retire because "I had already planned to retire when I reached 60," he said. "I was fed up with the discipline problems, although I had great rapport with kids." Jack realized he needed to retire when he fell asleep during a counseling session with a student. "We had played that weekend and I was exhausted," he remembered. "They had to shake me to wake me up. That's when I retired from the school system."

By that time, Jack had spent 18 years teaching physical education and coaching football and baseball, until he became a school counselor in 1980 and remained in that position until his retirement in 1992. The Hannahs were not really prepared to become full-time western singers. "We were athletes," said Jack. "That's how we thought of ourselves. But we also sang a lot; we just sang all the time. Joe and I have buried and married more people than we can count."

"For a couple of years, Lon did all the work, booking and promoting us," said Jack. "And it really wore him out. Then we got a guy who wanted to be an agent but he wasn't a good agent. Next we went with World Class Talent, an agency in Nashville, for about four or five years." "We worked harder on our instruments," said Joe. "I learned bass and we hired Richard Chon from the Fresno Philharmonic. I got the bass because I didn't want to just stand up there. I learned to play it over the Christmas vacation before we went to Elko. But I wasn't confident on bass at first; I was worried I wouldn't remember the words and harmony to the songs in addition to playing bass."

Jack hadn't written any western songs before they began recording for Warner Western, but the label wanted some original songs, so Jack—a natural writer—found songs starting to come to him:

"I was talking with Waddie Mitchell on the phone one day. And I asked him what he was doing. He said, 'What every cowboy does when it's 55 below zero. Up at the crack of dawn, pulling those calves in the air.' I put that conversation in a song and it became 'Great American Cowboy.' We sang that at Elko and after that the songs started coming."

Jack Hannah describes himself as a "recreational cowboy." He helps at a local ranch, but isn't a full-time working cowboy. He's also an avid historian who loves to read. "I have never been someone who sat in front of the TV," said Jack. "I stay busy with the church and giving back to the community. I read a lot of poetry and I'm a big fan of Robert Service, who wrote 'Sam McGee.' But I've also read Shakespeare, Chaucer, Burns, Wordsworth. I have a huge library.

"To me, writing songs is inspiration, it's not craft. Everything is grist for the mill. I have a wonderful memory and sometimes I'll have a song in my head before I write it down. For 'The Long X Brand,' that came from me spending time on the Long X Ranch. That whole song is real—I lived that whole song. The only song I totally made up was 'Santa Fe Lights.' Bill Thornbury walked in my house one day and started singing a melody and those words just came out."

"'From Whence Came the Cowboy' came out of a trip I took with six teachers to Elko. We got an $8,000 fund to send the teachers there. They had planned to go and laugh at the yokels, but within an hour they were crying and laughing. We bought $3,500 worth of material to put together a unit on cowboy poetry. Then one day we got a box full of literature on the cowboy from the University of Texas. As I read it I thought 'from whence came the cowboy.' It started as a poem—I had no intention of writing a song—but one day I was driving on the ranch, saying that poem to myself, when a melody came. When we recorded it I had to cut out a lot of the poem."

The time at World Class meant the group performed over 100 dates a year, including a trip to the Middle East, where they spent eight weeks as goodwill ambassadors for the American Information Agency. But after some time at World Class, they knew that wasn't the place for them. Willie Mathews, a friend and artist, knew Scott O'Malley in Colorado Springs and recommended the Sons look into O'Malley's organization. "We were impressed because nobody left him," said Joe. They joined with O'Malley, recorded for his Western Jubilee label and played dates booked by his agency.

"The people who like western music are good people. We've never been stiffed for a performance, although we've had to put some checks through twice. We've made a lot of friends and we love seeing them," although, Joe admits, "it's hard to get any sleep on the road because friends invite us out to dinner and to visit and we always like to go."

The Sons of the San Joaquin have no trouble making friends. And strangers have no trouble meeting the Sons. They've cut back a bit on their performances and Lon still teaches second grade in Visalia. But their sweet harmony still sends a chill through the audience when their voices blend.

Jack, Joe and Lon Hannah never imagined that life would ever take a turn down the trail of western music. But they feel their lives have been blessed by western music, showing them new trails to ride and introducing them to new friends. Western music has also been blessed. It's not often that men with the talent, background and character of the Sons of the San Joaquin come along.

SOURCES:

Sons of the San Joaquin. Phone interview with Jack Hannah and Joe Hannah, November 14, 2005.

_____. Phone interview with Lon Hannah, November 15, 2005.

39

Asleep at the Wheel

Western swing is an exciting, vibrant music that has influenced countless musicians and yet has barely survived since the mid–1950s. After Bob Wills, the group carrying the torch has been Asleep at the Wheel, formed around the time Merle Haggard released his *Best Damn Fiddle Player* salute to Wills and the Texas Playboys.

The group was formed by Ray Seifert, who grew up in suburban Philadelphia and changed his name to Ray Benson. (Actually, Benson is his middle name). While growing up, young Ray took lessons on piano and guitar and formed a folk group, The Four G's, with his older sister when he was nine; they sang "This Land Is Your Land" and other folk songs from the era that gave us the Kingston Trio and "Tom Dooley." In high school, Ray played tuba in the marching band and string bass in the school's orchestra and jazz band; when he was 16 he heard a Hank Williams recording of "Hey, Good Lookin'" and that turned his ear towards country.

Ray's sister attended Northeastern University in Boston and he would visit her there. That's how he met LeRoy Preston, and the two then decided to form a hippie country band. This was an era when the rednecks and the hippies did not get along and it was not hip for young people to like country music. That music was considered much too right-wing conservative for the left-wing liberalism of the late 1960s and early 1970s. But that did not deter Benson and Preston.

The decision to form the band inspired Ray to call his friend Reuben Gosfield, who lived in Columbia, Maryland, and attended Antioch College, and convince him to join the band. Gosfield was a dedicated blues fanatic who didn't wish to be converted; however, Benson played him "Move It on Over" by Hank Williams. On hearing the song, Gosfield had a conversion experience and agreed to join. In answer to the question of what instrument he should play? Benson replied that they needed a steel guitar player. So Gosfield learned the pedal steel and changed his name to Lucky Oceans. Also in Columbia, Maryland, were Larry and Lee Sigler, whose father owned a peach and apple orchard in Paw Paw, West Virginia. Sigler told Benson the group could stay there for free and rehearse if they helped fix up the place. Benson agreed and the band moved into a 200-year-old log cabin.

Benson loved George Jones and Merle Haggard and he bought their latest albums, which is how he came to purchase *The Best Damn Fiddle Player* album when it came out. The timing was perfect. "It was like the Rosetta Stone I'd been looking for," said Benson. "As much as I loved country music, the Nashville stuff didn't leave much room for instrumental solos and improvisation, and it didn't satisfy our love for the blues. Suddenly, here was a country music that incorporated both jazz solos and blues songs. We learned every

Asleep at the Wheel (photograph courtesy of Asleep at the Wheel).

song on that album and started playing them in every little roadhouse around the West Virginia panhandle."

The Sportsman's Club was Paw Paw's only nightclub, and the band, named Asleep at the Wheel because Lucky Oceans liked the phrase—"It's something you can't do," said Benson, "like Grateful Dead"—soon played there regularly. Then some folks from Medicine Ball Caravan visited the farm, stayed a few days, and invited Asleep down to open a show for them in Washington, D.C. Benson agreed and the group was soon popular in the D.C. area. This led to a fourth member, singer Chris O'Connell, who had been a secretary in Arlington—being added to the lineup.

Playing at Antioch College in Yellow Springs, Ohio, in 1969, a student there, George Frayne (aka Commander Cody) met Ray Benson, and the two kept in touch. Cody and his manager, Joe Kerr, encouraged Asleep at the Wheel to move to California. In 1971 the group moved to Oakland, where they played at the Longbranch Saloon in Berkeley. They also became the backup band for country artist Stoney Edwards. While playing in Berkeley one night, Jim Haber walked in and told them they needed a piano player. They agreed and he was hired; he changed his name to Floyd Domino.

Asleep at the Wheel was an exciting live act in the Bay Area, which led to a recording contract with United Artists and their first album, *Comin' at You*. Epic was their next label and delivered their second album, *Asleep at the Wheel*. Although they generated a lot of excitement when they performed live, they didn't really generate a lot of record sales. One of the major problems was that country radio just didn't play any western swing. It was the "Nashville Sound" and that wasn't music you danced to; instead, you sat down and listened to it.

Things weren't going well in California—the group weren't really making ends meet—so in February 1974, after finishing a job in San Jose, California, at two in the morning, they headed out to Austin, Texas. With encouragement from Doug Sahm and Willie Nelson, they picked that town because of the large number of live music venues and because Texas, the birthplace of western swing, was more open to the kind of music they played.

That move led to years of frustrating success. The Wheel charmed crowds wherever they played—audiences loved them. They were nominated—and won—top awards, but never could make enough money to survive. The problem was (and is) that it's extremely difficult to support a large group of musicians on the road. And western swing, to really be done well, needs a lot of musicians for that full, thick sound that permeates a dance hall. Oh yes—that was another problem. Dancing wasn't really in style in country music either. Audiences were used to sitting and listening to an act. Western swing ain't something you just sit and listen to—except when you take the occasional breather from dancing. It was the age-old conflict of art versus commerce. Asleep at the Wheel loved their music and were committed to doing it but couldn't make enough money to sustain themselves or the sound they were after.

There were some other problems as well. Around 1980 the core of the band crashed and burned—a result of drugs, booze and burnout from being on the road 300 days a year. When the smoke cleared, the band limped along; but by 1981 Ray Benson was the only original member left standing.

Still, Asleep at the Wheel survived and kept going. There were important changes. The concept of a "band" with all for one and one for all was gone. Benson set up the group with himself as the owner and the rest as employees. As musicians came and went—there have been well over 100 different "wheels" through the years—Benson hired them on a salary and fit them in. While each new member changes the overall sound somewhat, Benson's core musical sensibility keeps it all together. Inside his head is the "book" of songs that they perform.

It is an amazingly broad cross section of songs that "define" Asleep at the Wheel. They remain rooted in western swing but that music incorporates country, blues, jazz, boogie woogie and pop into its repertoire. Western swing demands good songs, played so that people can dance. The other criterion is that the songs must allow musicians to play takeoffs or solos and improvise musical phrases off the basic structure of a song. Western swing is a jazz musician playing country or western music or both and nobody has done it better or longer than Asleep at the Wheel.

Benson had to learn how to be an organizer and a businessman, which is what a bandleader is. He's also had to develop revenue streams outside of the band. He's done that by building Bismeaux Studio in Austin, by producing other acts, and by learning how to niche market Asleep in order to assure a touring base and album sales.

In the pantheon of American music, Asleep at the Wheel falls under the category of country and yet, they've never received much airplay on country radio, the major outlet for that music. Their biggest hit, "The Letter That Johnny Walker Read," reached number ten in 1975. Without big radio hits, you don't have big album sales. And without big hits you don't get the big bucks for personal appearances all across the nation.

So how does a western swing group survive in this day and time? "Barely," answers Ray. "It's tough. There's a lot of western swing activity in the southwest—the Playboy groups and Hot Club of Cowtown and others. But it's a tough road and Asleep wouldn't survive if we were just a western swing group. We do a lot more than that now."

The number of members is down to six—a good number to support on the road. "I'd rather have a couple more—we used to have eight, then seven," said Benson. "On the other hand, I like the smaller number for musical reasons—we're more versatile."

Benson's role has changed through the years. He used to be a member of a band but now he's organizer, talent scout, bandleader and manager of a group. He has to keep his ear open constantly for new musicians in case someone drops out. "I hear about guys mostly through the grapevine," said Benson. "I'm always looking for new talent." He's also expanded his horizons quite a bit. Besides his studio in Austin and working with Cracker Barrel on some niche market items, he's produced acts such as Suzy Bogguss, Pam Tillis, Ricky Van Shelton, done tribute albums to Bob Wills and produced commercials for Budweiser.

"When I graduated from high school I said I wanted to be a Renaissance Man," quipped Benson. "It was a smart aleck answer, but it's what I've done. My sister says I should be a poster child for ADHD. My interests run far and wide."

Asleep at the Wheel runs far and wide as well and there's no sign that the Wheel is gonna stop rolling.

SOURCE:

Benson, Ray. Phone interview with the author, June 7, 2002.

40

Wylie and the Wild West

Wylie Gustafson was born and raised on a ranch in Conrad, Montana, up near the Canadian border, but he didn't really appreciate it at the time. He took a turn at big city living away from the ranch and somewhere along the way discovered that he longed for what he had left behind. Somehow, he didn't imagine it would be that way during his childhood years. The Gustafsons raised beef cattle—Angus, Hereford and some Charolais. "Dad would breed, so we had a lot of black cows with white faces," remembered Wylie. "We had about five hundred mother cows on ten to fifteen acres, depending on the lease agreements."

The family had music in their home. "Dad played the guitar and sang old folk and western songs like Burl Ives songs and 'Strawberry Roan,' 'The Little Red Hen' and 'The Lilac Bush,'" remembered Wylie. "He'd sing 'Beautiful Brown Eyes' and he liked Jim Reeves, so he sang some Jim Reeves songs. We grew up listening to him a lot and on weekends we would take turns dancing to 'Skip to My Lou' with my sister. There was only one girl in the family so we had to share.

"Dad got us into music and taught me my first chords—G, C and D," continued Wylie. "He taught me to play 'Old Blue'—you know, 'I got a dog and his name is Blue, betcha five dollars he's a good dog too.' There's only two chords in that song so it's easy to learn.

"We were ranch kids—didn't have time for much other than working. We'd get up a couple hours before sunup because we had a twenty-mike trek from winter to summer pastures and we did that twice a year. As soon as it was light enough, we'd round 'em up and it was usually cold, rainy and windy and a lot of hard work. I thought, *There's got to be a better life than this*. When I was eighteen I'd had enough of the ranch life."

Wylie grew up listening to the radio—KMON from Great Falls, a station in Shelby, Montana, and another one in Alberta. "It was a little bit of everything," said Wylie. "They'd play a lot of West Coast country—Buck Owens and Merle Haggard—and then some pop music, like the Beatles or the Everly Brothers. I don't think they followed a playlist so I heard a little bit of everything."

Wylie's older brother had a band in high school so that's how Wylie got his big break, playing bass in his brother's band. "We were a rock and roll band," said Wylie. "I always loved music with a beat and a good rhythm. We played dance music with a strong rhythmic beat.

We played lots of Johnny Cash, like 'Folsom Prison' and 'I Walk the Line,' 'Tiger by the Tail' by Buck Owens, 'White Line Fever' by Merle Haggard, 'I Saw Her Standing There' by the Beatles and 'Satisfaction' by the Rolling Stones. I never cared much for 'Takin' Care of Business' by Bachman Turner Overdrive, but we'd play it because people always requested it. We did some Hank Sr. songs. In fact, the first album I bought was a *Greatest Hits* album by Hank Williams and the first song I learned on my own was 'Kaw-Liga.'"

Wylie freely admits what most successful musicians later deny: he got into music to attract girls. "I was a pretty shy kid at school and awkward around girls, but I discovered I could be appealing if I was in a band." Wylie also said he "always loved music, the melodies just fascinated me."

Wylie and the Wild West (photograph by Bill Watts, courtesy of Wylie Gustaffson).

"I'm not embarrassed to say that I grew up in the rock and roll era," Wylie continued. "That's as much a part of us—the strong beat, a strong rhythm in the songs and artists like the Rolling Stones and Beatles—as western and country music. We played what the kids wanted to hear and what we needed to play in order to get hired. We did a lot of good rock and roll. I always loved those old Sun Records artists like Jerry Lee Lewis." Wylie's band played Sadie Hawkins dances, proms, high school dances, local events and community affairs.

The musical highlight of his high school band years came on July 4, 1976, when his band played their first big concert as the opening act for the Mission Mountain Wood Band. "They were a hippie bluegrass band and they were our idols—local guys done good," remembers Wylie. "They'd been on *Hee Haw*, so opening for them was a big deal. The problem was that I was supposed to be team roping with my brother that day and I had to tell him I couldn't do it. He was real mad at me for that. But I was fifteen and playing in front of about a thousand people was a real big deal then."

After high school Wylie went to the University of Montana for a couple of years and was in a band there. "We were playing six nights a week," said Wylie. "It was a four piece band—two guitars, a bass and drums. We had a booking agency in Missoula that booked us throughout Montana, Idaho, North and South Dakota—the northwest area. We made good money, I paid for two years of college by doing that, and I've got to say that's where I cut my teeth as an entertainer. Sometimes you had to figure out how to enjoy playing in front of two drunks. We played for four or five hours at a time, six nights a week—mostly college bars. We'd get maybe two weeks off during the year."

The band recorded three albums that they sold off the stage. "That got me interested in trying to make a living playing music," said Wylie, who played in that band for six years, until 1986, when he moved to Los Angeles to pursue his music career. "I'd gotten burnt out," he said.

In L.A. he didn't want to play rock and roll because he'd grown to love old, traditional country music. He visited a "great old vinyl store" and started buying some old country music: "Elton Britt's yodel albums, Jimmie Rodgers, every old Merle Haggard and Buck

Owens album that I could find, the Sons of the Pioneers because I wanted to know the history of the music. I like music with a strong beat and Rosie Flores and Dwight Yoakum were happening about that time."

He found some good rockabilly groups in Orange County like Dave Alvin and the Blasters and Russell Scott and the Red Hots. At the Palomino in North Hollywood there was Ronnie Mack's Barn Dance each Tuesday night where eight different acts performed original material for twenty minutes each. "That's where you could meet others who were interested in country music," said Wylie. "And that's where I met Ray Doyle, my guitar player, who's been with me for twenty years. We struck up a conversation and discovered we both loved Elton Britt's yodels and traditional country music."

In 1989 Wylie and The Wild West did their first public performance at the Palomino. Playing with Wylie was guitarist Will Ray, "who played a telecaster chicken pickin' style of guitar." Will was in the Hellecasters, an instrumental group that played Telecaster guitars and produced the first two Wylie and the Wild West albums.

In 1990 Wylie did a good studio-produced demo of three songs in the "honky-tonk country" style that aimed for Dwight Yoakam's audience. For his day job he worked as the manager of an attorneys' office in L.A. He'd started as a courier and, he said, "They discovered I knew how to use a library so I spent a lot of time at the UCLA library looking up cases and articles. They did a lot of medical malpractice suits so I found information on that for them."

He received a credit card in the mail that gave him a $7,000 line of credit "so I decided to do a video. I'd met some videographers and spent that $7,000 to get three people up to the ranch to do a video on 'This Time,' a song my brother wrote. It was a West Coast mid tempo type shuffle song." Wylie sent the video to CMT at a time when that channel was trying to fill up 24 hours a day with videos and the major labels weren't releasing enough videos for them to do that. That was during the winter of 1991–1992. CMT played the video, received some requests and had a good response. Wylie had a manager in L.A. at the time who told him he needed to do an album, so he added seven more songs to that studio demo and had an album. He managed to get distribution from Oh Boy Records in Nashville, the label that had John Prine. Oh Boy got him into Walmart and some radio airplay. The major labels weren't interested in signing him, though. "It just wasn't radio music," said Wylie. "And that's what they were looking for. We were doing honky-tonk country music."

On every album Wylie did a cowboy song. He'd done "I'm Gonna Be a Cowboy" by Marty Robbins and the Eddy Arnold classic "Cattle Call." Then, in 1995, he said he went to Elko for the Gathering "and saw for the first time all these cowboy poets and singers and realized there was an audience for cowboy music. I had no inking that something like that even existed and it changed my life. That's when I knew there was an audience who wanted to hear this kind of music and I realized I could make a living playing the music I loved, so I started writing and recording more cowboy music.

"In 1995 I started making a living playing music. That's when I quit my day job in L.A. at the law firm. I'd paid off the $7,000 I owed the credit card company and knew I couldn't continue to play in L.A. because most of those clubs were 'pay for play.' You had to pay them in order to play."

In 1996 Wylie moved from L.A. to eastern Washington, which is where his wife was from. He started buying land from her family and his dad gave him his first horse. That led him back into the ranching life. But he still went to L.A. now and then to record commercials. "I was one of only a few yodelers in Los Angeles and there was an advertising company that called me to do yodels on some commercials," said Wylie. "The work was good and some ended up on national TV. In 1996 Yahoo called me for their commercial, so I went down to

L.A. and spent five or ten minutes working on a yodel for them. I did a couple and they picked one. That's the only hit I've ever written. I've spent twenty years trying to write a hit song and that's the only one so far." But that Yahoo yodel put Wylie on the map. It's been a nice calling card ever since.

In 1997 he did an album, *Total Yodel*, that was picked up by Rounder Records. David Skepner, the former manager of Riders in the Sky, became his manager after seeing him at a showcase in Nashville, and The Buddy Lee Agency booked him on a lot of fair dates.

In the meantime, he got into ranching. "Dad gave me a quarter horse," said Wylie. "Then we started buying horses from relatives and we got into cutting horses and developed a cutting horse business, breeding and training them."

It's a busy busy life. "Ranching is a full-time job," said Wylie. "I almost go crazy in the summers when we have to get in our first hay cutting. I've got to get 200 tons of hay for the cutting horses. I have a couple of employees but I'm still in charge and have to do a lot of manual work. I have to make all the decisions—like with the irrigation. But there's something about this western lifestyle that's very appealing. You work eighteen-hour days and you're worn out but it's worth the long hours and hard work. There's so much fulfillment and enjoyment in this life. Hard work is just part of it. I would rather work hard on a ranch than sit in an office from nine to five. I thought when I was eighteen that there was a better life, but after a few years away I wanted to get back to it."

Wylie and his wife, Kimberley, have developed a cutting horse business at the Cross Three Quarter Horse Ranch in Dusty, Washington. "I get a lot of fulfillment working with horses," said Wylie. "They require a lot of patience and it's a lifelong learning process. Training cutting horses is the most detailed, tedious work; they're like trained athletes and there's not much room for error in the training process. If you keep your mind open it'll only take about two hundred years to become a good horseman. But when you can drop your reins when you're in front of a cow and have your horse work that cow—well, there's nothing like it."

The Gustafsons have a resident trainer who takes clients. Then, Wylie and Kimberley train too. "We train to compete in cutting horse contests," said Wylie. "Eventually we'll sell some of them but a few we won't because they're family members. You can't do it as a hobby. Every day when I'm home I'm down at the barn. In the summer I only work with two horses; in the winter I can work with four or five. We go to clinics all the time and try to put ourselves in front of the best cutting horse trainers."

Wylie stays double booked most of the time: playing music and working on his ranch. "Summer is a busy time, there's lots of festivals and lots of opportunities," said Wylie. "During the Fall we go to a lot of cutting horse events. Pretty much every weekend I'm gone from the ranch. I always have a need to be out on the road but sometimes it's hard to drive past that mailbox."

Can someone make a living playing western music? "Absolutely," said Wylie. "I can only name a handful that do—Dave Stamey, Riders in the Sky, Michael Martin Murphey, Ian Tyson, Sons of the San Joaquin, Don Edwards and Red Steagall. It's kind of a short list, but it's out there."

And how do you do it? "It's hard—a lot of hard work," said Wylie. "It's not one specific thing. It's mainly staying together and sticking with it for the long haul. All of us have taken a bit of a different route. The Sons of the San Joaquin have a loyal, older audience while Riders in the Sky has a family-based audience, and we have a younger audience. I think the key is finding your audience. It's taken me a long time to develop an audience who will drive out of their local region to come hear us play.

"You can make a career playing this music. We're not the only ones doing it. But to make a living at it we have to be plugged into a lot of things. We do state fairs and music festivals. We appeal to the folk audience with the Jimmie Rodgers and yodeling songs. Then there's the cowboy gatherings. We can fit into all these types of venues, but we have to be flexible and be able to do different sets for different audiences."

Wylie's Wild West is Ray Doyle and Scot Wilburn. Doyle plays guitar and sings harmony and has been with Wylie for over twenty years. They formed a kinship when they met at Ronnie Mack's Barn Dance in 1988 and discovered they both owned *Yodel Songs*, an album by Elton Britt. Scot Wilburn plays steel guitar and fiddle. "We were with the William Morris Agency, Buddy Lee and a handful of other agencies out of Nashville and mostly we spent our time trying to find someone to make those phone calls rather than making them ourselves," said Wylie. "Now, we do our own booking, I have an assistant who does that. We're at the point now where most of our business is repeat business, so it's setting up the date, getting the fee worked up and scheduling."

As for finding new business, "people find out about us through a lot of different outlets," said Wylie. "We've been lucky to get on XM radio and that has helped, but the most important thing about our music is word of mouth. A friend might have a CD they buy at one of our concerts and they love it and play it for their friend who happens to book a cowboy gathering or equestrian event. Being around for over twenty years means there are some loyal fans. Also the Internet has helped tremendously in selling CDs and having people find out about us.

"It used to be that the only way to find an artist was to track them down through their booking agency. Now with the Internet it's easy to find the artist, hear a snippet of their music and know who we are. What I love about cowboy music is that people are such loyal fans. About once a week in the summer somebody will drive up our driveway—usually some older folks in an RV—just to meet me and I always make it a point to spend some time with them."

Wylie makes a living playing cowboy music but says, "I still don't know what cowboy music is because the cowboys I hang out with—hard core cowboys—listen to stuff that's all over the map. They like everything from AC/DC to Ian Tyson to George Strait—everybody loves George Strait. To define cowboy music today is hard to do. As a cowboy band I'm bound to the traditions and respect for where it came from and I consider myself a music historian. I really feel it's important to find a contemporary element in whatever we do. Ian Tyson has done that like no other musician has. He has been a voice for the Western lifestyle. I'd like to think we're still trying to do the same thing.

"I get so much inspiration writing songs; I'm trying to write songs for those who are living this lifestyle. This music rings true for cowboys and equestrians who are making a living on ranches or embracing this lifestyle. I found this little niche; I perform, sell CDs and it's working. I don't know if there's a formula but it takes a lot of hanging in there. But I'm doing what's true to my heart.

"We still play a lot of dances; when we play gatherings we often play the dance on Friday nights. That's what we do at Elko. There's a dance element with what we do. The main shows are more acoustic with lyrics and lots of cowboy poetry.

"It's not about making money and selling a million albums. It's about making a living in order to keep doing it. It's finding that audience our music speaks to. It's never going to be a huge audience, but it's a loyal audience."

SOURCE:

Wylie and the Wild West (Wylie Gustafson). Phone interview with the author, July 7, 2008.

41

R.W. Hampton, Riding for His Own Brand

The family ranch in America is struggling. It's difficult to make a living and it doesn't make much economic sense because the expenses and costs can quickly exceed the income. But the lifestyle is priceless. Unfortunately, those who live on family ranches in the West are often voiceless, so it's been up to western singers and cowboy poets to promote ranching culture and the way of life. Also, it's often been the singers and poets who have been able to sustain the cowboy lifestyle in these economic hard times because they're picking up outside income.

R.W. Hampton has a small family ranch in New Mexico. It is a life he loves and is devoted to. His family is a ranching family; his children help on the ranch and R.W. and his wife, Lisa, wouldn't trade that lifestyle for gold. But it's the singing and the show biz side of his life that keeps that small ranch going. On the other side of the coin, that small family ranch is the foundation for the songs, acting and show biz side that keeps R.W. Hampton going.

Richard Wade Hampton—known during his early years as Little Dicky—was born in Houston on June 17, 1957, but he doesn't remember a thing about the city. He was named after Wade Hampton, a cavalry leader in the Civil War who served under J.E.B. Stuart and rose through the ranks to become a lieutenant general, then later governor of South Carolina and then a U.S. Senator.

Hampton's father was in the air force and served in the Air Defense Command, and jobs in the service involve moving around. So the first town Dicky remembers is Great Falls, Montana—"Charlie Russell country," he says. They didn't stay there long, either, and because his father was worried he would be sent to some really out-of-the-way place—people in Air Defense Command manned outposts all over the world—he mustered out of the air force and the family settled in Sherman, Texas, a small town located just south of the Oklahoma state line, where he took a job as a salesman for Mrs. Tucker's Shortening.

"If my parents had any musical ability, they never revealed it," said Hampton. "But we always had music in the house. We had records by Jo Stafford, Frank Sinatra, Tony Bennett and Eddy Arnold. At supper time, they always put on some music to play." There may have been a way that Hampton secretly "inherited" a musical gene: he reports that when his mother was very pregnant with him, she attended the Houston Livestock Show and Rodeo, where Gene Autry performed.

Dicky joined the Boy Scouts and excelled (he is an Eagle Scout). During his high school years "Dicky" became "Dick." A turning point in his life came after his second two-week trip during the summer of 1974 out to Philmont, the Boy Scout ranch near Cimarron, New Mexico. The ranch, located in the Sangre de Cristo Mountains, has 137,500 acres where scouts engage in high adventure 100-mile backcountry treks over a two-week period. Dick worked at Philmont for three summers, 1974, 1975, 1976, with their livestock. His jobs included helping take care of the 350 ranch horses kept for scouts and working with their herd of Herefords.

Meanwhile, back in Texas the Hampton family moved to Richardson, a suburb of Dallas, where his father worked as a salesman for Anderson-Clayton Foods. Dick had a horse, boarded at a stable run by Walter Pittman just outside of town, and Dick used to ride his bicycle there in order to ride his horse. "It seemed like everybody had a horse back, then," remembers Hampton. "And every little town had a rodeo."

Hampton graduated from high school in 1975 and "just wanted to be a cowboy." He worked for several large ranches in New Mexico, including the Red River Ranch. "There are two kinds of employees on those big ranches," remembered Hampton. "Young single guys got hired in the spring and fall for rounding up cattle and breaking horses. The married guys had more permanent jobs year round."

Hampton was "living the dream," he said. "I had a three-speed Chevy pickup, a secondhand saddle and an Ovation guitar." That's about all he owned but he had no problem making a living. "I was making about $300 a month with a $60 a month payment on my pickup and there was nothing else to spend money on," he remembered.

From the Red River Ranch he moved to the Spade Ranch, northwest of Tucumcari, where he worked for a couple of years. He was always a hard worker and when he was hired the foreman usually told him, "You're hired for the spring and then we'll see how it goes." It always seemed to go pretty well and he remembered something his father always told him: "Don't ever leave a place you can't go back to." That allowed Hampton to go back to some ranches for a second hire when he needed a job.

"Dick" became "R.W." on the Fulton Ranch because the cook's name was Dick Shepherd, and you can't have two people with the same name on a ranch. He's been R.W. ever since, but old friends from way back still call him Dick.

Music, for Hampton, started with a Harmony guitar and country music on the radio. During the early 1970s, as Hampton entered his teen years, Merle Haggard, Johnny Cash, Conway Twitty, Charley Pride and Marty Robbins ruled the airwaves. Most of their songs were fairly easy to learn, so Hampton sat on the edge of his bed and played and sang. Sometimes his brother or father would walk down the hall and shut the door to his bedroom.

Hampton liked Lefty Frizzell, so he sang in that high, piercing, soulful voice. In the early seventies Lefty was on the radio with songs like "Railroad Lady," "I Never Go Around Mirrors" and a song that Merle Haggard wrote, "Life's Like Poetry." He especially loved Marty Robbins and especially the song "Man Walks Amongst Us." Hampton loved the classic Robbins songs like "El Paso," "Don't Worry," "and "Devil Woman," as well as Robbins hits during Hampton's teenage years like "My Woman, My Woman, My Wife," "El Paso City" and "Among My Souvenirs."

Then there was John Denver, who was not only popular with country audiences, but also had a young, pop following as well. Hampton did not play in a band. Instead, he played in the courtyard at school, where he attracted girls with songs like "Take Me Home, Country Roads," "Sunshine on my Shoulders," "Annie's Song" and "Back Home Again."

On the ranches where he worked, there were no TV sets in the bunkhouses where he stayed and sometimes no electricity. Hampton played, sang and began to write songs simply to entertain himself. He didn't play for gatherings of cowboys, although sometimes a cowboy—while playing cards—might yell over to him, "Play that song you wrote again." It gave him an inner joy, but it never let him dream of stardom. On the ranches, Hampton went out each day and either worked cattle or started colts.

The first time R.W. Hampton ever walked on a stage and sang to an audience was in 1978 when Dub Waldrup, the manager of the Spade Ranch, invited him to a cattlemen's awards program in Lubbock to sing "Little Joe, the Wrangler." Waldrup had heard Hampton sing the song and knew one of the honorees, Albert Mitchell, loved that song.

"There was Texas ranch royalty in that room," remembered Hampton. "People from the big ranches—guys I'd heard of—were there. I only played that one song but I remember thinking, *I like this*." That performance led to invitations to other cattlemen's gatherings. Hampton was told, "We'll get you time off, a motel room and we'll feed you. We'll treat you so many ways you're bound to like one of 'em." And indeed they did treat him, which led to his performing at more of these functions through the years.

At the Cowboy Symposium, organized by Alvin Davis in Lubbock, Texas, Hampton was invited to sing, and some folks from Adobe Records in Shallowwater, Texas, were there. They invited him to record his second album, *The One I Could Never Ride*, at Lanny Fiel's studio in Lubbock.

R.W. Hampton (photograph courtesy of R.W. Hampton).

As far as professional advancement, Hampton was lost. "I didn't know how to get gigs," he said. "I was totally at the mercy of people who heard me." Often, someone would be in the audience who was involved in a cowboy festival, so he'd get invited to play there.

If it was a bumpy ride to get in front of an audience, back on the home front there were a batch of potholes and speed bumps as well. Hampton had gotten married in 1981 and his first child was born in 1986. He continued to work on large ranches and generally lived in "a fairly decent house" out on a line camp. It was a busy life, looking after that section of the ranch, but the social life was still important. "I remember we'd spend a whole lot of time, usually on a Friday or Saturday, driving to somebody's house or a school gymnasium where there'd be a barbecue or dance or some music. Then we'd drive back in time to take care of the morning chores." When you live that far out, no drive is too far for some socializing.

His first wife, Denise, never really discouraged him but he wasn't encouraged either. "Her idea was that she wished it would work but chances are it wouldn't. It was something to get out of my system or be a nice hobby. Well, I'm not a hobby guy," said Hampton. It's hard enough to make it in music and if you don't have someone pulling with you a hundred and ten percent, well, the odds get a lot longer. A performer needs emotional support— there's a lot of rejection and frustration in the music business—and without a life partner fully behind you, the frustrations and discouragements multiply and build into a giant obstacle. Work was another problem; festivals want to book you well ahead of time but a ranch foreman was likely to say (and did), "Well, when we get up to that date, if we're ahead of the work then you can take a few days off."

Trying to ride for a ranch's brand was a struggle and so was his marriage, which ended in 1995. Still, Hampton trudged on, raising his daughter and two boys on his own.

Back in 1988 "I decided I'd go for it," said Hampton. "I found a place where I could live and traded work for a home on the Flying M Ranch. I sought outside ranch work and became a day working cowboy—a week here, three or four days there—so that I could slip away and play when the calls came in."

Hampton played Elko around 1986 and that event gave him a new perspective on performing. "I didn't know any other place where I could sing for that many people," he said. He met some people backstage like Gary Brown, who worked on the festivals in Visalia and Santa Clarita and booked him on the Rogue River Festival. That led to some breaks but, still, "the phone didn't ring much."

Part of the problem was that Hampton was deeply immersed in a culture that said you don't go out and seek fame and success; it should come to you. Promoting yourself is uncomfortable and unwelcome and real cowboys don't do it; instead, they feel that praise and honors should come on their own, unsolicited.

"That's kinda the way it is in western music," said Hampton. "You're not supposed to promote yourself and I'm fine with that. I don't like doing it and I really don't like other people doing it that much." But this is a world where success is something you go for; you form a game plan, set goals and work towards them. He who waits for success to come will generally end up sitting and waiting their whole life.

Shortly after the album on Adobe, the label chose to leave the record business. However, John Parkin and Bob Coffee, two of Don Edwards' friends in Fort Worth, liked R.W. and decided to put up the money for him to record a third album. Parkin and Coffee told him that if he made enough money on it he could pay them back, but there was no timetable.

That album, recorded in Garland, Texas, and produced by Rich O'Brien, was released ten years after his first album, *Travelin' Light*, and contained the song "Born to Be a Cowboy." "I had the idea because I thought that being a cowboy was every boy's dream," said R.W. "And so I wrote the song around that idea."

The album found itself on Michael Martin Murphey's tour bus and Hampton remembers two of Murphey's band members, Gary Roller and Leroy Featherstone, telling him how much they loved "Born to Be a Cowboy." Later, Murphey called him before recording the song and talked to him about editing it—it was originally seven minutes long—for commercial considerations on Murphey's album.

Hampton's one man play, *The Last Cowboy*, evolved from a raspy throat. "My brother lined up a gig at Poor David's Pub in Dallas," remembered Hampton, "and I was losing my voice; it was about played out. So that night I did more talking than usual, told some cowboy stories and some magic happened. Around that time Hal Holbrook was touring the country with his one man play on Mark Twain, so the idea of a one man play was in the air. We talked to David Marquis, a playwright, and he has a theater background so he came up with the idea of making this character the *last* cowboy. And then my brother thought it should be a kind of spirit—that this guy grew up in Tennessee and moved to Texas after Lee surrendered at Appomattox. That put him where the cowboy evolved with the cattle drives and then on to the singing cowboys. We raised some seed money and put it on in Dallas for a summer run and wanted to take it to New York for off Broadway but the money dried up so that never happened. Years later, my wife, Lisa, thought we should record it as an album—

hit some of the high points in the story and all of the songs—and I wasn't too excited about it until we got into the studio. Our producer, Rich O'Brien, caught Lisa's vision right away and eventually that led to our first Wrangler Award." Hampton still performs the one man show on occasion.

That dramatic side of Hampton has also shown up in his movie work. He first appeared in a TV special, *Kenny Rogers and the American Cowboy*. R.W. was involved in ranch scenes as well as concert scenes. He sang "Ghost Riders in the Sky" and then Rogers sang "Sweet Baby James." Six years after that special, Kenny Rogers was doing a CBS movie of the week and Ken Kragen, Rogers' manager, tracked Hampton down, telling him, "You're hard to find!"

The movie called for Hampton to sing "Ghost Riders" again but that could not be his only appearance in the movie because his character needed to be developed. "We worked for a month on the movie," said Hampton, "and the two worlds really came together. I played a character called 'R.W.' and joined the Screen Actor's Guild. They paid me union scale and I thought they paid me more money than a person should make for doing what I was doing. So I decided to pursue that."

Hampton had the support of a Hollywood agent but most of his calls came from production companies that knew about his work. He appeared in some spaghetti westerns, "usually playing a bad guy," directed by Terrence Hill and worked with Kris Kristofferson on the HBO movie *The Tracker*. "Kris is a gem," said R.W., "a genius. He not only knew his own lines but he knew everybody else's lines. He was incredibly dedicated and professional, always on time and nobody ever waited for him. I was always impressed by his intelligence."

Along the trail, R.W. tried marriage again, and this time it was meant to be. Lisa has been a great source of strength and support for him. Ironically, he met her father first. "Lisa's dad is a real gregarious guy, a larger than life person. You always know when he's in the room," said R.W. "I met him backstage at Elko one year and he kept saying, in a loud voice, 'You're a helluva singer!' A few years later he came to the Rogue River Roundup in Medford, Oregon, with his daughter. She captured my eye, my heart and my soul." R.W. had three kids from his first marriage and Lisa had one child; together they added two more.

There's a difference between being an artist or musician and being an entertainer. R.W. Hampton always appreciated and admired entertainers. "I know some people say that all they want to do is play music and sing even if they can't make a living," said Hampton. "I'm not one of those people. I could never see myself sitting in a Holiday Inn lounge with a drum machine playing night after night."

Hampton went to country music shows and learned from Marty Robbins and Merle Haggard about entertainment. "I saw Marty Robbins at a dinner theater in Dallas," said Hampton. "And I managed to get backstage and had a wonderful visit with him. He was so versatile and could really entertain an audience. He's the one who got me into entertainment and having fun on stage. I felt that a dinner theater was a great place to play. I also saw Merle Haggard a number of times and realized that dimension in him."

R.W. was also inspired by Tony Bennett. "Lisa and I went to the Houston Livestock Show and Rodeo," remembers R.W. "There were 58,000 people and Tony came out and stood on a stage the size of a postage stamp with his trio in front of a rodeo crowd. He didn't wear a cowboy hat or try to sing cowboy songs. He just sang and the crowd ate it up." There's a strong message to be who you are and do what you do—no matter where you are or who is in the audience. Tony Bennett delivered that message to R.W. with his performance in Houston.

R.W. and Lisa were living on the Flying M Ranch in a camp but yearned for a place of their own. "We talked about a new life and a new place. Lisa was fully supportive; she wanted to be a partner in my life and in my dream," said R.W. "So we came about 100 miles west of where we started and looked around. We found the Clearview Ranch and we bought it." It's a small, family ranch—a working ranch—and it is both a physical and spiritual home to R.W. Hampton. It's a bit of his paradise on earth, although he openly admits that paradise has its share of problems.

"Ranches across America are really struggling," said R.W. "The price of beef keeps fluctuating. You start them on grass and then send them to a feedlot and the price of grain has gone up—some of that due to corn being used for ethenol—and then transportation has gone up. Diesel fuel going over $5 a gallon in some places was a blow. Global warming or whatever you want to call it is nothing new, draught cycles have been going on out here for a long while. We didn't get enough snow on the mountains this past winter and we haven't had much rain, so we decided not to run any cattle this year."

R.W.'s ranch takes on steers after they've been weaned and grazes then until around October. The steers usually go from about 450 pounds to 800 pounds. The Hamptons get paid by weight, so much for so many pounds. This minimizes the risk for them.

"There's people with deeded ranches that have been in their family for over a hundred years and they're in danger of disappearing," said R.W. "They've lost portions of their place because of inheritance taxes and it's just hard to make a living. We used to feed our country but we don't anymore. There's cheap food coming in from outside our country and that hurts the family ranch, which can't compete with those cheap prices. It's like we've got a certain number of gigs for western singers but if all of a sudden western singers start coming in from all over the world and they're charging less—we can't make a living.

"The job of the modern day rancher is in jeopardy. He is the most highly skilled and most underpaid worker around. You need to know about a lot of things to work on a ranch. But the ranch jobs are drying up. It used to be that you could always get hired on the big ranches but they're not employing as many cowboys as they used to. They just can't afford to."

When you live on the land, the weather is always a concern. It's got to rain the right amount at the right time and then not rain at the right time—and the weather seldom works that way. "We live and die by weather patterns," said R.W. "Whenever I fly somewhere, I check into the hotel and turn on the weather channel."

"Lisa came from a background in real estate," said R.W. "So she was used to selling people what they didn't want or need and that fit right in with helping me get gigs." He laughed. "Before we got married I would leave with a guitar, suitcase and plastic grocery sack of CDs. I did no accounting and gave most of them away. She said, 'Let me take this over,' and when she did we started making money from CD sales. Sometimes the money we made on CD sales is more than the fee I received."

With Lisa's help, R.W.'s career rose to a new level, but to go higher he needed an outside manager. Both came to that realization at the same time. "We were both in the bathroom one morning—each in our own mirror—and she said, 'We gotta talk,' and I said, 'We gotta talk,' and we both said, 'We can't do this anymore; it's gotten too big' That's exactly how that happened."

R.W. had been talking with Scott O'Malley for a while and he also talked with a few others, but the name Brian Ferriman kept coming up. R.W. knew of his work with Brenn Hill and was impressed. Finally, R.W. called him and Brian flew to Albuquerque and they met. Brian listened to R.W.'s dreams and ideas and agreed to manage him, saying, "I don't exactly know what will happen, but let's try it."

"Brian has such great expertise," said R.W. "Cowboy festivals were my world and at those, you get a set fee and usually about 20 minutes to play. They run you on and off like you're in a cattle chute and if the person ahead of you takes up too much time, then you've got only ten minutes. Brian said, 'You can't really develop your show like that.'

"Brian got me into things where what you are paid is negotiable. We started playing performance halls and then I became spokesman for Atwood's Ranch and Home Superstores, which are in the Midwest. I could never have done that without Brian. And a lot of other things came where people said they had always wanted me but didn't think they could get me. Brian made the phone calls to do those things. He also got us a larger presence on the Web and exposure in Europe."

R.W. has played the east side of the big river a few times but wants to expand his audience over there. "There's an audience not being reached," he said. "Most of my shows are in the West but there's no reason that the cowboy can't draw a crowd in other places."

R.W. Hampton did not start out looking for an audience; an audience found him. When that audience first found him, it gave R.W. a taste of what being a singer of western songs and ranching culture could be. "I'm probably fairly driven in an understated way," said R.W. That seems to be a nice combination for western music, which doesn't like it when performers seem too pushy or ambitious.

Success never arrives solo and if someone isn't pushing their own career, then others must be around to lend a hand. R.W. Hampton has been blessed to have people like Don Edwards, Charlie Daniels, Ian Tyson, Dave Corlew and Red Steagall on his side. They've all played an important part in his life and have been supportive in tangible, solid ways.

The life of a western singer is like a long, hard, dusty cattle drive. There are problems and pitfalls every step of the way and the payoff comes only at the end of the drive, once the goods have been delivered. It's a trail where endurance and an unshakeable belief that you're doing what God has put you on this earth to do are what keep you going. No matter what happens, what setbacks occur, life is meaningful and fulfilled when you live your mission in life.

"My faith is important," said R.W. "God has given me some talent and I want to use it. My family is also important, so giving up my family is not part of the plan. But I believe there's bound to be some way to make this all happen in a family atmosphere."

That's the trail that R.W. Hampton rides, and no one doubts that the goods will always be delivered.

SOURCE:

Hampton, R.W. Phone interview with the author, August 21, 2009.

42

Waddie Mitchell, Cowboy Poet

A long, cold winter and a box of books. That's what it took to start Waddie Mitchell on the trail to being a cowboy poet. Sometimes a classroom ain't the best place to get an education. Sometimes a person has to be locked into some misery to discover happiness. Some people have to be cornered into learning, tricked into searching before the light of enlightenment clicks on. That's what happened to Waddie back on Christmas 1966.

He dropped out of school when he was 16 and went to work as a cowboy on the Seven S Ranch in Elko County where he was one of the few cowboys hired for the winter, a time when the ranch usually trims its hands to "just enough" until spring. Winter in Elko can be tough and lonesome. Christmas 1966 was the first Christmas Waddie had spent away from home, so he was glad when two boxes arrived from his mom and dad. Waddie needed some overshoes, a new coat and a new lasso rope—dried cotton rope—and he hoped that those were in the boxes that arrived. Since Waddie wasn't at home he didn't have to wait until Christmas morning to open those boxes so he tore into them right after they arrived. His heart sank when he realized those boxes contained books: *The Harvard Classics*. Waddie thought his parents were digging into him a bit for quitting school and he didn't appreciate it.

But the winters are long and cold and a body gets mighty lonesome in the bunkhouse. So through "sheer boredom" young Waddie Mitchell picked up one of the books and leafed through it until he found a story that looked interesting. He's not sure what that first one was but it might have been *Tarzan* by Edgar Rice Burroughs. He read it and then read another and another. Here was a guy who groaned through "literature" when he was in school but a thirst for knowledge, a hunger for learning and a love of literature took over until Waddie had read every single story in those volumes. He couldn't have received a better education for a poet if he had gone to the real Harvard. "It was the turning point of my life," said Waddie, and added, "I've still got those books."

Waddie Mitchell was born in Elko, Nevada, on August 22, 1950, and was a working cowboy during twenty-six years of his life. He grew up on a ranch that was about 60 miles from town—33 of those miles a dirt road—and quit school because he had to board in town in order to attend school and that took him away from the life he loved: cowboying, or "buckarooing," as it is known in Nevada.

The house he grew up in is now the "Sherman House," the home of the Elko Chamber of Commerce. It used to take an hour and a half to get from that house into town and now it's parked right in the middle of town. It is a large, impressive log structure situated right on Idaho Avenue, the main thoroughfare of Elko, close to the convention center where much of the annual cowboy poetry gathering is held.

Waddie's dad was a rancher who ran mostly Herefords on his range, although there were some Jerseys (for milk) "and a few exotics," according to Waddie. Waddie and his four sisters grew up on the ranch, which covered about 46,000 acres and had four or five cowboys working on it.

In 1970, Waddie's sister, who was in college in Boulder, Colorado, sent him a Kris Kristofferson album for his birthday. That album was Kristofferson's first and it featured the early hits Kristofferson had written like "Help Me Make It Through the Night," "For the Good Times" and "Sunday Morning Coming Down." But the album also had songs that showed Kristofferson as a song poet: "Blame It on the Stones," "To Beat the Devil," "The Best of All Possible Worlds," "The Law Is for the Protection of the People," "Casey's Last Ride," "Just the Other Side of Nowhere," "Darby's Castle" and "Duvalier's Dream."

Waddie Mitchell didn't have a record player—or even electricity—but the lyrics were on the album so Waddie read them and fell in love with Kristofferson's poetry. Since there was no electrical entertainment out on the chuck wagon where he worked, Waddie memorized those lyrics of Kristofferson and kept himself entertained by reciting them to himself. He can still recite lyrics from the back of that album. It was another step in Waddie Mitchell's path to becoming a cowboy poet.

In 1970, when Waddie was 20, he was drafted into the army; by that time he had gone through those *Harvard Classics* twice and was halfway through a third time. He did basic training at Fort Knox, Kentucky, and then, after a tour in Vietnam, landed in Colorado, near Fort Carson towards Penrose. There, he served his time in the army by working on a ranch where the horses for the mounted color guard were housed. There were also about 100 dude horses to rent and about another 100 horses that military personnel owned and kept there.

After he mustered out of the service, Waddie spent about a year in La Junta in southern Colorado after he married a girl from that area; her father was a cowpuncher. Waddie had been around a bit; before the army he'd cowboyed in Arizona and Oregon. But after about a year in Colorado it was time to head back to Nevada.

In Nevada, Waddie had friends going to school so he signed up under the GI Bill. Since he always liked to draw, one of the classes he took was Art, where the teacher was Sarah Sweetwater. Sarah took an interest in Waddie and encouraged him in his creative venture. Sweetwater "put on an art in the park deal in Elko," said Waddie and she asked him to demonstrate braiding rawhide for visitors. A friend of his twisted horsehair. "There were some old timers telling stories," remembered Waddie, "so I was asked to go over there and recite some poetry." That was the first time he recited poetry in public and that was when he met Hal Cannon, who knew Sarah Sweetwater.

"Hal became very interested," said Waddie. "People have an idea of what a cowboy is supposed to be and usually that came from television and movies and novels. They think of a cowboy with a guitar and singing but in twenty-six years of being a professional cowboy, I only ran into two cowboys who had guitars and only one of them would ever take it out and play it. And all he knew was Beach Boys songs and stuff like that." On the other hand, he "knew a lot of cowboys who were talking and telling stories and if a guy knew a poem, then he was welcome to tell it," said Waddie. "It was really entertainment."

Books were not uncommon for cowboys but whatever they carried was in their sack, so things could get mussed up. "But telling stories was something you carried in your head. I believe that's a need of human beings one way or another. Not as important as food, water and shelter—but right after that," Waddie said.

Waddie Mitchell was living the buckaroo life out on a remote ranch during the early 1980s. There was no electricity. "But if you've never had electricity, you don't miss it," said

Waddie. "If you live in a house that runs on electricity and the current goes out, then it's a pain in the butt. But if you don't have it then you just live that way."

His first child, a son, was born in 1976, then a daughter and then another by the time the first Elko Gathering was held in 1985. Waddie and his wife had two more children after Elko—five in all—but "it's a hard life," said Waddie and his wife eventually left him.

Before that first Elko Gathering, Hal Cannon came out to Waddie's ranch and listened to him recite some of his poetry. Waddie also introduced him to other cowboys writing poetry. Hal was intrigued; Waddie was the first cowboy he found who wrote poetry. He soon found out there were others. Hal talked to Waddie about putting on a poetry reading in Elko. They decided that the end of January was the best time because this was a break in the ranching life; cows had calved by this time but it was too cold to get out into the fields. Waddie knew of other cowboys who wrote poetry. "When you work with a guy you get to know him pretty well," said Waddie. "And if a guy was writing poetry, well, that knowledge would usually come out." Hal Cannon contacted some of those cowboys that Waddie knew as well as fellow folklorists and invited them to come to Elko, Nevada, at the end of January 1985 to listen to cowboys recite their poetry.

Waddie Mitchel (photograph by Donald Kallaus, courtesy of Scott O'Malley Agency).

Waddie Mitchell is the type of guy who's always willing to help a friend. So Waddie was at the Elko convention center bright and early on the first morning of that initial Gathering, helping set up chairs in one of the small, side rooms at the Convention Center. He helped set up about 100 chairs, with no idea of how many would be filled. Truth be told, he thought he'd set up too many. Then the cowboys, ranchers and folklorists came and those 100 chairs weren't nearly enough. Neither was the room big enough, so they moved into the auditorium, which seats 900. Fortunately, there was nothing else booked at the Elko Convention Center that weekend so the 2,000 or so who showed up at least had some extra room.

Hal Cannon had his hands full just keeping the program running during that first Elko Gathering. Waddie was the spark that ignited Hal's interest in cowboy poetry, so he was scheduled to be the first to recite his poetry. He recited "The Death of Dan McGrew," about a prospector in the far north who dies and is cremated. When someone opens the door to the furnace, Dan glowers at him, ordering him to shut it because it's the first time he's ever been warm. Waddie caught the attention of other poets and news media who covered the event. Word spread that Waddie Mitchell was a dang good cowboy poet and a talent to be reckoned with.

Elko came along at a fortuitous time for Waddie; it got him and his poems some attention and led to his being one of the first artists—along with Don Edwards and the Sons of the San Joaquin—signed to Warner Western, the label started by Jim Ed Norman in Nashville after Michael Martin Murphey's success with his first cowboy album. Murphey brought Waddie to Jim Ed's attention and Waddie was the first and only cowboy poet signed to that label.

Waddie recorded those Warner Western albums in Nashville and was booked by Terry Cline at World Class Talent. Waddie was sent out to open for country artists like Clint Black and Vince Gill. "But it was just awkward and uncomfortable," said Waddie. "People came to hear Clint Black or whoever was playing and they weren't in the mood to hear cowboy poetry and it was hard to explain what I did at the time so I got thrown into difficult situations." Still, he managed to appear on *The Tonight Show Starring Johnny Carson* four times and his poetry was increasingly recognized. But the situation at Warner Western wasn't working out. The corporation wasn't seeing big profits from this venture and the cowboy artists had a hard time fitting into the world of Nashville country music where big sales depended on having a hit song on country radio.

Waddie tried his hand at writing songs: "I wrote some with the songwriters from the publisher Little Big Town but that kind of writing was not my process at all." (Little Big Town was owned by Kerry O'Neil, who was also an investor in Warner Western.)

Warner Western folded and the cowboy artists walked away from the venture, a bit disappointed and frustrated but much wiser. The Warner Western experience didn't hurt anyone and gave three careers a major boost. Those artists were adrift when Waddie received a call from Willie Matthews telling him about a friend in Colorado who might be interested in what he was doing. Willie gave Waddie Scott O'Malley's phone number and Waddie gave him a call. Scott told him he wasn't really interested in taking on anybody new but agreed to come to a show Waddie was scheduled to do in Santa Rosa, California.

Waddie called Don Edwards and the Sons of the San Joaquin, told them about O'Malley and invited them to the Santa Rosa show. They all performed and met together after the show: "We sat down in a booth and Scott said he was very interested. We laid some rules down; we had just walked away from a sixty-seven-page contract and I wanted to work with a guy who could look me in the eye and shake my hand." Scott agreed. "We've never raised an eyebrow," said Waddie about the agreement during the ensuing years.

When creativity is embedded in the soul of a true artist, that creativity will find a way to "bust loose." Genius will escape if given opportunity. In college classrooms the professors of literature make poetry a puzzle to unlock. It is foreboding, full of mysteries and indecipherable blooh hah and it's no wonder kids run away from it. There's always more hidden than what meets the eye. But in real everyday life, poems rhyme and tell stories and everyday people write poems. Waddie Mitchell did not study poetry and literature in a classroom; he learned literature from *The Harvard Classics* and the poetry of Kris Kristofferson and others. These initial encounters led him to read other poets, like Lawrence Ferlinghetti, Gary Snyder, Robert Service, Edgar Allan Poe, Walt Whitman and Badger Clark. Waddie didn't read the western novels of Zane Grey or Louis L'Amour. He started with the classics and he stayed there.

Waddie Mitchell always loved hanging around cowboys. He claims that he started reciting poetry when he was around seven years old and remembers old cowboys also reciting poetry. He also loved the stories old cowboys told—rambling, ambling pieces that sometimes had a point and sometimes didn't. But it was a way to entertain and be entertained. There were tall tales and true stories, stories they'd heard passed down and stories from their own lives and experiences.

Lawrence Ferlinghetti is a "Beat Poet" from the 1960s. His *Coney Island of the Mind*, published in 1958, is a landmark book that has sold over a million copies and has been translated into nine languages. Ferlinghetti's bookstore, City Lights Booksellers in San Francisco, was a gathering place for early beat poets; his publishing company, City Lights Publishers, published books by Allen Ginsberg, William Carlos Williams, Gregory Corso, Kenneth Rexroth, Kenneth Patchen, Denise Levertov and Robert Duncan. Probably the most famous publication was Allen Ginsberg's "Howl," which was seized by the police in 1956 and Ferlinghetti was arrested on obscenity charges. He was acquitted in October 1957.

Waddie Mitchell had a book signing at City Lights and remembers Ferlinghetti telling him that his generation "had taken poetry away from the American people. He was almost guilty about it," remembered Waddie. "Poetry became something that the elitists got ahold of and now you almost got to read a book about it to understand it." That's not how Waddie Mitchell approaches his poetry. "If nobody understands it, you haven't done your job," said Waddie.

Sometimes it's just time for something. For cowboy poetry, the mid-1980s was the beginning of the time for cowboys to gather and recite their poetry while the world outside of cowboys and ranchers gathered to listen. As more people became aware of cowboy poetry, more people began writing poetry until there are now thousands of poets writing about the West and the western experience. There're old guys and young guys, women and girls, working cowboys, weekend cowboys, show business cowboys and city folks who dress up like cowboys. Each finds a hunger in their soul to write cowboy poetry and recite it at gatherings based on the Elko model held all over the West.

Waddie has witnessed this firsthand a number of times. "I've had people come up to me in their late forties with almost a tear in their eye," said Waddie. "They'd tell me, 'I was looking for this all my life' and 'this has changed my life.' It's changed the way they raise their kids. It's amazing what literature can do. Once people just like those people—down-to-earth folks—show that you can write poetry and recite it then it kinda inspires them to do what they want to do. They've told me, 'I didn't know I wanted to be a cowboy,' but then they're 55 or so and they discover this way of life."

Waddie is a bit mystified by his success, although he feels incredibly blessed and thankful for it. He stopped ranching and started touring as a cowboy poet at a critical time in his life. After twenty-six years of cowboying, his back was just about gone. "The doctors told me they'd done all they could do for me. When you're young you think you're bullet proof and a cowboy don't complain, you just grit your teeth. And that's what I did until those doctors made me feel duly stupid for doing it. There were five disintegrating vertebrae when I quit cowboying full time."

Waddie remarried—his wife is the daughter of actor and comic Buddy Hackett—and Buddy sent him to a back specialist who gave him exercises to do. Waddie's wife informed him he was "doing yoga" as he did his stretching and strengthening exercises. "It's worked," said Waddie. "The last four or five years are the first time I've been out of pain for I don't know how long."

The poems don't come easily for Waddie. "I'll work quite a while on a story in my head, like where I'm going to go with it and the best way to tell a story," said Waddie. "There's a million different ways to tell the same story. I like to do it succinctly. There's a definite beginning, a rise and a summing up at the end. I like an ending that really slaps people across the face. I work a long time in getting that story in my head and then I sit down with a yellow legal pad and write it out."

The writing is an important step in the evolution of one of Waddie's poems, but he then has to recite it. "It's trial and error," said Waddie. "I never let it get published until I recite it. When I recite there's sometimes a single word that has to be changed because it makes a difference. I may lose a phrase or two or maybe even a stanza or two. I kinda edit as the story is being told. Sometimes a poem just ain't working and I have to drop it."

"I'm more of a storyteller than a poet in the poetry world," said Waddie, who admits he's never submitted a poem to *Poetry* magazine or tried to court the elite world of academic poets. "To me, a poem is a story and then it's like a crossword puzzle. I've written some poems where the essence of them are words that create a mood but mostly I'm interested in stories." "I like a turn of phrase," said Waddie, who admits he writes more to a stride or rhythm of the words than to a musical tune.

Reading keeps Waddie Mitchell going. "I love my books and my library," he said and who admits that he's always got "a bunch of books going at the same time." At the time we talked, the book sitting in Waddie's lap was *Love in the Driest Season: A Family Memoir* by Neely Tucker, a book about adopting an orphan from Zimbabwe. He'd just finished *When a Crocodile Eats the Sun: A Memoir of Africa* by Peter Godwin, another book about Zimbabwe. He loved Bill Bryson's *Short History of Nearly Everything* and was also reading *The Great Upheaval: America and the Birth of the Modern World, 1788–1800* by Jay Winik, and *Will the Circle Be Unbroken* by Paul Kingsberry, a book on the history of country music.

Waddie Mitchell lives in a big house on a 720-acre spread near Elko. His poetry provided that house and land and he is eternally grateful. "It is delightful for me and gives me the sustenance to continue doing what I'm doing." He and Baxter Black are the two most prominent cowboy poets and Waddie seems perplexed that so many want to hear him recite. And it's not just in the west—about 35 percent of his bookings come from the East, places like Martha's Vineyard and Florida.

The poetry of Waddie Mitchell is poetry that doesn't need to be picked apart. You like it or you don't. It doesn't aim to have twenty levels of meaning: it aims for one strong meaning. It's like a Norman Rockwell painting: What you see is what you get. Waddie doesn't want to offend people, but he wants to make them think and ask questions. During the Olympic Games held in Salt Lake City in 2002, Waddie's poem "That No Quit Attitude" was heard. Here in that poem is the essence of Waddie Mitchell, cowboy poet:

> I believe, like dogs and horses, we're all born with resolution
> And, like muscles and good habits, it needs use and exercise.
> If left dormant, it's in jeopardy of lost evolution
> For eventually it shrivels up and atrophies and dies.
>
> But, when flexed, it blossoms heroes and a source of inspiration
> For we all recognize that virtue in that "no quit" attitude
> And it proves its attributes in competition and vocation
> Which evokes appreciation and a show of gratitude.
>
> And since mankind started walking, it's been swifter, higher, stronger
> As if pushed by some deep need to keep their limits unconfined
> Almost thriving, always striving towards things bigger, better, longer
> In an unrelenting pursuit of perfection, redefined.
> And in this world of soft complacence there are those among the masses
> Who will readily give all to see a job or dream fulfilled.
> It's a trait that's void of prejudice toward races, sex or classes
> Just demanding its possessor be of valor and strong will.

As Waddie and his pardner bring the cattle home, Waddie also brings the poem home:

> I'm convinced that "no quit" attitude will always persevere
>   And that's the essence and the promise and the crown of human kind.

In "Story with a Moral," Waddie used internal rhymes. Here is a sample verse:

Near some quakin' asp trees, I had caught in the breeze
A stench that was raunchy and mean,
And I reckoned as how it might be the old cow,
So I rode to a bend in the stream.

Notice the number of multisyllable words in "That No Quit Attitude" and how they flow through the "hard" sounds of words that have a "d" or "k" and then move into the softer sounds of words that have an "h" or a "p" or an "m." In "Story with a Moral" Waddie takes one-syllable words and uses them like steps marching toward his destination—which happens to be an old dead cow in a stream. Those are some of the marks of a great poet. (Waddie absorbed a lot of the rhythm and use of hard and soft sounds when listening to some Chinese poetry that had been translated.) The language comes alive when presented in Waddie's thick, slow western drawl and the effect holds an audience spellbound.

When people stumbled onto Elko, it was something they were longing to find even though most were not even aware of their search. Elko was like a life raft in the wide open ocean of the West. There were cowboys drowning in a creative drought and the poetry recited at Elko saved them. Elko was the impetus for a "Western Renaissance" that brought together poets, singers and all kinds of cowboys. For cowboys who wrote poems, it became an inspiration, a destination, and a vocation.

Waddie Mitchell is reluctant to take a lot of credit for Elko; he insists he was just one of a number of poets who showed up at that first Gathering and has been showing up ever since. But he became the symbol of Elko, the man on the poster for cowboy poetry and the shining example for what cowboy poetry is all about.

Waddie Mitchell is an open-minded man with firm convictions. He is a man who accepts others who are different, yet he is comfortable being who he is and doing what he does. He is a man who will jump in to help another with a chore or just something that needs to be done. He wears a distinctive wide brim hat, a hat style he wore from his pre–Elko days.

Waddie Mitchell wears the mantle of "cowboy poet" with an ease and conviction that tells the world that here is a man doing what he was born to do. And, like that cowboy hat, he wears it well.

SOURCE:

Mitchell, Waddie. Phone interview with the author, February 20, 2009.

43

Chris LeDoux

Chris LeDoux and his wife, Peg, were driving south from their ranch in Kaycee, Wyoming, to Casper when he heard his name sung on the radio. It was an unknown singer out of Nashville named Garth Brooks and the song was Garth's first hit, "Much Too Young (To Feel This Damn Old)." Chris had never heard of Garth Brooks and never even knew a song with his name in it existed until it came on the radio. "Hard to stay on the road," said Chris, who admitted it was "a shock" and an "oh wow" moment in his life. That song was the biggest break Chris LeDoux ever got in the music business, and it launched his career from being an artist on an independent label, trying to sell a few CDs, to a multimillion-selling artist.

Chris LeDoux grew up "all over" because his father was in the air force, and the family moved a lot—Long Island, Mississippi, France, Philadelphia, Texas and Wyoming. Chris got on his first bucking horse in Cartright, Oklahoma, when he was around 13 at a small community rodeo. "My father talked to the guy in charge," said Chris. "It was too late to enter but he said I could ride an 'exhibition.' I didn't know what 'exhibition' was."

Chris loved the experience and went on to ride in a number of rodeos, winning the Little Britches Rodeo Bareback World Championship in 1964, the Wyoming State High School Bareback Bronc Championship in 1967, the National Intercollegiate Bareback Riding Championship in 1969 and the Bareback Bronc Championship trophy in 1976.

The first record Chris ever bought was a 45 of "Big Iron" by Marty Robbins. "We went down to the store and asked the guy what was something good and he said, 'This is new.' I think he even played it for us," said Chris. His first guitar came when his mother bought him a Harmony instrument. She also bought a chord book for him and he sat down and learned to play. That guitar is still with him, but it's hanging on a wall now, all in pieces. "It got smashed while I was in college," he said.

The first songs he played were country—"Your Cheatin' Heart" by Hank Williams and some Buck Owens numbers. Then he started writing songs; his first composition was "Participally Phrase" because he was having trouble in High School English learning about participles.

Of his days with the rodeo, Chris said, "I was just into riding." But he'd recorded four songs in Nashville before he got married, then recorded some others in Wyoming after he'd gotten married and that was his first album. He "always had a few in the trunk" when he went to rodeos, but didn't spend much time trying to perform or sell them.

"Then my parents got involved," said Chris. His father, who had been a bomber pilot during World War II, retired and settled in Mt. Juliet, Tennessee, just outside of Nashville, and organized a record label, publishing and the basics of a career in the music industry. Chris LeDoux's albums soon became a cult favorite among rodeo cowboys and other lovers of western music; but as far as the rest of the recording industry, the albums really weren't a blip on the radar screen.

During his rodeo days, Chris performed only once at a rodeo. Then, in the late seventies and early eighties, he got a little more serious about performing. "We'd mail letters to a chamber of commerce or anybody we could when there was a rodeo or fair to see if we could get some bookings," remembers Chris. "Sometimes a letter would get answered and we'd play. And every now and then a phone call would come out of the blue."

The reason Chris got more serious about his music career was because he was in danger of losing his ranch. "We got into ranching after I was married and thought we knew what we were doing and that we could make it. Then in 1978 the interest rate shot up to twenty-two percent—we had one of those variable rates—and the bottom fell out of the value of land. It looked like we were going down a blind, dark alley."

The ranch in Kaycee stayed afloat because Chris's father-in-law put in some money and because Chris began earning a little bit of money performing. Then that song came on the radio. Eight months later, he and Garth were both booked into the same club in California, which is where they first met.

"It was a magical evening," said Chris. "We got to visit and talk a lot. It was a small stage and just to see his magic, hear his songs and see how he connected with people—it was incredible." Because of Garth, Chris was signed to Capitol Records—Garth's label—and began to sell in big numbers. The crowds at his shows increased and he began playing "a nice mix" of concert halls, fairs and rodeos. He still had a working ranch in Wyoming, running Angus cattle with some red bulls, but he was playing on the road more.

That situation lasted for a number of years until a few years ago when he started feeling bad—"little bouts of the flu and it got worse"—and went to a doctor. Chris was handed some heavy news: he needed a liver transplant if he was going to survive. As soon as Garth Brooks heard about that, he called Chris and told him, "I'm donating part of my liver to you." Chris was overwhelmed, "speechless," but it wasn't a match. However, a donor was found and the operation was a success.

"My health is up and down," said Chris. "It probably always will be, but I'm pretty much O.K. and can do most of the things I used to do." The lessons that he learned was that "you never know," he said. "I'd gotten to the point in life where I felt like I could coast, and then that hit me. Thanks to a good doctor and a donor and the man upstairs, I'm healed."

Was there any great revelation that came out of all this? "No, but I still do a lot of asking," said Chris. "I don't know why this all happened to me but I feel now I should sorta be a positive influence with my life and music now. But I'm not going to beat the drum over some cause. I really don't know what life is all about—life is a strange thing—but I do know how lucky most of us are, while some are really suffering."

Chris LeDoux died on March 9, 2005.

SOURCE:

LeDoux, Chris. Phone interview with the author, May 14, 2003.

44

George Strait

George Strait may be the true heir to Roy, Gene, Tex and all the other singing cowboys of the 1930s and 1940s. Strait dresses the part. He proudly wears his cowboy hat and boots and lives the part as well. He owns a ranch in Texas and sponsors the biggest team roping event in the country. He's recorded a number of songs about cowboys and the West, including "Amarillo by Morning," "The Cowboy Rides Away," "I Can Still Make Cheyenne," "Cowboys Like Us" and "How 'Bout Them Cowgirls." He's starred in a western movie, *Pure Country*, and, like Roy Rogers and Gene Autry, has made the West and cowboys part of contemporary America.

George Harvey Strait was born in Poteet, Texas, on May 18, 1952, the son of John Strait, a junior high school math teacher. He grew up in Pearsall, about 60 miles southwest of San Antonio and about 40 miles northeast from his grandfather's ranch in Big Wells, Texas.

When George was in the fourth grade his parents divorced; his mother took his sister and moved on while George and his brother, Buddy, stayed with their father. Strait's grandfather owned a 2,000-acre cattle ranch outside of Big Wells and George and his brother and their Dad went down there most weekends and during the summers to work on that ranch.

When Strait was in high school during the late 1960s the Beatles took the music world by storm and he was a Beatles fan. He graduated from high school in 1970 and enrolled in college but he didn't seem to fit in there. At the end of his first semester, on December 4, 1970, he eloped to Mexico with his high school sweetheart, Norma Voss, and they were married. A few weeks later they stated their vows again in a Texas church.

The marriage and lack of direction in college led George to join the army in 1971, where he ended up stationed in Hawaii and worked in the payroll office. George Strait didn't grow up wanting to be a singer; in fact, he never really thought about it until he was in the army. That's when he bought a cheap guitar and some songbooks that showed diagrams of chords and taught himself to play.

Strait jammed a bit with some army buddies but it didn't amount to much until the general at the base decided there should be four bands formed: one for country music, one for rock 'n' roll, one for soul and one for Hawaiian music. Strait auditioned for "Rambling Country" and landed that gig. It changed his life. During his final year in the army Strait played in that country band and "didn't even have to wear army clothes," he said. Strait got serious about country music and began buying records to learn songs. Hank Williams, George Jones and Merle Haggard were his big influences and Haggard's album of Bob Wills music, *Tribute to the Best Damn Fiddle Player in the World*, opened his eyes and ears to western swing.

By the time he ended his army tour he was dreaming of life as a country singer wearing a cowboy hat.

In 1975 Strait mustered out of the army but remained in Hawaii for about six months, trying to make a living singing in clubs. By that point Strait and his wife had a young daughter. The club singing didn't work out so the family moved back to Texas. In San Marcos, located between San Antonio and Austin, he enrolled at Southwest Texas State University, the alma mater of President Lyndon B. Johnson. There, he attended college on the G.I. Bill, received a stipend from the government for his education and played music at nights.

Soon after Strait registered for his classes he posted a note on campus that read "Country singer needs band." The band "Stoney Ridge" just happened to need a singer so the two got together and formed "Ace in the Hole." They played their initial gig during his first semester on a Wednesday night, October 14, at the Cheatham Street Warehouse in San Marcos. The price of admission was 50 cents, no charge for ladies. The club was located beside a railroad track, so every now and then a train came barreling by and drowned out the band. They soon became the regular Wednesday night band; members included Tom Foote, Mike Daily, and Terry Hale, who have remained with Strait through the years.

Strait also played at Gruene Hall once or twice a month. His first gig there was on a Sunday afternoon because owner Pat Molak had never heard the band and wanted to check them out before booking them on a weekend gig. He passed that audition too and soon became one of the most popular local and regional acts in southeast Texas.

Strait met Darrell Staedtler, a songwriter who had moved back to Texas from Nashville in the mid-1970s, and the two became friends. In 1977 Staedtler and Strait, along with Kent Finlay, owner of the Cheatham Street Warehouse, came to Nashville, where Strait recorded six demos for Chappell Music, Staedtler's publisher. The three hoped to get Strait a record deal doing Staedtler's songs, so they enlisted top session players. However, the demos didn't attract much attention from the Nashville big shots and Strait "came back to Texas with [his] tail between [his] legs."

In 1979 Strait graduated with a degree in agricultural education and landed a job as foreman of a cattle ranch near San Marcos. He continued to play Texas clubs in about a 200 mile radius of San Marcos. Strait spent the next four years playing Texas honky-tonks at night, perfecting his Texas swing sound, while he worked as foreman of a cattle ranch by day. Unlike most who sing about cowboys and the west, George Strait has lived the cowboy life; he's the Real Deal.

Texas had a continuing appeal through the 1970s and early 1980s. The movie *The Last Picture Show* (1971), the novels of Larry McMurtry, including his classic *Lonesome Dove* (1985) and then the TV mini-series (1989), the James Michener opus novel *Texas* (1985), the movie *Best Little Whorehouse in Texas* (1982) and the TV show, *Dallas* (1978-1991 and the number one ranked show in America) all put Texas in the media spotlight and popularized cowboys and those wearing cowboy hats and boots. The Dallas Cowboys were "America's Team" and the oil business was going strong

In country music, Texas came to the forefront in the early seventies when Willie Nelson moved back after his Nashville home had burned. Establishing his base in Austin, Willie quickly became a folk hero and then a major national star in country music, heading the "Outlaw Movement" that made Willie and Waylon Jennings major country stars and brought the cowboy back in country music. *The Outlaws* album was released in 1976 and those cowboys wore a black hat and made the cowboy a contemporary figure whose lifestyle would not be the subject of a Roy Rogers movie. Strait claims he was not influenced by the Outlaw movement. However, he was the beneficiary of it, as it drew attention to the music and performers coming out of Texas wearing cowboy hats.

In 1979 the movie *The Electric Horseman* was released starring Robert Redford and Willie Nelson as Las Vegas cowboys; in 1980 Willie starred in *Honeysuckle Rose*, a movie about country music cowboys on tour. Then, on June 6, 1980, *Urban Cowboy* was released as the Texas music movement peaked in 1980 and 1981 with the urban cowboy craze that popularized the nightlife of thousands of Texans who danced, partied, drank Lone Star beer and rode mechanical bulls.

In the late 1970s Strait had gone to Houston and cut three songs for Big D Records, the label owned by Pappy Dailey, who had discovered and produced George Jones. That connection came because Dailey's grandson, Mike, was the steel player in Strait's band. The songs were all written by Strait. The first, "I Just Can't Go on Dying Like This," was recorded in June 1976 at the Ray Doggett Studio. "(That Don't Change) The Way I Feel About You" was recorded in May 1978 in Soundmaster Studio, and "I Don't Want to Talk It Over Anymore" was recorded in April 1979 in Soundmaster Studio. The sessions were produced by Don Dailey, Mike's dad, and featured Mike Daily on steel, Tom Foote on drums, Terry Hale on bass, Bill Mabry on fiddle and Strait on guitar and vocals. The songs were good but not quite at the level of Nashville professionals. Strait, who has never been known as a songwriter, showed promise on these tunes but it was obvious he had some work to do on his songwriting before he reached the major league level.

In 1980 George Strait was 27 years old and had a job offer with a large ranching operation in Uvalde, Texas, designing cattle facilities. He dreamed of Nashville and singing country music but wasn't sure he could make a go of it. Still, it was worth one more shot.

Strait had played at the Prairie Rose, a club owned by Erv Woolsey during the late 1970s. Woolsey had worked for ABC and MCA Records in Nashville before going back to Texas to open that club. Woolsey was impressed with Strait's talent and the two kept in touch. Woolsey wanted to get back into the music industry and left Texas to take a job in Chicago, where he worked in promotion for MCA Records. In Chicago he received a call from Strait asking to help him get one more shot. Woolsey's friend, Blake Mevis, had produced hits on the Kendalls and Vern Gosdin so Woolsey lined him up with Mevis for a session. They recorded three songs on that session, "Blame It on Mexico," "Nobody in His Right Mind (Would've Left Her)" and "A Perfect Lie."

Woolsey played the demos for Jim Foglesong, head of the MCA Nashville label and Ron Chancey, vice-president of A&R. Both passed on them. Woolsey urged Ron Chancey, who produced the Oak Ridge Boys and was vice-president of A&R for MCA Records, to go to San Marcos and watch Strait perform. Chancey went and liked Strait's voice and looks but didn't believe the western swing he performed was commercial for country radio.

Strait continued to play but was frustrated because his first experiences with Nashville hadn't turned out well. He listened to the radio and learned more songs. Meanwhile, Woolsey himself wanted to get back to Nashville and soon did so with MCA Records, where he became vice president of promotion.

The songs that Strait recorded in Houston and his Chappell demos piqued the interest of publisher Tom Collins, who told Woolsey that if Strait cut songs from his publishing company, Pi-Gem, he would finance the session. Strait and producer Blake Mevis went into RCA Studio B, located right behind the Pi-Gem offices, and recorded four songs, including "Unwound."

"The demo of 'Unwound' was horrible," said Woolsey, who heard songwriter Dean Dillon singing the demo. "But we decided to give it a shot." Dillon was a well-known songwriter in Nashville who was recording for RCA at the time. He had charted three songs by the end of 1980, including "Nobody in His Right Mind (Would've Left Her)" which later became a hit for Strait.

Woolsey played the session for Ron Chancey, who went back down to San Marcos and watched Strait perform again. This time, Chancey agreed to sign Strait to a singles deal in February 1981. Strait joined a roster that had Loretta Lynn, Conway Twitty, the Oak Ridge Boys, Merle Haggard and Tanya Tucker.

After Strait was signed to MCA, the label executives and career advisors talked to him about taking off his cowboy hat and toning down the western look but he refused, saying something along the lines of "what you see is what you get." Strait reasoned that he is what he is: "The minute you start changing yourself, you're on the road to screwing up completely."

George Strait was signed to a recording contract at the height of the *Urban Cowboy* craze, which brought country music and cowboys to a large pop audience, sold a lot of cowboy hats and boots, and made Texas a hip place to be. In that movie John Travolta starred as a modern day cowboy who worked in the oil industry in Houston during the day and rode mechanical bulls at night in Gilley's, a club that catered to cowboys who drove pickup trucks, loved to drink beer, danced the "Cotton-Eyed Joe" and cherished their free-spirited independence and devil-may-care attitude.

George Strait (photograph courtesy of Packy Smith).

The music from *Urban Cowboy* topped the country charts, and Strait's career capitalized on the urban cowboy phenomena but George was different. While the urban cowboy audience wanted a pop-influenced version of country music, Strait's music was classic Texas country—western swing and honky-tonk.

Erv Woolsey's job was "promotion," getting records on the radio. He knew that the shift to a pop-country sound had left a number of disc jockeys in Texas and the Southwest hungry for traditional country records. Meanwhile, Strait was still working as a ranch foreman when "Unwound" hit the radio airwaves. Strait decided he needed to hit the road to promote the record, which entered the charts two days before Strait's 29th birthday. Strait played at Fan Fair in Nashville in June and went into the studio to record songs for an album. During the evenings the group played in a hotel lounge while cutting tracks during the day.

"Unwound" reached number six on the country charts. His next single, also written by Dean Dillon and Frank Dycus, was "Down and Out" and reached number 16 on the charts, then "If You're Thinking You Want a Stranger (There's One Coming Home)" made it to number three. Strait's fourth single was his first number one. "Fool Hearted Memory" was featured in the movie *The Soldier* and was followed by "Marina Del Ray" and then "Amarillo by Morning," a breakthrough single about a rodeo rider that only reached number four but firmly established Strait's credentials as a singer linked to cowboys and the West. The song was originally recorded by Terry Stafford, and Strait had sung it in Texas clubs for a number of years.

Strait and his band hit the road touring, opened some dates for Ray Price and visited radio stations, making friends with the DJs. Back in the 1930s radio didn't play records; instead, there were live "barn dances" that featured country music as well as morning and noon hour shows for country performers. In order to achieve regular exposure, the movies were the best outlet, so the key to the success of the recordings of Roy Rogers and Gene Autry was singing songs in their movies. The increase in independent radio stations with disc jockey shows made radio airplay (and DJs) more important in the 1940s. With the advent of television in the 1950s and the "Top 40 Format" for radio, getting a hit single on radio became the key to popularizing an artist.

If Roy and Gene had to nurture their careers in the 1980s and 1990s they would have done what George Strait did: release a series of hit singles for radio, follow up by recording albums and promote them through extensive touring and if the opportunity for a movie came along take it. Instead of a string of movies, George Strait had a string of radio hits. The opportunity for a movie came along in the early 1990s.

On October 23, 1992, the movie *Pure Country* debuted and earned $2.7 million during its opening weekend; eventually the movie did $15 million in total ticket sales and has remained a popular video/DVD for fans to purchase. It's also been on late night TV a number of times.

Like the movies starring Roy Rogers and Gene Autry, Strait's character is a cowboy in contemporary times. Strait played Dusty Chandler, a singing star who walks away from fame and goes back to his native Texas where he falls in love with a pretty female ranch owner who doesn't know he's a star.

Strait was reluctant to do a movie but Colonel Tom Parker, who managed Elvis Presley, encouraged him because it would broaden his career. Strait initially wondered what a movie could do for his career and asked, "What do I have to gain? I sell a lot of albums. I got a great life. I go out and do seventy-five concerts a year, and I sell out most of them. And I don't know how to act." But producer Jerry Weintraub developed a movie idea with screenwriter Rex McGee, who was told there were two requirements for the movie: (1) Strait had to sing ten songs and (2) he had to rope something. The movie was directed by Christopher Cain and shot in Texas and Las Vegas in 43 days. The album was produced by Tony Brown, the first time Strait was paired with this legendary producer who continues to produce Strait's albums.

Not many get to live life on their own terms, but George Strait lives his life mostly on his own terms. He rarely gives interviews and when he does the interview generally concludes that Strait is rather "bland." The stories end up being a recitation of his career totals: lots of number ones hit singles, millions of albums sold, awards awards and more awards and honors from the Country Music Association, the Academy of Country Music and numerous others.

The essence of George Strait is that he's a Man of Texas, specifically South Texas. He has a ranch near San Antonio and spends a lot of time there. Like Will Rogers, he is obsessed with roping and there are times during the year when he has a rope in his hand more than he has a guitar. He started a team roping contest in Kingsville, Texas, in 1982 that is now held in San Antonio and is the biggest team roping event in the Rodeo world.

Part of George Strait is a contemporary man, but the inner core is a throwback to the 19th century when the West was filled with real-life cowboys. Of course, Strait has the advantage of owning the ranch and hiring help to keep it going so he can keep his music career on track.

George Strait's ranch is in Cotulla, about 50 miles southeast of San Antonio; he also has a home in that city. At the beginning of his career Strait contemplated moving to Nashville for the sake of his career but he and his manager, Erv Woolsey, decided there was no need to do that. After all, it's a fairly short plane ride from San Antonio to Nashville, making it easy to travel to Nashville when business demands it. Instead, Strait has remained a Texan through and through.

"Texas is home, and I love it here," said Strait. "I love it, every part of it, from the South Texas brush country, the Hill country where I went to college (Southwest Texas State University) to the mountains of West Texas, the piney woods, the high plains and the coast. We've got it all. But at heart, I'm a brush popper."

Although he loves to rope ("I pretty much rope every day when I'm home on the ranch") he didn't get into roping until he went back to college in 1975. On his grandfather's ranch, the cowboys penned the cattle so there was no need to rope, but once George discovered roping he couldn't stop twirling that lariat.

George Strait did not grow up watching the movies of Roy Rogers and Gene Autry; by the time he was born the singing cowboy movie era was over. He is western in the most bona fide way—he was born in Texas, grew up working on a ranch and now owns his own ranch. Like Roy and Gene his music reaches a large, national audience and his personal appearances attract legions of fans. He's proud to wear a cowboy hat and proud to call himself a cowboy. You can't get any more western than that.

Sources:

Strait, George. File at Frist Library and Archive at Country Music Foundation, Nashville, Tennessee.
Woolsey, Irv. Phone interview with the author, November 26, 2007.

45

Country Music, Cowboys and The West

The cowboy is deeply imbedded in country music. In fact, the most enduring symbols of country music are the cowboy and the West. The first image of country music was the hillbilly or mountaineer, but with the introduction of the singing cowboy movies in the 1930s country music received its first positive image and national exposure. Since that time cowboys and country music have been linked, although the primary link through the years has been clothes more than songs.

The cowboy first became a figure in show business during Buffalo Bill's Wild West Shows when Buck Taylor was promoted as a cowboy hero. Although the "real" cowboy is a manual laborer, looking after cattle and doing ranch chores, the creation of the cowboy as a mythic, heroic figure meant that he had to leave the ranch and cows. This happened through dime novels during the 19th century, stage shows, western novels and songs where the cowboy is both performer and subject of an idealized, romantic West.

Throughout the 20th century country music grew to become part of America's musical mainstream. To do this it had to shed the image of "hillbilly," which was a term applied to the early music and performers. During the 1930s the image of the cowboy replaced the mountaineers as country performers—led by the singing cowboys in the movies—increasingly wore western outfits on stage.

As country music has grown from a pastime of amateurs into a national industry, its performers, recordings and business have been documented by trade magazines such as *Billboard*. In June 1949 *Billboard* renamed two of its record charts. "Race" was changed to "Rhythm and Blues" and "Folk" was changed to "Country and Western." At that time the charts reflected juke box airplay, sales and radio airplay. "Country and Western" was replaced by "C&W" in 1956. In October 1958 "Hot C&W Sides" was the name of the singles chart until November 1962 when it became the "Hot Country Singles" chart. So the period when the music was officially called "Country and "Western" or "C&W" was from 1949 to 1962.

In 1949, the year "Folk" became "Country and Western," there were some very big "western" records: "Mule Train" and "Riders in the Sky" were hits on both the "Pop" and "Country and Western" charts. There were five different versions of "Mule Train" that charted and four different versions of "Riders in the Sky." Bing Crosby and Vaughn Monroe had hits with both songs.

In 1944, the first year of the "Folk" charts, the western songs charted were "You're from Texas," "Mexican Joe," "Pistol Packin' Mama," "Rosalita," and "Texas Blues," while "Don't

Fence Me In," "Down in the Valley" "Jingle Jangle Jingle," "Pistol Packin' Mama," "Rosalita," "San Fernando Valley," "Texas Polka," and "You're from Texas" were all on the pop charts.

In 1945 "Don't Fence Me In," "Gonna Build a Big Fence Around Texas," "Oklahoma Hills," and "Sioux City Sue" were on the folk chart, and on the pop charts that year were "Along the Navajo Trail," "Don't Fence Me In," "Northwest Passage," "On The Atchison, Topeka, and the Santa Fe," "Sioux City Sue" and "Three Caballeros."

The trend of more "western" songs being on the pop charts than on the folk charts continued through 1949. Major western hits included "I Want to Be a Cowboy's Sweetheart," "(Oh Why, Oh Why, Did I Ever Leave) Wyoming," "Cool Water," "My Adobe Hacienda," "Ragtime Cowboy Joe," "That's What I Like About the West," "Blue Shadows on the Trail," "Buttons and Bows," "Pecos Bill," and "Tumbling Tumbleweeds."

During the 1950s, there really wasn't much "western" in "Country and Western" music as reflected by radio airplay. In 1950 Roy Rogers had a chart record with "Stampede," in 1951 there was "Cherokee Boogie" by Moon Mullican, in 1952 there was "The Gold Rush Is Over" by Hank Snow and "Indian Love Call" by Slim Whitman. In 1953 there was "Mexican Joe" by Jim Reeves. In 1954 there was "The Singing Hills" by Slim Whitman, in 1955 "The Ballad of Davy Crockett" by both Mac Wiseman and Tennessee Ernie Ford (and on the pop charts by Bill Hayes and Fess Parker), "Cattle Call" by both Eddy Arnold and Slim Whitman and "Yellow Rose of Texas" by Ernest Tubb. In 1956 and 1957 there were no western themed records on the country charts. In 1958 there was "Squaws Along the Yukon" by Hank Thompson. In 1959 there were five western themed songs on the chart: "Don't Take Your Guns to Town" by Johnny Cash, "El Paso" by Marty Robbins, "Half-Breed" by Marvin Rainwater, "Hanging Tree" by Marty Robbins, and "John Wesley Hardin" by Jimmie Skinner. Both "Don't Take Your Guns to Town" and "El Paso" became number one on the charts and "El Paso" won the third Grammy Award for Country Song of the Year.

In 1960 there was "Amigo's Guitar" by Kitty Wells, "Big Iron" by Marty Robbins and "Riverboat Gambler" by Jimmie Skinner. In 1961 there was "Oklahoma Hills" by Hank Thompson, "The Rebel: Johnny Yuma" by Johnny Cash and "San Antonio Rose" by Floyd Cramer. In 1962 there was "Adios Amigo" by Jim Reeves, "Cow Town" by Webb Pierce, "The Comancheros" by Claude King and "Where the Old Red River Flows" by Jimmie Davis.

During the period of 1949–1962 when "country" was labeled "country and western," many argue that country was dominated by western, or at least held a prominent spot in country music. However, that cannot be proven by the *Billboard* charts.

"Western" music *was* dominant on television. In 1949 *Hopalong Cassidy* and *The Lone Ranger* became regular network programs (although Hopalong Cassidy's old movies had been shown regularly on TV the previous year). These were the first two regularly scheduled network westerns. *The William Tell Overture* is neither country nor western, but for most of those who grew up during this period it has a strong western connotation because it was the theme song of *The Lone Ranger*.

In 1951 Gene Autry began his regular network TV series and generally sang a song on each show. *The Roy Rogers Show*, (1951–1957), always ended with Roy and Dale singing "Happy Trails," a song that became one of the most popular western songs of all time and yet was never a chart record from radio airplay. It became a western standard primarily through exposure on television.

Other TV shows with recognizable western theme songs were *Gunsmoke, Cheyenne*, and *The Life and Legend of Wyatt Earp*, which all debuted in 1955. *Wagon Train, Sugarfoot, Maverick*, and *Have Gun, Will Travel* debuted in 1957 (the latter show introduced the "Paladin" theme); and *Rawhide* and *Bonanza* debuted in 1959. The theme for *Bonanza* was on the pop chart in 1961 (#19), played by Al Caiola and His Orchestra. Caiola also had a pop chart record in 1960 with "The Magnificent Seven" (#35). In 1968 two movie themes were on the pop charts, by Hugo Montenegro and His Orchestra and Chorus: "The Good, the Bad and the Ugly" (#2) and "Hang 'Em High" (#82). These last four songs were all instrumentals.

The period 1955–1963 was the era of the TV western, and western shows were plentiful and popular. This period also coincided with the era when "country and western" was the term applied to what is now called "country" music. The 1962–1963 season marked the end of the heyday of the TV western, although *Bonanza* remained a popular TV show (often ranked number one with viewers) throughout the 1960s.

Many of those who count western music as an important part of their formative years were born during the 1920–1944 period when the singing cowboys were still in the movies (the last singing western was produced in 1954). For those born in 1945 or later, the TV western was generally more influential than singing cowboy movies, although Roy Rogers and Gene Autry continued to influence TV audiences after their movie careers were finished.

Television and the movies were more influential in exposing western music—and the idea of the cowboy as a heroic figure—to a broad, general audience than radio airplay during these years, although radio was certainly important. But those who claim that country music used to be dominated by western songs—or at least that country music on the radio contained a significant amount of western music—are confusing the music they heard on TV with what was on the radio.

Radio was going through major changes during the 1948–1960 period as television became part of American homes. When the networks dominated radio programming, country music was heard on barn dances or live variety shows aimed at a rural audience. Country music dominated these shows but there were also comedians, square dances and smooth pop-type groups. After World War II there were more radio stations licensed and these shows were dominated by disc jockeys with their own shows. Radio featured block programming, with a country show perhaps several hours a day, while a pop music show was on several hours a day. As the 1950s progressed there was an increasing number of shows featuring rhythm and blues. When "Top 40<in> programming was introduced in the mid-1950s where a radio station programmed only one type of music, playing the top hits, country music saw a dramatic decrease in airplay as rock 'n' roll became the dominant radio format. It was not until the 1970s that country stations gained a significant portion of radio formats.

During the 1940s the top ten country artists who received most airplay (on jukeboxes or radio) were Eddy Arnold, Ernest Tubb, Bob Wills, Al Dexter, Red Foley, Gene Autry, Jimmy Wakely, Tex Ritter, Tex Williams and Merle Travis. Of the top 50 artists during the 1940s there were some who have been labeled western artists such as the Sons of the Pioneers (#12), Spade Cooley (#18), Johnny Bond (#26), Wesley Tuttle (#27), Roy Rogers (#35), Bob Atcher (#40) and Carson Robison (#50). However, the artists labeled "western" recorded a wide variety of material. For example, Gene Autry's biggest hits were Christmas songs ("Here Comes Santa Claus" and "Rudolph, the Red-Nosed Reindeer"); the Sons of the Pioneers' biggest chart records included "Stars and Stripes on Iwo Jima," "Baby Doll," "Cigarettes, Whusky, and Wild Wild Women" and "Room Full of Roses." Roy Rogers' biggest chart record was "A Little White Cross on the Hill," and Tex Ritter's number one records during the 1940s were "I'm Wastin' My Tears On You," "You Two Timed Me One Time Too Often" and "You Will Have to Pay."

During the 1950s the top ten country artists, based on radio airplay reflected by the *Billboard* charts, were (in descending order) Webb Pierce, Eddy Arnold, Hank Snow, Carl Smith, Red Foley, Hank Williams, Ernest Tubb, Elvis Presley, Johnny Cash and Kitty Wells.

Marty Robbins—who recorded a wide variety of songs—and Gene Autry (at #41) are the only artists who could be remotely considered "western," but Autry's radio hits in the 1950s were "Rudolph," "Peter Cottontail," and "Frosty the Snow Man."

The most popular country music show on television during the 1950s was *The Ozark Jubilee*, hosted by Red Foley. Tennessee Ernie Ford and Jimmy Dean also had popular television shows during the 1950s but none of these could be considered "western." It was only in southern California that TV programs such as *Hometown Jamboree, Hollywood Barn Dance*, and *Town Hall Party* featured a "western" image. Looking back at the musical landscape in the early 1960s it seems logical that country and western would drop the western from its label simply because that label did not fit what was being played on the radio. The theme songs for TV westerns were generally written by "pop" writers who worked in TV and the movies in Los Angeles and were not released on records to radio. It was not until the 1970s that cowboys and the West would be a significant part of country music recordings.

The 1960s were a turbulent time in America. There was a social and cultural revolution, dominated by the issues of the Cold War, the atomic bomb, civil rights and the Vietnam War. The earliest baby boomers, born roughly between 1943 and 1954, grew up watching TV when westerns dominated that media. However, the second group of baby boomers, born from 1955 to 1964, did not grow up watching Roy and Dale on TV. Instead, the westerns that dominated TV land were "adult" westerns like *Gunsmoke* and *Bonanza*. Musically, the first group was impacted by Elvis and the Beatles, while the second group's musical heroes tended to be rock artists like Jimi Hendrix, Janis Joplin, Jim Morrison and others who emerged from the mid-1960s on. It was not an era of "Happy Trails."

In country music, Roger Miller became a major star in the mid-1960s. Then the "Nashville sound," led by Eddy Arnold, Jim Reeves, Patsy Cline and Ray Price featured a smooth, pop oriented style of country music. None of these artists wore cowboy hats; some of them even wore tuxedoes.

In 1969 the biggest country hits that had anything "west" in them were "Wichita Lineman" and "By the Time I Get to Phoenix" by Glen Campbell and "Your Squaw is on the Warpath" by Loretta Lynn. In 1969 it was "Okie From Muskogee" by Merle Haggard and "Running Bear" by Sonny James. The early 1970s continued this trend with "Is Anybody Goin' to San Antone" by Charley Pride in 1970 and "Ridin' My Thumb to Mexico" by Johnny Rodriguez in 1973.

Then, in 1974, there were a number of country songs that featured the term "cowboy" or talked about the western life. Some of these songs were "All Around Cowboy of 1964" by Buddy Alan, "Amarillo by Morning" by Terry Stafford, "Counterfeit Cowboy" by Dave Dudley, "Last of the Sunshine Cowboys" by Eddy Raven, "She's in Love with a Rodeo Man" by Johnny Russell and "Whatever Happened To Randolph Scott" by the Statler Brothers.

In 1975 the cowboy was back in the saddle in country music, led by Willie Nelson and Waylon Jennings and the "Outlaw Movement." Willie Nelson moved back to Texas in the early 1970s and found a thriving musical scene in Austin where young long-haired hippies wore cowboy hats and drank beer next to rednecks who also wore cowboy hats and drank beer. In fact, many Texans never took off their cowboy hats during the 1960s and early 1970s. Willie Nelson had a number one hit with "Blue Eyes Crying in the Rain" in 1975, while Waylon Jennings, who embraced his Texas roots in the 1970s by putting on a cowboy hat, released an album in 1972 titled *Ladies Love Outlaws*.

During 1975 Waylon had hits with "Bob Wills Is Still the King" and "Let's All Help the Cowboy (Sing the Blues)." Other hit country songs that embraced cowboys and the West were "Rhinestone Cowboy" by Glen Campbell (#1), "Bandy the Rodeo Clown" by Moe Bandy (#7) and "Ride 'Em Cowboy" by Paul Davis (#47 country and #23 pop).

In 1976 the seminal album *The Outlaws,* featuring Willie Nelson, Waylon Jennings, Jessi Colter and Tompall Glaser, was released and cowboys were riding high in country music. Hit singles that year included "El Paso City" by Marty Robbins (#1), "Cherokee Maiden" by Merle Haggard (#1), "Faster Horses (The Cowboy and the Poet)" by Tom T. Hall (#1), "Can You Hear Those Pioneers" by Rex Allen Jr. (#17), "Lone Star Beer and Bob Wills Music" by Red Steagall (#11), "Vaya Con Dios" by Freddy Fender (#7), and the first version of "Mamas Don't Let Your Babies Grow Up to Be Cowboys" by its writer, Ed Bruce (#15).

In 1977 there was "Cowboys Ain't Supposed to Cry" by Moe Bandy, "Desperado" by Johnny Rodriguez, "I Got the Hoss" by Mel Tillis, "Luckenback, Texas (Back to the Basics of Love)" by Waylon Jennings and "Adios Amigo" by Marty Robbins. In 1978 there was Waylon and Willie's version of "Mamas Don't Let Your Babies Grow Up to Be Cowboys," "Cowboys Don't Get Lucky All the Time" by Gene Watson and "Don't You Think This Outlaw Bit's Done Got Out of Hand" by Waylon Jennings. In 1979 there was "Coca Cola Cowboy" by Mel Tillis, "Down On the Rio Grande" by Johnny Rodriguez, "Riders in the Sky" by Johnny Cash, "Send Me Down to Tucson" by Mel Tillis and "Tulsa Time" by Don Williams. In each of these years there were a number of other songs that talked about "cowboys" or embraced the West.

The trend continued through the early 1980s, helped along by the movie *Urban Cowboy*, which made cowboys fashionable all over the United States. You would think that fans of cowboys and the West would rejoice; instead, many of them were mad. This wasn't the same cowboy they'd grown up with, the cowboys with white hats who lived cleanly and always did the just and honorable thing. Instead, these cowboys were outlaws and renegades, intent on doing their own thing and going their own way. If they played hard rock music they were still a cowboy because they had the cowboy attitude, which tended towards free living, free loving, hard drinking, some toking and, above all, full independence—while discarding social graces—and an in-your-face rejection of polite society while driving a pick up truck and flaunting nonconformist lifestyles.

At the end of 1977 the group Riders in the Sky was formed when three young men came together on a Monday night and sang cowboy songs to a nearly empty bar. They enjoyed it so much they decided to try singing cowboy songs for a living. It was barely a living those first few years but in 1983 Riders in the Sky landed on The Nashville Network (TNN), a cable channel out of Nashville. By this time the Riders had recorded several albums, were members of the Grand Ole Opry and had made several significant television appearances. As hosts of *Tumbleweed Theater* they introduced western movies to the nation. As their careers progressed they starred in *Riders Radio Theater*, a show on National Public Radio (NPR), and toured constantly. Aside from the Sons of the Pioneers and a few groups performing at chuck wagons, there was no western music to be heard by audiences anywhere.

The success of the Riders coincided with a renewed interest in the West from Michael Martin Murphey, who had a number of country hits in addition to his pop hits "Wildfire" and "Carolina in the Pines." In 1970 Murphey moved to Austin, Texas, and in 1972 his song "Geronimo's Cadillac" was on the charts. His follow-up album was *Cosmic Cowboy*, a term that seemed to fit the Austin movement. In 1986 he started West Fest, the first of the big western festivals which featured cowboy culture and western music. In 1988 and 1989 a number of western festivals, patterned roughly after West Fest, were started.

In 1989 country music saw the introduction of artists such as Garth Brooks, Clint Black, and Alan Jackson. George Strait, Ricky Van Shelton and Reba McEntire were going strong and all of the guys wore cowboy hats. Known as the "Hat Acts" they embraced the western image. The cowboy was firmly back in country music. That same year the Western Music

Association was formed in Las Vegas, an outgrowth of a gathering the year before of fans of the Sons of the Pioneers. The formation of the Western Music Association was the first time western music was defined as a separate genre. Prior to that time the music had some fans but no trade organization and no voice that united those fans.

Western music is a subgenre of what is now known as country music. The same is true of bluegrass. The roots of all these genres are the same: musically they are descended from British folk ballads which came across the Atlantic to the Appalachian region. There were many folk songs or songs with no known authorship which were passed on down through the years, with singers making changes in the lyrics or fiddlers making changes in the melodies.

Another source is songs written for the stage, originally minstrel shows but later everything from the Broadway stage in New York to traveling performers. As this music progressed it was generally handed down from performer to performer until the recording industry developed in the late 19th century. Although there were songs recorded that originated in the folk tradition, the music now known as country was not recorded until the 1920s. The first commercially successful recording was "Little Old Log Cabin Down the Lane" by Fiddlin' John Carson in Atlanta in 1923. The first commercially successful recording of a western song was "When the Work's All Done This Fall" by Carl Sprague in 1925.

What became known as country music was originally labeled "old familiar tunes," "old favorites" and "folk" music. Originally a music performed by string bands comprising a fiddle, a banjo and a guitar, the music evolved into a genre where professionals dominated the field. During the 1930s the music grew because of its exposure on radio barn dances and its exposure in the movies via the singing cowboys. After World War II there were essentially five different directions the music was headed: (1) western swing, which was based on the West Coast and was the most commercially successful in terms of record sales; (2) the singing cowboys, who continued to star in movies; (3) the acoustic string band sound that evolved into bluegrass through the efforts of Bill Monroe and banjo player Earl Scruggs, who gave the music its defining sound; (4) honky-tonk music, which came out of the bars in Texas; and (5) the smooth, pop oriented sound that played down the "twang" and sought to reach the largest possible audience.

As the 1940s ended and the 1950s began, western swing virtually died out, there were no longer any singing cowboy movies, the string band sound became firmly established as a subgenre of country music called bluegrass, and the "honky-tonk" and "smooth" sound competed for commercial acceptance. Country music articulates the white working class. As that group moved into the cities and suburbs and became part of the middle class, the country music industry became part of mainstream American music balancing between the "honky-tonk" or "traditional" sound that appealed to the working class and the "smooth, pop-oriented" sound that appealed to a broader cross section of middle class Americans.

The formation of the Western Music Association essentially created another subgenre of country music called western music. It had a lot in common with bluegrass because both bluegrass and western music remained true to their heritage, while country music reflected the market. In that sense, both western and bluegrass are more static in their music, preferring to stick with the old than venture into the new while country music has constantly evolved, absorbing musical trends from pop, rock 'n' roll, rhythm and blues and show tunes.

Each new generation wants a music of its own. This fact is generally reflected in the pop/rock world, where teenagers of the day flock to a new group of stars. Musically, the sounds tend to be more adventuresome, stretching the boundaries of the previous generation.

The teenager is a key factor when studying the commercial music industry. Generally, when someone is around the age of 15, music becomes an incredibly important part of their life, leading them to bond with friends of similar taste. This important period generally covers the ages of approximately 15–24, and for the rest of their lives people will measure current music against the music they loved and became attached to during this period. Needless to say, no music will quite measure up to the music of their youth.

Country music tends to attract those over 30 years of age after they no longer relate to the pop music of the day. These "converts" want a music that reminds them of the music of their youth, so if country music can somehow incorporate the sounds of the pop and rock music of 15–20 years earlier then it will continue to attract new followers. For this reason, the sounds of contemporary country music tend to embrace and reflect the pop-rock world of 15–20 years earlier.

For those who grow up listening to country music, a similar pattern emerges. However, these fans tend to grow disgruntled with contemporary country music because the sound has evolved from the time they first became attached to it.

This is both a blessing and curse for those who listen to country music. On one hand, it is a growing, vibrant music that continues to be commercially successful, attracting the largest age span of fans of any genre (18–65, although the 30–65 demographic dominates). On the other hand, it leaves the long-time fans forever frustrated because the music doesn't sound like it used to when they first became attached to it. This factor is a key reason for the emergence of the Western Music Association and western music from the 1980s. Country music brought the cowboy back into mainstream America during the 1970s, but it wasn't the sound of the earlier western music done by the Sons of the Pioneers and the original singing cowboys.

Country music has welcomed cowboys and the West into its camp; many country artists wear cowboy hats and the themes of cowboys and the West resonate through country songs. Western music aficionados have not been as welcoming; they insist on stressing the differences between western and country music. This has been a problem when trying to explain the differences between country and western to an audience that lumps them together.

The essential difference lies in the lyrics. In a set of liner notes, O.J. Sikes focused on the lyrics as the key difference and noted that the lyrics in western songs "describe rural, outdoor scenes or events found West of the Mississippi: a cowboy and his horse on the trail or herding cattle, rodeos, Western wildlife, desert sunsets, rolling prairies, deep canyons, tumbleweeds and cactus." Sikes further states that "country music lyrics usually describe events that occur indoors, interpersonal relationships like family ties, lost love and such." Musically, western music tends to be an acoustic music, and country music is electric, or at least has an electric lead and steel guitar, bass and drums. Although in terms of melody and harmony country and western are almost identical, contemporary country absorbs the influence of pop music, while western remains rooted in the sounds of country music of the 1930s and 1940s.

Some apologists for the western genre insist that country music is full of "cheating and drinking" songs and musically is "too much like rock." There is a bit of truth there; the terms "horse," "ride," "saddle," "gun" and "rodeo" sometimes have sexual overtones in country songs. However, country music is seen by many of its adherents as a music that embraces family values through positive love songs and recordings that emphasize family, children and a positive lifestyle.

The cowboy in contemporary country music tends to be a individual living in today's world while the cowboy in western songs tends to be either a historical figure living in the past or a contemporary individual living far away from the world of cities, suburbs, traffic and Walmarts.

The major sticking point that the advocates of western music have against country music is parked at the intersection of "art" and "commerce." Those in the world of country music also wrestle with this every day and also feel frustrations. Basically, the music industry does not judge music on aesthetic grounds. Instead it judges music with a commercial criteria: If it sells it's good, if it don't it ain't. There are a lot of wonderful artists, songs, etc., that do not sell in large numbers, so the major entertainment corporations must move on to what is commercial on a national scale. This frustrates those in a genre, such as western music, who argue for the intrinsic beauty of the music rather than face the commercial limitations.

There is the undying belief in the western music community that millions of people would love western music if only they had the opportunity to hear this music but that opportunity is blocked by the major record labels, which control access to radio and television. There is an antipathy towards "Nashville," which tends to be a catch-all term of all they dislike, are frustrated with and abhor about the music business and country music in particular. And so they intensify their efforts to distance themselves from country music and the country music industry.

In truth, a music is defined by the audience. The audience for western music is also, to a large extent, the audience for country music. That's the reason that those inside the world of western music see a huge difference between country and western and those outside this inner circle see the two as parts of the entire spectrum of country music.

The die-hard fans and aficionados of western music will never accept that western music is part of the world of country music or be satisfied when audiences confuse the differences or continue to see a world of "country and western" music instead of a world of "country" and "western" music. Either way, the image of the cowboy and the West will continue play a key role in shaping the image of both country and western music.

SOURCES:

Whitburn, Joel. *Top Country Songs, 1944–2005*. Menomonee Falls, WI: Record Research, 2005.
_____. *Top Country Albums, 1964–1997*. Menomonee Falls, WI: Record Research, 1997.
_____. *Pop Hits: Singles & Albums, 1940–1954*. Menomonee Falls, WI: Record Research, 2002.
_____. *Top Pop Singles, 1955–2002*. Menomonee Falls, WI: Record Research, 2003.

46

The West on the Music Charts

Trade magazines have kept charts of music recordings as well as sheet music since the late 19th century. The following list comprises songs that embrace the cowboy or the West or both. In the first group of songs listed, there was no differentiation between "pop" and other genres; generally, what was most popular was "pop" and that was listed. In 1944 *Billboard* magazine instituted its first charts for "folk" music, which would later be known as "country." During the 1944–1954 period I have listed both "folk" and "pop" songs that feature cowboys or the West or both. From 1955 forward I only use the country charts to show the appeal of cowboys and the West in the country genre.

In compiling this list I have cast the widest net possible. I have used songs about historical cowboys as well as contemporary cowboys, cities and states west of the Mississippi and the general indication of "western lifestyles," past and present, to determine which songs to include. There are numerous recordings included that may be challenged as to whether or not they are "truly" western or embrace the West. However, it's to be hoped this list will generate an appreciation of how much the image of cowboys and the West have affected popular and country music.

I have used Joel Whitburn's books based on the *Billboard* charts to compile this list. While there are numerous songs that have been written, included on albums or perhaps just sung to admiring fans that are wonderful examples of cowboys and the influence of the West, I have established the basic criterion that the songs included here must have received commercial acceptance to the point that the recording has been documented on a trade music chart in *Billboard* magazine, indicating a fairly wide public acceptance.

In this list, under the year the recording was on the charts, I have listed the song and the artist as well as the highest position reached on the chart.

Chart Songs with a Cowboy or Western Theme, 1896–1944:

1896

"You've Been a Good Ole Wagon but You Done Broke Down" by Len Spencer (#2)

1900

"San Francisco Sadie" by Dan Quinn (#3)

1904

"Navajo" by Billy Murray (#1); "Navajo" by Harry Macdonough (#3); "Navajo" by J.W. Myers (#3)

1905

"Down Where the Silv'ry Mohawk Flows" by Harry Anthony (#7); "Down Where the Silv'ry Mohawk Flows" by Haydn Quartet (#4); "My Little Canoe" by Grace Nelson (#7); "My Little Canoe" by Haydn Quartet (#2); "My Little Canoe" by Henry Burr (#3)

1906

"Cheyenne (Shy Ann)" by Billy Murray (#2); "Paddle Your Own Canoe" by Arthur Collins and Byron Harlan (#8)

1907

"Red Wing (An Indian Fable)" by Frank Stanley and Henry Burr (#2); "San Antonio (Cowboy Song)" by Billy Murray (#3)

1908

"When It's Moonlight on the Prairie" by the Haydn Quartet (#35)

1909

"Yip-I-Addy-I-Ay!" by Arthur Collins and Byron Harlan (#7); "Yip-I-Addy-I-Ay!" by Blanche King (34)

1910

"Down in Sunshine Valley" by Billy Murray and the Haydn Quartet (#4); "My Prairie Song Bird" by Frank Stanley and Henry Burr (#9)

1912

"Down In Sunshine Valley" by Henry Burr and Albert Campbell (#8); "Oh That Navajo Rug" by American Quartet (#9); "Ragtime Cowboy Joe" by Bob Roberts (#1); "Till the Sands of the Desert Grow Cold" by Donald Chalmers (#5)

1913

"Till the Sands of the Desert Grow Cold" by Alan Turner (#1); "Till the Sands of the Desert

Grow Cold" by Frank Croxton (#9); "Trail of the Lonesome Pine" by Elsie Baker and James F. Harrison (#9); "Trail of the Lonesome Pine" by Henry Burr and Albert Campbell (#1)

1914

"California and You" by Henry Burr & Albert Campbell (#8); "California and You" by Irving Kaufman (#4); "Little Grey Home in the West" by Charles Harrison (#4); "Little Grey Home in the West" by Maggie Teyte (#5); "When It's Moonlight on the Alamo" by the Peerless Quartet (#4)

1915

"Cows May Come, Cows May Go, but the Bull Goes on Forever" by the Peerless Quartet (#8); "Hello Frisco!" by Elida Morris and Sam Ash (#3); "Hello Frisco!" by Olive Kline and Reinald Werrenrath (#1); "There's a Long, Long Trail" by Charles Harrison (#9)

1916

"There's a Long, Long Trail" by James F. Harrison and James Reed (#1)

1917

"There's a Long, Long Trail" by James F. Harrison and James Reed (#3); "There's a Long, Long Trail" by John McCormack (#3)

1918

"There's a Long, Long Trail" by Oscar Seagle and Columbia Stellar Quartet (#4)

1919

"There's a Long, Long Trail" by Riccardo Stracciari (#10)

1920

"Barefoot Trail" by John McCormack (#6)

1921

"Wyoming (Lullaby)" by Charles Hart (#7)

1922

"California" by Van & Schenck (#5); "On the Alamo" by Isham Jones (#1)

1923

"Rose of the Rio Grande" by Marion Harris (#3)

1924

"California, Here I Come" by Al Jolson (#1); "California, Here I Come" by California Ramblers (#10); "California, Here I Come" by Georgie Price (#7); "Covered Wagon Days" by Ted Weems (#10); "Covered Wagon Days" by Vincent Lopez (#5); "Home in Pasadena" by Billy Murray and Ed Smalle (#15); "In a Covered Wagon with You" by Benson Orchestra of Chicago (#8); "Roamin' to Wyomin'" by the California Ramblers (#10)

1925

"Indian Love Call" by Louis Reisman (#6); "Indian Love Call" by Paul Whiteman (#3); "West of The Great Divide" by Henry Burr (#13)

1926

"Horses" by George Olsen (#2); "Horses" by The Georgians (#13)

1927

"Desert Song" by Nat Shilkret (#19); "In a Little Spanish Town" by Ben Selvin (#4); "In a Little Spanish Town" by Paul Whiteman (#1); "In a Little Spanish Town" by Sam Lanin (#12)

1929

"Gay Caballero" by Frank Crumit (#2); "Return of the Gay Caballero" by Frank Crumit (#19); "Utah Trail" by Ford and Glenn (#9); "Utah Trail" by Frank Luther and Carson Robison (#19); "I'm the Medicine Man for the Blues" by Ted Lewis (#10)

1930

"Somewhere In Old Wyoming" by Ben Selvin (#10); "Under A Texas Moon" by Guy Lombardo (#5); "When It's Springtime In The Rockies" by Ben Selvin (#1); "When It's Springtime In The Rockies" by Ford and Glenn (#14); "When It's Springtime In The Rockies" by Hilo Hawaiian Orchestra (#1); "When It's Springtime In The Rockies" by Ray Miller (#5); "When The Bloom Is On The Sage" by the Beverly Hill Billies (#7)

1932

"On The Trail" ("Grand Canyon Suite") by Paul Whiteman (#13); "California Medley" by Red Nichols (#20)

1933

"California, Here I Come" by Claude Hopkins (#17); "Home On The Range" by Bing Crosby (#18); "The Last Round-Up" by Bing Crosby (#2); "The Last Round-Up" by Conrad Thibault (#18); "The Last Round-Up" by Don Bestor (#2); "The Last Round-Up" by Gene Autry (#12); "The Last Round-Up" by George Olsen (#1); "The Last Round-Up" by Guy Lombardo (#1); "The Last Round-Up" by Victor Young (#3)

1934

"Amapola" by the Castillians (#20); "Night on the Desert" by Leo Reisman (#10); "On the Wrong Side of the Fence" by Jan Garber (#15); "Tumbling Tumbleweeds" by Sons of the Pioneers (#13); "Wagon Wheels" by Paul Whiteman (#1)

1935

"East of the Sun (And West of the Moon)" by Tom Coakley (#1); "Ole Faithful" by Gene Autry (#10); "Take Me Back to My Boots and Saddle" by Tommy Dorsey (#4); "Take Me Back to My Boots and Saddle" by Victor Young (#20); "Tumbling Tumbleweeds" by Gene Autry (#10); "Wah-Hoo!" by Paul Whiteman (#36); "Wah-Hoo!" by Top Hatters (#15)

1936

"Empty Saddles" by Bing Crosby (#8); "I Wanna Be a Cowboy's Sweetheart" by Patsy Montana (#10); "Saddle Your Blues to a Wild Mustang" by Paul Whiteman (#19); "San Francisco" by Tommy Dorsey (#10); "Springtime in the Rockies" by Benny Goodman (#2); "I'm Shooting High" by Jan Garber (#3); "I'm Shooting High" by Little Jack Little (#15)

1937

"Indian Love Call" by Jeanette MacDonald and Nelson Eddy (#8); "My Little Buckaroo" by Bing Crosby (#19); "On a Little Dream Ranch" by Dick Robertson (#14); "On a Little Dream Ranch" by Russ Morgan (#13); "There's a Ranch in the Sky" by Jan Garber (#19)

1938

"Colorado Sunset" by Lawrence Welk (#17); "Hi-Yo, Silver" by Jan Savitt (#14); "Hi-Yo, Silver" by Roy Rogers (#13); "Indian Love Call" by Artie Shaw (#6); "It's a Lonely Trail (When You're Travelin' All Alone)" by Guy Lombardo (#7); "Mexicali Rose" by Bing Crosby (#3); "Rancho Grande" by Dick Robertson (#5); "Silver on the Sage" by Will Osborne (#20); "There's a Gold Mine in the Sky" by Bing Crosby (#6); "There's a Gold Mine in the Sky" by Horace Heidt (#5); "There's a Gold Mine in the Sky" by Isham Jones (#13)

1939

"Alla En El Rancho Grande" by Bing Crosby (#6); "Cherokee" by Charlie Barnet (#15); "Dawn on the Desert" by Tommy Dorsey (#13); "It's a Lonely Trail (When You're Travelin' All Alone)" by Bing Crosby (#17); "Ragtime Cowboy Joe" by Pinky Tomlin (#14); "Rainbow Valley" by Dick Jurgens (#17); "San Antonio Rose" by Bob Wills (#15); "South of the Border" by Gene Autry (#12); "South of the Border" by Guy Lombardo (#8); "South of the Border" by Shep Fields (#1); "South of the Border" by Tony Martin (#16); "Tumbling Tumbleweeds" by Glen Gray (#17)

1940

"Adios, Marquita Linda" by Artie Shaw (#18); "Back in the Saddle Again" by Art Kassel (#24); "Call of the Canyon" by Glenn Miller (#10); "Call of the Canyon" by Tommy Dorsey

(#14); "Gaucho Serenade" by Dick Todd (#4); "Gaucho Serenade" by Eddy Duchin (#17); "Gaucho Serenade" by Glenn Miller (#8); "Leanin' on the Ole Top Rail" by Bob Crosby (#7); "Leanin' on the Ole Top Rail" by Ozzie Nelson (#16); "Sierra Sue" by Bing Crosby (#1); "Sierra Sue" by Glenn Miller (#17); "Singing Hills" by Bing Crosby (#3); "Singing Hills" by Dick Todd (#16); "South of the Border" by Ambrose (#8); "Tumbling Tumbleweeds" by Bing Crosby (#12); "Yodelin' Jive" by Bing Crosby and the Andrews Sisters (#4)

1941

"Adios": Glenn Miller (#13); "Along the Santa Fe Trail" by Bing Crosby (#4); "Along the Santa Fe Trail" by Dick Jurgens (#6); "Along the Santa Fe Trail" by Glenn Miller (#7); "Along the Santa Fe Trail" by Sammy Kaye (#9); "Amapola" by Jimmy Dorsey (#1); "Cool Water" by Sons of the Pioneers (#25); "Cowboy Serenade" by Glenn Miller (#15); "Cowboy Serenade" by Kay Kyser (#13); "Lone Star Trail" by Bing Crosby (#23); "My Adobe Hacienda" by Louise Massey (#23); "New San Antonio Rose" by Bing Crosby (#7); "New San Antonio Rose" by Bob Wills (#11)

1942

"Deep in the Heart of Texas" by Alvino Rey (#1); "Deep in the Heart of Texas" by Bing Crosby (#3); "Deep in the Heart of Texas" by Horace Heidt (#7); "Deep in the Heart of Texas" by Ted Weems (#23); "Deep in the Heart of Texas" by The Merry Macs (#11); "Idaho" by Alvino Rey (#3); "Idaho" by Benny Goodman (#4); "Jingle Jangle Jingle" by Freddy Martin (#15); "Jingle Jangle Jingle" by Gene Autry (#14); "Jingle Jangle Jingle" by Kay Kyser (#1)

1943

"Home in San Antone" by Bob Wills (#21); "New San Antonio Rose" by Bob Wills (#19); "Pistol Packin' Mama" by Al Dexter (#1); "Pistol Packin' Mama" by Bing Crosby and the Andrews Sisters (#2); "Touch of Texas" by Freddy Martin (#12)

Country and Pop Charts with Cowboy or Western Themes, 1944–1954

1944

"Don't Fence Me In" by Bing Crosby and the Andrews Sisters (#1 Pop); "Down in the Valley" by the Andrews Sisters (#20 Pop); "Jingle Jangle Jingle" by The Merry Macs (#4 Pop); "Mexico Joe" by Ivie Anderson with Ceele Burke (#16 Pop, #4 Country); "New San Antonio Rose" by Bob Wills (#3 Country); "Pistol Packin' Mama" by Al Dexter (#1 Country); "Pistol Packin' Mama" by Bing Crosby and The Andrews Sisters (#1 Country); "Roly-Poly" by Bob Wills (#3 Country); "Rosalita" by Al Dexter (#1 Country; #29 Pop); "San Fernando Valley" by Bing Crosby (#1 Pop); "San Fernando Valley" by Johnny Mercer (#21 Pop); "Texas Blues" by Foy Willing (#3 Country); "Texas Polka" by Martha Tilton (#30 Pop); "You're from Texas" by Bob Wills (#1 Country; #14 Pop)

1945

"Along the Navajo Trail" by Bing Crosby and the Andrews Sisters (#2 Pop); "Along the Navajo Trail" by Dinah Shore (#7 Pop); "Along the Navajo Trail" by Gene Krupa (#7 Pop); "Don't Fence Me In" by Gene Autry (#4 Country); "Don't Fence Me In" by Hoarce Heidt (#10 Pop); "Don't Fence Me In" by Kate Smith (#8 Pop); "Don't Fence Me In" by Sammy Kaye (#4 Pop); "Gonna Build a Big Fence Around Texas" by Gene Autry (#2 Country); "Northwest Passage" by Woody Herman (#13 Pop); "Oklahoma Hills" by Jack Guthrie (#1 Country); "On the Atchison, Topeka, and the Santa Fe" by Bing Crosby (33 Pop); "On the Atchison, Topeka, and the Santa Fe" by Johnny Mercer (#1 Pop); "On the Atchison, Topeka, and the Santa Fe" by Judy Garland (#10 Pop); "On the Atchison, Topeka, and the Santa Fe" by Tommy Dorsey (#6 Pop); "On the Atchison, Topeka, and the Santa Fe" by Tommy Tucker (#10 Pop); "Sioux City Sue" by Dick Thomas (#1 Country Charts; #16 Pop); "Three Caballeros" by Bing Crosby and the Andrews Sisters (#8 Pop)

1946

"Blue Texas Moonlight" by Elton Britt (#6 Country); "California Polka" by Tex Williams (#4 Country); "I Want to Be a Cowboy's Sweetheart" by Rosalie Allen (#5 Country); "New Spanish Two-Step" by Bob Wills (#20 Pop); "Sioux City Sue" by Bing Crosby (#3 Pop); "Sioux City Sue" by The Hoosier Hot Shots & Two Ton Baker (#2 Country); "Sioux City Sue" by Tiny Hill (#3 Country); "Sioux City Sue" by Tony Pastor (#10 Pop); "Sioux City Sue" by Zeke Manners: (#2 Country); "Texas Playboy Rag" by Bob Wills: (#2 Country)

1947

"(Oh Why, Oh Why, Did I Ever Leave) Wyoming" by Dick Jurgens (#14 Pop; #4 Country); "Across the Alley from the Alamo" by The Mills Brothers (#2 Pop); "Across the Alley from the Alamo by Stan Kenton (#11 Pop); "Across the Alley from the Alamo" by Woody Herman (#12 Pop); "Bob Wills Boogie" by Bob Wills (#4 Country); "Cool Water" by Sons of the Pioneers (#4 Country); "I Tipped My Hat (And Slowly Rode Away)" by Harry James (#21 Pop); "My Adobe Hacienda" by Billy Williams (#13 Pop); "My Adobe Hacienda" by Eddy Howard (#2 Pop); "My Adobe Hacienda" by Kenny Baker (#16 Pop); "My Adobe Hacienda" by Louise Massey (#16 Pop); "My Adobe Hacienda" by The Dinning Sisters (#9 Pop); "On the Old Spanish Trail" by Eddy Howard (#23 Pop); "Ragtime Cowboy Joe" by Eddy Howard (#16 Pop); "Ragtime Cowboy Joe" by Eddy Howard (#5 Country); "Red Wing (An Indian Fable)" by Sam Donohue (#9 Pop); "Teardrops in My Heart" by Sons of the Pioneers (#4 Country); "That's What I Like About the West" by Tex Williams (#4 Country)

1948

"(Treasure of) Sierra Madre" by Buddy Clark (#23 Pop); "(Treasure of) Sierra Madre" by Freddy Martin (#23 Pop); "160 Acres" by Bing Crosby and the Andrews Sisters (#23 Pop); "Adios" by Glenn Miller (#28 Pop); "At the Flying 'W'" by Elliot Lawrence (#21 Pop); "Blue Shadows on the Trail" by Bing Crosby (#48 Pop); "Blue Shadows on the Trail" by Vaughn Monroe (#26 Pop); "Boy from Texas" by Nat "King" Cole (#24 Pop); "Buttons and Bows" by Betty Garrett (#8 Pop); "Buttons and Bows" by Betty Jane Rhodes (#9 Pop); "Buttons and Bows" by Dinah Shore (#1 Pop); "Buttons and Bows" by Evelyn Knight (#14 Pop); "Buttons and Bows" by Gene Autry (#17 Country; #17 Pop); "Buttons and Bows" by the Dinning Sisters (#5 Pop); "Cigarettes, Whusky and Wild, Wild Women" by Red Ingle (#15 Pop); "Cool Water" by Sons of the Pioneers" (#7 Country); "Cool Water" by Vaughn Monroe with Sons of the Pioneers (#9 Pop); "Deck of Cards" by Phil Harris (#20 Pop); "Deck of Cards" by T. Texas Tyler (#20 Pop); "Great Long Pistol" by Jerry Irby: (#10 Country); "Oklahoma Waltz" by Johnny Bond (#9 Country); "Pass That Peace Pipe" by Bing Crosby (#21 Pop); "Pass That Peace Pipe" by Margaret Whiting (#8 Pop); "Pecos Bill" by Roy Rogers (#13 Country); "Pecos Bill" by Tex Ritter: (#15 Country); "Rye Whiskey" by Tex Ritter (#9 Country); "Tacos, Enchiladas, and Beans" By Sam Donohue (#21 Pop); "Texarkana Baby" by Eddy Arnold (#1 Country); "Texarkana Baby" Eddy Arnold (#18 Pop); "Texarkana Baby" by Bob Wills (#15 Country); "Tumbling Tumbleweeds" by Sons of the Pioneers (#11 Country)

1949

"Mule Train" by Bing Crosby (#4 Pop); "Mule Train" by Frankie Laine (#1 Pop); "Mule Train" by Gordon MacRae (#14 Pop); "Mule Train" by Tennessee Ernie Ford (#9 Pop; #1 Country); "Mule Train" by Vaughn Monroe (#10 Pop); "Ragtime Cowboy Joe" by Jo Stafford (#10 Pop); "Riders in the Sky" by Bing Crosby (#14 Pop); "Riders in the Sky" by Burl Ives (#21 Pop; #8 Country); "Riders in the Sky" by Peggy Lee (#2 Pop); "Riders in the Sky" by Vaughn Monroe (#1 Pop; #2 Country); "Sister of Sioux City Sue" by Dick Thomas (#1 Country)

1950

"Buffalo Billy" by Roberta Quinlan (#22 Pop); "Our Little Ranch House" by Guy Lombardo (#19 Pop); "Place Where I Worship (Is the Wide Open Spaces)" by Al Morgan (#29 Pop); "Stampede" by Roy Rogers (#8 Country)

1951

"Across the Wide Missouri" by Hugo Winterhalter (#21) (Pop Charts); "Across the Wide Missouri" by Paul Weston (#19) (Pop Charts); "Cherokee Boogie" by Moon Mullican (#7) (Country Charts); "Down the Trail of Achin' Hearts" by Patti Page (#17) (Pop Charts); "On Top of Old Smoky" by Percy Faith with Burl Ives (#10) (Pop Charts); "On Top of Old Smoky" by the Weavers (#2 Pop); "On Top of Old Smoky" by Vaughn Monroe (#8 Pop; #8 Country); "Slow Poke" by Roberta Lee (#13 Pop); "The Roving Kind" by Rex Allen (#20 Country)

1952

"Adios" by Gisele MacKenzie (#14 Pop); "Fandango" by Hugo Winterhalter (#30 Pop); "Gold Rush Is Over" by Hank Snow (#2 Country); "High Noon (Do Not Forsake Me)" by Frankie Lane (#5 Pop); "High Noon (Do Not Forsake Me)" by Tex Ritter (#12 Country: #12 Pop); "Idaho State Fair" by Vaughn Monroe (#20 Pop); "Indian Love Call" by Slim Whitman (#9 Pop; #2 Country); "Slow Poke" by Arthur Godfrey (#12 Pop); "Slow Poke" by Hawkshaw Hawkins (#26 Pop); "Slow Poke" by Helen O'Connell (#8 Pop); "Slow Poke" by Pee Wee King (#1 Pop); "Slow Poke" by Ralph Flanagan (#6 Pop); "Slow Poke" by Tiny Hill (#28 Pop)

1953

"A-L-B-U-Q-U-E-R-Q-U-E" by Ralph Flanagan (#18 Pop); "Gambler's Guitar" by Jim Lowe (#26 Pop); "Gambler's Guitar" by Rusty Draper (#6 Pop); "Kaw-Liga" by Dolores Gray (#23 Pop); "Kaw-Liga" by Hank Williams (#1 Country; #23 Pop); "Mexican Joe" by Jim Reeves (#1 Country); "On The Trail (Grand Canyon Suite)" Ray Anthony (#26 Pop); "Shane (The Call of the Far Away Hills)" by Paul Weston (#29 Pop); "South of the Border" by Frank Sinatra (#18 Pop); "Vaya Con Dios (May God Be with You)" by Les Paul and Mary Ford (#1 Pop); "Wild Horses" by Perry Como (#6 Pop); "Wild Horses" by Ray Anthony (#28 Pop)

1954

"In a Little Spanish Town" by David Carroll (#29 Pop); "On the Alamo" by Norman Petty Trio (#29 Pop); "Padre" by Lola Dee with Stubby and The Buccaneers (#25 Pop); "Singing Hills" by Slim Whitman (#4 Country); "The Bandit" by Percy Faith (#25 Pop); "The Bandit" by Tex Ritter (#30 Country; #30 Pop); "The Bandit" by The Johnston Brothers (#26) (Pop Charts)

Country Charts 1955–2005

1955

"Ballad of Davy Crockett" by Mac Wiseman (#10); "Ballad of Davy Crockett" by Tennessee Ernie Ford (#4); "Cattle Call" by Eddy Arnold (#1); "Cattle Call" by Slim Whitman (#11); "Yellow Rose of Texas" by Ernest Tubb (#7)

1956

None

1957

None

1958

"Squaws Along the Yukon" by Hank Thompson (#2)

1959

"Don't Take Your Guns to Town" by Johnny Cash (#1); "El Paso" by Marty Robbins" (#1); "Half-Breed" by Marvin Rainwater: (#16); "Hanging Tree" by Marty Robbins (#15); "John Wesley Hardin" by Jimmie Skinner (#17)

1960

"Amigo's Guitar" by Kitty Wells (#5); "Big Iron" by Marty Robbins (#5); "Riverboat Gambler" by Jimmie Skinner (#14)

1961

"Oklahoma Hills" by Hank Thompson (#7); "The Rebel: Johnny Yuma" by Johnny Cash (#24); "San Antonio Rose" by Floyd Cramer (#8)

1962

"Adios Amigo" by Jim Reeves (#2); "Cow Town" by Webb Pierce (#5); "Don't Go Near the Indians" by Rex Allen (#4); "The Comancheros" by Claude King (#7); "Where the Old Red River Flows" by Jimmie Davis (#15)

1963

"Abilene" by George Hamilton IV (#1); "The Man Who Robbed the Bank at Santa Fe" by Hank Snow (#9); "Cowboy Boots" by Dave Dudley (#3); "Old Showboat" by Stonewall Jackson (#8); "T for Texas" by Grandpa Jones (#5); "The Matador" by Johnny Cash (#2)

1964

"Cowboy in the Continental Suit" by Marty Robbins (#3); "Cross the Brazos at Waco" by Billy Walker (#2); "Fort Worth, Dallas or Houston" by George Hamilton IV (#9); "Girl from Spanish Town" by Marty Robbins (#15); "Ringo" by Lorne Green (#21)

1965

"Buckaroo" by Buck Owens and the Buckaroos (#1); "Kansas City Star" by Roger Miller (#7); "Matamoros" by Billy Walker (#8); "Sons of Katie Elder" by Johnny Cash (#10); "Waltz Across Texas" by Ernest Tubb (#34)

1966

"This Gun Don't Care" by Wanda Jackson (#46); "Waco" by Lorne Green (#50)

1967

"Ballad of Waterhole #3 (Code of the West)" by Roger Miller (#27); "California Up Tight Band" by Flatt & Scruggs (#20); "Dallas" by Vern Stovall (#58); "In Del Rio" by Billy Walker (#18); "Ramblin' Man" by Ray Pennington (#29); "Ride, Ride, Ride" by Lynn Anderson (#36); "San Antonio" by Willie Nelson (#50); "The Storm" by Jim Reeves (#16); "Wheels Fell Off the Wagon Again" by Johnny Dollar (#47); "Cherokee Strip" by Bob Beckham (#73)

1968

"By the Time I Get to Phoenix" by Glen Campbell (#2); "By the Time You Get to Phoenix" by Wanda Jackson (#46); "California Sunshine" by Rusty Draper (#70); "Going Out to Tulsa" by Johnny Seay (#68); "I Hope I Like Mexico Blues" by Dallas Frazier (#59); "Phoenix Flash" by Stan Hitchcock (#60); "Plastic Saddle" by Nat Stuckey (#9); "Reno" by Dottie West (#19); "Roses to Reno" by Bob Bishop (#42); "Texas Tea" by Dee Mullins (#51); "Texas" by Tex Ritter (#69); "Wichita Lineman" by Glen Campbell (#1); "Your Squaw Is on the Warpath" by Loretta Lynn (#3)

1969

"Back Side of Dallas" by Jeannie C. Riley (#33); "Back to Denver" by George Hamilton IV (#26); "California Cotton Fields" by Dallas Frazier (#45); "California Girl (And the Tennessee Square)" by Tompall & the Glaser Brothers (#11); "Canadian Pacific" by George Hamilton IV (#25); "Gotta Get to Oklahoma (Cause California's Gettin' to Me)" by The Hagers (#41); "Kaw-Liga" by Charley Pride (#3); "Moffett, Oklahoma" by Charlie Walker (#44); "Okie from Muskogee" by Merle Haggard (#1); "Oklahoma Home Brew" by Hank Thompson (#60); "Running Bear" by Sonny James (#1); "Something's Wrong in California" by Waylon Jennings (#19); "True Grit" by Glen Campbell (#9); "Who Do I Know in Dallas" by Kenny Price (#64); "Wicked California" by Tompall and the Glaser Brothers (#24)

1970

"California Grapevine" by Freddie Hart (#68); "Cowboy Convention" by Buddy Alan and Don Rich (#19); "Great White Horse" by Buck Owens and Susan Raye (#8); "Is Anybody Goin' to San Antone" by Charley Pride (#1); "Kansas City Song" by Buck Owens (#2); "Long Long Texas Road" by Roy Drusky (#5)

1971

"By the Time I Get to Phoenix" by Glen Campbell and Anne Murray (#40); "(Don't Let the Sun Set On You) Tulsa" by Waylon Jennings (#16); "Dozen Pairs of Boots" by Del Reeves (#31); "Honky-Tonk Stardust Cowboy" by Bill Rice (#51); "Houston Blues" by Jeannie C. Riley (#47); "Indian Lake" by Freddy Weller (#3); "Padre" by Marty Robbins (#5); "Tulsa County" by Anita Carter (#41); "West Texas Highway" by George Hamilton IV (#23)

1972

"Throw a Rope Around the Wind" by Red Lane (#66); "Country Western Truck Drivin' Singer" by Red Simpson (#62); "Do You Remember These" by Statler Brothers (#2); "Oklahoma Sunday Morning" by Glen Campbell (#15)

1973

"Bad, Bad, Bad Cowboy" by Tompall Glaser (#77); "California Is Just Mississippi" by Billy Mize (#99); "Colorado Country Morning" by Tennessee Ernie Ford (#70); "Hoppy's Gone" by Roger Miller (#42); "Riders in the Sky" by Roy Clark (#27); "Ridin' My Thumb to Mexico" by Johnny Rodriguez (#1); "Some Old California Memory" by Henson Cargill (#28); "Uneasy Rider" by Charlie Daniels (#67)

1974

"All Around Cowboy of 1964" by Buddy Alan (#67); "Amarillo by Morning" by Terry Stafford (#31); "Bob, All the Playboys and Me" by Dorsey Burnette (#69); "Counterfeit Cowboy" by

Dave Dudley (#61); "Dallas" by Connie Smith (#35); "From Tennessee to Texas" by Johnny Bush (#48); "Great Mail Robbery" by Rex Allen Jr. (#63); "Houston (I'm Comin' to See You)" by Glen Campbell (#20); "Just Another Cowboy Song" by Doyle Holly (#69); "Last of the Sunshine Cowboys" by Eddy Raven (#63); "She's in Love with a Rodeo Man" by Johnny Russell (#39); "Texas Law Sez" by Tompall Glaser (#74); "There's Still a Lot of Love in San Antone" by Darrel McCall (#48); "Two Gun Daddy" by Marty Robbins (#39) "Whatever Happened to Randolph Scott" by the Statler Brothers (#22)

1975

"Bandy the Rodeo Clown" by Moe Bandy (#7); "Bob Wills Is Still the King" by Waylon Jennings ((#1); "Colorado Country Morning" by Hank Snow (#95); "Cowboy and the Lady" by Patsy Sledd (#90); "Cowboy Like You" by Hecklels (#91); "Cowboy" by Eddy Arnold (#13); "Cowboys and Daddys" by Bobby Bare (#29); "Here I Am in Dallas" by Faron Young (#16); "Hoppy, Gene and Me" by Roy Rogers (#15); "I Love a Rodeo" by Roger Miller (#57); "Indian Creek" by Porter Wagoner: (#96); "Indian Giver" by Billy Larkin (#34); "Indian Love Call" by Ray Stevens (#38); "Jo and the Cowboy" by Johnny Duncan (#26); "Last of the Outlaws" by Chuck Price (#54); "Let's All Help the Cowboy (Sing the Blues)" by Waylon Jennings (#2); "Padre" by Judy Lynn (#92); "Rhinestone Cowboy" by Glen Campbell (#1); "Ride 'Em Cowboy" by Paul Davis (#47); "Roly-Poly" by Carl Smith (#97); "San Antonio Stroll" by Tanya Tucker; "She Talked a Lot About Texas" by Cal Smith (#13); "Shotgun Rider" by Marty Robbins (#55); "Someday Soon" by Kathy Barnes (#39); "This Is My Year for Mexico" by Crystal Gayle (#21); "Western Man" by La Costa (#11)

1976

"(Great American) Classic Cowboy" by Penny DeHaven (#83); "All the King's Horses" by Lynn Anderson (#20); "Are They Gonna Make Us Outlaws Again" by James Talley (#61); "Asphalt Cowboy" by Hank Thompson (#72); "Back in the Saddle Again" by Sonny James (#14); "California Okie" by Buck Owens (#43); "Can You Hear Those Pioneers" by Rex Allen Jr. (#17); "Cherokee Maiden" by Merle Haggard (#1); "Colorado Call" by Shad O'Hea (#85); "Cowboy Peyton Place" by Doug Sahm (#100); "Disco Tex" by Little David Wilkins (#75); "El Paso City" by Marty Robbins (#1); "The End Is Not in Sight (The Cowboy Tune)" by the Amazing Rhythm Aces (#12); "Faster Horses (The Cowboy and the Poet)" by Tom T. Hall (#1); "Four Wheel Cowboy" by C.W. McCall (#88); "I Can Almost See Houston from Here" by Katy Moffatt (#83); "I'll Be Your San Antone Rose" by Dottsy (#12); "I've Rode with the Best" by Jim Ed Brown (#65); "Indian Nation" by Billy Thunderkloud (#74); "Jesus Is the Same in California" by Lloyd Goodson (#80); "Ladies Love Outlaws" by Jimmy Rabbitt and Renegade (#80); "Littlest Cowboy Rides Again" by Ed Bruce (#32); "Lone Star Beer and Bob Wills Music" by Red Steagall (#11); "Lonesome Is a Cowboy" by Mundo Earwood (#70); "Mamas Don't Let Your Babies Grow Up to Be Cowboys" by Ed Bruce (#15); "Oh Those Texas Women" by Gene Davis (#97); "Oklahoma Sunshine" by Pat Boone (#86); "Rodeo Cowboy" by Lynn Anderson (#44); "Rye Whiskey" by Chuck Price (#81); "San Antonio Stroll" by Maury Finnery (#F?); "T for Texas" by Tompall and His Outlaw Band (#36); "Teardrops in My Heart" by Rex Allen Jr. (#18); "Texas on a Saturday Night" by Bill Green (#94); "Texas Woman" by Pat Boone (#34); "Texas-1947" by Johnny Cash (#35); "Texas" by the Charlie Daniels Band (#36); "Vaya Con Dios" by Freddy Fender (#7); "Waltz Across Texas" by Maury Finney (#81); "Wichita Jail" by the Charlie Daniels Band: (#22)

1977

"Abilene" by Sonny James (#24); "Adios Amigo" by Marty Robbins (#4); "Billy the Kid" by the Charlie Daniels Band (#75); "California Lady" by Randy Barlow (#31); "Cherokee Fiddle" by Michael Murphey (#58); "Cowboy and the Lady" by Bobby Goldsboro (#85); "Cowboy and the Lady" by Tommy Cash (#63); "Cowboys Ain't Supposed to Cry" by Moe Bandy (#13); "Desperado" by Johnny Rodriguez (#5); "Genuine Texas Good Guy" by Jerry Green (#96); "Here's to the Horses" by Mack Vickery (#94); "I Got the Hoss" by Mel Tillis (#3); "I'm Giving You Denver" by Jean Shepard (#74); "If You Ever Get to Houston (Look Me Down)" by Don Gibson (#16); "It's a Cowboy Lovin' Night" by Tanya Tucker (#7); "Last Gunfighter Ballad" by Johnny Cash (#38); "Luckenback, Texas (Back to the Basics of Love)" by Waylon Jennings (#1); "Mexican Love Songs" by Linda Hargrove (#61); "Miles and Miles of Texas" by Asleep at the Wheel (#38); "Ridin' Rainbows" by Tanya Tucker (#12); "Rodeo Bum" by Mel Street (#56); "Texas Angel" by Jacky Ward (#31); "Texas Tea" by Leroy Van Dyke (#77); "Twenty-Four Hours from Tulsa" by Randy Barlow (#18); "When I Die, Just Let Me Go to Texas" by Ed Bruce (#52); "Y'All Come Back Saloon" by the Oak Ridge Boys

1978

"Ain't No California" by Mel Tillis (#4); "Bob's Got a Swing Band in Heaven" by Red Steagall (#63); "Carlena and Jose Gomez" by Billy Walker (#57); "Colorado Kool-Aid" by Johnny Paycheck (#50); "Cowboys Don't Get Lucky All the Time" by Gene Watson (#11); "Don't You Think This Outlaw Bit's Done Got Out of Hand" by Waylon Jennings (#5); "Even Cowgirls Get the Blues" by La Costa (#79); "Half My Heart's in Texas" by Ernest Tubb (#79); "Hello Mexico (And Adios Baby to You)" by Johnny Duncan (#4); "Hurt as Big as Texas" by Randy Cornor (#100); "I Want a Little Cowboy" by Jerry Abbott (#63); "Mamas Don't Let your Babies Grow Up to Be Cowboys" by Waylon Jennings and Willie Nelson (#1); "Rider in the Rain" by Randy Newman (#78); "Texas Me and You" by Asleep At the Wheel (#75); "This Is a Holdup" by Ronnie McDowell (#39)

1979

"All Around Cowboy" by Marty Robbins (#16); "All the Gold in California" by Larry Gatlin & the Gatlin Brothers (#1); "Buenas Dias Argentina" by Marty Robbins (#25); "Cabello Diablo (Devil Horse)" by Chris LeDoux (#98); "California" by Glen Campbell (#45); "Coca Cola Cowboy" by Mel Tillis (#1); "Cowboy Singer" by Sonny Curtis (#77); "Dallas Cowboys" by Charley Pride (#89); "Don't Feel Like the Lone Ranger" by Leon Everette (#33); "Down on the Rio Grande" by Johnny Rodriguez (#6); "Eyes as Big as Dallas" by Wynn Stewart (#37); "He's a Cowboy from Texas" by Ronnie McDowell (#68); "Hello Texas" by Brian Collins (#94); "I Got Western Pride" by Ray Frushay (#93); "Medicine Woman" by Kenny O'Dell (#32); "My Guns Are Loaded" by Bonnie Tyler (#86); "My Own Kind of Hat" by Merle Haggard (#4); "Outlaws and Lone Star Beer" by C.W. McCall (#81); "Outlaw's Prayer" by Johnny Paycheck (#27); "Riders in the Sky" by Johnny Cash (#2); "Rodle-Odeo-Home" by Arnie Rue (#74); "Salute to the Duke" by Paul Ott (#87); "Send Me Down to Tucson" by Mel Tillis (#2); "Texas (When I Die)" by Tanya Tucker (#5); "Tulsa Time" by Don Williams (#1); "Waltz Across Texas" by Ernest Tubb (#56); "When Our Love Began (Cowboys and Indians)" by George James (#95)

1980

"Another Texas Song" by Eddy Raven (#34); "Arizona Highway" by Tim Rex and Oklahoma (#87); "Arizona Whiz" by George Burns (#80); "Bourbon Cowboy" by Jim Seal (#79); "Bull Rider" by Johnny Cash (#66); "Cactus and a Rose" by Gary Stewart (#48); "California Calling" by Dennis Smith (#94); "Colorado Country Morning" by Pat Boone (#60); "Cowboy Stomp!" by Spurzz (#76); "Cowboys and Clowns" by Ronnie Milsap: (#1); "Cowboys Are Common as Sin" by Max D. Barnes (#68); "Cowgirl and the Dandy" by Brenda Lee (#10); "Dallas" by Floyd Cramer (#32); "Dancin' Cowboys" by the Bellamy Brothers (#1); "Even Cowgirls Get the Blues" by Lynn Anderson 26); "I Musta Died and Gone to Texas" by the Amazing Rhythm Aces (#77); "Kaw-Liga" by Hank Williams, Jr. (#12); "Last Cowboy Song" by Ed Bruce (#12); "Let Jesse Rob the Train" by Buck Owens (#22); "Little Ground in Texas" by the Capitals (#29); "Lost in Austin" by Freddy Weller (#45); "Love Is a Warm Cowboy" by Buck Owens (#42); "Mamas Don't Let Your Cowboys Grow Up to Be Babies" by Tony Joe White (#91); "Mexico Winter" by Bobby Hood (#85); "Molly (And the Texas Rain)" by Sonny Wright (#91); "My Heroes Have Always Been Cowboys" by Willie Nelson (#1); "Pecos Promenade" by Tanya Tucker (#10); "Real Cowboy (You Say You're)" by Billy "Crash Craddock (#20); "Ride That Bull (Big Bertha)" by Marlow Tackett (#92); "Ride, Concrete Cowboy, Ride" by Roy Rogers (#80); "Rodeo Eyes" by Zella Lehr (#25); "San Antonio Medley" by Curtis Potter and Darrell McCall (#89); "Saturday Night in Dallas" by Kenny Seratt (#54); "Shotgun Rider" by Joe Sun (#23); "Sweet Mother Texas" by Eddy Raven (#44); "Ten Seconds in the Saddle" by Chris LeDoux (#96); "Texas Bound and Flyin'" by Jerry Reed (#26); "Texas in My Rear View Mirror" by Mac Davis (#9); "Texas Tea" by Orion (#68); "That's the Way a Cowboy Rocks and Rolls" by Jacky Ward (#7); "Too Old To Play Cowboy" by Razzy Bailey (#13); "Tumbleweed" by Sylvia (#10); "Yippy Cry Yi" by Rex Allen Jr. (#25); "Why Don't You Go to Dallas" by Peggy Sue (#93); "Wild Bull Rider" by Hoyt Axton (#21); "Your Body Is an Outlaw" by Mel Tillis (#3)

1981

"After Texas" by Roy Head (#75); "Cherokee Country" by Solid Gold Band (#47); "Cow Patti" by Jim Stafford (#65); "Cowboy and the Lady" by John Denver (#50); "Cowboy" by Larry Dalton (#82); "Cowboys Don't Shoot Straight (Like They Used To)" by Tammy Wynette (#21); "Here's to the Horses" by Johnny Russell (#49); "Houston Blue" by David Rogers (#88); "Lonestar Cowboy" by Donna Fargo (#73); "Matador" by Sylvia (#7); "Mexican Girl" by Michael Tate (#93); "New York Cowboy" by the Nashville Superpickers (#83); "Rode Hard and Put Up Wet" by Johnny Lee (#52); "Rodeo Girls" by Tanya Tucker (#83); "Round-Up Saloon" by Bobby Goldsboro (#31); "Teardrops in My Heart" by Marty Robins (#45); "Texas Cowboy Night" by Mel Tillis and Nancy Sinatra (#23); "Texas Ida Red" by David Houston (#69); "Texas State Of Mind" by David Frizzell and Shelly West (#9); "Texas Women" by Hank Williams Jr. (#1); "Urban Cowboys, Outlaws, Cavaleers" by James Marvell (#94); "Waltzes and Western Swing" by Donnie Rohrs (#85); "You're the Reason God Made Oklahoma" by David Frizzell and Shelly West (#1); "Your Daddy Don't Live in Heaven (He's in Houston)" by Michael Ballew (#67)

1982

"Alice in Dallas (Sweet Texas)" by Wyvon Alexander (#82); "Bandera, Texas" by Solid Gold Band (65); "Bull Smith Can't Dance the Cotton-Eyed Joe" by Wolfpack (#88); "Cherokee

Boogie" by BR5-49 (#44); "Cherokee Fiddle" by Johnny Lee (#10); "Cowboy in a Three Piece Business Suit" by Rex Allen Jr. (#44); "Get in Line Reggae Cowboy" by the Bellamy Brothers (#21); "Kansas City Lights" by Steve Wariner (#15); "Last of the Silver Screen Cowboys" by Rex Allen Jr. (#43); "Midnight Rodeo" by Leon Everette (#9); "Oklahoma Crude" by the Corbin/Hanner Band (#49); "Ride, Cowboy Ride" by Rex Allen Jr. (#85); "Rodeo Clown" by Mac Davis (#37); "Rodeo Romeo" by Moe Bandy (#10); "Slow Texas Dancing" by Donna Hazard (#76); "Someday Soon" by Moe Bandy (#21); "Who Do You Know in California" by Eddy Raven (#11)

1983

"Amarillo by Morning" by George Strait (#4); "Cowboy's Dream" by Mel Tillis (#49); "Dallas" by the Bama Band (#54); "Houston (Means I'm One Day Closer to You)" by Larry Gatlin and The Gatlin Brothers (#1); "I Spent the Night in the Heart of Texas" by Marlow Tackett (#56); "My First Taste of Texas" by Ed Bruce (#6); "Pancho and Lefty" by Willie Nelson and Merle Haggard (#1); "San Antonio Rose" by Ray Price (#70); "Smokin' in the Rockies" by Gary Stewart and Dean Dillon; "Somewhere in Texas" by Ray Price (#55); "There's Still a Lot of Love in San Antone" by Connie Hanson with Darrell McCall (#83); "This Cowboy's Hat" by Porter Wagoner (#35); "Tulsa Ballroom" by Dottie West (#40); "Wayward Wind" by James Galway with Sylvia (#57); "Wild Montana Skies" by John Denver and Emmylou Harris (#14); "Child of the Fifties" by the Statler Brothers (#17)

1984

"Colorado Christmas" by the Nitty Gritty Dirt Band (#93); "Cowgirl in a Coupe DeVille" by Terry Gregory (#75); "Deep in the Arms of Texas" by Con Hunley (#75); "Denver" by the Gatlin Brothers (#7); "Dream on Texas Ladie" by Rex Allen Jr. (#18); "Ride 'Em Cowboy" by David Allan Coe (#48); "God Must Be a Cowboy" by Dan Seals (#10); "I Got Mexico" by Eddy Raven (#1); "If You're Gonna Play in Texas" by Alabama (#1); "Lady Takes the Cowboy Everytime" by the Gatlin Brothers (#3); "Oklahoma Heart" by Becky Hobbs (#46); "Renosa" by Katy Moffatt (#82); "Ride 'Em Cowboy" by Juice Newton (#32); "Shoot First, Ask Questions Later" by James & Michael Younger (#65); "Somebody Buy This Cowgirl a Beer" by Shelly West (#34); "Yellow Rose" by Johnny Lee and Lane Brody (#1)

1985

"California Sleeping" by Loy Blanton (#77); "California Road" by Mel Tillis (#61); "California" by Keith Stegall (#13); "Cowboy Rides Away" by George Strait (#5); "Desperados Waiting for a Train" by The Highwaymen (#15); "Does Fort Worth Ever Cross Your Mind" by George Strait (#1); "Don't Call Him a Cowboy" by Conway Twitty (#1); "Hottest 'Ex' In Texas" by Becky Hobbs (#37); "Houston Heartache" by Mason Dixon (#76); "I Wanna Be a Cowboy 'Til I Die" by Jim Collins (#59); "Mexico" by Backtrack/John Hunt (#94); "Reno and Me" by Bobby Bare (#76); "This Ain't Dallas" by Hank Williams Jr. (#4); "Tokyo, Oklahoma" by John Anderson (#30)

1986

"Cowpoke" by Glen Campbell (#38); "Desperado Love" by Conway Twitty (#1); "Even Cowgirls Get the Blues" by Johnny Cash and Waylon Jennings (#35); "Everything That Glitters

(Is Not Gold)" by Dan Seals (#1); "Farther Down the Line" by Lyle Lovett (#21); "Friend in California" by Merle Haggard (#9); "Heartache the Size of Texas" by the Vega Brothers (#54); "Lights of Albuquerque" by Jim Glaser (#40); "Makin' Up for Lost Time (The Dallas Lovers' Song)" by Crystal Gayle and Gary Morris (#1); "Modern Day Cowboy" by Jay Clark (#75); "Oklahoma Borderline" by Vince Gill (#9); "Reno Bound" by Southern Pacific (#86); "She Wants to Marry a Cowboy" by James Younger and Michael Younger (#65); "Texas Moon" by Johnny Duncan (#81); "Tonight We Ride" by Michael Martin Murphey (#26)

1987

"67 Miles to Cow Town" by Hollie Hughes (#75); "All My Ex's Live in Texas" by George Strait (#1); "Boogie Back to Texas" by Asleep at the Wheel (#53); "Colorado Moon" by Tim Malchak (#37); "Cowboy Man" by Lyle Lovett (#10); "Geronimo's Cadillac" by Jeff Stevens and The Bullets (#53); "Girls Ride Horses Too" by Judy Rodman (#7); "Going to California" by Danny Shirley (#81); "I Don't Feel Much Like a Cowboy Tonight" by Gene Stroman (#74); "Just a Kid from Texas" by Dann Rogers (#78); "Just Try Texas" by Mike Lord (#94); "Like an Oklahoma Morning" by Tony McGill (#76); "Lone Star State of Mind" by Nanci Griffith (#36); "No Easy Horses" by Schuyler, Knobloch and Bickhardt (#19); "Ponies" by Michael Johnson (#26); "Senorita" by Don Williams (#9); "South of the Border" by Clay Blaker (#91); "Tanya Montana" by David Allan Coe (#62); "W. Lee O'Daniel (And the Light Crust Dough Boys)" by Johnny Cash (#72); "Way Down Texas Way" by Asleep at the Wheel (#39); "Weekend Cowboys" by Marty Haggard (#75)

1988

"Boots (These Boots Are Made for Walking)" by Brenda Cole (#84); "Dallas Darlin'" by Norm Schaffer (#77); "High Ridin' Heroes" by David Lynn Jones with Waylon Jennings (#14); "Hollywood Heroes" by Hunter Cain (#82); "I Want to Be a Cowboy's Sweetheart" by Suzy Bogguss (#77); "Lost in Austin" by Kenny Blair (#84); "Missin' Texas" by Kim Grayson (#65); "Santa Fe" by the Bellamy Brothers (#5); "Texas in 1880" by Foster and Lloyd (#18); "Where the Rocky Mountains Touch the Morning Sun" by Randy Vanwarmer (#72); "Wild Texas Rose" by Billy Walker (#79)

1989

"You and the Horse (That You Rode In On)" by Patsy Cole (#91); "Beneath the Texas Moon" by J.C. Crowley (#55); "California Blue" by Roy Orbison (#51); "California Wine" by Mark Murphey (#96); "Coast of Colorado" by Skip Ewing (#15); "Cowboy Hat in Dallas" by the Charlie Daniels Band (#36); "Frontier Justice" by Cee Cee Chapman and Santa Fe (#51); "Houston Solution" by Ronnie Milsap (#4); "I'm in Love and He's in Dallas" by Marie Osmond (#59); "Lonestar Lonesome" by Terry Stafford (#89); "Longneck Lone Star (And Two Step Dancin')" by Diana Sicily Currey (#91); "Modern Day Cowboy" by John Marriott (#92); "Much Too Young to Feel This Damn Old" by Garth Brooks (#8); "Old Coyote Town" by Don Williams (#5); "Planet Texas" by Kenny Rogers (#30); "Thank the Cowboy for the Ride" by Tammy Wynette (#66); "To a San Antone Rose" by Steve Douglas (#91)

1990

"Cowboy Logic" by Michael Martin Murphey (#52); "Oklahoma Swing" by Vince Gill (#13); "She Came from Fort Worth" by Kathy Mattea (#2); "This Ain't My First Rodeo" by Vern Gosdin (#14); "Under the Gun" by Suzy Bogguss (#72); "Western Girls" by Marty Stuart (#20)

1991

"Ballad of Davy Crockett" by the Kentucky Headhunters (#49); "Blame It on Texas" by Mark Chesnutt (#5); "Concrete Cowboy" by the Corbin/Hanner Band (#59); "Cowboys Don't Cry" by Dude Mowrey (#65); "Hold On Partner" by Roy Rogers and Clint Black (#42); "Let the Cowboy Dance" by Michael Martin Murphey; "One Less Pony" by Sawyer Brown (#70); "Rodeo" by Garth Brooks (#3); "Someday Soon" by Suzy Bogguss (#12); "This Cowboy's Hat" by Chris LeDoux (#63)

1992

"Boot Scootin' Boogie" by Brooks & Dunn (#1); "Cowboy Beat" by Bellamy Brothers (#23); "Dallas" by Alan Jackson (#1); "Faster Gun" by Great Plains (#41); "Ridin' for a Fall" by Chris LeDoux (#72); "Whatcha Gonna Do with a Cowboy" by Chris LeDoux (with Garth Brooks) (#7); "Workin' Man's Dollar" by Chris LeDoux (#69)

1993

"Under This Old Hat" by Chris LeDoux (#54); "Cadillac Ranch" by Chris LeDoux (#18); "Cowboy Boogie" by Randy Travis (#46); "Cowboy's Born with a Broken Heart" by Boy Howdy (#12); "Desperado" by Clint Black (#54); "God Blessed Texas" by Little Texas (#4); "Heartland" by George Strait (#1); "Let That Pony Run" by Pam Tillis (#4); "Reno" by Doug Supernaw (#4); "Should've Been a Cowboy" by Toby Keith (#1); "Texas Tattoo" by The Gibson/Miller Band (#22)

1994

"Cowboy Band" by Billy Dean (#24); "Cowboys Don't Cry" by Daron Norwood (#24); "Indian Outlaw" by Tim McGraw (#8); "Mamas Don't Let Your Babies Grow Up to Be Cowboys" by the Gibson/Miller Band (#49); "Red and Rio Grande" by Doug Supernaw (#23); "Ride 'em High, Ride 'em Low" by Brooks and Dunn (#73); "Rope The Moon" by John Michael Montgomery (#4); "Western Flyer" by Western Flyer (#61); "What The Cowgirls Do" by Vince Gill (#2)

1995

"Amy's Back in Austin" by Little Texas (#4); "Clown In Your Rodeo" by Kathy Mattea (#20); "Dallas Days and Fort Worth Nights" by Chris LeDoux (#68); "Fastest Horse in a One Horse Town" by Billy Ray Cyrus (#75); "Sea of Cowboy Hats" by Chely Wright (#56); "Texas Tornado" by Tracy Lawrence (#1); "Whose Bed Have Your Boots Been Under?" by Shania Twain (#11)

1996

"Beaches of Cheyenne" by Garth Brooks (#1); "Cowboy Love" by John Michael Montgomery (#4); "Don't Touch My Hat" by Lyle Lovett 68); "I Can Still Make Cheyenne" by George Strait (#4); "Long Tall Texan" by the Beach Boys and Doug Supernaw (#69); "Santa Got Lost in Texas" by Jeff Carson (#70); "Stars Over Texas" by Tracy Lawrence (#2); "Tangled Up in Texas" by Frazier River (#67); "There's a Girl in Texas" by Trace Adkins (#20); "Trail of Tears" by Billy Ray Cyrus (#69); "When Cowboys Didn't Dance" by Lonestar (#45)

1997

"Cowboy Cadillac" by Garth Brooks (#52); "Every Cowboy's Dream" by Rhett Akins (#51); "How a Cowgirl Says Goodbye" by Tracy Lawrence (#4); "Long Trail of Tears" by George Ducas (#55); "Tell Me Something Bad About Tulsa" by Noel Haggard (#75); "Texas Diary" by James T. Horn (#72); "Wichita Lineman" by Wade Hayes (#55)

1998

"Back in the Saddle" by Matraca Berg (#51); "Bang a Drum" by Chris LeDoux with Jon Bon Jovi (#68); "Buckaroo" by Lee Ann Womack (#27); "Day That She Left Tulsa (In a Chevy)" by Wade Hayes (#5); "I'm a Cowboy" by Bill Engvall (#60); "Little Red Rodeo" by Collin Raye (#3); "Texas Size Heartache" by Joe Diffie (#4); "Yippy Ky Yay" by Lila McCann (#63)

1999

"Albuquerque" by Sons of the Desert (#58); "Cattle Call" by Eddy Arnold with LeAnn Rimes (#18); "Cowboy Cadillac" by Confederate Railroad (#70); "Horse to Mexico" by Trini Triggs (#53); "John Wayne Walking Away" by Lari White (#64); "My Own Kind of Hat" by Alan Jackson (#71); "On Earth as It Is in Texas" by Deryl Dodd (#71); "Senorita Margarita" by Tim McGraw (#74); "South of Santa Fe" by Brooks & Dunn (#41); "Stampede" by Chris LeDoux (#66)

2000

"Cactus in a Coffee Can" by Jerry Kilgore (#73); "Cowboy Take Me Away" by the Dixie Chicks (#1); "It Never Rains in Southern California" by Trent Summar (#74); "Meanwhile Back at the Ranch" by the Clark Family Experience (#18); "Merry Christmas from Texas Y'all" by Tracy Byrd (#55); "Roly-Poly" by Asleep at the Wheel with the Dixie Chicks (#65); "Up North (Down South, Back East, Out West)" by Wade Hayes (#48); "You Can Leave Your Hat On" by Ty Herndon (#72)

2001

"Arizona Rain" by 3 of Hearts (#59); "Austin" by Blake Shelton (#1); "Cowboy Christmas" by Clay Walker (#70); "Cowboys Don't Cry" by Eddy Raven (#60); "I Drove Her to Dallas" by Tyler England (#53); "Laredo" by Chris Cagle (#8); "Oklahoma" by Billy Gilman (#33); "Telluride" by Tim McGraw (#52); "Texas in 1880" by Radney Foster with Pat Green (#54); "Texas on My Mind" by Pat Green and Cory Morrow (#60); "Wild Horses" by Garth Brooks (#7)

2002

"Cowboy in Me" by Tim McGraw (#1)

2003

"Beer for My Horses" by Toby Keith with Willie Nelson (#1); "Cowboys Like Us" by George Strait (#2); "Playboys of the Southwestern World" by Blake Shelton (#24); "Tell Me Something Bad About Tulsa" by George Strait (#11)

2004

"Cowgirls" by Kerry Harvick (#45); "Good Year for the Outlaw" by Jeffrey Steele (#54); "Save a Horse (Ride a Cowboy)" by Big & Rich (#11); "Texas Plates" by Kellie Coffey (#24); "Wild West Show" by Big & Rich (#21)

2005

"I Want a Cowboy" by Katrina Elam (#59); "Nothin' but Cowboy Boots" by Blue County (#38); "Oklahoma-Texas Line" by Rascal Flatts (#53); "Somewhere Between Texas and Mexico" by Pat Green (#42)

Sources

Whitburn, Joel. *Pop Memories 1890–1954: The History of American Popular Music*. Menomonee Falls, Wisconsin: record Research Inc., 1986.

Whitburn, Joel. *Top Country Songs 1944–2005*. Menomonee Falls, Wisconsin, 2005.

Bibliography

Adams, Les, and Buck Rainey. *Shoot-Em-Ups: The Complete Reference Guide to Westerns of the Sound Era*. Waynesville, NC: World of Yesterday, 1978.
Allen, Rex. *My Life: Sunrise to Sunset*. As told to Paula Simpson Witt and Snuff Garrett. Scottsdale, AZ: RexGarRus, 1989.
Allen, Rex, Jr. Personal interview with the author, May 31, 2006, Nashville, Tennessee.
Anderson, Liz. Telephone interview with the author, May 11, 2007.
Anderson, Lynn. Telephone interview with the author, May 9, 2007.
Arnold, Eddy. Personal interview with the author, March 18, 2005.
Autry, Gene. *Back in the Saddle Again*. With Mickey Herskowitz. Garden City, NY: Doubleday, 1976.
Benson, Ray. Telephone interview with the author, June 7, 2002.
Bentinck, Henry. "The Nation's Barn Dance." *Radio Guide* 4, no. 2 (November 11, 1934).
Bergreen, Laurence. *Capone: The Man and the Era*. New York: Touchstone/Simon & Schuster, 1994.
Berry, Chad, ed. *The Hayloft Gang: The Story of the National Barn Dance*. Urbana: University of Illinois Press, 2008.
Biggar, George C. "The National Barn Dance." In *Country Music Who's Who*.
_____. July 13, 1964. Letter. Country Music Foundation.
Bill, Edgar L. Letter dated March 1953. Country Music Foundation.
Block, Alex Ben. "Salute to Republic Entertainment." *Hollywood Reporter*, October 24, 1995.
Bond, Johnny. "Gene Autry: 'Champion.'" Manuscript in the Country Music Foundation archives.
_____. Interview at Country Music Foundation, Oral History Music Project.
_____. *Reflections: The Autobiography of Johnny Bond*. Los Angeles: John Edwards Memorial Foundation, 1976.
Brooks, Tim, and Earle Marsh. *The Complete Directory to Prime Time Network TV Shows, 1946-Present*. 8th ed. New York: Ballantine, 2003.
Buscombe, Richard. *The BFI Companion to the Western*. New York: Atheneum, 1988.
Cameron, Ian, and Douglas Pye, eds. *The Book of Westerns*. New York: Continuum, 1996.
Carman, Bob, and Dan Scapperotti. *Roy Rogers: King of the Cowboys: A Film Guide*. Privately published, 1970 and 2000.
Carr, Patrick, ed. *The Illustrated History of Country Music*. New York: Dolphin, 1980.
Cash, Johnny. *Man in Black*. Grand Rapids, MI: Zondervan, 1975.
_____, with Patrick Carr. *Cash: The Autobiography*. York: HarperCollins, 1997.
Country Music Magazine. *The Comprehensive Country Music Encyclopedia*. New York: Crown, 1994.
Cusic, Don. *The Cowboy Way: The Amazing True Adventures of Riders in the Sky*. Lexington: University Press of Kentucky, 2003.
_____. *Cowboys and the Wild West: An A to Z Guide from the Chisholm Trail to the Silver Screen*. New York: Facts on File, 1994.
_____. *Discovering Country Music*. Westport, CT: Praeger, 2008.
_____. *Eddy Arnold: I'll Hold You in My Heart*. Nashville, TN: Rutledge Hill, 1997.
_____. *Gene Autry: His Life and Career*. Jefferson, NC: McFarland, 2007.
_____. *Johnny Cash: The Songs*. New York: Thunder's Mouth, 2005.

Daniel, Wayne W. "Gene Autry: America's Number 1 Singing Cowboy." *Nostalgia Digest* (February/March 2003): 6–14.
Dary, David. *Cowboy Culture: A Saga of Five Centuries.* Lawrence: University Press of Kansas, 1981, 1989.
Davis, Elise Miller. *The Answer Is God: The Inspiring Personal Story of Dale Evans and Roy Rogers.* New York: McGraw-Hill, 1955.
Doherty, Thomas. *Pre-Code Hollywood: Sex, Immorality, and Insurrection in American Cinema 1930–1934.* New York: Columbia University Press, 1999.
Dunning, John. *On the Air: The Encyclopedia of Old-Time Radio.* New York: Oxford University Press, 1998.
Edwards, Don. *Classic Cowboy Songs from the Minstrel of the Range.* Salt Lake City, UT: Gibbs-Smith, 1994.
_____. Telephone interview with the author, March 2, 2004.
_____. *Saddle Songs: A Cowboy Songbag.* Colorado Springs, CO: Sevenshoux Enterprises, 2003.
Evans, James. *Prairie Farmer and W.L.S.: The Burridge D. Butler Years.* Urbana: University of Illinois Press, 1969.
Everson, William K. *History of the Western Film.* Secaucus, NJ: Citadel Press, 1969.
Eyles, Allen. *The Western.* Cranbury, NJ: A.S. Barnes, 1975.
Fenin, George N., and William K. Everson. *The Western from Silents to the Seventies.* New York: Penguin, 1977.
Frank, Marie. Interview. Oral History Project. Country Music Foundation.
Gail, Belinda. Personal interview with the author, November 16, 2002, in Las Vegas, Nevada.
George-Warren, Holly. *Cowboy: How Hollywood Invented the Wild West.* Pleasantville, NY: Reader's Digest Books, 2002.
_____. *Public Cowboy No. 1: The Life and Times of Gene Autry.* New York: Oxford University Press, 2007.
Giddens, Gary. *Bing Crosby: A Pocketful of Dreams: The Early Years, 1903–1940.* Boston: Little, Brown, 2001.
Grabman, Sandra. *Pat Buttram: The Rocking Chair Humorist.* Boalsburg, PA: Bear Mano Media, 2006.
Green, Douglas B. "Gene Autry." In *Stars of Country Music,* edited by Bill C. Malone and Judith McCulloh. Urbana: University of Illinois Press, 1975.
_____. *Singing Cowboys.* Salt Lake City, UT: Gibbs-Smith, 2006
_____. *Singing in the Saddle: The History of the Singing Cowboy.* Nashville, TN: Country Music Foundation Press and Vanderbilt University Press, 2002.
Griffis, Ken. *Hear My Song: The Story of the Celebrated Sons of the Pioneers.* Northglenn, CO: Norken, 2001.
Hale, Monte. Personal interview with the author, March 25, 2001, in Los Angeles, California
Hall, Wade. *Hell-Bent for Music: The Life of Pee Wee King.* Lexington: University Press of Kentucky, 1996.
Hamblen, Suze. Interview by the author, March 23, 2001, in Santa Clarita, California.
Haslam, Gerald W. *Workin' Man Blues: Country Music in California.* Berkeley and Los Angeles: University of California Press, 1999.
Hill, Brenn Hill. Telephone interview with the author, December 4, 2001.
Hopper, Lawrence. *Bob Nolan: A Biographical Guide and Annotations to the Lyric Archive at the University of North Carolina, Chapel Hill.* Limited publication by Paul Lawrence Hopper, 2000.
Horstman, Dorothy. *Sing Your Heart Out, Country Boy: Classic Country Songs and Their Inside Stories by the People Who Wrote Them.* New York: Dutton, 1975.
Hot Club of Cowtown. Personal interview with the author, March 7, 2002, in Nashville, Tennessee.
Hurst, Richard Maurice. *Republic Studios: Between Poverty Row and the Majors.* Metuchen, NJ: Scarecrow Press, 1979.
Jones, Loyal. *Country Music Humorists and Comedians.* Urbana: University of Illinois Press, 2008.
Kazanjian, Howard, and Chris Enns. *Happy Trails: A Pictorial Celebration of the Life and Times of Roy Rogers and Dale Evans.* Guilford, CT: Twodot/Globe Pequot, 2005.
_____ and _____. *The Cowboy and the Senorita: A Biography of Roy Rogers and Dale Evans.* Guilford, CT: Twodot, 2005.
Kingsbury, Paul, ed. *The Encyclopedia of Country Music.* New York: Oxford University Press, 1998.
_____, and Alan Axelrod, eds. *Country: The Music and the Musicians.* New York: Abbeville Press, 1988.
La Chapelle, Peter. *Proud to Be an Okie: Cultural Politics, Country Music, and Migration to Southern California.* Berkeley: University of California Press, 2007.

Lackmann, Ron. *Same Time—Same Station: An A-Z Guide to Radio from Jack Benny to Howard Stern.* New York: Facts on File, 1996.
LeDoux, Chris. Telephone interview with the author, May 14, 2003.
Lee, Katie. *Ten Thousand Goddam Cattle: A History of the American Cowboy in Song, Story, and Verse.* Flagstaff, AZ: Northland Press, 1977.
Lemann, Nicholas. *The Promised Land: The Great Black Migration and How It Changed America.* New York: Vintage, 1991.
Lightfoot, William E. "Belle of the Barn Dance: Reminiscing with Lulu Belle Wiseman Stamey." *Journal of Country Music* 12, no. 1: 2–15.
_____. "From Radio Queen to Raleigh: Conversations with Lulu Belle: Part I." *Old Time Country* 6, no. 2 (Summer 1989): 4–10.
_____. "From Radio Queen to Raleigh: Conversations with Lulu Belle: Part II." *Old Time Country* 6, no. 3 (Fall 1989): 3–11.
Logsdon, Guy. *"The Whorehouse Bells Were Ringing" and Other Songs Cowboys Sing.* Urbana: University of Illinois Press, 1989.
Lomax, John A., and Alan Lomax. *Cowboy Songs and Other Frontier Ballads.* New York: Collier, 1986.
Loy, R. Philip. *Westerns and American Culture, 1930–1955.* Jefferson, NC: McFarland, 2001.
Magers, Boyd. *Gene Autry Westerns: America's Favorite Cowboy.* Madison, NC: Empire, 2007.
Malone, Bill C. *Country Music, U.S.A.* Austin: University of Texas Press, 1968.
_____. *Don't Get Above Your Raisin': Country Music and the Southern Working Class.* Urbana: University of Illinois Press, 2002.
_____. *Singing Cowboys and Musical Mountaineers: Southern Culture and the Roots of Country Music.* Athens: University of Georgia Press, 1993.
_____, and Judith McCullough, eds. *Stars of Country Music.* Urbana: University of Illinois Press, 1975.
Marvin, Frankie. Interview at Country Music Foundation, Oral History Music Project.
McCloud, Barry, ed. *Definitive Country: The Ultimate Encyclopedia of Country Music and Its Performers.* New York: Perigree, 1995.
McCusker, Kristine M. *Lonesome Cowgirls and Honky-Tonk Angels: The Women of Barn Dance Radio.* Urbana: University of Illinois Press, 2008.
McElvaine, Robert S. *The Great Depression: America, 1929–1941.* New York: Times, 1984.
Montana, Patsy. *Patsy Montana: The Cowboy's Sweetheart.* With Jane Frost. Jefferson, NC: McFarland, 2002.
Morris, Edward. "New, Improved, Homogenized: Country Radio Since 1950." In *Country: The Music and the Musicians.* New York: Abbeville Press, 1988.
Morris, Georgia, and Mark Pollards. *Roy Rogers: King of the Cowboys.* San Francisco: Collins/HarperCollins, 1994.
Murphey, Michael Martin. Personal interview with the author, February 19, 2002, in Nashville, Tennessee.
Nelson, Ken. *My First 90 Years Plus 3.* Pittsburgh: Dorrance, 2007.
Oermann, Robert K. *America's Music: The Roots of Country.* Atlanta, GA: Turner, 1996.
Ohrlin, Glenn. *The Hell-Bound Train: A Cowboy Songbook.* Urbana: University of Illinois Press, 1973.
O'Neal, Bill. *Tex Ritter: America's Most Beloved Cowboy.* Austin, TX: Eakin Press, 1998.
_____, and Fred Goodwin. *The Sons of the Pioneers.* Austin, TX: Eakin Press, 2001.
Phillips, Robert W. *Roy Rogers: A Biography, Radio History, Television Career Chronicle, Discography, Filmography, Comicography, Merchandising and Advertising History, Collectibles Description, Bibliography and Index.* Jefferson, NC: McFarland, 1995.
_____. *Singing Cowboy Stars.* Salt Lake City, UT: Gibbs Smith, 1994.
Porterfield, Nolan. *Jimmie Rodgers: The Life and Times of America's Blue Yodeler.* Urbana: University of Illinois Press, 1979.
_____. *Last Cavalier: The Life and Times of John A. Lomax.* Urbana: University of Illinois Press, 1996.
Riders in the Sky (Too Slim, Ranger Doug and Woody Paul). *Riders in the Sky: The Book.* With Texas Bix Bender. Salt Lake City, UT: Biggs Smith, Peregrine Smith, 1992.
Rogers, Dale Evans. *Rainbow on a Hard Trail: Her Story of Life and Love.* With Norman B. Rohrer. Grand Rapids, MI: Fleming H. Revell, 1999.
Rogers, Dusty. Personal interview with the author, February 16, 2008, in Branson, Missouri.
Rogers, Roy, and Dale Evans. *Happy Trails: Our Life Story.* With Jane Stern and Michael Stern. New York: Simon & Schuster, 1994.
_____ and _____. *Happy Trails: The Story of Roy Rogers and Dale Evans.* With Carlton Stowers. Waco, TX: Word, 1979.

Rogers, Roy, Jr. *Growing Up with Roy & Dale*. With Karen Ann Wojahn. Ventura, CA: Regal, 1986.
Rogers-Barnett, Cheryl. *Cowboy Princess: Life with My Parents, Roy Rogers and Dale Evans*. With Frank Thompson. Lanham, MD: Taylor Trade, 2003.
Rothel, David. *The Gene Autry Book*. Madison, NC: Empire, 1988.
_____. *The Roy Rogers Book*. Madison, NC: Empire, 1996.
_____. *The Singing Cowboys*. Cranbury, NJ: A.S. Barnes, 1978.
_____. *Those Great Cowboy Sidekicks*. Waynesville, NC: WOY Publications, 1984.
Rumble, John Woodruff. "Fred Rose and the Development of the Nashville Music Industry, 1942–1954." PhD diss., Vanderbilt University, 1980.
Russell, Tony. *Country Music Originals: The Legends and the Lost*. New York: Oxford University Press, 2007.
_____. *Country Music Records: A Discography, 1921–1942*. New York: Oxford University Press, 2004.
Satherley, Art. Interview at Country Music Foundation, Oral History Music Project.
Savage, William W., Jr. *Singing Cowboys and All That Jazz: A Short History of Popular Music in Oklahoma*. Norman: University of Oklahoma Press, 1983.
Seemann, Charlie. "Gene Autry." *The Journal of the American Academy for the Preservation of Old-Time Country Music*, no. 22 (August 1994).
Slatta, Richard. *Cowboys of the Americas*. New Haven, CT: Yale University Press, 1990.
Smith, Jon Guyot. "A Brief Assessment of Gene Autry's Role in the Development of Country Music." Originally published in "Gene Autry's Friends" and copied for the author.
_____. "Smiley Burnette: Gentle Genius Who Was Gene Autry's Pal." Originally published in "Gene Autry's Friends" and copied for author.
_____. "Smiley Burnette: It's Nice to Be Important, but More Important to Be Nice." *DISCoveries* (April 1994): 26–30.
Smith, Packy, and Ed Husle, eds. *Don Miller's Hollywood Corral: A Comprehensive B Western Roundup*. Burbank, CA: Riverwood Press, 1993.
Smith, Richard Norton. *The Colonel: The Life and Legend of Robert R. McCormick, 1880–1955*. Evanston, IL: Northwestern University Press, 1997.
Sons of the San Joaquin. Telephone interview with Jack Hannah and Joe Hannah, November 14, 2005; interview with Lon Hannah, November 15, 2005.
Stambler, Irwin, and Grelun Landon. *Country Music: The Encyclopedia*. New York: St. Martin's Press, 1997.
Stamper, Pete. *It All Happened in Renfro Valley*. Lexington: University Press of Kentucky, 1999.
Steagall, Red. Telephone interview with the author, May 23, 2005.
Stowers, Carlton. *The Story of Roy Rogers and Dale Evans: Happy Trails*. Carmel, NY: Guideposts, 1979.
Summers, Neil. *The First Official TV Western Book*. Vienna, WV: Old West Shop, 1987.
_____. *The Official TV Western Book*. Vol 2. Vienna, WV: Old West Shop, 1989.
_____. *The Official TV Western Book*. Vol 3. Vienna, WV Old West Shop, 1991.
Thompson, Vern. Telephone interview with the author, December 11, 2002.
Thorp, N. Howard "Jack." *Songs of the Cowboys*. New York: Clarkson N. Potter, 1966.
Tinsley, Jim Bob. *For a Cowboy Has To Sing*. Orlando: University of Central Florida Press, 1991.
_____. *He Was Singin' This Song*. Orlando: University of Central Florida Press, 1981.
Townsend, Charles R. *San Antonio Rose: The Life and Music of Bob Wills*. Urbana: University of Illinois Press, 1986.
Tuska, Jon. *The American West in Film: Critical Approaches to the Western*. Westport, CT: Greenwood Press, 1985.
_____. *The Filming of the West*. New York: Doubleday, 1976.
_____. *The Vanishing Legion: A History of Mascot Pictures, 1927–1935*. Jefferson, NC: McFarland, 1982.
Tuttle, Marilyn. Telephone interview with the author, November 29 and November 30, 2006.
Tuttle, Wesley. Personal interview with the author, January, 3, 2001, in Los Angeles, California.
Tyson, Ian. *I Never Sold My Saddle*. With Colin Escott. Vancouver, B.C.: Douglas & McIntyre, 1997.
_____. Telephone interview with the author, March 2, 2005.
Vaughn, Gerald F. *Ray Whitley: Country-Western Music Master and Film Star*. Newark, DE: Privately published by the author, 1973.
Wakely, Linda Lee. *See Ya Up There, Baby: The Jimmy Wakely Story*. Canoga Park, CA: Shasta Records, 1992.
Ward, Geoffrey C. *The West: An Illustrated History*. Boston: Little, Brown, 1996.
Warren, Dale. Telephone interview with the author, September 17, 2002.

Western, Johnny. Telephone interview with the author, August 31, 2005.
Whitburn, Joel. *Pop Hits: Singles & Albums 1940–1954*. Menomonee Falls, WI: Record Research, 2002.
_____. *Top Country Albums, 1964–1997*. Menomonee Falls, WI: Record Research, 1997.
_____. *Top Country Songs, 1944–2005*. Menomonee Falls, WI: Record Research, 2005.
_____. *Top Pop Singles, 1955–2002*. Menomonee Falls, WI: Record Research, 2003.
White, John I. *Git Along Little Dogies: Songs and Songmakers of the American West*. Urbana: University of Illinois Press, 1975.
White, Raymond E. *King of the Cowboys, Queen of the West: Roy Rogers and Dale Evans*. Madison: University of Wisconsin Press/Popular Press, 2005.
Whitley, Ray. Country Music Foundation Oral History Project. Interviewer: Douglas B. Green, March 30, 1975.
_____. Country Music Foundation Oral History Project. Interviewer: Douglas B. Green, July 1, 1974.
_____. Country Music Foundation Oral History Project. Interviewer: Murray Nash, June 8, 1978.
Willing, Sharon Lee. *No One to Cry To: A Long, Hard Ride into the Sunset with Foy Willing of the Riders of the Purple Sage*. Tucson: Wheatmark, 2007.
WLS Family Album, 1933. Published by WLS, The Prairie Farmer Station, 1230 West Washington Boulevard, Chicago, Illinois.
Wolfe, Charles K. *Classic Country: Legends of Country Music*. New York: Routledge, 2001.
_____. "The Triumph of the Hills: Country Radio, 1920–1950." In *Country: The Music and the Musicians*. New York: Abbeville Press, 1988.
Wylie and the Wild West (Wylie Gustafson). Telephone interview with the author, July 7, 2008.
Yoggy, Gary. *Riding the Western Range: The Rise and Fall of the Western on Television*. Jefferson, NC: McFarland, 1995.
_____, ed. *Back in the Saddle: Essays on Western Film and Television Actors*. Jefferson, NC: McFarland, 1998.

Index

A&M Records 184
Abbott, Jerry 244
ABC/Dot Records 161
ABC Records 161, 220
"Abilene" 241, 244
AC/DC (group) 201
Academy Award 87, 105, 106, 126
Academy of Country and Western Music 84, 222
Acrobat Ranch (TV show) 148
"Across the Alley from the Alamo" 238
Across the Rio Grande (film) 63
"Across the Wide Missouri" 239
Acuff, Roy 70, 87, 95, 143, 146, 183
Acuff-Rose Publishing 112
"Adios" 237, 238, 239
"Adios Amigo" 145, 225, 228, 241, 244
"Adios, Marquita Linda" 236
Adkins, Trace 249
Adobe Records 204, 205
Adventures of Champion (TV show) 148
Adventures of Jim Bowie (TV show) 147
Adventures of Kit Carson (TV show) 148
Adventures of Rin Tin Tin (TV show) 147
"Afraid" 98
"After Sundown" 112
"After Texas" 245
"Ages and Ages Ago" 47, 48
"Aha, San Antone" 38
"Ain't No California" 244
"Ain't No Need to Worry" 22
Akavoff, Mike 161
Akins, Rhett 249
Alabama (group) 125, 246
Aladdin Lamp Company 108
The Alamo (film) 105
Alan, Buddy 227, 242
The Alaskans (TV show) 148
"A-L-B-U-Q-U-E-R-Q-U-E" 240
"Albuquerque" 249
Alexander, Wyvon Alexander 245

"Alice in Dallas (Sweet Texas)" 245
"All Alone Each Night" 42
"All Around Cowboy" 244
"All Around Cowboy of 1964" 227, 242
"All My Ex's Live in Texas" 247
"All the Gold in California" 244
"All the King's Horses" 243
"Alla en El Rancho Grande" 236
Allegheny Uprising (film) 104
Allen, Bob 144
Allen, Bonnie Linder 98
Allen, Deanna 173
Allen, Jules Vern 13, 17, 82, 165
Allen, Rex 2, 14, 31, 46, 52, 97–99, 155, 159, 171, 173, 174, 175, 239, 241
Allen, Rex, Jr. 2, 99, 170–175, 228, 243, 245, 246
Allen, Rosalie 72, 238
Allen, Steve 97, 135
Allen, Virginia 99
Allison, Joe 161
Allsup, Tommy 110
"Along the Navajo Trail" 225, 238
"Along the Santa Fe Trail" 113, 237
Alvino Rey 68, 237
"Amapola" 236, 237
"Amarillo by Morning" 218, 221, 227, 242, 246
The Amazing Rhythm Aces 243, 245
Ambrose 237
Ameche, Don 35
"An American Boy Grows Up" 106
The American Quartet 233
The American Record Corporation 8, 18, 25, 28, 42, 47, 86, 109, 152
Ames, Ed 106
Ames Brothers 73, 187
"Amigo's Guitar" 225, 240
"Among My Souvenirs" 203
Amos Publishing 161
"Amy's Back in Austin" 248
Anderson, Broncho Billy 6
Anderson, Casey 176
Anderson, Ivie 237

Anderson, John 246
Anderson, Lee "Carrot Top" 76
Anderson, Liz 176, 179, 180
Anderson, Lynn 176–180, 241, 243, 245
Andrews Sisters 112, 237, 238
Andy Parker and the Plainsmen *see* Parker, Andy
Angel and the Badman (film) 104
Annett, Bernie 134
Annie Get Your Gun (musical) 37
Annie Oakley (TV show) 148, 155, 156
"Annie's Song" 203
"Another Goodbye Song" 172
"Another Man Done Gone" 149
"Another Texas Song" 245
Anson Weeks Orchestra 34
"The Answer to the Last Letter" 132
Anthony, Harry 233
Anthony, Ray 240
Antioch College 193, 194
"Anytime" 58
"Apache Tears" 150
"Are They Gonna Make Us Outlaws Again" 243
Argosy Productions 104
"A-Ridin' Old Paint" 86
The Arizona Cowboy (film) 98, 173
"Arizona Highway" 245
"Arizona Rain" 249
"Arizona Whiz" 245
Arkie the Arkansas Woodchopper 12, 17, 41
Armstrong, Louis 165
Arnold, Eddy 26, 52, 70, 73, 95, 137, 139, 143, 199, 202, 225, 226, 227, 239, 240, 243, 249
Arnspiger, Herman 108
Art Kassel 236
Ash, Sam 234
Asleep at the Wheel 193–196, 244, 247, 249
"Asphalt Cowboy" 243
Astair, Fred 35
"At the Flying 'W'" 238
Atcher, Bob 14, 226

257

Index

Atchison, Tex 39, 45
Atkins, Chet 133, 176
"Austin" 249
Austin, Gene 61, 168
Austin, Texas 122, 194, 219, 227
Austin City Limits (TV show) 115
Autry, Gene 1, 8, 12, 13, 14, 15, 16, 17, 18–24, 19, 20, 21, 22–24, 25, 26, 27, 28, 29, 30, 31, 34, 37, 39, 41, 44, 45, 46, 47, 49, 51, 52, 54, 59, 60, 62, 63, 65, 66, 67, 68–69, 70, 71, 73, 78, 79, 80, 81, 82, 84, 86, 89, 91, 92, 94, 95, 96, 97, 98, 100, 103, 104, 113, 114, 117, 126, 142, 143, 146, 147, 148, 156, 155, 156, 157, 158, 165, 168, 171, 174, 175, 177, 186, 189, 202, 218, 222, 223, 225, 226, 227, 235, 236, 237, 238, 239
Autry, Ina Mae 19, 80, 155
Autry, Jackie 94, 96
Avalon, Frankie 105
Axton, Hoyt 245

"Baby Doll" 226
Bacall, Lauren 106
Bach 164
Bachman Turner Overdrive 197
"Back Home Again" 203
"Back in the Saddle Again 17, 47, 48, 66, 67, 236, 243, 249
"Back Side of Dallas" 242
Back to Bataan (film) 104
"Back to Denver" 242
"Backslider's Wine" 124
"Bad, Bad, Bad Cowboy" 242
"Bad News" 149
Bailey, Razzy 245
Baker, Bob 14, 28, 52
Baker, Howard 87
Baker, Kenny 238
Baker, Two Ton 238
Bakewell, Bill 37
Balcom, Stuart 162
"Ball of John Chisum" 106
"Ballad of Davey Crockett" 17, 225, 240, 248
"The Ballad of Floyd Collins" 126
"The Ballad of Ira Hayes" 149, 150
"The Ballad of the Alamo" 105
"the Ballad of the Green Beret" 106
"Ballad of the War Wagon" 106
"Ballad of Waterhole #3 (Code of the West)" 241
Ballew, Michael 245
Ballie, Kathy 172
The Bama Band 246
Bamby, George 54, 55
Bancroft, George 103
"Bandera, Texas 245
"The Bandit" 240
Bandy, Moe 227, 228, 243, 244, 246
"Bandy the Rodeo Clown" 227, 243
"Bang a Drum" 249
"Barbara Allen 12, 50
The Barber of Seville (opera) 189
Bare, Bobby 177, 243, 246
"Barefoot Trail" 234
Barlow, Randy 244

Barnes, Kathy 243
Barnes, Max D. 245
Barnet, Charlie 236
Barry, Don 37
Baseball Hall of Fame 188
Bat Masterson (TV show) 148
Bates, George 146
Baxter, Les 63
Baxter, Warner 7
"Be Honest with Me" 60, 67
The Beach Boys 210, 249
"Beaches of Cheyenne" 170, 249
Bearsville Records 184
"The Beast in Men" 152
The Beatles 126, 152, 171, 183, 197, 198, 218, 227
The Beautiful Blonde from Bashful Bend (film) 55
"Beautiful Brown Eyes" 60, 197
Beck, Jim 130, 131, 132, 134, 135
Beckham, Bob 241
"Beer and Skittles" 42
"Beer for My Horses" 250
Begg, Bill 156
The Bellamy Brothers 245, 246, 247, 248
Bells of San Angelo (film) 37
Benchley, Robert 17
Bender, Bill 165
"Beneath the Texas Moon" 247
Bennett, Tony 139, 202, 206, 236, 237
Benson, Ray 95, 193, 194, 196
Benson Orchestra of Chicago 235
Berg, Matraca 249
Bergen, Edgar 35
Berle, Milton 135
Berlin, Irving 55
Berriman, Brian 207
Best Little Whorehouse in Texas (musical) 219
"The Best of All Possible Worlds" 210
Bestor, Don 235
Beverly Hill Billies (group) 4, 82, 89, 90, 235
The Beverly Hillbillies (TV show) 81
"Beyond the Last Mile" 132
"Beyond the Sunset" 72
"The Bible Tells Me So" 38
Biblow, Twylla 185
Big & Rich 250
Big D Jamboree 131
Big D Records 220
"Big Foot" 150
"Big Girls Don't Cry" 177
"Big Iron" 144, 216, 225, 240
Big Jake (film) 106
Big Jim McClain (film) 105
"Big Rock Candy Mountain No. 2" 82
The Big Show (film) 27, 34
The Big Stampede (film) 102
The Big Trail (film) 101, 102
Biggar, George 40
Bigger, Jimmy 134
Billboard 12, 16, 60, 112, 124, 135, 140, 145, 147, 150, 161, 177, 226

"Billy the Kid" 244
"Bird on a Wire" 152
Bishop, Bob 241
Bismeaux Studio (Austin) 195
Black, Baxter 162
Black, Clint 125, 212, 228, 248
Black Saddle (TV show) 148
Blair, Kenny 247
Blake, Norman 168
Blake, Robert 95
"Blame It on Mexico" 220
"Blame It on Texas" 248
"Blame It on the Stones" 210
Blanton, Loy 246
Blood Alley (film) 105
"Blue Canadian Rockies" 73
Blue County (group) 250
"Blue Eyed Elaine" 67
"Blue Eyes Crying in the Rain" 227
"Blue Prairie" 189
"Blue Shadows on the Trail" 155, 225, 238
Blue Sky Boys 40
Blue Steel (film) 102
"Blue Texas Moonlight" 238
Bluebird Records 39
Bluebonnet Records 40
BMI 42
"Bob, All the Playboys and Me" 242
"Bob Wills Boogie" 238
"Bob Wills Is Still the King" 227, 243
Bobby Benson's Adventures (CBS radio show) 14
"Bob's Got a Swing Band in Heaven" 244
Bogguss, Suzy 196, 247, 248
La Bohème (opera) 189
Boles, Jim 68
Bonanza (TV show) 17, 63, 148, 225, 226, 227
Bond, Johnny 52, 55, 57, 61, 62, 63, 65–71, 74, 76, 77, 86, 91, 92, 114, 155, 157, 172, 226, 239
Bonner, M.J. 12
"Bonnie Blue Flag" 105
"Boogie Back to Texas" 247
Boone, Richard 106, 156, 157
Boot Records 184
"Boot Scootin' Boogie" 248
"Boots and Saddle" 86
Boots and Saddles (TV show) 156
"Boots (These Boots Are Made for Walking)" 247
Border G-Men (film) 48
Bordertown Trails (film) 80
Borge, Victor 63
"Born to Be a Cowboy" 205
Born to the West (film) 103
Boston Gardens Rodeo 66, 165
"Bourbon Cowboy" 245
Bowen, Jimmy 160, 161
The Bowery Boys 102
"Boy from Texas" 238
Boy Howdy (group) 248
"The Boy in Blue" 82
Boy Scouts (Philmont) 203
Boyd, William 47

Index

BR5–49 246
Bradbury, Bill 100
Bradbury, Robert North 100
Bradley, C.M. 133
Bradley, Owen 133, 135
Bradley Recording Studio (Nashville) 135
Brady, Pat 29, 30, 31, 90
Brand of Fear (film) 63
Brave Eagle (TV show) 148
Brennan, Walter 105
Brentwood Records 120
"Bridge Over Troubled Waters" 152
Briner, George 124
Brinkley, Dr. John R. 15
Britt, Elton 72, 74, 165, 198, 199, 238
Brock, William 87, 88
Brody, Lane 246
Brokaw, Tom 175
Broken Arrow (TV show) 147
"Broken Down Merry-Go-Round" 60
Bronco (TV show) 148
Bronco Buster (film) 27
Brooks, Garth 170, 216, 217, 125, 228, 247, 248, 249
Brooks & Dunn 248, 249
The Brothers Four 105
Brown, Durwood 108
Brown, Gary 205
Brown, Jim Ed 243
Brown, Joe E. 36
Brown, Johnny Mack 63, 102, 103
Brown, Mark 87
Brown, Mary 175
Brown, Milton 108, 109, 113, 131
Brown, Tony 222
Brubeck, Dave 126
Bruce, Ed 228, 243, 244, 245, 246
Brunswick Records 4, 108, 109, 112
"Brush Those Tears from Your Eyes" 58
Bryant, Anita 70
Bryant, Boudleaux 16
Bryson, Bill 214
"Bubbles in My Beer" 73
"Buckaroo" 241, 249
Buddy Lee Agency 200
Buena Vista Records 99
"Buenas Dias Argentina" 244
Buffalo Bill Jr. (TV show) 148, 155, 156
Buffalo Bill's Wild West Show 6, 19, 224
"Buffalo Billy" 239
"Bull Rider" 245
"Bull Smith Can't Dance the Cotton-Eyed Joe" 245
Bullet Records 131
"Bunkhouse Jamboree" 42
Burdette, Lew 187
Burke, Ceele 237
Burn 'Em Up Barnes (serial) 18
Burnette, Dorsey 242
Burnette, Smiley 14, 19, 20, 21, 22, 23, 24, 25, 26, 28, 39, 42, 66, 79–81, 90, 156
Burns, George 245

Burns, Robert 191
Burr, Henry 233, 234, 235
Burroughs, Edgar Rice 209
Burrus Mill and Elevator Company 108
"Bury Me Not on the Lone Prairie" 104, 150
Bush, Johnny 243
"A Bushel and a Peck" 60
Busse, Hi Pickets 171
"Busted" 149
Butcher, Dwight 47
Butler, Burridge 12
"Buttons and Bows" 177, 225, 238, 239
Buttram, Pat 17, 68, 69, 80, 98
Butts, R. Dale 34, 35, 36
"By the Time I Get to Phoenix" 227, 241, 242, 244
Byrd, Tracy 249

Cachet Records 151
"Cactus and a Rose" 245
"Cactus in a Coffee Can" 249
"Cadillac Ranch" 248
Cagle, Chris 249
Cahill, US. Marshal (film) 106
Cain, Christopher 222
Cain, Hunter 247
Cain's Ballroom (Tulsa) 109
Caiola, Al and His Orchestra 226
"Cajon Stomp" 28
Calamity Jane 3
Caldwell, Dick 185
Caldwell, Hank 54, 55
"A Calico Apron, and a Gingham Gown" 54
"California" 234, 244, 246
"California and You" 234
"California Blue" 247
"California Calling" 245
"California Cotton Fields" 242
"California Girl (And the Tennessee Square)" 242
"California Grapevine" 242
"California, Here I Come" 235
"California Is Just Mississippi" 242
"California Lady" 244
The California Mail (film) 27
"California Medley" 235
"California Okie" 243
"California Polka" 238
The California Ramblers 235
"California Road" 246
"California Sleeping" 246
"California Sunshine" 241
"California Up Tight Band" 241
"California Wine" 247
"Call of the Canyon" 236
"Call the Lord and He'll Be There" 135
Callahan Brothers 15
Camel Caravan 29
Cameron, Rod 48
Camp, Chuck 119
Campbell, Albert 233 234
Campbell, Glen 106, 139, 161, 175, 227, 241, 242, 243, 244, 246

"Can You Hear Those Pioneers" 170, 175, 228, 243
"Canadian Pacific" 242
Canadian Songwriters Hall of Fame 186
Cannon, Hal 167, 185, 190, 210, 211
Canova Family 56
Cansler, Larry 124
The Capitals 245
Capitol Records 12, 54, 58, 60, 76, 86, 91, 92, 161, 217
Card, Ken 47
"The Caretaker" 148
Carey, Harry 102
Carey, MacDonald 35
Cargill, Henson 242
Carillo, Leo 55
"Carlena and Jose Gomez" 244
Carlton College 154
Carmichael, Hoagy 55, 173
Carnegie Hall 158, 159, 183
"Carolina in the Pines" 124, 228
Carr, Trem 103
Carradine, John 103
Carroll, David 240
Carroll, Earl 76
Carson, Fiddlin' John 12, 50, 229
Carson, Jeff 249
Carson, Johnny 157, 212
Carson, Ken 30
Carson, Sunset 80
Carter, Anita 242
Carter, June 149
Carter, Walter 52
Carter Family 15, 50, 97, 131, 146, 165
Caruso 187
Casanova in Burlesque (film) 36
"Casey" 186
"Casey Jones" 149
"Casey's Last Ride" 210
Cash, Carrie 146
Cash, John Carter 146, 151
Cash, Johnny 52, 106, 146–153, 156, 157, 159, 165, 197, 203, 225, 226, 228, 240, 241, 243, 244, 245, 246, 247
Cash, Roy 148
Cash, Tommy 244
Cass County Boys 68, 70, 155, 165
The Castillians 236
Castle Studio (Nashville) 133, 135
Castleman, Boomer 122
"Cattle Call" 60, 105, 166, 199, 225, 240, 249
Caviness, Claude 136, 137
CBS Records 29, 124, 178, 179
Cedarwood Publishing 139
Cee Cee Chapman & Santa Fe 247
CFTO (Toronto) 184
"Chain Around the Flowers" 122
"Chain Gang" 124
Chalmers, Donald 233
Chancey, Ron 220, 221
Chappell Music Publishing 219
Charles, Ray 73, 160
Charlie Chan 102

Index

Charlie the Lonesome Cougar (film) 98
Chart Records 178, 277
Chase, Borden 104
"Chattanoogie Shoeshine Boy" 133
Cheer Up and Smile (film) 101
Cheney, Jack 61, 65
"Cherokee" 236
"Cherokee Boogie" 225, 239, 245
"Cherokee Country" 245
"Cherokee Fiddle" 124, 244, 246
"Cherokee Maiden" 73, 243
"Cherokee Strip" 241
Chesnutt, Mark 248
Chesterfield Pictures 103
"Chewing Chawing Gum" 14
"Cheyenne (Shy Ann)" 233
Cheyenne (TV show) 17, 63, 147, 148, 225
Chicago 8, 12, 25, 29, 34, 36, 37, 38, 39, 40, 42, 46, 47, 62, 98
Chicago Cubs 188
Chicago World's Fair 6, 45
"Child of the Fifties" 246
"Children Go Where I Send Thee" 151
"China Doll" 73
Chisum (film) 106
CHNS (Halifax, Nova Scotia) 14
Chon, Richard 191
Chornowol, Adrian 185
Chrisman, Paul *see* Paul, Woody
Churchill, Berton 103
Churchill, Max 162
"Cigarettes, Whusky, and Wild Wild Women" 226, 239
"Cimarron" 60, 65, 66, 71
Cimarron (film) 7
"Cindy" 105
The Cisco Kid 7, 102, 148
"City Lights" 136
City Lights Publishers 213
Clark, Badger 212
Clark, Buddy 238
Clark, Cottonseed (real name Clark Fulks) 57
Clark, Jay 247
Clark, Roy 242
The Clark Family Experience 249
Clement, Zeke 13, 15
"Clementine" 113
Clift, Montgomery 104
Cline, Patsy 227
"Clown in Your Rodeo" 248
CMA Awards 70
Coakley, Tom 236
"Coast of Colorado" 247
Coast Records 54
"Coca Cola Cowboy" 228, 244
Cochran, Hank 137
Cody, Buffalo Bill 3, 6
Coe, David Allan 246, 247
Coffee, Bob 205
Coffey, Kellie 250
Cohen, Paul 92, 131, 132
Cole, Brenda 247
Cole, Nat "King" 238
Cole, Patsy 247
Collins, Arthur 233

Collins, Bill 115
Collins, Brian 244
Collins, Carr 16
Collins, Jim 246
Collins, Judy 183
Collins, Tom 220
"Colorado Blues" 39
"Colorado Call" 243
"Colorado Christmas" 246
"Colorado Country Morning" 242, 243, 245
"Colorado Kool-Aid" 244
"Colorado Moon" 247
"Colorado Sunset" 236
Colorado Sunset (film) 29
Colt .45 (TV show) 148
Colter, Jessi 228
Columbia Pictures 30, 37, 57, 63, 92, 138, 140
Columbia Records 109, 110, 131, 132, 135, 138, 139, 140, 144, 147, 149, 151, 156, 178, 185; Columbia Okeh 57
Columbia Stellar Quartet 234
"The Comancheros" 106, 225, 241
The Comancheros (film) 106
Combine Publishing 139
Commander Cody (George Frayne) 194
Como, Perry 55, 143, 187, 240
"Concrete Cowboy" 248
Confederate Railroad 249
The Conqueror (film) 105
Conqueror Records 42
Consolidated Film Industries 18, 103
Cook, Ronnie 119
"Cool Water" 14, 26, 67, 93, 170, 174, 186, 225, 237, 238, 239
Cooley, Spade 54, 129, 226
Cooper, Gary 7
Cooper, Merian 104
Coral Records 63, 92
The Corbin/Hanner Band 246, 248
Corlew, Dave 208
Corner, Randy 244
Corrigan Ray "Crash" Corrigan 52, 63, 102
La Costa 243, 244
Cotner, Carl 68, 69, 70, 156
Cotton, Carolina 54
"Cotton-Eyed Joe" 221
"Counterfeit Cowboy" 227, 242
Country Music Association 87, 152, 199, 222
Country Music DJ Hall of Fame 158
Country Music Foundation 115
Country Music Hall of Fame 70, 71, 74, 87, 151
Country Song Roundup 72
"Country Western Truck Drivin' Singer" 242
Cousin Emmy 15
The Covered Wagon (film) 7
"Covered Wagon Days" 235
Covered Wagon Jubilee (radio show) 83
"Cow Patti" 245

"Cow Town" 225, 241
Cowan, Edgar 182
"Cowboy" 243, 245
The Cowboy and the Senorita (film) 30, 36
"Cowboy and the Lady" 243, 244, 245
"Cowboy Band" 248
"Cowboy Beat" 248
"Cowboy Boogie" 248
"Cowboy Boots" 241
"Cowboy Cadillac" 249
"Cowboy Christmas" 249
The Cowboy Church 84
"Cowboy Convention" 242
Cowboy Corner (radio show) 162
Cowboy Hall of Fame 94
"Cowboy Hat in Dallas" 247
"Cowboy in a Three Piece Business Suit" 170, 246
"The Cowboy in Me" 250
"Cowboy in the Continental Suit" 241
"Cowboy Jack" 39
"Cowboy Joe" 82
"Cowboy Like You" 243
"Cowboy Logic" 248
"Cowboy Love" 249
"Cowboy Man" 247
"Cowboy Peyton Place" 243
"The Cowboy Rides Away" 218, 246
"Cowboy Serenade" 237
"Cowboy Singer" 244
"Cowboy Stomp!" 245
Cowboy Symposium (Lubbock, TX) 204
"Cowboy Take Me Away" 249
Cowboy Theatre (TV show) 148
"Cowboys Ain't Supposed to Cry" 228, 244
"Cowboys and Clowns" 245
"Cowboys and Daddys" 243
"Cowboys Are Common as Sin" 245
"Cowboy's Born with a Broken Heart" 248
"The Cowboy's Christmas Ball" 86
"Cowboys Don't Cry" 248, 249
"Cowboys Don't Get Lucky All the Time" 228, 244
"Cowboys Don't Shoot Straight (Like They Used To)" 245
"Cowboy's Dream" 246
"Cowboy's Lament" 16
"Cowboys Like Us" 218, 250
"Cowboy's Night Herd Song" 28
"Cowgirl and the Dandy" 245
Cowgirl Hall of Fame 42
"Cowgirl in a Coupe DeVille" 246
"Cowgirls" 250
"Cowpoke" 236
"Cows May Come, Cows May Go, But the Bull Goes on Forever" 234
Cox, Marie 76
Craddock, Billy "Crash Craddock" 245

Cramer, Floyd 134, 135, 225, 241, 245
Crawford, Blackie 134
"Crazy Arms" 135, 136, 137
Crazy Water Crystals 14, 16, 47, 56
Cripple Creek Bar-Room (film) 6
Crockett, John 13
Crosby, Bing 13, 27, 35, 42, 55, 61, 63, 73, 112–113, 187, 224, 235, 236, 237, 238, 239
Crosby, Bob 63, 113
Cross, Hugh 14, 40
"Cross the Brazos at Waco" 241
Crowley, J.C. 247
Croxton, Frank 234
Crumit, Frank 235
"Cry" 178
"Cry, Cry, Cry" 147
"Crying in the Chapel" 98
Currey, Diana Sicily 247
Curtis, Ken 30, 31, 54, 57, 59, 105
Curtis, Sonny 244
"Custer" 150
Cyrus, Billy Ray 248, 249

Dailey, Don 220
Dailey, Mike 219, 220
Dailey, Pappy 220
Dailey, Rennie 90, 91
Dakota (film) 104
Dalhart, Vernon 50, 56, 126, 165
"Dallas" 241, 243, 245, 246, 248
Dallas (TV show) 219
"Dallas Cowboys" 244
Dallas Cowboys (football team) 219
"Dallas Darlin'" 247
"Dallas Days and Fort Worth Nights" 248
Dalton, Larry 245
Dancer, Toby 185
Dances with Wolves (film) 126
"Dancin' Cowboys" 245
"Dang Me" 137
Daniel, W. Leo 82
Daniels, Charlie (The Charlie Daniels Band) 162, 208, 242, 243, 244, 247
"Danny Boy" 137, 138, 139
Darby, Ken 106
"Darby's Castle" 210
The Dark Command (film) 104
Darling, Denver 14, 16, 72
"Daughter of Jole Blon" 68
Dave Alvin and the Blasters 199
Davis, Alvin 204
Davis, Clive 138, 149
Davis, Gail 155
Davis, Gene 243
Davis, Jimmie 45, 67, 225, 241
Davis, Joan 27
Davis, Mac 245, 246
Davis, Paul 227, 243
Davis, Rufe 56, 70
Davis, Stu 132
Davy Crockett (TV show) 105
Dawidziak, Mark 144
"Dawn on the Desert" 236
The Dawn Rider (film) 102

Day, Jimmy 134, 135, 138
"Day That She Left Tulsa (in a Chevy)" 249
Dean, Billy 248
Dean, Eddie 14, 54, 55, 57, 63, 68, 74, 75, 76, 77, 114, 157
Dean, James 49
Dean, Jimmy 57, 58, 68, 76, 96, 227
"The Death of Dan McGrew" 211
Death Valley Days (NBC radio show) 13, 54
Decca Records 25, 31, 45, 47, 48, 58, 73, 83, 86, 92, 98, 112, 131, 132, 135
"Deck of Cards" 239
Dee, Lola with Stubby and the Buccaneers 240
"Deep in the Arms of Texas" 246
"Deep in the Heart of Texas" 113, 237
DeHaven, Penny 243
"Delia's Gone" 152
Delmore Brothers 40, 91
Denning, Doc 190
Dennis, Jimmy 134
Denny, Jim 139
"Denver" 246
Denver, John 203, 245, 246
"Desert Song" 235
The Desert Trail (film) 102
"Desperado" 170, 228, 244, 248
"Desperado Love" 246
"Desperados Waiting for a Train" 246
Destry Rides Again (film) 104
"Detour" 92
"Devil Woman" 203
Devine, Andy 103
DeVol, Hank 63
Dew, Eddie 80
Dew, Joan 142
DeWitt, Jack 135
DeWitt, Lew 173
Dexter, Al 73, 112, 226, 237
The DeZurik Sisters 14
Dick Powell's Zane Grey Theatre (TV show) 147, 148
Dickens, Little Jimmy 144
Dido (group) 186
Dietrich, Marlene 35
Diffie, Joe 249
Dillon, Dean 220, 221, 246
The Dining Sisters 17, 238, 239
Dinning, Lu 77
"Disco Tex" 243
"Disenchanted" 124
Disneyland Records 99
"Distant Drums" 73
"Divorce Me C.O.D." 68
The Dixie Chicks 249
"Do Lord" 121
"Do You Remember These" 242
Dr. Quinn, Medicine Woman (TV show) 151
Dodd, Deryl 249
"Does Fort Worth Ever Cross Your Mind" 246
Dolenz, Mickey 122

Dollar, Johnny 241
Domino, Fats 131
Domino, Floyd (b. Jim Haber) 194
Donohue, Sam 238, 239
"Don't Be Ashamed of Your Age" 73
"Don't Bite the Hand That's Feeding You" 60, 67
"Don't Call Him a Cowboy" 246
"Don't Count the Rainy Days" 124
"Don't Fall in Love with a Cowboy" 37
"Don't Feel Like the Lone Ranger" 244
"Don't Fence Me In" 225, 237, 238
Don't Fence Me In (film) 95
"Don't Go Near the Indians" 99, 241
"Don't It Make You Want to Go Home" 178
"Don't Let the Stars Get in Your eyes" 133
"(Don't Let the Sun Set on You) Tulsa" 242
"Don't Step on Mother's Roses" 148
"Don't Take Your Guns to Town" 147, 148, 150, 225, 240
"Don't Touch My Hat" 249
"Don't You Think This Outlaw Bit's Done Got Out of Hand" 228, 244
"Don't Worry" 203
Dooley, Buddy 76
"Dorraine of Ponchartrain" 149
Dorsey, Jimmy 54, 113, 135, 237
Dorsey, Tommy 54, 113, 135, 236, 238
Doss, Tommy "Spike" 30
Dot Records 161
Dottsy 243
Doublemint Chewing Gum 16
Douglas, Steve 247
"Down and Out" 221
"Down by the Glenside" 105
Down Dakota Way (film) 30
"Down in Old Santa Fe" 19
"Down in Sunshine Valley" 233
"Down in the Valley" 225, 237
Down Mexico Way (film) 29
Down Missouri Way (film) 75
"Down on the Rio Grande" 228, 244
"Down the Trail of Achin' Hearts" 239
"Down Where the Silv'ry Mohawk Flows" 233
Doyle, Ray 199, 201
"Dozen Pairs of Boots" 242
Dozier, Bill 156
"Draggin' the Bow" 42
Drake, Pete 166
Draper, Rusty 240, 241
Drasnow, Hecky 68
"Dream Baby" 73
"Dream on Texas Ladies" 246
"Drift Away" 178
"Drifting Back to Dixie" 82
The Drifting Cowboys 133, 134, 138
"Drive On" 152

"Drums" 150
Drums Along the Mohawk (film) 104
Drusky, Roy 242
Ducas, George 249
Duchin, Eddy 237
"Dude Cowboy" 42
Dude Martin's Roundup (radio show) 54
Dudley, Dave 227, 241, 243
Dulle, Joe 166
Duncan, Johnny 243, 244, 247
Duncan, Robert 213
Duncan, Tommy 109, 110, 112
Dunn, Holly 124
The Durango Kid 80, 92
Durante, Jimmy 35, 37
"Dust" 29
"Dusty Skies" 73
"Duvalier's Dream" 210
Dycus, Frank 221
Dylan, Bob 122, 123, 126, 149, 151, 183, 184

The Eagles 170
Earles, Vivian 57
Earwood, Mundo 243
"East of the Sun (And West of the Moon)" 236
Eastern Slope Records 185
Eastwood, Clint 124
Eaton, Joe 34
Ebsen, Buddy 98
Eddy, Nelson 75, 236
Edelman, Irving 59
Edison, Thomas 6
Edwards, Dayle 166
Edwards, Don 2, 12, 99, 117, 125, 162, 164–169, 185, 200, 205, 208, 211
Edwards, Kathy Jean Davis 167
Edwards, Stoney 194
Eight to the Bar (ABC radio show) 58
Eiland, F.L. 73
Eipper, Laura 144
El Dorado (film) 106
"El Paso" 126, 144, 145, 203
"El Paso City" 145, 203, 228, 243
"El Rancho Grande (My Ranch) 113
Elam, Katrina 250
Elder, Otis 47
The Electric Horseman (film) 220
Elektra Records 161
Elko Cowboy Poetry Gathering 158, 160, 162, 167, 181, 185, 190, 191, 201, 205, 206, 211
Elliott, "Wild Bill" 86
Emery, Ralph 125
EMI America Records 124
Emmons, Buddy 138
"Empty Saddles" 67, 112, 236
"The End Is Not in Sight (The Cowboy Tune)" 243
"End of the Trail" 81
England, Tyler 249
English, Wes 119
Engvall, Bill 249
Epic Records 178, 194

Epiphone Guitars 52
"The Erie Canal" 105
Evans, Dale 2, 17, 33–38, 46, 58, 104, 114, 155, 171, 172, 179, 204, 225, 227
"Even Cowgirls Get the Blues" 178, 244, 245, 246
Everette, Leon 244, 246
Everly Brothers 40, 197
"Every Cowboy's Dream" 249
"Everyday in the Saddle" 86
"Everything That Glitters (Is Not Gold)" 246
Ewing, Skip 247
"Eyes as Big as Dallas" 244

Fabian 106
"A Face in the Crowd" 124
"Face the Flag" 106
Faith, Percy 239, 240
"Fandango" 239
The Far Frontier (film) 58
Fargo, Donna 245
Farr, Hugh 27, 165
Farr, Karl 27, 165
Farr Brothers 28, 29, 30, 117, 168
"Farther Down the Line" 247
"Faster Gun" 248
"Faster Horses (The Cowboy and the Poet)" 228, 243
"Fastest Horse in a One Horse Town" 248
Faulkner, Roy "Lonesome Cowboy" 15
Featherstone, Leroy 205
"Felina" 145
Fender, Freddy 228, 243
Ferguson, Gene 149
Ferlinghetti, Lawrence 212
Ferriman, Brian 208
Festival of the West 175
"Fetch Me Down My Trusty .45" 81
Fibber McGee and Molly (radio show) 45
"Fiddlin' Man" 124
Fields, Jimmy 132
Fields, Shep 236
The Fighting Kentuckian (film) 104
The Fighting Legion (film) 8
The Fighting Seabees (film) 104
Finlay, Kent 219
Finney, Maury 243
First National Pictures 102
"The First Time Ever I Saw Your Face" 152
Fisher, George "Shug" 14, 30, 31
Fisk University 150
"Five Feet High and Rising" 148
Flack, Roberta 152
Flame of the Barbary Coast (film) 104
Flanagan, Ralph 187, 239, 240
Flatt & Scruggs 241
"Flattery Will Get You Everywhere" 177
Fletcher, Curley 18
Flick, A.J. 98
Flores, Al 134

Flores, Rosie 199
"Flow Gently, Sweet Afton" 148
Flying Tigers (film) 104
Flying W Wranglers 119–120
Foglesong, Jim 161, 220
Foley Red 14, 28, 39, 42, 52, 92, 132, 133, 226, 227
"Folsom Prison Blues" 147, 197
Fontana, D.J. 134
"Fool Hearted Memory" 221
"Fool Me" 178
"The Fool's Paradise" 71
Foote, Tom 219, 220
"For the Good Times" 139, 140, 210
Foran, Dick 24, 27, 28, 30, 104
Ford, Glenn 109
Ford, John 101, 103, 104, 105
Ford, Mary (Coleen Summers) 58, 68, 76, 240
Ford, Tennessee Ernie 71, 225, 227, 239, 240, 242
Ford, Whitey (Duke of Paducah) 13, 42
Ford and Glenn 235
The Foreman Phillips Show (ABC radio show) 76
"Forever More" 60
Fort Apache (film) 104
Fort Worth 108, 162, 163, 164, 166, 167, 180, 185, 205
Fort Worth Cats 189
"Fort Worth, Dallas or Houston" 241
Foster, Fred 139
Foster, Radney 249
Foster, Uncle Gus 131
Foster and Lloyd 247
"Four Strong Winds" 182, 184
"Four Wheel Cowboy" 243
Fox, Curley: and Texas Ruby 40; and the Tennessee Firecrackers 16
Fox, Thomas 33, 34
Fox Studio 101
Foy Willing and the Riders of the Purple Sage *see* Willing, Foy
Francks, Don 182
Frank, J.L. 15, 16, 20, 45, 79
"Frankie's Man, Johnny" 148
Franks, Tillman 134
Frazee, Jane 30, 37
Frazier, Dallas 241, 242
Frazier River 249
Fresno State University 87, 188, 189
"Friend in California" 247
Friesen, Orrin 158
Frizzell, David 245
Frizzell, Lefty 131, 132, 134, 203
Frog Millhouse *see* Burnette, Smiley
"Froggy Went A-Courtin'" 60
"From Tennessee to Texas" 243
"From the Word Go" 124
"From Whence Came the Cowboy" 191
Frontier Doctor (TV show) 98
"Frontier Justice" 247
The Frontiersmen 171
"Frosty the Snow Man" 227

Frushay, Ray 244
Fulks, Clark 57
"Full Moon in Baghdad" 180
Fury (TV show) 148

Gallico, Al 178
Galway, James 246
"Gambler's Guitar" 240
"The Game of Triangles" 177
"Games People Play" 178
Gannaway, Al 17
Ganong, Arthur 131
Garber, Jan 236
Garland, Judy 75, 238
Garner, Bonnie 179
Garrett, Betty 238
Garrett, Snuff 99
Gashouse Gang 189
Gate O'Horn (Chicago) 182
Gatlin, Larry (and the Gatlin Brothers) 244, 246
"Gaucho Serenade" 237
Gay, Connie B. 17
"Gay Caballero" 235
Gayle, Crystal 243, 247
"Gentle Annie" 103
"Genuine Texas Good Guy" 244
The Georgians 235
Gerde's Folk City 182
"Geronimo's Cadillac" 123, 228, 247
The Gershwins 55
"Get Along Home, Cindy 56
"Get Along Little Dogies" 86
"Get in Line Reggae Cowboy" 246
"Ghost Riders in the Sky" 154, 174, 206
Giant (film) 49
Gibson, Arbie 42
Gibson, Don 244
Gibson, Hoot 102
Gibson Guitars 49, 51, 52
The Gibson/Miller Band 248
Gill, Vince 212, 247, 248
Gillette, Lee 91, 92
Gilley, Mickey 73
Gilley's Club 221
Gilman, Billy 249
Ginsberg, Allen 213
Girardi, Paul 59
"Girl from Spanish Town" 241
"The Girl I Left Behind Me" 105
"The Girl That I Love in My Dreams" 24
Girl Trouble (film) 35
Girls of the Gold West 2, 14, 16, 39–40, 164–169, 45, 52
"Girls Ride Horses Too" 247
"Give Me More, More More" 155
"Give My Love to Rose" 150, 152
Glaser, Dick 161
Glaser, Jim 247
Glaser, Tompall 228, 242, 243; and the Glaser Brothers 242
GMG Pictures 95, 110
Go West Young Lady (film) 109
Gobel, Georgie 13
"God Blessed Texas" 248
"God Must Be a Cowboy" 246

Godfrey, Arthur 239
"The Gods Were Angry with Me" 60
Godwin, Peter 214
"Going Out to Tulsa" 241
"Going to California" 247
"Going to Memphis" 149
"The Gold Rush Is Over" 73, 225, 239
Golden Boot Award 84
The Golden Stallion (film) 30
Golden West Cowboys 15, 16
Goldsboro, Bobby 244, 245
Goldsmith, Tumbleweed Tommy 115
Goldtown Ghost Riders (film) 80
"Gone and Left Me Blues" 60
Gone Country (play) 173, 174
Gone with the Wind (film) 104
"Gonna Build a Big Fence Around Texas" 225, 238
Good, Dollie 39, 45
Good, Millie 39, 45
"The Good, the Bad and the Ugly" 226
The Good, the Bad and the Ugly (film) 17
"The Good Things" 106
"Good Year for the Outlaw" 250
"Goodbye" 172
"Goodbye, Little Darlin', Goodbye" 113
Goodbye, Mr. Chips (film) 104
"Goodbye, My Little Cherokee" 86
"Goodbye Old Paint" 86
Goodman, Benny 54, 113
"Goodnight Irene" 147
Goodson, Lloyd 243
Gore, Albert 87
Gosdin, Vern 220, 248
Gosfield, Reuben 193 (Lucky Oceans)
"Gospel Boogie" 151
"Gotta Get to Oklahoma (Cause California's Gettin' to Me)" 242
Grable, Betty 55
Grammy Award 117, 160, 178, 225
Grand Canyon Suite 56
Grand Canyon Trail (film) 58
Grand Ole Opry 12, 15, 16, 51, 87, 95, 115, 126, 132, 133, 134, 139, 143, 144, 228
Grant, Kirby 57
Grant, Marshall 147
The Grateful Dead 183, 194
Grauman's Chinese Theater 57, 102
Gray, Dolores 240
Gray, Glen 236
Grayson, Kim 247
"Grazing in Greener Pastures" 140
"(Great American) Classic Cowboy" 243
"Great American Cowboy" 191
Great Depression 25, 26, 47, 52, 72, 83, 86, 97, 154, 187
"Great Long Pistol" 239
"Great Mail Robbery" 172, 243

Great Plains (group) 248
"The Great Speckled Bird" 148, 149
The Great Speckled Bird (group) 183, 184
The Great Train Robbery (film) 6
"Great White Horse" 242
"The Greatest Cowboy of Them All" 152
Green, Bill 243
Green, Douglas B. (Ranger Doug) 12, 48, 115, 117, 158, 190
Green, Jerry 244
Green, Lorne 241
Green, Pat 249, 250
The Green Berets (film) 106
"Green Green Grass of Home" 137
"Green Grow the Lilacs" 150
Green Grow the Lilacs (play) 86
"The Green Leaves of Summer" 105
Greene, Jack 73
Greenspoon, Danny 186
Gregory, Terry 246
Grey, Zane 57, 212
Griffin, Rex 132
Griffis, Ken 46
Griffith, Nanci 247
Grossman, Albert 182, 183, 184
Gruene Hall 219
Gruhn, George 52
Guard, Dave 106
"Guitar Polka" 72
"Gulf Coast Blues" 108
Gunga Din (film) 104
Guns and Guitars (film) 154
Gunsmoke (TV show) 63, 147, 148, 156, 157, 225, 227
Gustafson, Kimberley 200
Gustafson, Wylie 197–200; *see also* Wylie and the Wild West
Guthrie, Jack 238
Guthrie, Woody 126

Hackett, Buddy 213
Haden, Russell 92
"Hadie Brown" 28
Hafstad, Ralph 154
The Hagers 242
Haggard, Marty 247
Haggard, Merle 106, 111, 185, 192, 197, 198, 203, 206, 218, 221, 227, 228, 242, 243, 244, 246, 247
Haggard, Noel 249
Hagler, Skeeter 162
Haldeman, Oakley 68
Hale, Joanne 95, 96
Hale, Monte 2, 31, 48, 58, 94–96, 98, 164–169
Hale, Terry 219, 220
Haley, Bill and the Comets 17
"Half-Breed" 225, 240
"Half My Heart's in Texas" 244
Hall, Harry 27
Hall, Tom T. 228, 243
Hall of Great Westerners 162
Hamblen, Suze (Veeva Ellen Daniels) 77, 83

Hamblin, Stuart 14, 28, 45, 75, 77, 82–85, 89, 90, 91
Hamilburg, Mitch 80, 155, 156
Hamilton, George, IV 241, 242
Hampton, Denise 204
Hampton, Lisa 205, 206, 207
Hampton, R.W. 202–208
Hampton, Wade 202
"Hang 'Em High" 226
"Hang Your Head in Shame" 58
"Hanging Tree" 225, 240
"Hank and Joe and Me" 148, 149
Hannah, Jack 187–192
Hannah, Joe 187–192
Hannah, Lon 187–192
Hannah, Lon, Sr. 187
Hanson, Connie 246
"Happy to Be with You" 149
"Happy Trails" 17, 38, 56, 58, 225, 227
Hardin, John Wesley 150
"Hardin Wouldn't Run" 150
Hargrove, Linda 244
Harlan, Byron 233
Harmony guitar 50, 203
Harrell, Scotty 59, 61, 65, 66
Harris, Emmylou 52, 73, 246
Harris, Marion 234
Harris, Phil 239
Harrison, Charles 234
Harrison, James F. 234
Hart, Charles 234
Hart, Freddie 242
Hart, Guy 51
Hart, William S. 6, 7
Harte, Bret 39
Harvey Girls (film) 77
Harvick, Kerry 250
Haunted Gold (film) 102
Have Gun, Will Travel (TV show) 63, 147, 148, 156, 225
"Have I Told You Lately That I Love You?" 14, 58
Hawkins, Hawkshaw 239
Hawks, Howard 105
Hay, George D. 12, 134
Haycox, Ernest 103
Haydn Quartet 233
Hayes, Bill 225
Hayes, Gabby 36
Hayes, Wade 249
Hayton, Lennie 113
Hayward, Susan 155
Hazard, Donna 246
"He Taught Me How to Yodel" 72
"He Was a Traveling Man" 79
Head, Roy 245
"Heart Aching Blues" 132
Heart of the Rockies (film) 58
"Heartache the Size of Texas" 247
"Heartbreak Hotel" 135, 137
"Heartland" 248
Heather, Jean 16
"Heaven Says Hello" 73
Heckle, Texas Bob 142, 143
The Heckles 243
"He'd Still Love Me" 177
Hee Haw (TV show) 198
Heidt, Horace 236, 237, 238

Heldorado (film) 37
"Hello Frisco!" 234
"Hello Mexico (and Adios Baby to You)" 244
"Hello Texas" 244
Helms, Don 133, 134
"Help" 171
"Help Me Make It Through the Night" 140, 210
Hendrix, Jimi 227
Henning, Paul 81
Heppler, Bob 134
Here Comes Elmer (film) 36
"Here Comes Santa Claus" 30, 68, 226
"Here I Am in Dallas" 243
"Here We Go Again" 160, 161
"Here's to the Horses" 244, 245
"Here's to the Ladies" 105
Herman, Woody 113, 238
Herndon, Ty 249
"He's a Cowboy from Texas" 244
"Hey, Good Lookin'" 193
"Hey La La" 132
"Hey Mr. Bluebird 73
"Hey Porter" 147
"Hiawatha's Vision" 150
Hickok, Wild Bill 3
Hicks, Johnny 131
High Noon (film) 87, 105
"High Noon Theme (Do Not Forsake Me, Oh My Darlin')" 17, 239
"High Ridin' Heroes" 246
The Highwaymen 73, 246
Hildebrandt, Jeff 159
Hill, Brenn 207
Hill, Terrence 206
Hill, Tiny 238, 239
Hill, Tommy 134
"The Hills of Old Wyomin'" 86
Hilo Hawaiian Orchestra 235
Hitchcock, Stan 241
Hitchhike to Happiness (film) 36
"Hitler Lives" 72
"Hi-Yo, Silver" 236
Hobbs, Becky 246
Hoch, Inton 105
Hoffman, Sam 83
Holbrook, Hal 205
"Hold On, Little Dogies, Hold On" 81
"Hold On Partner" 248
"Hold That Critter Down" 28
"Hold to God's Unchanging Hand" 73
Holiday Inn (film) 35
Holloway, Sterling 80
Holly, Doyle 243
Hollywood Barn Dance (radio show) 14, 16, 54, 57, 68; on TV 227
"Hollywood Heroes" 247
Hollywood Walk of Fame 84
Holmes, Floyd "Salty" 45
Holt, Tim 47, 48, 52, 103
Home in Oklahoma (film) 36
"Home in Pasadena" 235
"Home in San Antone" 237

"A Home in the Meadow" 106
"Home on the Range" 112, 235
"Home Sweet Home in Texas" 39
Homer and Jethro 40
Hometown Jamboree (TV show) 227
Hondo (film) 105
"The Honey Song" 42
Honeysuckle Rose (film) 220
"Honky Tonk Stardust Cowboy" 242
Hood, Bobby 245
Hoosier Holiday (film) 36
Hoosier Hot Shots 17, 42, 238
Hootenanny (TV show) 182
Hooven, Herb 165
Hopalong Cassidy 159
Hopalong Cassidy (TV show) 148, 225
Hopalong Cassidy Returns (film) 48
Hope, Bob 63, 177, 178
Hopkins, Claude 235
Hopkins, Lightnin' 126
"Hoppy, Gene and Me" 243
"Hoppy's Gone" 242
Horn, James T. 249
The Horse Soldiers (film) 105
"Horse to Mexico" 249
The Horse Whisperer (film) 167
"Horses" 235
Horton, Johnny 105, 150
Horwitz, Will 15
Hot Club of Cowtown 195
"Hot Rod Lincoln" 71
Hotel de Paree (TV show) 148
"Hottest 'Ex' in Texas" 246
Houston, David 245
"Houston Blue" 245
"Houston Blues" 242
"Houston Heartache" 246
"Houston (I'm Comin' to See You)" 243
Houston Livestock Show and Rodeo 94, 202, 206
"Houston (Means I'm One Day Closer to You)" 246
"Houston Solution" 247
"How a Cowgirl Says Goodbye" 249
"How 'Bout Them Cowgirls" 218
"How Can I Unlove You" 178
"How Many Biscuits Can You Eat?" 14
How the West Was Won (film) 106
Howard, Eddy 238
Howard, Harlan 137
Howard, Ron 106
Howard, Van (Howard Vandevender) 134, 135, 136
Howdy Doody (TV show) 148
"Howl" 213
Huffaker, Clair 106
Huges, Hollie 247
Humphrey, Babe 119
Hunchback of Notre Dame (film) 104
Hunley, Con 246
Huntsman, Ron 162
"Hurt" 152
Hurt, Chick 45

"Hurt as Big as Texas" 244
"The Hyphen" 106

"I Can Almost See Houston from Here" 243
"I Can Still Make Cheyenne" 218, 249
"I Can't Escape from You" 133
"I Don't Care" 73
"I Don't Feel Much Like a Cowboy Tonight" 247
"I Don't Wanna Play House" 178
"I Don't Want to Be Free" 60
"I Dreamed That My Daddy Come Home" 91
"I Drove Her to Dallas" 249
"I Feel Good, I Feel Bad" 122
"I Found You Just in Time" 178
"I Get the Short End Every Time" 132
"I Got Mexico" 246
"I Got Stripes" 148, 149
"I Got the Hoss" 228, 244
"I Got Western Pride" 244
"I Hang My Head and Cry" 47, 48
"I Hope I Like Mexico Blues" 241
"I Just Can't Go on Dying Like This" 220
"I Know I'll Never Win Your Love Again" 133
"I Left My Love" 105
"I Lost the Only Love I Knew" 133
"I Love a Rodeo" 243
"I Love My Daddy, Too" 45
"I Love You So Much It Hurts" 60
"I Made a Mistake and I'm Sorry" 132
"I Musta Died and Gone to Texas" 245
"I Never Go Around Mirrors" 203
"I Never Promised You a Rose Garden" 178
"I Ride an Old Paint" 150
"I Saw Her Standing There" 197
"I Saw My Castles Fall Today" 132
"I Spent the Night in the Heart of Texas" 246
"I Still Miss Someone" 147, 148
"I Tipped My Hat (and Slowly Rode Away)" 238
"I Walk the Line" 147, 157, 181, 197
"I Wanna Be a Cowboy 'Til I Die" 246
"I Wanna Be a Western Cowgirl" 46
"I Want a Cowboy" 250
"I Want a Little Cowboy" 244
"I Want to Be a Cowboy's Dream Girl" 45
"I Want to Be a Cowboy's Sweetheart" 44, 45, 46, 72, 225, 236, 238, 247
"I Want to Go Home" 148
"I Wish I Had a Nickel" 60
"I Won't Go Huntin' with You Jake (But I'll Go Chasin' Women)" 84
"I Won't Mention It Again" 140
"I Wonder Where You Are Tonight" 60, 71
Ian and Sylvia 182, 183, 185
The Ian Tyson Show (TV show) 184
"I'd Rather Be Sorry" 140
"Idaho" 237
"Idaho State Fair" 239
"If I Kiss You (Will You go Away)" 177
"If You Ever Get to Houston (Look Me Down)" 244
"If You Knew" 106
"If You're Ever Lonely Darling" 132
"If You're Gonna Play in Texas" 246
"If You're Thinking You Want a Stranger" 221
"I'll Be a Cowboy Till I Die" 57
"I'll Be Your San Antone Rose" 243
"I'll Go on Alone" 144
"I'll Go Ridin' Down That Texas Trail" 81
"I'll Take You Home Again, Kathleen" 104
"I'm a Barefooted Mama" 42
"I'm a Cowboy" 249
"I'm a Do-Right Cowboy" 86
"I'm a Natural Born Cowboy" 86
"I'm a Newborn Man" 151
"I'm an Old Cowhand (From the Rio Grande)" 112
"I'm Getting Good at Missing You (Solitaire)" 172
"I'm Giving You Denver" 244
"I'm Gonna Be a Cowboy" 199
"I'm Gonna Miss You, Girl" 124
"I'm Gonna Try to Be That Way" 151
"I'm in Love and He's in Dallas" 247
"I'm Oscar, I'm Pete" 80
"I'm Sending You Red Roses" 60
"I'm Shooting High" 236
"I'm So Lonesome I Could Cry" 152
"I'm Stickin' with You" 160
"I'm the Medicine Man for the Blues" 235
"I'm Wastin' My Tears on You" 226
"I'm Wishing for the One I Love" 90
Imperial Records 131, 134
"In a Covered Wagon with You" 235
"In a Little Spanish Town" 235, 240
"In Del Rio" 241
"In My Life" 152, 171
In Old Arizona (film) 7
In Old California (film) 104
In Old Monterey (film) 29
In Old Oklahoma (film) 36, 104
In Old Santa Fe (film) 19, 20, 25, 51, 80
"In Person" 177
"In the Baggage Coach Ahead" 56
"In the Misty Moonlight" 73
The Incredible Journey (film) 98
"Indian Creek" 243
"Indian Giver" 243
"Indian Lake" 242
"Indian Love Call" 225, 235, 236, 239, 243
"Indian Nation" 243, 248
Ingle, Red 239
"Invitation to the Blues" 136
Irby, Jerry 239
The Iron Horse (film) 7
Irving Berlin, Inc. 112
"Is Anybody Goin' to San Antone" 227, 242
Island in the Sky (film) 105
Isley, Phil 94
"It Is No Secret (What God Can Do)" 72, 84
"It Makes No Difference Now" 45, 67
"It Never Rains in Southern California" 249
"It Wasn't God Who Made Honky-tonk Angels" 177
"It's a Cowboy Lovin' Night" 244
"It's a Lonely Trail (When You're Travelin' All Alone)" 236
"It's Indian Summer" 81
"It's My Lazy day" 80, 81
"It's Over" 171
"I've Been Everywhere" 177
"I've Done the Best I Could" 86
"I've Got to Hurry, Hurry, Hurry" 133
"I've Rode with the Best" 243
Ives, Burl 197, 239

J. Walter Thompson Agency 67
Jackson, Alan 125, 228, 248, 249
Jackson, Stonewall 241
Jackson, Tommy 135
Jackson, Wanda 241
Jacobs, Jake 189
James, George 244
James, Harry 54, 187, 238
James, Sonny 73, 227, 242, 243, 244
James, Will 165, 181
The Jazz Singer (film) 7
"Jealous Lies" 131
Jean, Norman 177
"Jeannie with the Light Brown hair" 103
Jefferson, Blind Lemon 168
Jefferson Airplane 183
Jeffries, Jim 131
Jenkins, Carl 133
Jennings, Waylon 114, 118, 158, 159, 184, 219, 227, 228, 242, 246, 247
"Jesus Is the Same in California" 243
"Jim, I Wore a Tie Today" 73
"Jingle Jangle Jingle" 86, 225, 237
JMI Records 99
"Jo and the Cowboy" 243
Joco Records 155

"John Henry" 149
"John Wayne Walking Away" 249
"John Wesley Hardin" 225, 240
Johnny Ringo (TV show) 148
Johns, August Wayne 34
Johnson, Betty 70
Johnson, Elsie 132
Johnson, Pres. Lyndon B. 219
Johnson, Michael 247
Johnson, Sleepy 112
Johnson, Col. W.T. 47, 51
Johnston, Bob 123, 124
Johnston, W. Ray 94, 103
The Johnston Brothers 240
"The Johnstown Flood" 82
Jolson, Al 235
Jon Bon Jovi 249
Jones, Buck 102
Jones, David Lynn 247
Jones, Dick 155, 156, 157
Jones, George 193, 218, 220
Jones, Grandpa 241
Jones, Isham 234, 236
Jones, Nora 160
Jones, Stan 115
Joplin, Janis 227
Junior Rodeo (TV show) 148
Jurgens, Dick 236, 237, 238
"Just a Kid from Texas" 247
"Just Another Cowboy Song" 243
"Just the Other Side of Nowhere" 210
"Just Try Texas" 247

"Kansas City Lights" 246
"Kansas City Song" 242
"Kansas City Star" 241
Kapp Records 110
Kaufman, Irving 234
"Kaw-Liga" 198, 240, 242, 245
Kaye, Sammy Kaye 237, 238
KDHL (Northfield, MN) 154
"Keep Me in Mind" 178
"Keeping Up Appearances" 177
Keith, Toby 170, 248, 250
Kelly, Joe 17
The Kendalls 220
Kennedy, Jerry 140
Kenny Rogers and the American Cowboy (TV show) 206
Kenton, Stan 76, 238
The Kentucky Headhunters 248
Kerouac, Jack 182
Kerr, Anita 138
Kerr, Joe 194
KFDI (Wichita, KS) 158
KFI (Los Angeles) 13, 90, 92
KFJF (Kansas City) 12
KFOX (Los Angeles) 16, 29
KFPI (Milford, Kansas) 39
KFRU (Bristow, OK) 12
KFWB (Los Angeles) 14, 27, 90
KGER (Los Angeles) 26
KGKB (Palestine, TX) 56
KGMP (Elk City, OK) 54
KGO (San Francisco) 54
KHJ (Los Angeles) 16, 29
KICA (Clovis, NM) 134
KIL (St. Louis) 39

Kilgore, Jerry 249
Kilgore, Merle 149
Killen, Buddy 133, 135
Kincaid, Bradley 12, 40, 41, 50, 51
King, Blanche 233
King, Claude 106, 225, 241
King, Dusty 55
King, Pee Wee (and the Golden West Cowboys) 15, 16, 239
King of the Cowboys (film) 29
King of the Pecos (film) 103
"King of the Road" 137
King Records (131)
King Sisters (Donna, Alice, Yvonne and Louise) 68
Kingsberry, Paul 214
Kingston, Al 102
The Kingston Trio 96, 182, 193
Kirchener, Don 122, 123
Kirk, Jack 24, 100
KLIF (Dallas) 131
Kline, Olive 234
KMBC (Kansas City) 14, 41
KMIC (Los Angeles) 82
KMJ (Fresno, CA) 13
KMON (Great Falls, MT) 197
KMOX (St. Louis) 39
KMPC (Los Angeles) 14
KMTR (now KLAC) 29, 44, 82, 83, 109
Knapp, Evalyn 19
Knight, Evelyn 238
Knight, Fuzzy 98
Knox, Buddy 160
KNX (Los Angeles) 13, 29, 45, 68
Koki, Sam 28
KOY (Phoenix) 97
KPHO (Phoenix) 143
Kragen, Ken 206
Krall, Diana 73
Kramer, Fred 112
Kristofferson, Kris 139, 140, 151, 184, 201, 206, 212
KRLD (Dallas) 131
Kruble, Leroy 55
Krupa, Gene 238
KTHS (Hot Springs, ARK) 46
KTLA (Los Angeles) 70
KTM (Los Angeles) 14
KTOK (Stillwater, OK) 61
KTSA San Antonio 13
"Kum Ba Yah" 121
Kuykendall, Dan 87
KVOO (Tulsa, OK) 12, 13, 25, 109
KWEM (Memphis, TN) 146
Kyser, Kay 237

Labour, Fred (Too Slim) 115, 116
LaBour, Roberta 116
Ladd, Alan 105
"Ladies Love Outlaws" 243
Lady for the Night (film) 104
"Lady Takes the Cowboy Every Time" 246
Laemmle, Carl 19
LaFarge, Peter 149, 150
Laine, Frankie 239
Lair, John 40
Lamar, Howard 168

L'Amour, Louis 105, 212
Landau, Marty 172
Lane, Jerry 177
Lane, Red 242
Lanier, Don 160, 161
Lanin, Sam 235
Lanny Fiel's Studio (Lubbock) 204
Laramie (TV show) 148
"Laredo" 249
Larkin, Billy 243
Las Vegas 60, 63, 76, 166, 173, 174, 175, 190
Lash of the West (TV show) 148
The Last Command (film) 105
The Last Cowboy (play) 205
"Last Cowboy Song" 245
"Last Gunfighter Ballad" 244
"Last of the Outlaws" 243
Last of the Pony Riders (film) 69, 80
"Last of the Silver Screen Cowboys" 99, 170, 246
"Last of the Sunshine Cowboys" 227, 243
The Last Picture Show (film) 219
"The Last Roundup" 67, 112, 235
Law, Don 131, 135, 150
"The Law Is for the Protection of the People" 210
Law of the Plainsman (TV show) 148
Lawless Code (film) 63
The Lawless Frontier (film) 102, 103
The Lawless Range (film) 103
The Lawman (TV show) 148
Lawrence, Elliot 238
Lawrence, Tracy 248, 249
Lawrence Welk Show (TV) 177
Layman, Zora 14
"Lead Me Father" 147
"Leanin' on the Ole Top Rail" 237
Ledford, Lily May 13, 39
LeDoux, Chris 46, 216–217, 244, 245, 248, 249
LeDoux, Peg 216
Lee, Brenda 138, 177, 245
Lee, Dickie 115
Lee, Johnny 245, 246
Lee, Peggy 239
Lee, Roberta 239
Lee, Spike 95
LeFevre, Jimmy and His Saddle Pals 90
Leftcourt, Leo 156
Lefton, Abe 67
"Legend of John Henry's Hammer" 149
The Legend of Lobo (film) 98
Le Grand, Allen 144
Lehr, Sammy 58
Lehr, Zella 245
Lennon Sisters 177
"Let Jesse Rob the Train" 245
"Let Me Talk to you" 135
"Let Old Mother Nature Have Her Way" 155
"Let That Pony Run" 248
"Let the Cowboy Dance" 248
"Let the Train Whistle Blow" 152

Index

"Let's All Help the Cowboy (Sing the Blues)" 227, 243
"Let's Go Roaming Around the Range" 81
"Let's Go to Church (Next Sunday Morning)" 60
"The Letter That Johnny Walker Read" 195
Levertov, Denise 213
Levine, Nat 18, 19, 20, 24, 25, 102, 103
Lewis, C.S. 121
Lewis, Jerry Lee 198
Lewis, Ted 235
Lewis, Texas Jim 14
The Lewis and Clark Expedition 122
Liberty Pictures 103, 110
Life and Legend of Wyatt Earp (TV show) 17, 63, 147, 148, 225
"Life's Like Poetry" 203
Light Crust Doughboys 16, 61, 82, 113, 131
Lightnin' Express (film) 44
"Lights of Albuquerque" 247
Lights of Old Santa Fe (film) 36
"Like a Soldier" 152
"Like an Oklahoma Morning" 247
Likona, Terry 115
"The Lilac Bush" 197
"Listen to a Country Song" 178
Little, Jack 236
Little Big Town Publisher 212
"Little Buffalo Bill" 155
Little Doc Roberts Traveling Medicine Show 61
"Little Grey Home in the West" 234
"Little Ground in Texas" 245
"Little Joe, the Wrangler" 204
Little Miss Broadway (film) 75
"Little Ole Log Cabin Down the Lane" 12, 229
"Little Rag Doll" 83
"The Little Red Hen" 197
"Little Red Rodeo" 249
"Little Rosewood Casket" 56
Little Texas (group) 248
"A Little White Cross on the Hill" 226
"Littlest Cowboy Rides Again" 243
The Littlest Rebel (film) 75
Livingston, Bob 80, 103, 123
Log Cabin Dude Ranch (radio show) 42
Lohr, Paul 116
Lomax, John 11, 164, 167
Lombardo, Guy 235, 236, 239
"The Lone Cowboy" 79
The Lone Ranger (TV show) 147, 148, 225
"Lone Star Beer and Bob Wills Music" 228, 243
"Lone Star State of Mind" 247
"Lone Star Trail" 73, 237
"Lonely River" 47, 48
"Lonely Street" 171, 172
The Lonely Trail (film) 103
"Lonesome Cowgirl" 39

Lonesome Dove (novel) 219
"Lonesome Is a Cowboy" 243
Lonestar (group) 249
"Lonestar Cowboy" 245
"Lonestar Lonesome" 247
"A Long Line of Love" 124, 190
"Long Long Texas Road" 242
"Long Tall Texan" 249
"Long Trail of Tears" 249
The Longest Day (film) 106
Longfellow, Henry Wadsworth 150
"Longneck Lone Star (And Two Step Dancin')" 247
Lopez, Vincent 234
"Lopez the Bandit" 83
Lord, Mike 247
Los Angeles Angels 31, 188, 189
Los Canyon Rangers (group) 78
"Lost in Austin" 245, 247
Louise Massey and the Westerners *see* Massey, Louise
Louisiana Hayride 46, 134
"Love Affairs" 124
"Love Is a Warm Cowboy" 245
Love Me Tender (film) 135
"Love Song in 32 Bars" 71
"Love Song of the Waterfall" 28
"Love Without End" 186
Lovett, Lyle 247, 249
Lowe, Jim 240
Lubbock, Texas 204
"Luckenbach, Texas (Back to the Basics of Love)" 228, 244
Lucky Stars Radio Show 83
The Lucky Texan (film) 102
The Lucky U Ranch (radio show) 30, 31
Lulu Belle and Scotty, 14, 17, 39, 40, 91, 98
Luther, Frank 14, 56, 236
Lynn, Judy 243
Lynn, Loretta 221, 227, 242

Mabie, Milt 42
Mabry, Bill 220
MacDonald, Jeanette 75, 236
Macdonough, Harry 233
Mack Sennett Studios 103
MacKenzie, Gisele 239
MacKintosh and T.J. (film) 31
MacRae, Gordon 239
Madison Square Garden 51, 62, 66, 68
Magnificent Seven (film) 17
Maher, Wally 68
Majestic Pictures 103
Majestic Records 58
"Make the World Go Away" 137
"Makin' Up for Lost Time (The Dallas Lovers' Song)" 247
Malchak, Tim 247
Malone, Bill C. 16
"Mama Don't 'Low No Music in Here" 19, 79, 80
"Mama Spank" 177
"Mamas Don't Let Your Babies Grow Up to Be Cowboys" 114, 228, 243, 244, 248, 245
"A Man Called Peter" 135

The Man from Monterey (film) 102
The Man from U.N.C.L.E. (TV show) 157
Man from Utah (film) 102
"A Man Gets to Thinking" 106
"The Man on the Hill" 148
"Man Walks Amongst Us" 203
"The Man Who Couldn't Cry" 152
"The Man Who Robbed the Bank at Santa Fe" 241
("The Man Who Shot) Liberty Valance" 106
The Man Who Shot Liberty Valance (film) 106
Mandrell, Barbara 173
Manners, Zeke 72, 238
"The Mansion on the Hill" 124
Maphis, Joe 14, 76, 92
Maphis, Rose Lee 76, 77, 92
Marcos, Peter 156
"Maria Elena" 60
"Marina Del Ray" 221
"Marine's Let's Go" 98
Markey, Patrick 167
Marquis, David 205
Marriott, John 247
Martin, Bob 135
Martin, Dean 73, 105
Martin, Dude 55
Martin, Freddy 237, 238
Martin, Grady 138
Martin, Pepper 189
Martin, Tony 187, 236
Martin, Troy 131, 132, 135
Martin Guitars 51, 52
Marvell, James 245
Marvin, Frankie 68
Marvin, Johnny 29, 61, 63
Mascot Pictures 8, 18, 24, 25, 102, 103
Mason Dixon 246
Massey, Allen 41, 42
Massey, Curt 41, 42
Massey, Louise and the Westerners 2, 14, 16, 41–43, 98, 237, 238
"The Matador" 149, 241, 245
"Matamoros" 241
"Matilda Higgins" 79
Mattea, Kathy 248
Matthews, Melva 184, 192
Matthews, Willie 212
Maverick (TV show) 17, 63, 148, 225, 245
Maynard, Ken 8, 18, 20, 25, 26, 51, 80, 102
MCA Booking Agency 109
MCA Records 116, 161, 220, 221
McAluiffe, Harry (Big Slim and the Lone Star Cowboy) 16
McBride, Leonard 132
McCall, C.W. 243, 244
McCall, Darrel 243, 245, 246
McCallum, Paul 167
McCann, Lila 249
McCarthy, Charlie 35
McClintock (film) 106
McCluskey, William "Bill" 39, 40
McCormack, John 234
McCoy, Tim 102

McDonald, Slim 131
McDowell, Ronnie 244
McEntire, Reba 125, 162, 173, 228
McGhee, Brownie 126
McGill, Tony 247
McGraw, Tim 248, 249, 250
McIntire, John 14
McKinley, Pres. William 6
McLemore, Ed 131
McMahon, Gary 190
McMichen, Clayton 15
McMurtry, Larry 219
McVey, Tyler 68
"Me and My Broken Heart" 172
"Mean as Hell" 150
"Meanwhile Back at the Ranch" 249
Mears, Martha 30
Medicine Ball Caravan 194
"Medicine Woman" 244
Meek, Donald 103
Meglin, Ethel 75
Meiklejohn, Bill 35
"A Melody from the Sky" 86
Melody Ranch (CBS radio show) 16, 24, 29, 30, 48, 62, 66, 67, 68, 69, 155, 165
Melody Ranch (film) 80
Melody Ranch (TV show) 70
Melody Trail (film) 27
Memphis Chicks 189
Mercer, Johnny 112, 237, 238
Mercury Records 98, 99, 135, 140
MerleFest 168
"Merry Christmas from Texas Y'all" 249
The Merry Macs 91, 237
Mevis, Blake 220
"Mexicali Rose" 67, 236
"Mexican Girl" 245
"Mexican Joe" 224, 225, 240
"Mexican Love Songs" 244
"Mexico" 246
"Mexico Joe" 237
"Mexico Winter" 245
MGM Pictures 101
MGM Records 95
MGM Studio 172
Michener, James 219
Midnight Frolic (radio show) 26
"Midnight Rodeo" 246
Midwestern Hayride (Cincinnati TV show) 17, 40
"Mighty Lak a Rose" 33
"Miles and Miles of Texas" 244
Miller, Glenn 54, 113, 164, 187, 236, 237, 238
Miller, Mitch 156
Miller, Ray 235
Miller, Roger 136, 137, 227, 241, 242, 243
Mills, Jay Orchestra 34
The Mills Brothers 238
Milsap, Ronnie 245, 247
Milwaukee Braves 187
"Mine All Mine" 60
"Mis Raices Estan Aqui" 106
Miskulin, Joey 115, 117, 118
"Miss Molly 73

"Missin' Texas" 247
Mission Mountain Wood Band 198
"The Missouri Waltz" 89
Mr. Smith Goes to Washington (film) 104
Mitchell, Albert 204
Mitchell, Thomas 103
Mitchell, Waddie 125, 162, 167, 185, 191, 201, 209–215
Mitchum, Robert 106
Mix, Tom 7, 18, 101, 165
Mize, Billy 70, 242
"Mocking Bird Hill" 72
"Modern Day Cowboy" 247
Moffatt, Katy 124, 243, 246
"Moffett, Oklahoma" 242
"Moisture" 186
Molak, Pat 219
"Molly (And the Texas Rain)" 245
"Mona Lisa" 60
The Monk lonious 126
The Monkees 122, 123
Monogram Pictures 42, 63, 94, 100, 102, 103
Monroe, Bill 229
Monroe, Vaughn 154, 224, 238, 239
Montana, Patsy 2, 13, 14, 15, 39, 44–46, 56, 72, 98, 117, 236
"Montana Plains" 45, 46
Montenegro, Hugo 226
Montgomery, John Michael 248, 249
Montgomery Ward 51
Monument Records 139
Monument Valley 103, 105
Mooney, Ralph 135
"Moonlight on the Prairie" 25
Moore, Gary 37
Moore, Grace 39
Moore, Robin 106
Moore, Scotty 52
Morgan, Al 239
Morgan, Charlie 54
Morgan, George 73
Morgan, Jaye P. 54
Morgan, Russ 236
Morris, Elida 234
Morrison, Jim 227
Morrison, Van 73
Morrow, Cory 249
Morton, Gary 167
"Mother, May I" 177
"Move It on Over" 193
"Move on In and Stay" 133
Mowrey, Dude 248
MTV 152
"Much Too Young (to Feel This Damn Old)" 216, 247
"Mule Train" 224, 239
Mullican, Moon 225, 239
Mullins, Cam 138, 140
Mullins, Dee 241
Murphey, Mark 247
Murphey, Michael Martin 2, 46, 121–128, 167, 171, 190, 200, 205, 211, 228, 244, 247, 248
Murphey, Ryan 124
Murphy, Joaquin 54
Murray, Anne 242

Murray, Billy 233, 235
Music Country USA (TV show) 162
Music Row 135
Mutual Broadcasting System 29, 30
"My Adobe Hacienda" 42, 225, 237, 238
"My Blue Heaven" 168
"My Brown Eyed Texas Rose" 82
"My First Taste of Texas" 246
My Friend Flicka (film) 147
"My Gal Is Purple" 105
"My Grandfather's Clock" 148, 149
"My Guns Are Loaded" 244
"My Heart Cries to You" 60
"My Heroes Have Always Been Cowboys" 245
"My Little Buckaroo" 236
"My Little Canoe" 233
"My Love Is a Rider" 39
"My Lulu" 103
"My Mary" 82
"My Old Scrapbook" 133
"My Own Kind of Hat" 244, 249
"My Prairie Song Bird" 233
"My Rifle, My Pony and Me" 105
"My Shoes Keep Walking Back to You" 136
"My Treasure" 147
"My Woman, My Woman, My Wife" 203
Myers, J.W. 233
Mystery Mountain (serial) 8, 19, 20, 80

N Bar K Musical Showroom (ABC radio show) 58
NASCAR 145
Nash, Bill 140
Nashville 107, 110, 112, 115, 120, 133, 135, 136, 139, 142, 144, 149, 149, 161, 166, 168, 172, 173, 174, 176, 177, 179, 183, 184, 185, 191, 193, 199, 211, 212, 219, 220
Nashville Songwriters Hall of Fame 74, 84
Nashville Sound 129, 137, 194, 227
Nashville Superpickers (group) 245
Nation, Buck 15, 47
Nation, Tex Ann 47
National Barn Dance (film) 16
National Barn Dance (WLS: Chicago) 8, 12, 16, 25, 29, 36, 37, 39, 40, 42, 47, 50, 79, 98
National Cowboy and Western Heritage Museum 99, 162, 163
National Cowgirl Hall of Fame 46
National Jamboree 72
National Public Radio (NPR) 228
"Navajo" 233
"Navajo Rug" 185
'Neath the Arizona Skies (film) 102
Nelson, Grace 233
Nelson, Ozzie 237
Nelson, Ricky 105
Nelson, Willie Nelson 114, 118, 136, 137, 175, 184, 194, 219, 220,

227, 228, 241, 244, 245, 246, 250
Nesmith, Michael 122
"Never" 76, 92
"Never Coming Back Again" 172
"Never Givin' Up on Love" 124
New Christy Minstrels 122
New Frontier (film) 104
"New San Antonio Rose" 112, 237
"New Spanish Two-Step" 238
"New York Cowboy" 245
Newman, Randy 244
Newport Folk Festival 182
Newton, Juice 246
Newton, Wayne 140
"The Next Voice You Hear" 73
Nichols, Bill "Slumber" 26, 27
Nichols, Red 235
"Night Life" 137
"Night on the Desert" 236
The Nightrider (film) 157
Nine Inch Nails 152
Nitty Gritty Dirt Band 122, 246
"No Easy Horses" 247
"No, No, No (I'd Rather Be Free)" 172
"No One to Cry To" 58
"Nobody in His Right Mind (Would've Left Her)" 220
Nolan, Bob 14, 26, 28, 30, 77, 93, 113, 114, 115, 117, 171, 186
Norman, Jim Ed 211
North of '36 (film) 7
North Texas Agricultural College 130
North Texas State University 121
"North to Alaska" 106
North to Alaska (film) 105
Northeastern University 193
"Northwest Passage" 225, 238
Northwest Rebellion (group) 184
Northwestern University 86
Norwood, Daron 248
"Not Another Time" 177
"Nothin' but Cowboy Boots" 250
Nudie the Rodeo Tailor 155

"O Come, Angel Band" 151
The Oak Ridge Boys 220, 221, 244
Oakley, Annie 6
Oatman, Mike 162
O'Brien, George 47, 47
O'Brien, Rich 205, 206
Oceans, Lucky 193, 194
O'Connell, Chris 194
O'Connell, Helen 239
O'Connor, Mark 171
O'Daniel, W. Lee "Pappy" 15, 108, 131
O'Dell, Kenny 244
Odetta 182
Oh Boy Records 199
"Oh Bury Me Not" 152
"Oh That Navajo Rug" 233
"Oh Those Texas Women" 243
"Oh, What a Beautiful Morning" 36
"(Oh Why, Oh Why, Did I Ever Leave) Wyoming" 225, 238

O'Hea, Shad 243
"Okie from Muskogee" 227, 242
"Oklahoma" 249
Oklahoma (musical) 29, 36, 86
"Oklahoma Borderline" 247
"Oklahoma Crude" 246
"Oklahoma Heart" 246
"Oklahoma Hills" 155, 225, 238, 241
"Oklahoma Home Brew" 242
"Oklahoma Sunday Morning" 242
"Oklahoma Sunshine" 243
"Oklahoma Swing" 248
"Oklahoma-Texas Line" 250
"Oklahoma Waltz" 71
"Oklahoma Waltz" 239
"Old Apache Squaw" 148, 149, 150
The Old Barn Dance (film) 28
"Old Blue" 197
"Old Cheyenne" 185
"Old Chisholm Trail" 39, 168
The Old Corral (film) 27
"The Old Covered Wagon" 81
"Old Coyote Town" 247
"An Old Fashioned Tree" 68
"Old Glory Blowout 6
"The Old Hen Cackl'd and the Rooster's Gonna Crow" 12
The Old Homestead (film) 27
"Old Pinto" 42
"Old Showboat" 241
Old Time Country Music Hall of Fame 159
The Old Wyoming Trail (film) 28
"Ole Faithful" 236
Olsen, George 235
Olson, James S. 101, 102, 104, 107
O'Malley, Scott 192, 207, 212
"On a Little Dream Ranch" 236
"On Earth as It Is in Texas" 249
"On the Alamo" 234, 240
"On the Atchison, Topeka, and the Santa Fe" 225, 238
"On the Old Spanish Trail" 238
"On the Strings of My Lonesome Guitar" 81
"On the Trail" ("Grand Canyon Suite") 235, 240
"On the Wrong Side of the Fence" 236
"On Top of Old Smoky" 239
On Top of Old Smoky (film) 80
"One Has My Name (The Other Has My Heart)" 60
"160 Acres" 238
"One Less Pony" 248
"One More Ride" 147
"One Morning in May" 186
"The One on the Right Is on the Left" 149
O'Neil, Kerry 212
"Orange Blossom Special" 149
Orbison, Roy 73, 139, 247
Orchestra Wives (film) 35
Orion 245
Osborne, Mel 61, 65
Osborne, Will 236
Osmond, Marie 247
Ott, Paul 244

Otto Gray & His Oklahoma Cowboys 12, 13, 15
"Our House Is Not a Home" 177
"Our Little Ranch House" 239
"Out on the Lone Prairie" 86
Outlaw Movement 114, 227
"Outlaws and Lone Star Beer" 244
"Outlaw's Prayer" 244
Ovation guitar 203
"Over the Next Hill" 151
Overland Stage Raiders (film) 103
Owens, Buck 161, 197, 199, 216, 242, 243, 245
Owens, Tex 14, 91
Ozark Jubilee (Springfield, Missouri, TV show) 17
The Ozark Jubilee (TV show) 227

Pacific Coast League 188
Pack Train (film) 80
"Paddle Your Own Canoe" 233
"Padre" 240, 242, 243
Page, Patti 55, 73, 239
Paige, Mabel 17
"Paladin Theme" 17, 156, 157, 159, 225
Palamino (North Hollywood club) 199
Paleface (film) 177
Pals of the Saddle (film) 103
"Pancho and Lefty" 170, 246
Paradise Canyon (film) 102
Paramount Pictures 16, 28, 34, 42, 48, 103
Parker, Andy (and the Plainsmen) 54–55, 92, 117
Parker, Charlie 126
Parker, Fess 225
Parker, Linda 39
Parker, Col. Tom 222
Parkin, John 205
"Party Doll" 160
"Pass That Peace Pipe" 239
Pastor, Tony 238
Patchen, Kenneth 213
Paul, Johnny 58, 59
Paul, Les 58, 76, 240
Paul, Woody (Paul Chrisman) 115, 117
Paycheck, Johnny 136, 137, 244
"Pecos Bill" 225, 239
"Pecos Promenade" 245
Peebles, Hap 158
Peer International Publishing 131, 135
The Peerless Quartet 234
"Peg Leg Jack" 79
Peggy Sue 245
Pennington, Ray 241
Penny, Hank 40, 91
Penny, Lee 42
"The People" 106
"People Will Say We're in Love" 36
"A Perfect Lie" 220
Perkins, Luther 147
Perryman, Lloyd 28, 29, 30, 114
"Peter Cottontail" 60, 227

Index

Peter, Paul and Mary 182
Peter Potter's Hollywood Barn Dance 16, 29
Peters, Bill 134
Peters, Lyman 82, 83
Petticoat Junction (TV show) 42, 81
Petty, Norman 240
Phantom Empire 8, 18, 20–24, 25, 26
Phantom Stallion (film) 31, 98
Phelps Brothers (Earl, Willie and Norman) 47
Phillips, Foreman 92
Phillips, Sam 147
"Phoenix Flash" 241
Pickard Family 15
Pickens, Slim 98, 171
"Pickin' Time" 147
Pierce, Webb Pierce 73, 136, 225, 226, 241
Pi-Gem publishing 220
"Pilgrims on the Way (Matthew's Song)" 124
The Pinafores 68
Pink Cadillac (film) 124
"Pistol Packin' Mama" 112, 224, 225, 237
Pitney, Gene 106
Pittman, Walter 203
Pittsburgh (film) 104
"Place Where I Worship (Is the Wide Open Spaces)" 239
The Plainsmen 54
"Planet Texas" 246
Plantation Party (NBC radio show) 42
"Plastic Saddle" 241
Platt, Louise 103
"Playboys of the Southwestern World" 250
"The Pledge of Allegiance" 106
Plumb, Neely 58, 59
Poe, Edgar Allan 212
"Ponies" 247
Pony Express (TV show) 148
"Poor Unlucky Cowboy" 83
"Poor Wayfarin' Stranger" 106
"Port of Lonely Hearts" 147
Porter, Edwin S. 6
Portis, Charles 106
Potter, Curtis 245
Potter, Peter 16
Powell, Dick 61
Powell, Eleanor 35
The Prairie Farmer (publication) 12
The Prairie Ramblers 14, 16, 39
Prairie Rose Wranglers 159
Prairie Stranger (film) 57
PRC Studio 54
Presley, Elvis 17, 52, 73, 126, 135, 144, 181, 222, 226, 227
Preston, LeRoy 193
Preston, Lew 57
Price, Chuck 243
Price, Georgie 235
Price, Janie Mae 139
Price, Kenny 242

Price, Ray 129–141, 161, 165, 221
Pride, Charley 203, 227, 242, 244
Prine, John 199
"The Prisoner's Song" 50
"Promises Promises" 177
Pruett, Jack 135
Pruett, Sammy 133
Pugh, Fred 58
Pulley, Ray 132
Pure Country (film) 218, 222
"Put Your Arms Around Me Honey" 104
"Put Your Little Shoes Away, Little Joe" 56

"Quicksilver" 72
The Quiet Man (film) 105
Quigley, Charles 17
Quinlan, Roberta 239
Quinn, Dan 233
Quirk, Charlie 29

Rabbitt, Jimmy and Renegade 243
"Radio Land" 124
Radio Scout (film) 27
"Ragtime Cowboy Joe" 225, 233, 236, 238, 239
"Railroad Lady" 203
"Rainbow Valley" 236
Rainbow Valley (film) 102
"Raining on the Mountain" 91
Rainwater, Marvin 225, 240
"Raise a Ruckus Tonight" 106
"Ramblin' Man" 241
Ramsey, Buck 162
Ranch Party (TV show) 77
"Rancho Grande" 236
Rancho Grande (film) 65
"Rancho Padre" 42
Randy Rides Alone (film) 102
Range Busters (serial) 62, 66
Range Feud (film) 102
Range Rider (TV show) 148, 156
Rascal Flatts 250
Raven, Eddy 172, 227, 243, 245, 249
Rawhide (TV show) 63, 148, 225
Ray, Johnnie 143
Ray, Will 199
Ray Doggett Studio 220
Raye, Collin 249
Raye, Susan 242
RCA (and RCA Victor) Records 70, 72, 135, 176, 177, 220
RCA Studio B 220
Reagan, President Ronald 14, 88
"Real Cowboy (You Say You're)" 245
Reap the Wild Wind (film) 104
"The Rebel Johnny Yuma" 149, 225, 241
The Rebel, Johnny Yuma (TV show) 17, 148
"Red and Rio Grande" 248
Red River (film) 104
Red River Dave 15
Red River Range (film) 103
Red Steagall Cowboy Gathering 162

"Red Wing (An Indian Fable)" 233, 238
"Redemption" 152
Redford, Robert 167, 168, 220
Reed, James 234
Reed, Jerry 245
Reeves, Del 242
Reeves, Jim 73, 197, 225, 227, 240, 241
"Reflections" 150,151
Reid, Don 173
Reid, Harold 173
Reinhart, Dick 57, 62, 66
The Reinsmen 99, 190
Reisman, Leo 236
"Remember Me" 14
"(Remember Me) I'm the One Who Loves You" 84
Ren Records 166
Renfro Valley Barn Dance (radio show) 39
"Reno" 241, 248
"Reno and Me" 246
"Reno Bound" 247
"Renosa" 246
Republic Pictures 8, 24, 28, 29, 30, 36, 37, 48, 58, 61, 80, 84, 94, 98, 100, 103, 104, 105
Republic Records 71
Resisman, Louis 235
The Restless Gun (TV show) 147
"Return of the Gay Caballero" 235
Reunion in France (film) 104
Reveille Roundup Program (NBC radio show) 42
Rex, Tim and Oklahoma 245
Rexroth, Kenneth 213
Reynolds, Burt 179
Reynolds, Debbie 106
Reynolds, George 133
"Rhinestone Cowboy" 227, 243
Rhodes, Betty Jane 238
Rhythm on the Range (film) 27
Rice, Bill 242
Rice, Darol 58, 59
Rice, Glen "Mr. Tallfeller" 14
Rice, Tony 168
Rich, Charlie 106
Rich, Don 242
Richardson, Ethel Park 14
Riddle, Nelson 63
"Ride, Concrete Cowboy, Ride" 245
"Ride, Cowboy, Ride" 170, 174, 175, 177, 246
"Ride 'Em Cowboy" 227, 243, 246
"Ride 'Em High, Ride 'Em Low" 248
Ride Him Cowboy (film) 102
"Ride, Ride, Ride" 241
"Ride That Bull (Big Bertha)" 245
"Rider in the Rain" 244
"Riders in the Sky" 224, 228, 239, 242, 244
Riders in the Sky 2, 46, 114–118, 158, 159, 170, 185, 190, 200, 228
Riders of Destiny (film) 100
Riders of the Purple Sage (novel) 57
"Ridin' All Day" 81

Index

"Ridin' Down That Old Texas Trail" 42
"Ridin' Down the Canyon" 19, 81, 113
"Ridin' Home" 25
"Ridin' for a Fall" 248
"Ridin' My Thumb to Mexico" 227, 242
"Ridin' Rainbows" 244
"Riding Old Paint Leading Old Bald" 83
The Rifleman (TV show) 63, 148
Riley, Jeannie C. 242
Rime, LeAnn 249
Rin Tin Tin (TV show) 148
Rinehart, Nolan "Cowboy Slim" 15
"Ring of Fire" 149
"Ringo" 241
"Rio Bravo" 105
Rio Bravo (film) 105
Rio Grande (film) 104, 105
Ritter, Dorothy 87
Ritter, Tex 1, 2, 14, 28, 31, 42, 47, 51, 52, 54, 55, 56, 63, 69, 71, 77, 86–88, 91, 92, 102, 109, 113, 114, 126, 150, 155, 166, 175, 186, 218, 226, 239, 240, 242
A River Runs Through It (film) 167
Riverboat (TV show) 148
"Riverboat Gambler" 225, 240
Rivers, Jerry 133, 134
Rivkin, Joe 34, 35
RKO Pictures 48
"The Road of No Return" 133
"Roamin' to Wyomin'" 235
"Roaming Cowboy" 15
Roaring Westward (film) 63
Robbins, Marty 105, 125, 126, 139, 142–145, 166, 199, 203, 206, 216, 225, 227, 228, 240, 241, 242, 243, 244, 245
Roberts, Bob 233
Roberts, Randy 101, 102, 104, 107
Robertson, Dick 236
Robertson, Texas Jim 14
Robinson, Bill "Bojangles 75
Robison, Carson 14, 56, 97, 226, 235
"Rock and Rye Polka" 42
"Rock Around the Clock" 17
Rockwell, Norman 214
Rocky Mountaineers 26
"Rocky Top" 177
"Rode Hard and Put Up Wet" 245
"Rodeo" 170, 248
Rodeo 163, 181, 176, 179, 220
"Rodeo Bum" 244
"Rodeo Clown" 246
"Rodeo Cowboy" 243
"Rodeo Eyes" 245
"Rodeo Girls" 245
"Rodeo Romeo" 246
"Rodeo Sweetheart" 46
Rodgers, Jesse 15
Rodgers, Jimmie 13, 15, 25, 44, 50, 61, 95, 97, 126, 131, 146, 149, 164, 168, 198, 201
Rodgers and Hammerstein 55

"Rodle-Odeo-Home" 244
Rodman, Judy 247
Rodriguez, Johnny 227, 228, 242, 244
Rogers, Buck 18
Rogers, Cheryl 36
Rogers, Dann 247
Rogers, David 245
Rogers, Dusty 172
Rogers, Ernest 16
Rogers, Kenny 73, 124, 206, 247
Rogers, Roy 1, 14, 16, 17, 25, 26, 27, 28, 29, 30, 31, 34, 35, 36, 37, 38, 46, 49, 51, 52, 54, 58, 60, 61, 63, 65, 80, 84, 86, 89, 90, 94, 95, 96, 98, 99, 104, 113, 114, 117, 126, 148, 154, 155, 156, 158, 159, 165, 170, 171, 172, 174, 175, 177, 179, 186, 187, 218, 222, 223, 225, 226, 227, 236, 239, 243, 245, 248
Rogers, Will 28, 222
Rogue River Festival 205
Rohrs, Donnie 245
Rolfe, Sam 156, 157
Roller, Gary 205
"Rollin' Nowhere" 124
The Rolling Stones 197, 198
"Roly-Poly" 237, 243, 249
Romero, Caesar 5
Ronnie Mack's Barn Dance 201
"Room Full of Roses" 226
Rooney, Jim 186
Rooney, Mickey 75
Roosevelt, Elliott 56
Roosevelt, Pres. Franklin D. 56, 62, 154
Roosevelt, Pres. Theodore 6
"Rope the Moon" 248
"Rosalita" 224, 225, 237
Rose, Fred 48, 68, 70, 112; as Floyd Jenkins 113
Rose, Paul 45
"Rose Garden" 177
"Rose of the Alamo" 72
"Rose of the Rio Grande" 234
"Roses to Reno" 241
The Rough Riders (TV show) 148
Rounder Records 200
"The Round-Up in Cheyenne" 79
"A Roundup Lullaby" 112
"Round-Up Saloon" 245
Rovin' Tumbleweeds (film) 29
"The Roving Kind" 239
Rowan, Peter 168
Royal Mounted Patrol (film) 57
Rubin, Rick 152
"Rudolph the Red Nosed Reindeer" 30, 68, 155, 226, 227
Rue, Arnie 244
Rundgren, Todd 184
"Running Bear" 227, 242
Rush, Art 35, 36
Russell, Charlie 202
Russell, Jane 75
Russell, Johnny 227, 243, 245
Russell, Tom 185
Russell Scott and the Red Hots 199

Rutherford, Ann 103
"Rye Whiskey" 239, 243
"Rye Whiskey, Rye Whiskey" 86

Sacred Records 77, 93
"Saddle Your Blues to a Wild Mustang" 47, 236
Sadler, SSgt. Barry 106
Saga of Death Valley (film) 61, 65
Sagebrush Trail (film) 102
Saginaw Trail (film) 80
Sahm, Doug 194, 243
"Sailor's Sweetheart" 45
St. Louis 45
"Salute to the Duke" 244
"Sam Hall" 86
"Sam McGee" poem 191
"The Same Old Me" 136
"San Antonio" 241
"San Antonio (Cowboy Song)" 233
"San Antonio Medley" 245
"San Antonio Rose" 112, 138, 225, 236, 241, 246
"San Antonio Stroll" 243
Sands of Iwo Jima (film) 104
"San Fernando Valley" 113, 225, 237
San Fernando Valley (film) 36
"San Francisco" 236
"San Francisco Sadie" 233
"Santa Fe" 247
"Santa Fe Lights" 191
Santa Fe Stampede (film) 103
"Santa Fe Trail" 16
"Santa Got Lost in Texas" 249
Satherley, Art 44, 68
"Satisfaction" 197
"Saturday Night in Dallas" 245
"Save a Horse (Ride a Cowboy)" 250
Savitt, Jan 236
Sawyer, Fern 180
Sawyer Brown 248
Scarborough, Cy 119
Schaffer, Norm 247
Schoen, Vic 113
Schuyler, Knobloch and Bickhardt 247
Scouts of the Plains (play) 3
Scruggs, Earl 229, 241
The Sea Chase (film) 105
"Sea of Cowboy Hats" 248
Seagle, Oscar 234
Seal, Jim 245
Seals, Dan 246, 247
"The Searchers" 105
The Searchers (film) 105
Sears, Roebuck & Co. 12, 25, 42, 50, 75, 79, 97, 146, 165
Seay, Johnny 241
Sells, Paul 57, 58
Selvin, Ben 58, 235
"Send Me Down to Tucson" 228, 244
Sennett, Mack 18
"Senorita" 247
"Senorita Margarita" 249
Seratt, Kenny 245

Index

Sergeant Preston of the Yukon (TV show) 147, 148
Service, Robert 191, 212
"Seven Beers with the Wrong Man" 73
"Seven Years with the Wrong Woman" 73
The Shadow (radio show) 201
Shakespeare 191
"Shall We Gather at the River" 103
Shane (film) 105
"Shane (The Call of the Far Away Hills)" 240
Shasta Records 63
Shaw, Artie 54, 236
"The She Buckaroo" 46
"She Came from Fort Worth" 248
"She Talked a Lot About Texas" 243
"She Wants to Marry a Cowboy" 247
She Wore a Yellow Ribbon (film) 104
Sheehan, Winifred "Winnie" 101
Shelton, Aaron 133
Shelton, Blake 249, 250
Shepard, Jean 244
Shepherd, Dick 203
The Sheriff of Cochise (TV show) 148
Sherman Hotel (Chicago) 12, 34
Sherrill, Billy 178
"She's Got to Be a Saint" 140
"She's in Love with a Rodeo Man" 227, 243
"The Shifting, Whispering Sands" 150
Shilkret, Nat 235
Shirley Danny 247
Sholes, Steve 73
"Shoot First, Ask Questions Later" 246
Shooting High (film) 80
The Shootist (film) 106
Shore, Dinah 238
"Shotgun Rider" 243, 245
"Shoulda Been a Cowboy" 170, 248
"Shy Anne from Old Cheyenne" 46
"Sick Sober and Sorry" 71
Siegel, Bugsy 76
Siegel, Sol 28
"Sierra Sue" 237
Sievert, Bud 59
Sigler, Larry 193
Sigler, Lee 193
"Signed, Sealed and Delivered" 60
Sikes, O.J. 230
"Silly Song" 90
"Silver Bell" 186
"Silver on the Sage" 113, 236
"Silver Spurs" 73
Simms, Harry 54
Simon and Garfunkel 152
Simpson, Red 242
Simpson-Witt, Paula 99
Sinatra, Frank 55, 113, 187, 202, 240
Sinatra, Nancy 161, 245
"Sing About Love" 178
"Sing, Cowboy, Sing" 86
"Sing Me a Song of the Saddle" 66
"The Singing Hills" 113, 225, 237, 240
"Singing the Blues" 144
Singing Vagabond (film) 27
"Sioux City Sue" 225, 238
"Sister of Sioux City Sue" 239
Six Flags Over Texas 166
"67 Miles to Cow Town" 247
Skepner, David 200
Skinner, Jimmie 225, 240
"Skip to My Lou" 197
"Skip to My Lou/Yellow Rose of Texas" 105
Sledd, Patsy 243
Slepka, Bill 61, 65
Slightly Static (film) 27
"Slipping Around" 60
Slippy McGee (film) 30, 37
Sloey, Al 58, 59
"Slow Poke" 239
"Slow Texas Dancing" 246
Small, Joe Austell 150
Smalle, Ed 235
Smith, Bessie 108
Smith, Cal 243
Smith, Carl 132, 137, 165, 226, 243
Smith, Connie 243
Smith, Dennis 245
Smith, Hal 137
Smith, John 158
Smith, Jon Guyot 79
Smith, Kate 238
Smith, Paul "Clem" 55
Smith, Sammi 140
Smith, Velma 137
"Smokin' in the Rockies" 246
Smoking Guns (film) 19
Snow, Hank 14, 73, 146, 225, 226, 239, 241, 243
Snow White and the Seven Dwarfs (film) 90
"So No More" 186
"So Round So Firm, So Fully Packed" 68
The Soldier (film) 221
Solid Gold Band 245
"Solitaire" 171
"Some Old California Memory" 242
"Somebody Buy This Cowgirl a Beer" 246
"Someday in Wyoming" 81
"Someday Soon" 183, 184, 243, 246, 248
"Someday You'll Call My Name" 60
"Someone" 86
"Something's Wrong in California" 242
"Sometime in Wyoming" 19
"Somewhere Between Texas and Mexico" 250
"Somewhere in Old Wyoming" 235
Somewhere in Sonora (film) 102
"Somewhere in Texas" 246
Song of Arizona (film) 36
"Song of the Bandit" 28
Song of the Caballero (film) 8
Song of the Gringo (film) 86
"Song of the Lariat" 42
"Song of the Range" 81
Song of the Range (film) 63
Song of the Saddle (film) 27
Song of the Sierra (film) 63, 92
"The Sons of Katie Elder" 149, 241
The Sons of Katie Elder (film) 106, 151
Sons of the Desert 249
"Sons of the Pioneers" 189
Sons of the Pioneers 2, 14, 15, 16, 25, 26–27, 28, 29, 30, 31, 34, 46, 49, 54, 58, 59, 60, 82, 83, 84, 89, 90, 93, 95, 104, 105, 113, 114, 115, 117, 119, 155, 165, 168, 186, 187, 190, 191, 199, 226, 228, 229, 230, 236, 237, 238, 239
Sons of the Saddle (film) 8
Sons of the San Joaquin 117, 125, 159, 167, 170, 187–192, 200, 211, 212
Soundmaster Studio 220
Sousa, John Philip 164
South, Joe 178
South of Caliente (film) 30, 37
"South of Santa Fe" 249
"South of the Border" 29, 62, 67, 236, 237, 240, 247
South of the Border (film) 29
Southern Pacific 247
Southwest Texas State University 219, 223
Spahn, Warren 187
Spencer, Len 232
Spencer, Tim 26, 27, 29, 30, 90, 114, 117
Spoilers of the Plains (film) 56, 58, 104
Sprague, Carl T. 13, 82, 126, 229
Spriggens, Deuce 30, 31, 54
"Springtime in the Rockies" 236
Spurzz 245
The Squaw Man (film) 6
"Squaws Along the Yukon" 225, 240
Staedtler, Darrell 219
Stafford, Jim 245
Stafford, Jo 55, 202, 239
Stafford, Terry 221, 227, 242, 247
Stagecoach (film) 103, 104
Stamey, Dave 200
"Stampede" 225, 239, 249
Stamps-Baxter School 56
Standard Radio 27
Stanley, Frank 233
The Star Packer (film) 102
Starday Records 81
Starr Outfitting Company 83
Starrett, Charles 28, 57, 63, 80, 92
"Stars and Stripes on Iwo Jima" 226
Stars of the Grand Ole Opry (TV show) 17
"Stars Over Texas" 249
"Started Out in Texas" 39
"Station L-O-V-E Signing Off" 72
Statler Brothers 172, 173, 175, 227, 242, 243, 246
"Statue in the Bay" 95

"Stay There 'Til I Get There" 178
Steagall, Red 2, 160–163, 200, 208, 228, 243, 244
Steel, Bob 102
Steele, Jeffrey 250
Stegall, Keith 246
Stein, Maury 58, 59
Stephenson, Joe 119
Stetson (hat) 62
Steve Donovan, Western Ranger (TV show) 148
Stevens, Jeff & the Bullets 247
Stevens, Ray 243
Stewart, James 106
Stewart, Lisa 172
Stewart, Wynn 244
"Still Taking Chances" 124
Stone, Cliffie 55, 57, 58, 59, 75, 89
Stone, Paul 168
Stony Plain Records 185
Stop Records 166
"The Storm" 241
"The Story of My Life" 144
"Story with a Moral" (poem) 215
Stout, Archie 105
Stovall, Vern Stovall 241
Stover, Everett 112
Stracciari, Riccardo 234
Strait, George 2, 125, 161, 185, 201, 218–223, 228, 246, 247, 248, 249, 250
Strait, Norman Voss 218
Strange, Glen 103
"Strawberry Roan" 166, 171, 197
Strawberry Roan (film) 18
Stream, Harold "Spook" 178
Street, Mel 244
"Streets of Laredo" 99, 150, 152, 174
Stroman, Gene 247
Stuart, J.E.B. 202
Stuart, Marty 248
Stuckey, Nat 241
Sugarfoot (TV show) 147, 148, 225
Sullivan, Ed 135
Sullivan, Joe
Summar, Trent 249
"Summer Wages" 185
Summers, Colleen (Mary Ford) 57, 76
Sun, Joe 245
Sun Records 147, 181, 198
"Sunday Morning Coming Down" 210
The Sunshine Girls 57, 76
Sunshine Ranch (radio show) 29
"Sunshine on My Shoulders" 203
Supernaw, Doug 248, 249
"Surrey with the Fringe on Top" 36
Susanna Pass (film) 30
Sutton, Glenn 178, 180
Swarthout, Glendon 106
"Sweet Genevieve" 104
"Sweet Leilani" 112
"Sweet Little Miss Blue Eyes" 135
"Sweet Mother Texas" 245
Sweetwater, Sarah 210
Swift Jewel Cowboys 14

Sylvia 245, 246
Synder, Gary 212

"T for Texas" 241, 243
Tackett, Marlow 245, 246
"Tacos, Enchiladas, and Beans" 239
The Tailormaids 76
"Take It as It Comes" 124
"Take Me Back to My Boots and Saddle" 112, 236
Take Me Back to Oklahoma (film) 109
"Take Me Home, Country Roads" 203
"Takin' Care of Business" 197
Tales of the Texas Rangers (TV show) 148
Tales of Wells Fargo (TV show) 63, 147, 148
"Talk to Your Heart" 133
"Talkin' to the Wrong Man" 124
"The Talking Leaves" 150
"The Tall Guys" 56
Tall in the Saddle (film) 104
Talley, James 243
"Tangled Up in Texas" 249
"Tanya Montana" 247
"Taps" 106
Tate, Michael 245
Taveres, Freddy 59
Taylor, Buck 6, 224
Taylor, Dub "Cannonball" 63, 91
Taylor, Jack 45
Taylor, Joe 182
"Tear After Tear" 99
"Teardrops in My Heart" 170, 238, 243, 245
Teeter, Buck 119
Telegraph Trail (film) 102
"Tell Me Something Bad About Tulsa" 249, 250
"Telling My Troubles to My Old Guitar" 60
"Telluride" 249
Temple, Shirley 75
"10 Little Bottles" 71
"Ten Seconds in the Saddle" 245
"Ten Thousand Cattle" 103
"Tennessee Babe" 105
"Tennessee Saturday Night" 71
"Tennessee Stud" 152
"Tennessee Yodel Polka" 72
"Tenting Tonight" 105
Terhune, Max 98
Terry, Gordon 157
Terry, Sonny 126
The Texan (TV show) 148
"Texarkana Baby" 239
"Texas" 240, 243
"Texas Angel" 244
"Texas Blues" 58, 224, 237
"Texas Bound and Flyin'" 245
Texas Centennial (Dallas) 27
Texas Cowboy Hall of Fame 163
"Texas Cowboy Night" 245
Texas Cyclone (film) 102
"Texas Diary" 249
"Texas Ida Red" 245
"Texas in 1880" 247, 249

"Texas in My Rear View Mirror" 245
"Texas Law Sez" 243
"Texas Me and You" 244
"Texas Moon" 247
"Texas–1947" 243
"Texas on a Saturday Night" 243
"Texas on My Mind" 249
"Texas Plains" 45, 83, 84
"Texas Plates" 250
"Texas Playboy Rag" 238
"Texas Polka" 225, 237
Texas Ruby 56, 91
"Texas Size Heartache" 249
Texas State Barn Dance 131
"Texas State of Mind" 245
Texas State Radio Network 56, 131
Texas Steers (film) 104
"Texas Tattoo" 248
"Texas Tea" 241, 244, 245
Texas Terror (film) 102
"Texas Tornado" 248
Texas Trail of Fame 162
"Texas (When I Die)" 244
"Texas Woman" 243
"Texas Women" 245
Texas Wranglers 16
Teyte, Maggie 234
"Thank the Cowboy for the Ride" 247
"(That Don't Change) the Way I Feel About You" 220
"That No Quit Attitude" (poem) 214, 215
"That Pioneer Mother of Mine" 28
"That Silver Haired Daddy of Mine" 13, 20, 25
"That's a No No" 177
"That's the Way a Cowboy Rocks and Rolls" 245
"That's What I Like About the West" 225, 238
"There Ain't Gonna Be No Me to Welcome You" 57
"There Are Strange Things Happening Everyday" 151
"There's a Girl in Texas " 249
"There's a Gold Mine in the Sky" 236
"There's a Long, Long Trail" 234
"There's a Ranch in the Sky" 236
"There's a Silver Moon on the Golden Gate" 39
"There's a Star Spangled Banner Waving Somewhere" 60
"There's Still a Lot of Love in San Antone" 243, 246
"These Are Not My People" 178
They Were Expendable (film) 104
Thibault, Conrad 235
"This Ain't Dallas" 246
"This Ain't My First Rodeo" 248
"This Cowboy's Hat" 246, 248
"This Gun Don't Care" 241
"This Is a Holdup" 244
"This Is My Year for Mexico" 243
"This Land Is Your Land" 193
"This Ole House" 84
"This Time" 199

Thomas, Dick 238, 239
Thompson, Hank 52, 131, 158, 156, 225, 240, 241, 242, 243
Thompson, Uncle Jimmy 12
Thompson, Vern 119, 120
Thornbury, Bill 191
Thorp, Jack 11, 164
Three Badmen (film) 7
"Three Caballeros" 225, 238
Three Godfathers (film) 104
Three Little Maids 39
Three Mesquiteers 103, 104
3 of Hearts (group) 249
"Three Sheets in the Wind" 71
Three Sheets to the Wind (radio show) 104
3:10 to Yuma film 105
"Throw a Rope Around the Wind" 242
"Throw a Saddle on a Star" 54
Thunderkloud, Billy 243
Tibbs, Casey 165
"The Tie That Binds" 56
"Tiger by the Tail" 197
"Till the End of the World" 60, 71
"Till the Sands of the Desert Grow Cold" 233, 234
Tillis, Mel 228, 244, 245, 246
Tillis, Pam 196, 248
Tilton, Martha 42, 237
Tim McCoy (TV show) 148
"Timber" 190
"Tiny Bubbles" 99
Tiomkin, Dmitri 105
TNN (The Nashville Network) 172, 228
"To a San Antone Rose" 247
"To Beat the Devil" 210
Todd, Dick 237
"Tokyo, Oklahoma" 246
"Tom Dooley" 182, 193
Tomlin, Pinky 236
The Tommy Hunter Show 184
"Tomorrow Never Comes" 71
"Tonight We Ride" 124, 247
"Too Late" 60
"Too Lee Rollum (I'm an Arizona Cowboy)" 98
"Too Much of You" 177
"Too Old to Play Cowboy" 245
The Top Hatters 236
"Top of the World" 178
Toronto Maple Leafs 189
"The Touch of God's Hand" 28
"Touch of Texas" 237
Town and Country Time (Washington D.C. radio show) 17
Town Hall Party (radio show) 69, 76, 77, 87, 92
Town Hall Party (TV show) 155, 227
The Tracker (HBO movie) 206
The Trail Beyond (film) 102
"Trail Dust" 54
"Trail of Tears" 249
"Trail of the Lonesome Pine" 234
"The Trail to Mexico" 103
Trailin' Trouble (film) 62, 66
The Train Robbers (film) 106

Travis, Merle 52, 55, 68, 69, 70, 76, 86, 91, 92, 155, 157, 226
Travis, Randy 125, 248
Travolta, John 221
"(Treasure of) Sierra Madre" 238
Tree Publishing 137
The Trespasser (film) 30, 37
Trevor, Claire 103
"Triflin' Gal" 73
Triggs, Trini 249
Trinity Broadcasting Network 38
Tritt, Travis 125
Trotter, John Scott 63, 113
Trouble Along the Way (film) 105
"True Grit" 242
True Grit (film) 106
Tubb, Ernest 67, 73, 143, 146, 225, 226, 240, 241, 244
Tucker, Neely 214
Tucker, Tanya 221, 243, 244, 245
Tucker, Tommy 238
"Tulsa Ballroom" 246
"Tulsa County" 242
"Tulsa Time" 228, 244
"Tumbleweed" 245
Tumbleweed Theater 115
"Tumbling Tumbleweeds" 14, 25, 26, 28, 67, 82, 93, 113, 168, 170, 174, 186, 225, 236, 237, 239
Tumbling Tumbleweeds (film) 8, 15, 18, 24, 26, 27, 80, 103
"Turn Me Around" 106
Turner, Big Al 131
Turner, Alan 233
Turner, Lana 75
Tuttle, Marilyn 75–78, 89, 92, 93
Tuttle, Wesley 2, 75, 76, 76, 77, 86, 87, 89–93, 157
Twain, Mark 205
Twain, Shania 248
Twentieth Century–Fox 28, 35
"Twenty-Four Hours from Tulsa" 244
"Twilight on the Trail" 113
Twitty, Conway 203, 221, 246
Two Fisted Law (film) 102
"Two Glasses Joe" 73
"Two Gun Daddy" 243
"Two Less Lonely People" 172
"The Two-Step Is Easy" 124
"Two Timin' Woman" 147
Tyler, Bonnie 244
Tyler, T. Texas 239
Tyson, Clay Dawson 183
Tyson, Ian 181–186, 200, 201, 208
Tyson, Sylvia 181, 182, 184

UCLA *see* University of California–Los Angeles
Ulrich, Louise 133
Uncle Ezra's Radio Station (radio show) 29
"Uncle Henry" 22
"Uncle Noah's Ark 20, 24, 80
Uncle Tom Murray's Hollywood Hillbillies 26
"Under a Texas Moon" 235
"Under Fiesta Stars" 67
"Under the Gun" 248

"Under This Old Hat" 248
Under Western Stars (film) 28
"Understand Your Man" 149
"Uneasy Rider" 242
"The Union Forever" 103
Union Pacific (TV show) 148
United Artists Publisher 161
United Artists Records 111, 194
Universal Pictures 8, 18, 19, 48, 103
University of California–Los Angeles 121, 122, 124, 199
University of Montana 198
University of Southern California 101
University of Texas 86, 192
University of Texas, Arlington 130
"Until Death Do Us Part" 132
"Unwound" 220, 221
"Up North (Down South, Back East, Out West)" 249
Urban Cowboy (film) 220, 221, 228
"Urban Cowboys, Outlaws, Cavaleers" 245
"Utah Trail" 235

Van & Schenck 234
Van Dyke, Leroy 175, 244
Vanguard Records 183
"The Vanishing Race" 150
Van Shelton, Ricky 125, 196, 228
Vanwarmer, Randy 247
Vass Family 14
Vaughn, Jerry 58, 59
Vaughn, Scott 119, 120
"Vaya Con Dios (May God Be with You)" 228, 240, 243
The Vega Brothers 247
Vickery, Mack 244
Victor Records 13, 31, 39, 45, 50
Vietnam 87, 106, 152, 172, 178, 183, 210, 227
Village Barn (film) 72
Village Barn (Greenwich Village club) 16
Vinopal, David 51
"The Violet and the Rose" 155
The Virginian (film) 7
The Virginian (novel) 6
Vocalion Records 112
Voice of Hollywood (film) 8

"W. Lee O'Daniel (and the Light Crust Dough Boys)" 247
"Waco" 241
WACO (Waco, TX) 56
Wade, Pete 134, 135
Wagnon, Bill 76, 92
Wagon Train (film) 147
Wagon Train (TV show) 30, 63, 148, 225
"Wagon Train" 81
"Wagon Wheels" 236
Wagoner, Porter 243, 246
Wagons West (film) 30
"Wah-Hoo" 47, 236
"Waiting for a Train" 149
Wake of the Red Witch (film) 104
Wakely, Jimmy 31, 49, 52, 54, 57, 60–65, 67, 76, 92, 114, 172, 226

Index

Waldrup, Dub 204
"Walk a Mile in My Shoes" 178
Walker, Billy 241, 244, 247
Walker, Charlie 242
Walker, Cindy 73–74
Walker, Clay 247, 249
Wallace, Jerry 73
Walsh, Raoul 101, 104
Walt Disney 90, 98, 105
"Waltz Across Texas" 241, 243, 244
"Waltz Time Melody" 42
"Waltzes and Western Swing" 245
"Wanderin'" 106
Wanted: Dead or Alive (TV show) 63, 148
War of the Wildcats (film) 36
The War Wagon (film) 106
Ward, Jacky 244, 245
Wariner, Steve 246
"Warm Red Wine" 73
Warner, James 104
Warner Brothers Records 49, 99, 102, 124, 125, 161, 170, 172, 190, 191
Warner Western Records 125, 161, 191, 211, 212
Warren, Dale 31, 59
Washington Cowboy (film) 28, 29
Water, Ocie 54
Watson, Gene 228, 244
Watts, Howard "Cedric Rainwater" 133
"Way Down Texas Way" 247
"Way Out There" 25
"The Way She Got Away" 135
Way Up Thar (film) 27
Wayne, John 24, 36, 63, 151, 100–107
"The Wayward Wind" 246
WBAP (Fort Worth, TX) 12, 16, 108
WCAU (Philadelphia) 98
WDZ (Tuscola, ILL) 79
"We Crossed Our Heart" 132
We Five (group) 184
"We Will Gather at the River" 105
"Weary Blues" 132
The Weavers 147, 239
"Wedding Bells" 60
"Weekend Cowboys" 247
Weems, Ted 235, 237
Weintraub, Jerry 222
Welk, Lawrence 177, 178, 236
Weller, Freddy 242, 245
Wellington, Larry 41, 42
Wells, Kitty 225, 226, 240
Werrenrath, Reinald 234
West, Dottie 241, 246
West, Shelly 245, 246
"West Fest" 228
West of the Divide (film) 102
"West of the Great Divide" 235
West Side Kid (film) 36
West Texas A&M 160
"West Texas Highway" 242

Western, Jo 158
Western, Johnny 69, 145–159, 170, 174
Western Channel 175
"Western Flyer" 248
Western Flyer (film) 248
"Western Girls" 248
Western Heritage Award 162, 206
Western Jubilee Records 192
"Western Man" 243
Western music 1, 2, 3, 11, 13, 14, 15, 17, 31, 55, 114, 116, 120, 142, 145, 162, 167, 168, 170, 171, 175, 179, 180, 185, 192, 205, 225, 226, 229, 230, 231
Western Music Association 46, 75, 78, 81, 84, 111, 114, 170, 190, 228, 229, 230
Western Music Hall of Fame 49, 74, 81, 84, 99, 111
Western Ranger (TV show) 148
Western Swing 1, 54, 108, 109, 110, 111, 113, 129, 137, 162, 163, 164, 165, 193, 195, 220, 229
The Western Way (magazine) 1
Westerners International 168
WestFest 126, 127, 167
Weston, Dick 27, 28
Weston, Paul 239, 240
Westward Ho! (film) 24, 100, 103
WFAA (Dallas) 34, 131
WGN Barn Dance (Chicago) 17
Whalin, June 109
Whalin, Kermit 109
WHAS (Louisville) 15, 20, 34
"What a Man My Man Is" 178
"What Am I Doin' Hangin' Round" 122
"What on Earth (Will You Do for Heaven's Sake)" 151
"What She Wants" 124
"What the Cowgirls Do" 248
"What Was Your Name in the States" 106
"Whatcha Gonna Do with a Cowboy" 248
"Whatever Happened to Randolph Scott" 227, 243
"What's Forever For?" 124
"Wheels Fell Off the Wagon Again" 241
"When Cowboys Didn't Dance" 249
"When I Die, Just Let Me Go to Texas" 244
"When It's Lamp Lighting Time in the Valley" 86
"When It's Moonlight on the Alamo" 234
"When It's Moonlight on the Prairie" 233, 235
"When My Blue Moon Turns to Gold Again" 74
"When Our Love Began (Cowboys and Indians)" 244
"When Papa Played the Dobro" 149
"When the Bloom Is on the Sage" 113, 235

"When the Flowers of Montana Were Blooming" 45
"When the Moon Shines Down on the Mountain" 82
"When the Work's All Done This Fall" 13, 82, 229
"When You and I Were Young Maggie Blues" 60
Where the Buffalo Roam (film) 42
"Where the Old Red River Flows" 225, 241
"Where the Rocky Mountains Touch the Morning Sun" 247
Whirlwind (film) 80
Whiskeyhill Singers 106
White, John I. 13
White, Lari 249
White, Lasses 94
White, Tony Joe 245
White Elephant Saloon (Fort Worth) 164, 166, 167, 185
"White Girl" 150
"White Line Fever" 197
"A White Sport Coat (and a Pink Carnation)" 144
Whiteman, Paul 235, 236
Whitford, Eldon 51
Whiting, Margaret 60, 239
Whitley, Ray 47–49, 51, 52, 56, 93, 95, 96, 114, 165
Whitman, Slim 225, 239, 240
Whitman, Walt 212
WHN Barn Dance (New York) 14, 86
WHO (Iowa Barn Dance Frolic in Des Moines) 14
"Who Do I Know in Dallas" 242
"Who Do You Know in California" 246
"Who's Gene Autry?" 146
"Whose Bed Have Your Boots Been Under?" 248
"Why Are You Marching, Son?" 106
"Why Don't You Go to Dallas" 245
"Why I Love Her" 106
"Why Me, Lord" 152
WIBW (Topeka, KS) 41
"Wichita Jail" 243
"Wichita Lineman" 227, 242, 249
"Wicked California" 242
"Wide Open Road" 147
Widener, June 57
Wigginton, Chuck 134
Wilburn, Scot 201
"Wild and Wicked World" 135
Wild Bill Hickok (TV show) 148
"Wild Bull Rider" 245
Wild Horse Rodeo (film) 28
"Wild Horses" 240, 249
"Wild Montana Skies" 246
"Wild Texas Rose" 247
"Wild West Show" 250
"Wildfire" 124, 228
Wiley, Bill 46, 118
Wilkins, Little David 243
"Will It Be Love by Morning" 124
"Will the Circle Be Unbroken" 131

Willcox Cowboy Hall of Fame 99
Willett, Slim 133
William Morris Agency 201
"William Tell Overture" 225
Williams, Audrey 132, 133
Williams, Billy 238
Williams, Doc 16
Williams, Don 228, 244, 247
Williams, Hank 46, 70, 132, 133, 134, 139, 146, 152, 189, 193, 198, 216, 218, 226, 240
Williams, Hank, Jr. 245, 246
Williams, Mentor 178, 179, 180
Williams, Tex 63, 126, 172, 226, 238
Williams, William Carlos 213
Williamson, Slim 177, 178
Willing, Foy (and the Riders of the Purple Sage) 2, 14, 56–59, 76, 117, 237
The Willis Brothers 14
Wills, Bob 61, 73, 108–111, 112, 113, 126, 129, 131, 137, 165, 185, 193, 196, 226, 236, 237, 238, 239
Wills, Johnnie Lee 109
"Wills Breakdown" 108
Winds of the Wasteland (film) 103
"Wings in the Morning" 151
Winik, Jay 214
Winkler, Daniel M. 36
Winter, Dale 34
Winterhalter, Hugo 239
Wiseman, Mac 225, 240
Wister, Owen 6
"With Love" 172
The Wizard of Oz (film) 104
WJJD (Chicago) 45
WJR (Detroit) 14
WKY (Oklahoma City) 61, 65, 66
WLS (Chicago) 8, 12, 13, 14, 17, 19, 25, 29, 36, 37, 39, 42, 45, 47, 50, 51, 98, 171
WLW (Cincinnati) 12, 14, 34, 40, 91
WMC (Memphis) 14, 34
WMCA (New York) 47, 56
WNEW (New York) 56
WOAI (San Antonio) 13
WOC (Davenport, Iowa) 14
Wolfe, Russ 119
Wolfpack (group) 245
Womack, Lee Ann 249
"Won't You Please Be Mine (Just for Today)" 133
Woolsey, Erv 220, 221, 222
WOR (New York) 14, 16, 86

Wordsworth 191
"Workin' Man's Dollar" 248
World Championship Rodeo 47
World Class Talent Agency 191, 192
World War I 181
World War II 17, 26, 29, 30, 36, 46, 47, 54, 58, 60, 63, 68, 80, 84, 92, 94, 104, 109, 110, 112, 113, 129, 130, 131, 142, 216, 226, 229
WOV (New York) 72
WOW (Omaha, Nebraska) 56
Wrangler Award *see* Western Heritage Award
WREC (Memphis) 33
"Wreck of the Old 97" 50
"Wreck on the Highway" 183
Wright, Chely 248
Wright, Jake 57
Wright, Sonny 245
Wrigley, P.K. 29, 62, 67, 69; Wrigley Chewing Gum Company 29
WSB (Cross Road Follies in Atlanta) 6, 12
WSM (Nashville) 12, 15, 51, 132, 133, 135, 143
WTTM (Trenton, N.J.) 97
Wuthering Heights (film) 104
W.W. and the Dixie Dance Kings (film) 179
WWBM Chicago 34
WWVA (Jamboree in Wheeling, WVA) 16
Wylie and the Wild West 197–201; *see also* Gustafson, Wylie
Wynette, Tammy 178, 245, 247
"Wyoming (Lullaby)" 234
Wyoming Outlaw (film) 104

XEAW (Monterrey, Mexico) 15
XED (Renosa, Tamaulipas) 15
XENT (Nuevo Laredo) 15
XEPN (Piedras Negras) 15
XER (Villa Acuna, Mexico) 39
XERA (Del Rio, Texas) 15

Yahoo 199
"Y'all Come Back Saloon" 244
Yancy Derringer (TV show) 148
Yankovic, Frank 115
Yates, Herbert J. 18, 19, 24, 25, 28, 29, 36, 42, 58, 94, 103, 104
"Yellow Rose" 246
"Yellow Rose of Texas" 225, 240
Yellow Rose of Texas (film) 36

"Yellow Stripes" 104
"Yes, Sir, That's My Baby" 89
"Yip-I-Addy-I-Ay!" 233
"Yippy Cry Yi" 245
"Yippy Ky Yay" 249
Yoakum, Dwight 199
"Yodelin' Jive" 238
"The Yodeling Cowboy" 90
"You and the Horse (That You Rode in On)" 247
"You Are My Sunshine" 45, 67, 73
"You Can Leave Your Hat On" 249
"You Done Me Wrong" 135
"You Don't Know Me" 73
"You Dreamer You" 148
"You Two Timed Me One Time Too Often" 91, 226
"You Were on My Mind" 184
"You Will Have to Pay" 226
"You Win Again" 133
Young, Faron 243
Young, Neil 184
Young, Victor 113, 235, 236
Young Mr. Lincoln (film) 104
Younger, James 246, 247
Younger, Michael 246, 247
"Your Body Is an Outlaw" 245
"Your Cheatin' Heart" 216
"Your Daddy Don't Live in Heaven (He's in Houston)" 245
"Your Good Girl's Gonna Go bad" 178
"Your Heart Is Too Crowded" 132
"Your Old Love Letters" 71
"Your Squaw Is on the Warpath" 227, 242
"Your Wedding Corsage" 131
"You're from Texas" 73, 224, 225, 237
"You're My Baby" ("Little Woolly Booger") 147
"You're My Man" 178
"You're the Best Thing That Ever Happened to Me" 140
"You're the Reason God Made Oklahoma" 245
"You're Under Arrest (For Stealing My heart)" 133
"You've Been a Good Ole Wagon But You Done Broke Down" 232
"You've Got My Troubles Now" 132

Ziegfeld, Florenz 76

www.ingramcontent.com/pod-product-compliance
Lightning Source LLC
Chambersburg PA
CBHW081545300426
44116CB00015B/2758